Media Business and Innovation

Series Editor

M. Friedrichsen, Stuttgart Media University, Germany and Humboldt School Digital Management University, Luxembourg/Berlin

More information about this series at
http://www.springer.com/series/11520

Gregory Ferrell Lowe • Charles Brown
Editors

Managing Media Firms and Industries

What's So Special About Media Management?

 Springer

Editors
Gregory Ferrell Lowe
School of Communications,
    Media & Theatre
University of Tampere
Tampere
Finland

Charles Brown
Faculty of Media, Arts and Design
University of Westminster
Northwick Park
United Kingdom

Media Business and Innovation
ISBN 978-3-319-08514-2   ISBN 978-3-319-08515-9   (eBook)
DOI 10.1007/978-3-319-08515-9

Library of Congress Control Number: 2015943676

Springer Cham Heidelberg New York Dordrecht London

Printed on acid-free paper

Springer International Publishing AG Switzerland is part of Springer Science+Business Media (www.springer.com)

Foreword

Why would anyone read this book? There are scores of excellent management books covering theories of the firm, business economics, governance, strategy, business models, organisational issues, marketing, customer service, leadership and personnel management. Based on established theory and practical experience, they provide substantive and valuable insight into the factors that influence managerial choices and offer practical advice for best practice in managing an enterprise. Many of these scholars draw parallels between industries and teach readers how to apply and use the knowledge their books contain.

This is important because management is management, no matter where it is practiced. The basic concerns and application of managerial work are the same across industries. The similarities in issues that managers confront make it possible to learn from management practices and processes in other industries. Although many people think media are different from other products and services, and that is true in key respects as this book demonstrates, they arrive at the erroneous conclusion that those differences necessarily imply that media management must also be different. This is especially characteristic among those who associate management exclusively with commercial activities, ignoring its applicability to social enterprises, public administration, non-governmental organisations and not-for-profit firms.

This brings us back to the question raised at the start: Why read *this* book? The answer is not in the main title but rather in the question posed in its subtitle: "What is so special about media management?" That is a question of central importance.

Analysis of and participation in media industries and markets, and their basic strategic and operational processes, can be well informed by general knowledge in management literature. But that alone has limits. Media tend to operate in environments and ecosystems that present challenges that are not germane to many other industries. Although management per se does not differ in media enterprises compared with other enterprises, how it is exercised, the unique dynamics of the particular settings in which it operates, and the factors that must be taken into consideration in making management decisions often differ significantly in the media firm.

There are plentiful examples of effective managers in one industry or another who failed after moving to manage a media firm and even when moving from one media industry to manage the enterprise in another media industry of a different type. Such failures often occurred because those managers could not, or did not, adequately consider the differences in managing a media firm or take into account distinctions that characterise these industries.

It is clear today that far better management is needed in media industries and firms than was necessary in the past. This is a vital concern because the configuration of the industries, their roles and choices in media use are all being dramatically altered. Managers need to strike an effective balance between developing their existing roles, structures and processes, that is to say the history and accomplishments of the past, and facilitating adaptation to the increasingly digital environment of the twenty-first century. They have to cope with varying perspectives and demands of different cultures within their organisations, with diverse cultures and subcultures in the operational environment. They have to operate in markets that are far more competitive than in the past because contents created by producers for different media are now converging onto the same platforms and because media consumers are also content makers these days. They have to engage in collaborations and value configurations that were not previously required. These are enormous challenges that require scholars and managers alike to draw on the best knowledge from general management studies and combine it with specific knowledge that is pertinent to managing a media firm—indeed to managing within and across media industries.

This book is a step towards bridging the gap between the various sources of knowledge that can inform media management. The contents build upon general management knowledge for multiple industries and knowledge that has been created by management scholars with specific application to media enterprises. The book reports a substantial and growing body of knowledge created by researchers and educators involved with media management as a specialisation, one that is comparatively young and has flourished in the past two decades.

The editors of this book, and the European Media Management Association that supported the project, have wrestled with questions regarding what should be included and who would contribute. They faced a range of difficult selections and choices and decided to focus on crucial, fundamental topics that inform the distinctiveness of media management. These include media governance and accountability, forms of media products and markets, the economic and political economic factors influencing their management, the growing emphasis on entre-preneurship and business models, the increasing roles of media audiences and issues in leading creative personnel and projects. In doing so, they have brought together internationally recognised scholars from media studies programmes and business schools who are noted for the insight and vision their work has produced in this field.

The book delivers on its aspiration to clarify how media are different from other industries and why its characteristics drive different types of policy and managerial decision making. It reveals what is known and, equally important, what remains to be discovered about media management in aspects that are crucial for theory development and in practical application. It points out the needs and the challenges for this field to develop an increased legitimacy, both in the academy and media industries. Crucially, it points out the need for critical analysis of theories and practices and their outcomes. This volume moves the development of the field forward another step, providing more evidence of its utility and vitality. This book is worthwhile reading because it provides inspiration for increased, focused inquiry and knowledge development.

Robert G. Picard
Reuters Institute,
University of Oxford,
Oxford, UK

Contents

1   Introduction: What's So Special About Media Management?. . . .   1
     Gregory Ferrell Lowe

Part I   Scholarship and Distinction

2   The Development of Media Management as an Academic
     Field: Tracing the Contents and Impact of Its Three Leading
     Journals.   23
     Leona Achtenhagen and Bozena Mierzejewska

3   Competencies of Media Managers: Are They Special?.   43
     Juan Pablo Artero and Juan Luis Manfredi

4   Convergence, Similarities and Distinctions in Management Across
     Media Industries.   61
     Paulo Faustino and Luísa Ribeiro

5   Media Management: A Critical Discipline?.   83
     Charles Brown

Part II   Governance and Accountability

6   A Stakeholder Approach to Media Governance.   103
     Anker Brink Lund

7   Obeying His Masters' Voices: Managing Independence
     and Accountability in Public Service Media Between
     Civil Society and State.   121
     Christian S. Nissen

8   Corporate Social Responsibility and Media Management:
     A Necessary Symbiosis.   143
     George Tsourvakas

9   Resources and Perspectives from Media Political Economy.   159
     Justin Schlosberg

Part III   Business and Economics

10   Managing in the Distinctive Economic Context of Media 175
Gillian Doyle

11   Entrepreneurial Venturing and Media Management 189
Andreas Will, Dennis Brüntje, and Britta Gossel

**12   Business Models of Media Industries: Describing and Promoting
Commodification** 207
M. Bjørn von Rimscha

13   Technology Management and Business Models 223
Gustavo Cardoso and José Moreno

Part IV   Products and Markets

14   Contents as Products in Media Markets 243
Mercedes Medina, Alfonso Sánchez-Tabernero, and Ángel Arrese

**15   The Audience as Product, Consumer, and Producer in the
Contemporary Media Marketplace** 261
Philip M. Napoli

16   Audience Experiences and Emotional Economy 277
Annette Hill

17   Dynamic Media Management Capabilities: A Case Study 293
John Oliver

Part V   Leadership and Labour

**18   Leadership in Media Organisations: Past Trends and Challenges
Ahead** 311
Ghislain Deslandes

19   Managing Media Workers 329
Mark Deuze

20   Managing Creativity in Media Organisations 343
Paul Dwyer

21   Projectification in the Media Industries 367
Rolf A. Lundin and Maria Norbäck

Introduction: What's So Special About Media Management?

Gregory Ferrell Lowe

1.1 A Young Field of Academic Specialisation

This is not a book about management theory per se. Although every chapter draws on some aspect of management theory, often multiple, the book is about exploring answers to a question with significant implications for developing a young field of emerging scholarship: *What's so special about media management*? If the answer is nothing, the field has dim prospects. We don't think that is true. If only based on the contents of this book, we feel confident there is enough that is unique for theory and practice in research about the management of media firms and industries to legitimate our contention that the field is reasonably distinctive.

The community of researchers, educators and practitioners involved with media management agree on the need to better define and describe what is distinctive and therefore valuable in this specialisation. That is important for advancing theory and supporting professionalism in practice. Many of the answers offered here are somewhat tentative. That is not surprising given the newness of the field. We don't see this as a problem because our collective intention is to stimulate scholarly discourse that will broaden and deepen understandings. This matters not only to our specialisation but, arguably, for theory development in the broader field of media studies.

Aside from a rich vein of scholarship in political economy, media studies have not prioritised organisational structure and managerial context. Mainly the focus has been on production, technology and power relations. As Jason Schlosberg demonstrates in Chap. 9, the potential for better connecting a heritage of relevant study in political economy with media management studies holds promise for development in both areas. This echoes remarks made earlier by Robert G. Picard (2008) about challenges and opportunities in grafting media studies onto management studies roots. We might take issue with the one directional nature of his

G.F. Lowe (✉)
School of Communication, Media and Theatre, University of Tampere, Tampere, Finland
e-mail: Greg.Lowe@uta.fi

© Springer International Publishing Switzerland 2016
G.F. Lowe, C. Brown (eds.), *Managing Media Firms and Industries*, Media
Business and Innovation, DOI 10.1007/978-3-319-08515-9_1

proposal and instead suppose that for this specialisation development depends as much on grafting management studies onto the roots of media studies.

The book's title supposes there is something "special" about media management. The contributors interrogate what that entails. Special can be variously understood. It can refer to something that is especially valuable and treasured because it is comparatively extraordinary. Special can be understood more generically to imply a notable degree of uniqueness, whether treasured or not. And the term can be a polite way of saying "abnormal".

Whether this field becomes uniquely valuable and treasured depends mainly on the quality of research and whether scholarship generates fresh insight that advances theory and matters to practice at the intersection of media studies and management studies. The book contents evidence good possibilities for achieving that over time. But as Küng (2007: 22) observed several years ago, "While the field is acquiring critical mass in terms of students and scholars, it has yet to establish an accepted set of theoretical foundations. It's literature is fragmented and diverse—a loose agglomeration". There are also problems in the field of management studies that are pertinent here. As Picard (2008: 4) observed, "One of the challenges of grafting to the root stock of management studies is that much of the origins of management theory and research were based on activities of manufacturing companies".

Thus, for the most part, the contents of this book suggest the second understanding of "special" is a more accurate description at this point. A scholarly community interested in the management of media firms is working on something comparatively unique but not yet widely treasured. As for the third option, many colleagues are located between business and media schools, and colleagues in media studies have sometimes been rather dismissive of the field as a focus better left to business schools (Chan-Olmsted, 2006: xvii). Not infrequently the field is viewed by colleagues on both sides of the aisle, i.e. in media studies and management studies, as an unusual if not somewhat "abnormal" area, and criticised by media scholars as administrative research.

That can be a fair criticism, but it is not something we feel uncomfortable with—much less ashamed about. As Kurt Lewin (1952) famously proposed, "there is nothing so practical as good theory". The importance of conducting research that has potential to benefit society is a necessary implication of the *social* sciences, and media are a vital aspect of much in social life today. Moreover, as discussed below, much of the funding for academic positions in the field is provided by grants from the industry and associated foundations. In that conjunction a practical orientation is inescapable. However, there is a pressing need for a more characteristic scepticism than is evident in most of what has been published in this field and a greater role for critical theory (see Chap. 5 by Charles Brown for pointed discussion). Conducting research and building theory that benefits practice is not a problem, but rather an asset that matters for achieving greater legitimacy. It is fair to say that conducting research that uncritically supports the corporate self-interests of media operators and fails to address questionable practices because of the field's dependence on industrial support, or because colleagues are keen to be accepted by the management science community, is problematic—not only for this field but for the academy more generally.

As Picard (2008: 2) has noted, "Media management courses in universities began in the mid twentieth century, but when one reviews those courses and the literature of media management studies through most of the past 50 years, one finds that it included media but very little management". That began to change at the turn of the twenty-first century as media management was recognised as having vital importance as a specialisation in its own right. To date, however, the field has a tangled if largely fruitful relationship with the older field of media economics, which began in the latter half of the 1970s and early 1980s. Most of the innovators involved in launching media management studies are internationally recognised media economists, e.g. Robert G. Picard, Alfonso Nieto, Karl Erik Gustafsson, Alan Albarran and Steven Wildman, to name a few of the best known. Most members of the European Media Management Association (emma), the sponsor for this book project, work in academic programmes that were launched after 2005. The newness of the field is evident, as well, in the large proportion of participants in annual emma conferences who are young faculty just beginning academic careers and Ph.D. students working on dissertations.

Academic programmes in media management are under development and many are not very secure, another indication of newness and also of uncertain value. Academic positions and programmes in this field are often funded by external grants rather than the internal budgets of academic institutions. Some of the early programmes, such as the pioneering effort at St. Gallen in Switzerland, were defunded some time ago because they lost external support (in that case from Bertelsmann, which was the main sponsor). The Media Group at the Business Research and Development Centre at the Turku School of Economics in Finland has disbanded, as well. The Media Management Center at Northwestern University in the USA, another early pioneering institution, has done better than most and has been the key driver for the International Media Management Academic Association (IMMAA), due especially to the work of John Lavine.

Most media management curricula are mainly, even exclusively, at the graduate level—typically as a specialised master's degree programme. In some cases it is only for Ph.D. studies, as at the Media Management and Transformation Center in the Jönköping International Business School in Sweden. Many programmes depend on a small faculty's (often one or two) aptitude in fundraising and maintaining industry support, as well as cultivating the support of wider faculties in cross-disciplinary arrangements (usually media and business schools). The location of media management in academic institutions straddles a range of divides with uncertain placement, again characteristic of emerging fields.

As Hirsch and Levin (1999) found in their research about the emergence of new fields and how paradigm shifts happen in older ones, in early development there is great interest—nearly obsessive—to develop definitions, heuristics and typologies that frame (or reframe) a field. After this period of "emerging excitement" when the new thing takes hold, there is a period of "validity challenge" as its credibility is interrogated. The third stage is "tidying up with typologies" as the concept is reconfigured and refined. This is followed by one of three outcomes in period four: (1) "override of challenges" meaning an umbrella concept is agreed to be valid and becomes the dominant paradigm; (2) "permanent issue", meaning there is no consensus and disagreement persists, perhaps endlessly; or (3) "construct collapse", meaning the new concept is scraped.

This field has so far been in the first period and the second is underway, overlapping with the third. We could expect this to last several years and to be followed by one of the three outcomes—hopefully the override of challenges. But should scholarship fail to advance theory that matters in both media and management studies, sadly the third outcome option is more likely.

1.2   Managing Media Complexity

As Küng (2007: 24) suggests, "The goal of studying media management must be to build a bridge between the general discipline of management and the specificities of the media industry and media organisations". We propose that what makes media management special has mainly to do with the kinds of products created and distributed by media companies, the types of people that do that work and the potential significance of the results in multiple dimensions (economic, cultural, social, political, technological). This is illustrated in Table 1.1, which encapsulates a general mapping of the field. Most of these elements are covered in this book by the various authors, although not in equal detail or comprehensively. We will come back to this point.

It is clear that media companies are not only financial enterprises—far from it. Of course the same can be said of other industries. The total value and social

Table 1.1 Illustrating the complexity of media industries

Products	People	Environment	Consequences
Public goods	Owners and investors	Instability	Social cohesion
Experience goods	Content makers	Uncertainty	Representation and portrayal
Talent goods	Managers	Fragmentation	Conditioning
Credence goods	Advertisers	Digitalization	Pluralism
Symbolic goods	Audiences	Convergence	Democracy
Dual market goods	Suppliers	Consolidation	Market dynamics
Multi-purpose goods	Partners/Alliances	Diverse contexts	Polarisation
Single production	Competitors	Legacies	Cultural roles
Series production	Regulators	Decline and growth	
Media/platforms	Foundations	Multi-sectoral	
Genres	NGOs and civil society		
Transmedia			

impact of everything from construction to transportation, from mining and refining to retail sales and industrial manufacturing, aren't only important for economic reasons. But media industries have a range of social responsibilities and a degree of social impact that seems exceptional.

Let's begin with the first column. Media companies make and distribute products and services (both) that are highly complex goods. They are at the same time symbolic goods, public goods, club goods, experience goods, talent goods, multipurpose goods and goods for dual markets. Chapter 14 by Mercedes Medina and her colleagues at the University of Navarra in Spain focuses on this as the core concern. A refrigerator might be more than an appliance, for instance it could be a symbolic good if one buys a particular brand and style as a fashion statement. But the product doesn't serve multiple purposes. A new restaurant is an experience good because one can't know its quality or value until having eaten at least one meal, and the product certainly depends in large part on the talent of the chef and kitchen team, but it is not a public good because the product is characterised by rivalry (one person can consume each meal and no one else). An expensive restaurant is more like a club good because many people are excluded by high price. Although goods produced by all industries have some of the features that are indicative of media goods, perhaps none have all of these features as a *characteristic* "package". Managing that package in creation, distribution and continual development requires a set of managerial skills, talents and processes that are commensurate with the tasks.

The management of media firms is uniquely challenging because the tasks are also complex. Media content is essential to the "soft power" of nations in the international arena (Nye, 2005). Some believe, for example, that Disney animated films have done more through the years to cultivate positive perceptions of America abroad than most diplomatic efforts and much of the nation's aid contributions (Fraser, 2003), although soft power can backfire (Fraser, 2008). Media play vital roles in the exercise of citizenship for the practice of democracy and have considerable potential to support a higher degree of general knowledge and educational achievement for a society, as well as contributing to the experience of its (typically rich) cultural heritage and the continual evolution of that (Christians, Glasser, McQuail, Nordenstreng, & White, 2009). One needs to acknowledge the media sector's contributions to employment, tax revenues and profits (Doyle, 2013; Picard, 2011). Media industries are typically mandated to fulfil functions that aren't good business but are the price of doing business. They are subject to regulations and legislation to a comparatively high degree, although more so in broadcasting and less in print (see Chap. 6 by Anker Brink Lund for insightful discussion in application to the public sector in European dual-market systems in broadcasting).

Media content has socially significant roles in shared processes of "working through" the meanings and implications of events, concepts and emotional consequences (Ellis, 2000)—what many now refer to as "the affective economy" (Annette Hill provides fascinating Chap. 16 on this topic). Each genre plays some role in a complex mediation process, from news reports that inform a public about an event, to current affairs discussions about it, to dramatic portrayals and enactments that humanise the event, and even to comedic relief that can reduce anxiety. Media content simultaneously connects people, reflects both distinctive and mutual concerns, and confronts all of us from time to time (Sullivan, 2013).

Systemic arrangements and platform features are much the same everywhere, but there are always distinctive aspects as a function of local languages, diverse cultures and heritage ways of life (McQuail, 2010). People use media for an astonishing range of activities and facilitations—to both bond and differentiate, to relax and work, to collaborate and compete, to contribute and profit, to approach and avoid, to advocate and critique and to question and answer. Media products are multipurpose goods.

A range of media goods entails one-off productions, especially characteristic in the production of films, books and audio recordings. Many others are serial productions, especially characteristic of newspapers, magazines and broadcast programming (Picard, 2011). These lines are not clear-cut, however. A book or motion picture that hits can be developed into a franchise that becomes a series, as evident in the Harry Potter phenomenon. Most media goods are produced as projects, and the projectification of content creation has become increasingly characteristic due to corporate downsizing, freelance contracting and the growth of an independent sector in most media markets (see Chap. 21 by Rolf Lundin and Maria Norbäck for detailed discussion).

A media enterprise functions in the public domain even when owned and operated as a private enterprise, and even more characteristically when positioned as a public utility (PSB) or community channel. Media scholarship features a rich heritage of discourse about the social responsibility of media firms with different schools of thought about the proper roles and obligations of media in society. The diversity in media systems reflects this complexity. Despite convergence and consolidation, there are still distinctive expectations for different media (and firms). Audiences and policy makers do not necessarily apply the same standards or criteria to newspapers, broadcasters, publishers and new media. What passes for good content in an individual blog might not pass muster for newspaper publication, and what works as a personal video posted on YouTube doesn't fulfil the expectations most people have for television. Publishers can specialise in narrow niches and that is perfectly acceptable, but newspapers are generally expected to provide a broad range of socially relevant services and often publish news and information that isn't profitable even when operating as hyper-local providers. Here we are touching on the fourth column with a concern about the consequences of mediation.

This unique importance is evident in many Western societies where media are the only industries with constitutional protections. In most democracies, freedom of the press is enshrined as a civic right that government is forbidden to obstruct. What is special about media management has a lot to do with what is special about the roles and functions of media in societies. Yet, there are different models for understanding the roles of media, and alternative normative frameworks for legitimating varied, even contending approaches to the structuring and functions of media systems (Christians et al., 2009). That suggests another dimension of what is special about media management: there will always be intriguing diversity in the arrangements, tasks and performance that characterise media firms and industries in different countries and regions, posing comparatively unique challenges for management work in these industries.

Media are also special due to the people that media firms employ, as well as the diverse and often contending interests of relevant stakeholders. Regarding media workers, there is not only enormous diversity in types of work and workers but employment trends that include especially the casualisation of labour agreements, outsourcing, downsizing and freelancing add another layer of complexity (see Chap. 19 by Mark Deuze for thoughtful discussion). Many workers involved with creating content are journalists or artists. Each has characteristic (if often stereotyped) personas that make managing such talent challenging and sometimes frustrating. Journalists are sceptical by disposition and training, often becoming more so as a result of calluses that develop from experience. It's rarely enough for a manager to "tell them how it is" and trust that compliance is forthcoming. Considerable effort at convincing is usually required. For their part, artists tend to resist rules and to resent authority, thinking that management stifles creativity. In Chap. 20, Paul Dwyer deals with relevant aspects and provides an illuminating example from the BBC in Britain.

In general, the population of media workers has comparatively high degrees of individual expertise across varied specialisations. They work as professionals and take codes of ethical practice seriously. Most prefer familiar routines for handling the complicated and demanding types of work required in media production (e.g. news reporting, scriptwriting, producing in formats, logging and editing footage, etc.), typically on deadline. That makes change difficult, even painful, because it wastes time and strikes at the core of professional identities, and because it makes doing the job more difficult under conditions of higher uncertainty. It is also difficult to manage talent because very often they find it impossible to explain what they do or how and why they do it well. Much of what they know is tacit knowledge, which also makes research challenging. Moreover, media workers must be able to work independently but also collaboratively. And the work of media production is characterised by contradictions that must be managed. News should be informative but also competitive (i.e. popular); quality matters, but so does being contented with "good enough" due to cost concerns; media production features high degrees of time-pressure and can be quite stressful. Professionals who take pride and pleasure in their creations don't take kindly to managers who want to change aspects they consider special, often quite personal.

Dealing with workers and other managers internal to a media firm is important for success as a media manager, but the range of constituencies with a stake in the media system and its operations is so much broader. Government cares about media for the social, political and economic aspects of its structural performance and because representation and portrayal have considerable impact on electoral results. Regulators must address the concerns of contending parties, allowing for (even catering to) the self-interested concerns of the industry while accommodating the diverse and often contrary interests of audiences, advertisers, manufacturers of electronic goods, national and international laws, etc. Advertisers are important to profitability, but don't inherently have the same interests as audiences. Even the "audience" concept is increasingly complicated: a general audience, niche or target audiences, listeners, viewers, users, producers, creators, etc. (Chap. 15 by Philip Napoli is enlightening here).

One also needs to factor in the dynamics of co-opetition that characterises industrial relations in media today. Independent production firms account for an increasing proportion of content as in-house production and staff shrink. As Porter (1980/2004) demonstrated in the "five forces" of competitive rivalry, suppliers and customers can also be collaborators or competitors—and the nature of which changes over time as conditions develop. That is characteristic of media industries where an independent or freelance supplier of content acts as a collaborator on one project but as a competitor in another—often enough at the same moment. Similarly the market situation as a whole is highly volatile these days as a consequence of convergence and consolidation that happens on a global scale.

Without question, then, the work of managing a media enterprise is characterised by high degrees of complexity in the kinds of goods produced, in the ways and means of production and in the diverse professionals on which the work depends. It is equally characterised by high degrees of uncertainty in the environment. As Table 1.1 illustrates, environmental conditions indicate that little to nothing can be taken for granted.

Media industries have a history of industrial structures (Berg, Lowe, & Brink Lund, 2014; Dimmick, 2003) that are either monopolies due to licensing and regulations premised on normative theories about what media are supposed to do and be responsible for in a society (e.g. social responsibility for PSB), or oligopolies due to characteristic dynamics for these industries (such as high fixed costs, high first copy costs, economies of scale, economies of scope and copyright regimes). If monopoly was historically characteristic of public (and also state) broadcasting, oligopoly continues to be the predominant structure in "competitive" contexts (Berg, 2012; Doyle, 2013; Picard, 2011).

The management of media firms was arguably underdeveloped because competition was limited, in many cases non-existent. The margins for media firms fattened on multiple revenue streams that include advertising, sponsorship, subscriptions, merchandising, market protections (subsidies, trade barriers and regulation) and restricted competition (either by design or default). The managers of media firms didn't need to be highly competent in many arenas of theory and practice that are keenly important now—e.g. strategic management, brand management, human resource management, innovation management, supply chain management, financial management, etc.

Since the late 1990s, and especially in conjunction with the general economic contraction since 2008, key trends that had been evident for some time have been magnified and accelerated, including disruption of industry structures and growing instability for legacy firms caused by the growth of web-based media and declines in mass media use by audiences and advertisers. Proliferation of media and channels is slicing the advertising cake into ever more slender portions. Classified advertising has declined dramatically as people instead use Craig's List and similar online services. Media markets are far less cohesive, and there are pressing concerns about the future of mass media, in particular, which tend to be dominated by large companies with significant economic resources and societal influence (Albarran & Mierzejewska, 2004; Baker, 2006; Noam, 2009) that therefore have been the major employers for media workers of all types. Today, however, entrepreneurialism is a growing trend in corporate strategy, individual career development and media management education (Chap. 11 by Andreas Will and his colleagues at Ilmaneu University of Technology in Germany focuses on this aspect).

Reading this book, it's clear there are many moving parts that are interdependent elements in the media ecology—a system of systems with a multiplicity of links featuring complex dynamics at the intersection between societies, markets, cultures, organisations and products. There is much differentiation within and between these parts and considerable variation in how they fit together. It is commonplace to acknowledge that how things are in this company or that country can't be generalised very far. But everywhere it is clearly true that media industries are in a period of turbulent change. Media firms must develop their dynamic capabilities for success in a context that now requires continuous adaptation; they must also rethink traditional business models and develop new and more integrated revenue streams (see Chap. 17 by John Oliver about dynamics capabilities and Chap. 12 by Bjørn von Rimscha about business models).

Even what counts as a "media company" is no longer certain; Google and Apple can be considered as such although neither is a content making enterprise (primarily, at least). There is a growing volume of non-institutional media actors engaged in production and distribution of content, as evident in blogging and user-generated content. Platform companies historically focused on distribution, like YouTube and Netflix, are becoming content makers. We also need to remember that we are not in fact dealing with "the" media industry, but rather with varied media industries. As Chap. 4 by Paulo Faustino and Luísa Ribeiro explains, differences between platforms and sectors pose significant challenges for managers across media—an issue of particular importance in consolidated media firms. Managers also struggle with a constant need to invest in new technologies and upgrades and to finance the training that is required to utilise and capitalise on those investments.

As a result, there are fewer and fewer parts of the media-society ecology that are "under control". Media managers no longer have the luxury of focusing on a narrow range of volatile aspects. Today this combination of *complexity, uncertainty and volatility* is characteristic and explains a lot of what is unique about media enterprises and therefore why their management is distinctively challenging.

1.3   Shortcomings and Challenges in Media Management Practice

Given the characteristic features of media markets, it isn't surprising that in many cases the management of media firms has not historically been predicated on expertise in managing. In these industries managers are often promoted due to success in content production. Good journalists become editors, successful actors become film directors, and great DJs become programme directors. In the former European PSB monopolies, managers were political appointees, and even when not as often the case these days, their managers must deal with often subtle but persistent political pressures. Chapter 7 by Christian S. Nissen addresses these issues in some detail. In the USA there has long been a "revolving door" between corporate success and appointment to the Federal Communications Commission (FCC) and of FCC officials leaving for lucrative rewards in the industry (Calabrese & Mihal, 2011; Downie, 2011).

Sometimes employees that haven't been successful in content making are "promoted" to management positions in the big media firms, especially in Europe, rather than endure complications involved with sacking them given comparatively rigid labour structures. Even where structures are flexible, as in the USA, incompetent managers are sometimes kept on (if moved around) to avoid embarrassment. There is also a history of media managers who are mainly investors that launched or acquired media properties and took on their management. Managers of this type might know little about the media business per se, especially if they are external investors with speculative interest (see Chap. 3 by Juan Pablo Artero and Juan Manfredi for an overview and discussion about contemporary competencies). Such problems have not ended, but they are becoming less common. The stakes are too high and the competition too serious to tolerate managerial incompetence. Certainly there are legacy problems in some media companies that are big and old where managers are sometimes left in place for political reasons. But the importance of training and development among media managers is an evident trend.

There is also a heritage of managerial division in media firms, particularly in journalistic organisations where a deliberate separation between management arenas is typified where the General Director or CEO is responsible for business operations while an Editor in Chief or Programme Director is responsible for content production. The separation of powers is legitimated on the premise that news reporting requires a high degree of independence from business interests to ensure serving the critical, democratic functions of civil society. That pattern of editorial-business separation is questioned these days, and journalistic firms are less bashful about basing content decisions on business interests. One routinely hears newspaper publishers, especially, expounding on the necessary interdependence of editorial and commercial operations to ensure the long-term viability of the firm in an era of evident decline (in the West, at least).

There is evidence, however, that the dual-market nature of commercial news media exerts both explicit and implicit pressures when deciding what stories to cover and how to present or portray them. The FAIR organisation provides annual reports about this problem and its increasingly less subtle persistence (Fairness and Accuracy in Reporting, u.d). And Stavitsky (1995) observed that radio programme makers and journalists at National Public Radio [NPR] in the USA distrusted the intentions of audience researchers because they perceived "the guys in suits with charts" to represent the interests of corporate managers. Picard (2006) observed that an increasing percentage of news media content is not original and therefore not valuable to readers and viewers. Aggregated content is commercially cost effective, but only in the short run.

Even in non-journalistic firms, a characteristic tension between employees who are responsible for the business interests and those responsible for the artistic properties has long been notable. Aris and Bughin (2009) highlighted the generalisable nature of the problem between "sales" and "programming" in commercial broadcasting. Bilton (2011) emphasised the impact of digitalisation in current trends to soften this historic divide, but the problems persist due to the reality of multiple professions with distinctive subcultures working simultaneously but not always harmoniously within media firms. The various specialisations don't speak the same language or interpret the meaning of work or of the enterprise in the same ways. In fact, they may see things in antagonistic terms.

Removing or at least lessening the historic divide seems advisable, but media companies should develop an abiding and consistent appreciation for ethical dilemmas because these frequently test the metal of media managers. There is sustained need for a healthy understanding of, and respect for, what is now regarded as "corporate responsibility" but has a longer, deeper history as social responsibility in the media. This topic is considered in Chap. 8 by Georgios Tsourvakas. The responsibilities that media have to and for society are contested, but nonetheless considerable. Renewing the necessary balance between business and organisational interests with social and public interests is an increasingly pressing concern—as evident in discussions about journalistic ethics. Mixing and blurring content and business aspects can create enormous problems, as the phone-hacking scandal at News Corporation illustrates.

The historic lack of emphasis on excellence in media management practice, even a general standard of required competencies for managers, is understandable in light of the historically limited amounts of competition. But managerial competence in media firms is an issue of considerable importance today, as evident in the flourishing of media management programmes in a growing number of schools and universities—often funded in part or entirely by media firms and foundations. This brings us to consideration of research and education.

1.4 Summarising and Critiquing the Status of the Field

There has not been concerted effort at theorisation that is distinctive to media management scholarship, although much more has been done in the first and second columns of Table 1.1 than the other two. There is established research and discourse about the nature of media goods and a growing body of work about managing for innovation and entrepreneurialism. Although welcome, much of that is not about media management per se, but rather about the co-related field of media economics. One can't yet point to a body of theory that is unique to media management scholarship. On the plus side, the field is inherently cross-disciplinary. As Sylvia Chan-Olmsted observed, when responding to a request for fundamental literature in the field, the books and articles she recommends are "the 'borrowed' literatures from economics, management, sociology, marketing and many other areas" (Chan-Olmsted, 2006: xvii).

To date, this young field has mainly focused on applying management theory in research about media companies, in affect using media firms and industries as case studies. A review of two journals, the International Journal on Media Management and the Journal of Media Business Studies, makes this evident. Publications emphasise, for example, brand management in media firms, strategic management in media firms, innovation management in media firms, project management in media industries, new business models in the digital environment and so forth (see Chap. 2 by Achtenhagen and Mierzejewska for detailed examination).

Thus, our theoretical foundations are uncertain and highly fragmented and often rather weak as evident in the proportion of conference papers and journal publications that have been strongly descriptive studies. There is usually some theoretical framework, but this often feels "tacked on" rather than the guiding light and grounds for empirical testing. That is beginning to change as a growing proportion of the papers presented in recent conferences put more emphasis on crafting theoretical frames and conducting theory-driven research.

But it's also problematic that published work in our field too often fails to incorporate general scholarship from communication and media studies. This heritage is present by implication, especially in comparisons between mass media and new media and in the occasional application of critical and cultural approaches, but when reading journal articles it is striking how rarely even classic literature from communication and media scholarship is cited. The community seems more concerned with applying general management theory than with developing communications and media theory. Our perspective here is at odds with Küng (2007) who believed more management theory is what's needed and that there might even be an over-reliance on media scholarship. Perhaps that could have been true at the time, but it's not evidently accurate today. We also suggest that the field needs to pay far more attention to broad strands of philosophic thought (sociology, anthropology, political science, history, etc.) and to engage in more critical deliberation.

We hope this book helps stimulate such discourse. That is vital to create a discipline, which this isn't yet because there are no characteristic theories or cohesiveness in a shared body of knowledge already proven to be both distinctive and important. As long as media management scholars are mainly talking only with each other and not also being talked about by others, the field hasn't "arrived". That is not to imply that it is normatively negative to lack disciplinary status. "Ferment in the field", to use the phrase from an influential issue of the Journal of Communication (1983), is characteristic when a profound change is underway. Certainly little could be more profound that the launch and early development of a field. As the editors of that journal issue observed, "the emergence of a vital new discipline" depends on the development of "the dialogue of perspectives... [marking] the growth and rapid development of communications as a discipline, it's coming of age" (pp. 4–5). We need to encourage and engage a robust discourse about the scope, ingredients, dynamics and characteristic of media management theory.

Perhaps we are being too harsh in the effort to make our point. There is reason to think this specialisation has an importance that is likely to grow and might well contribute to the development of theory both in management and about media and pointedly at the intersection of the two. Table 1.1 suggests four areas of research with potential for that: (1) characteristic dynamics of media industries that require competence to manage highly complex goods (the product column in our table); (2) the characteristic complexity of relevant constituencies, as well as historic division between management and content making in media firms (the people column in our table); (3) the degree of uncertainty and instability that is uniquely challenging for these industries and thus for their management (the environment column in our table); and (4) the impact of media products on the nature and experience of social life (the consequences column in our table).

1.4.1   Media Management in Academic Institutions

In answering the question as to what is so special about media management, we must simultaneously consider what is different and especially valuable about the properties of media and what is unique and potentially important about scholarship in this field. The two aspects are interdependent. The book's premise focuses on what is special about managing a media firm that is different when compared with management in other industries. The editors have tried to ensure that each chapter addresses that key question. The premise also focuses on what is therefore special about this academic field, which is a crucial factor for longer-term sustainability.

What is (so far) special about media management as an academic field is a strong orientation towards practice with a keen interest in applied theory. Our faculties are working in areas that have real-world implications and pursue real-world impact. That is not surprising because media management programmes tend to be rooted either in business schools, which need tight links with companies and industries, or in media schools that often specialise in training students to be journalists or other specialists in content production. Curricula typically include student internships and temporary employment so students gain practical experience. We should continue to value and appreciate the importance of this. But to mature as a field of scholarship and one that produces fresh insight, our research needs to be more critical, more comparative and more collaborative.

One must be careful about the terms of reference. One researcher conceives of media firms mainly in the journalistic context while another conceives of this in TV production or book publishing or telecommunications. In fact we are not talking about "the" media industry, but rather a sector of broader economies (regional, national and international) that is comprised of various media industries. Moreover, media researchers in Europe should not neglect consideration of the public sector because in the northwest region especially PSB organisations are big and powerful with strong heritages.

American media management scholars typically conceive of media industries as commercial entities. Some find the European context strange, in the worse cases "inferior" to the American system. Meanwhile, Asian media management scholars and those in countries where the state has or had a strong authoritarian character, conceptualisation understandably has much to do with supporting state control or taking a critical stance opposed to that. The roles, responsibilities and risks of being a media manager vary across these contexts. American media firms don't have to deal as much or as often with policy issues in daily practice, while Asia media firms can court grave risk in being outspokenly critical of government authorities.

This field has enjoyed rapid growth in European and American universities and increasingly now also in Asia. Flourishing interest has encouraged graduate studies coursework in media studies curricula and a growing number of comprehensive programmes being offered in media management. This was recently evident in the strong interest to participate in a pre-conference on curricula and pedagogy during the 2014 emma event in Tallinn, Estonia. Whereas the organisers had expected 20 at most, in fact close to 45 participated from universities across Europe and from Asia. One also finds relevant courses increasingly offered in curricula at the undergraduate level. This suggests the field is increasingly recognised as having importance in the essentials for media-related education.

There are also more professorships in media management and economics advertised today, often funded with "soft money" provided by industry foundations. Media firms are keenly aware of the need for developing management competencies, and many are paying for senior and middle managers to receive specialised training. While much of this happens in executive MBA programmes that aren't only (or even mainly) focused on media enterprises, many emma members provide education services for industry executives and middle managers, and courses are often scheduled for weekends and evenings to accommodate those that must continue work alongside studies.

Certainly some proportion of the field's growth is the "flash in the pan" variety, meaning that high interest may not be matched by high commitment from some institutions. Some universities and polytechnic schools have undoubtedly added media management coursework because it's fresh and attractive to potential students, and thus partly serves a PR and marketing function. Serious investment is less evident. Moreover, adding coursework and faculty in this field can attract external funding from media companies and foundations. That's fine, but it's an open question as to whether this specialisation enjoys abiding and substantial institutional support to withstand the growing pains and arrive at a mature status eventually.

Soft money funding is an asset many universities need today, but it is also a potential liability because programmes are easier to start than sustain and some of the pioneers have disappeared (as discussed earlier). Professorships that depend on external funding to a high degree are vulnerable when it dries up, and that is especially problematic in a strained fiscal climate when universities are cutting back and cutting out so much, and given the fact that many working in this field are young faculty without tenure. Even though it is not a popular sentiment in some academic circles, it seems fair to note that any new programme or position must prove its value partly by its worth.

The contents of this book suggest that the degree to which the field of media management will flourish as an academic specialisation depends largely on how successful the community becomes in fundraising. But arguably, more important still is success in developing an insightful, influential and applicable body of relevant theory. That is the key to sustainability for any academic field and especially crucial for a young one. The authors in this book contribute varied perspectives from diverse schools of management thought and research that together suggest rich possibilities for accomplishing that. It is encouraging to read about so much relevant work being done across such a range of national, industrial and cross-disciplinary contexts. But there is not yet enough collaborative and comparative research being done or funded. Quite a lot of published works are case studies on particular companies in a few industries and in select countries, with findings that are difficult—often impossible—to generalise.

As a community, we aren't apparently looking at the same issues or phenomena across companies and countries or incorporating (as a rule) the diverse sectors comprising media systems (private commercial + public service + community alternative + company owned or sponsored). One should be concerned about the lack of focused research programmes and cumulative results that are comparative, comprehensive and also critical in character. Chapter 5 by Charles Brown makes the later point quite well and is substantiated in Chap. 9 by Justin Schlosberg. Küng (2007: 33) highlighted some of the consequences:

> Media management researchers to date have focused primarily on the external environ-
> ment, structural characteristics, industry output, and consumers. In addition, there is a
> substantial body of work applying rationalist strategy models, looking particularly at the
> content of media firms' strategies. The inevitable result is that understanding of the media
> industry is uneven, and that a number of important dimensions and developments in the
> field are under addressed.

1.4.2   Caveats

There are four caveats that we want to particularly highlight. First, we've not addressed media management in non-Western cultures and societies. Our view is grounded in European traditions, with useful contributions from the USA. This is not a normative position. We aren't implying a Western orientation is the ideal and ought to be the model everywhere. This was a deliberate decision keyed to the fact that the book is produced under the auspices of the *European* Media Management Association and most of our contributors are members. We expect dynamics and key competencies to vary for media firms and industries in the developing world. We anticipate more comprehensive understandings as publications from other regions and contexts emerge.

A second caveat has to do with the lack of research about community and alternative media. There is little published in media management literature about this third sector. Following Drucker (2007), we would expect rich differences in management dynamics and key competencies given the largely voluntary nature of work (where makers aren't always employees) and due to financial distinctions characteristic of fundraising for operators in the sector. There are seams that need stitching and holes that need filling in this new field.

A third limitation is the lack of as much remark about what is the *same* in media management as in the management of any kind of company. Although the book's thematic focus emphasises both sides (what is unique and what is not), the authors mainly deal with what is comparatively unique. This reflects a self-interested bias because authors and editors have vested professional interests in demonstrating the unique importance of our specialisation. This community is struggling to establish a new field, often against economic and institutional pressures that make positions vulnerable given its newness. Most contributors would agree that "of course" media management is special and "of course" it should be supported by home institutions and media industries. It is unsurprising that the substance as a whole tends to underemphasise the ways and degrees to which media management is little or not at all different from managing other kinds of firms—a point made by Knee, Greenwald and Seave (2009).

We certainly accept the "management realities". Whatever the means for generating revenue, every media firm is a financial organisation. Finances must be managed, and managers are accountable for how money is spent and what it produces or fails to produce. State media organisations are equally required to keep within budgetary limits and are responsible for financial accounting. Every organisation of much size is obliged to manage employees, generally understood as "human resources". Even the smallest outfits are concerned about developing the enterprise to ensure a sustainable future and support training to master new competencies and unfamiliar technologies or software packages. In these and other ways, the management of a media company is no different from what is required of professional managers for any organisation.

Although important, the similarities aren't really surprising or very revealing. They have little to offer in establishing what is uniquely important about this field of specialisation. The potential for contributing to the development of theory about media management—especially at their intersection—as well as the potential value produced for useful application depends on the ways and degrees to which media companies are different from other types.

As noted earlier, much of the scholarship one finds in our literature is derived from general management theories that are applied to media firms and industries. The giants on whose shoulders we stand include Michael Porter, Henry Mintzberg, Peter Drucker, Teresa Amabile and Clayton Christiansen, for instance. Obviously quite a lot of the work in managing a media firm is the same as for other industries;

elsewise, these bodies of theory would not be as popular as they evidently are in our work. But it would be useful if more scholarship in this field would challenge received management theory.

A fourth caveat is that we aren't able to deal in one volume with all areas of research and expertise, or even in detail with areas that are treated. We have included one chapter on many topics, each of which could merit a book in its own right. Although there is overlap between some chapters because media industry dynamics are a shared and persistent feature, allowing too much overlap would be redundant and grow tiresome. As editors, we've had to handle a characteristic conundrum: the impossibility of including everything that is relevant and the restriction of only being able to incorporate a comparatively limited treatment of anything. There are broad and significant areas of media management work that aren't dealt with here, for example, we have nothing about brand management or customer relationship management. We invited chapters about both, but weren't able to make it happen. The circle of experts in these areas in this field is still small, so options are correspondingly constrained.

From the outset, we have understood this to be a necessary limitation and conceived the book as a means for helping to facilitate a wider and deeper conversation at this critical juncture in the field's scholarly development. The book is intended to encourage a discourse of ferment about how to develop the field, both as a scientific practice and in practical application. In that light it is as legitimate to talk about what is not here and ought to be, as what is included and why that matters. We welcome critique about what has been missed and merits inclusion in future publications that we could hope this inaugural emma-sponsored publication might encourage.

1.4.3 The Editorial Process

It will be useful to briefly explain the editorial process. Lowe proposed the project at the 2012 Annual General Assembly of emma's conference, that year at the Corvinus University in Budapest. He was the newly elected president of the association, and Brown was the outgoing president. We agreed to collaborate as editors.

We originally thought to include chapters from managers but decided that would entail a different book with less value for academic purposes, which we consider crucial given the connection with emma. Few managers would have the time or the expertise in academic work to provide a suitable contribution. One notable exception in this volume is Christian S. Nissen, the former Director General of DR Denmark who has a strong academic background and is today an Adjunct Professor at the Copenhagen Business School (and winner of the emma Annual Award for Excellence in 2012). We decided this book should be primarily intended for academic readers as an effort to contribute to developing the field. Of course we hope thoughtful managers with intellectual interests in the field, especially specialists working as internal advisors and consultants, will find the book useful.

But we understand the pithy point made by Lucy Küng (2010: 55): "Academic material is, it seems, too abstract and too vague to be useful in practice, and full of impenetrable vocabulary". We have tried to lessen this problem, but it is partly unavoidable in a scholarly book.

The editorial process began with the publication of a Call for Chapter Proposals. We received a handful, mainly keyed to conference papers or already published books. We did not receive enough to build a collection. We therefore invited most of the authors in this volume, in each case with a specific focus. Roughly 20 % of those we invited declined, mainly due to lack of time. That explains why some important thinkers are regrettably not included in the collection. Although missed, in our estimation this hasn't harmed the value of the book. Although a few of the invited chapters did not work out in practice and were dropped, this did not happen often, and in each case the choice was as much with the author as the editors.

The editors reviewed the first draft of each chapter and provided extensive critique, suggestions and directions for development. The authors returned their revisions and the editors reviewed these drafts, as well. In many cases the second draft was of sufficient quality to be sent for peer review, double-blind method. In some cases a third draft was requested before this step. The authors received the peer review results and produced a third (or fourth) draft. In most cases this was the final draft, although in a few cases the editors requested minor adjustments to complete the project. The final draft was copy-edited by Lowe.

During the process, we received a few complaints from colleagues who had not been invited to contribute. We apologise for hurt feelings, but we couldn't include everything or everyone. We have based decisions on what seemed best for the book as a collection. The size is about where the limits extend before a multiple volume series would have been required, with significantly more work and higher costs. We hope the quality of the results will please the authors who have contributed, and that those who were disappointed at not being included will nonetheless find the book of value for their research and teaching.

We want to express our sincere appreciation to the authors who have done so much work in producing this volume, and such good work. This has been a demanding project. We think the results demonstrate the good quality of scholarly thinking that is percolating in this field today. As editors, we found it remarkably easy to work with the authors and were routinely impressed by the commitment and dedication they demonstrated throughout the project. A few authors have been frustrated that it has taken so long to complete the manuscript, and we have shared that feeling. But the approach we took was essential to guarantee the quality of scholarship and the validity of all the contributions when reporting professional accomplishments in annual evaluations that have a bearing on decisions about promotion. It was important that we demonstrate a process as rigorous and method-ical as for publication in an academic journal.

Finally, editors and authors alike thank you for reading and using this book, in whole and in part. We invite every reader to contribute to discourse that is vital for enriching the field. If reading the book encourages that, it will be well worth the considerable effort that has been involved in managing this media production.

References

Albarran, A. B., Chan-Olmsted, S. M., & Wirth, M. O. (2006). *Handbook of media management and economics*. Mahwah, NJ: Lawrence Erlbaum Associates.

Albarran, A. & Mierzejewska, B. (2004). *Media concentration in the US and European union: A comparative analysis*. Paper presented at the 6th World Media Economics and Management conference, Montreal, Canada, 12–15 May.

Aris, A., & Bughin, J. (2009). *Managing media companies: Harnessing creative value* (2nd ed.). Chichester: Wiley.

Baker, C. E. (2006). *Media concentration and democracy: Why ownership matters*. Cambridge: Cambridge University Press.

Berg, C. E. (2012). A matter of size: The importance of critical mass and the consequences of scarcity for television markets. Doctoral dissertation at the Copenhagen Business School: defended February 2013.

Berg, C. E., Lowe, G. F., & Brink Lund, A. (2014). A market failure perspective on value creation in PSM. In G. F. Lowe & F. Martin (Eds.), *The value of public service media*, RIPE@2013 (pp. 105–126).

Bilton, C. (2011). The management of the creative industries: From content to context. In M. Deuze (Ed.), *Managing media work* (pp. 31–42). Thousand Oaks, CA: Sage.

Calabrese, A., & Mihal, C. (2011). Liberal fictions: The public-private dichotomy in media policy. In J. Wasko, G. Murdoch, & H. Sousa (Eds.), *The handbook of political economy of communications* (pp. 238–239). Oxford: Wiley.

Chan-Olmsted, S. (2006). Preface remarks. In A. B. Albarran, S. M. Chan-Olmsted, & M. O. Wirth (Eds.), *Handbook of media management and economics*. Mahwah, NJ: Lawrence Erlbaum Associates.

Christians, C. G., Glasser, T. L., McQuail, D., Nordenstreng, K., & White, R. (2009). *Normative theories of the media: Journalism in democratic societies*. Chicago: University of Illinois Press.

Dimmick, J. W. (2003). *Media competition and coexistence: The theory of the niche*. Mahwah, NJ: Lawrence Erlbaum Associates.

Downie, J. (2011). New republic: The FCC's revolving door is shameless. National Public Radio, 20 May. Available at: http://www.npr.org/2011/05/20/136492206/new-republic-the-fccs-revolving-door-is-shameless

Doyle, G. (2013). *Understanding media economics* (2nd ed.). Thousand Oaks, CA: Sage.

Drucker, P. F. (2007). *The essential drucker*. Amsterdam: Butterworth-Heinemann, An Imprint of Elsevier.

Ellis, J. (2000). *Seeing things: Television in the age of uncertainty*. London: I.B. Tauris & Co.

Fairness and Accuracy in Reporting (u.d.), FAIR. Available at: www.fair.org

Ferment in the Field. (1983). *Journal of Communication, 33*(3) (Spl. Issue).

Fraser, M. (2003). *Weapons of mass distraction: Soft power and the American empire*. New York: Thomas Dunne Books, An Imprint of St. Martin's Press.

Fraser, M. (2008). American pop culture as soft power: Movies and broadcasting. In W. Yasushi & D. L. McConnell (Eds.), *Soft power superpowers: Cultural and national assets of Japan and the United States* (pp. 172–187). Amonk, NY: An East Gate Book from M.E. Sharp Inc.

Hirsch, P., & Levin, D. (1999). Umbrella advocates versus validity police: A life-cycle model. *Organizational Science, 10*(2), 199–212.

Knee, J. A., Greenwald, B. C., & Seave, A. (2009). *The curse of the mogul: What's wrong with the world's leading media companies*. New York: Portfolio.

Küng, L. (2007). Does media management matter? Establishing the scope, rationale and future research agenda for the discipline. *Journal of Media Business Studies, 4*(1), 21–39.

Küng, L. (2010). Why media managers are not interested in media management—and what we could do about it. *The International Journal on Media Management, 12*, 55–57.

Lewin, K. (1952). *Field theory in social science: Selected theoretical papers*. London: Tavistock.

McQuail, D. (2010). *McQuail's mass communication theory* (6th ed.). Thousand Oaks, CA: Sage.

Noam, E. M. (2009). *Media ownership and concentration in America.* New York: Oxford University Press.

Nye, J. S., Jr. (2005). *Soft power: The means to success in world politics.* New York: Public Affairs.

Picard, R. G. (2006). *Journalism, value creation and the future of news organizations.* (Working Paper #2006–4). Boston: Harvard University, Joan Shorenstein Center..

Picard, R. G. (2008) *Improving the harvest: Grafting media studies to management studies.* Remarks to the seminar Media Management as a New Academic Field: Reflections and Prospect for the Future. University of Tampere, Finland, 3–4 April.

Picard, R. G. (2011). *The economics and financing of media companies* (2nd ed.). New York: Fordham University Press.

Porter, M. E. (1980/2004). *Competitive strategy: Techniques for analyzing industries and competitors.* New York: Free Press.

Stavitsky, A. G. (1995) Guys in suits with charts: Audience research in U.S. public radio. *Journal of Broadcasting and Electronic Media,* Spring. Available at: http://www.aranet.com/library/pdf/doc-0088.pdf

Sullivan, J. L. (2013). *Media audiences: Effects, users, institutions and power.* Thousand Oaks, CA: Sage.

Part I
Scholarship and Distinction

The Development of Media Management as an Academic Field: Tracing the Contents and Impact of Its Three Leading Journals

2

Leona Achtenhagen and Bozena Mierzejewska

2.1 Introduction

Over the past two decades, media management has developed as an academic field that is positioned largely at the intersection of media/communication studies and business administration/economics. Scholars at communication school realise that it could be fruitful to more deeply investigate operational, organisational, managerial, financial, technological, institutional and economic contexts as these impact both opportunities and limitations for the production and development of media content. Similarly, scholars in business administration and economics realise that the media industries represent a fascinating context characterised by a number of specificities that are conducive for exploring and testing the contingencies, boundaries and limitations of existing theory and lend itself to the development of new theory.

The field appears to be maturing and it is useful to take stock. Based on Greenwood (1957), Hall (1968) and Wilensky (1964), Bird, Welsch, Astrachan and Pistui (2002) argue that three prerequisites must be achieved for an academic field to become recognised by other disciplines: (a) professional associations with communication sanctions, ethical codes and culture, (b) career opportunities and (c) systematic theory and an established body of literature. In established academic disciplines, professional associations operate through both formal and informal networks. This is evident in the field of media management scholarship today. The European Media Management Association (emma) has an annual conference

L. Achtenhagen (✉)
Media Management and Transformation Centre, Jönköping International Business School, Jönköping, Sweden
e-mail: acle@jibs.hj.se

B. Mierzejewska
School of Business, Fordham University, New York, NY, USA
e-mail: bmierzejewska@fordham.edu

© Springer International Publishing Switzerland 2016
G.F. Lowe, C. Brown (eds.), *Managing Media Firms and Industries*, Media Business and Innovation, DOI 10.1007/978-3-319-08515-9_2

23

and is enjoying growth in members also beyond Europe. In the USA, the Association for Education in Journalism and Mass Communication (AEJMC) has a division on media management and economics.[1]

The second criterion, career opportunities, refers to whether the expertise in the field leads to occupational positions and careers. Specialised master degree programmes in media management are offered at an increasing number of higher education institutions and research centres, and individual positions with the focus on media management are routinely published. That leaves little doubt about the fulfilment of this criterion.

Regarding the existence of systematic theory and an established body of literature, media management is developing at a brisk pace, but the field has not yet reached maturity on this criterion. Achievement is evident at national and international conferences and workshops and an increasing body of publications—both in books and journals. In view of the number of references that can be cited, it is evident that growth has taken place. However, the extent to which a systematic theory and body of literature has developed is not self-evident.

This chapter explores the scholarly state of the art in the field of media management and economics by systematically reviewing its three leading academic journals from their varied beginnings to 2013: the *Journal of Media Economics (JME)*, the *International Journal on Media Management (JMM)* and *Journal of Media Business Studies (JOMBS)*. Our primary focus is on the impact created by these journals for the development of theory and especially indications of systematic theory. We therefore selected articles that have been cited at least 10 times[2] in other works. Analysis clarifies which media sectors and topics are addressed in these articles and the methods they employed. Our sample extends for 25 years from the founding of JME in 1998–2013, the most recent complete year of journal publication.

We chose those journals for several reasons. First, we were guided by the observations of academic colleagues who have analysed the historical development of media management as an academic field and earlier indicated that these journals play an important role in its development (e.g. Albarran, 2006; Hollifield, 2001; Sylvie & Schmitz Weiss, 2012; Wirtz et al. 2013). Second, these journals are important for discourse in the media management field (Mierzejewska & Hollifield, 2006). The three journals have published a total of 1.057 research articles that have been cited 10.314 times, according to data collected through the 'Publish or Perish' software (available at www.harzing.com; assessed April 2013).

The chapter is structured as follows. In the next section, we profile the three academic journals, summarising their focus areas, their organisations and their editors and editorial boards. We then analyse our data, consisting firstly of the ten

---

[1] Several other regional or national academic associations support sections gathering scholars in media management. There is also a biennial World Media Economics and Management Conference that is an informal network, but not a formal association.

[2] As measured by the software 'Publish or Perish', accessed in March and April 2013.

most-cited articles published in each of the three journals and secondly of all articles published in one of these journals and cited ten times or more. We then draw conclusions and suggest some ways forward for developing the field, with special emphasis on the third prerequisite outlined above. This contribution takes stock of the development of media management as an academic field and proposes how scholars in the field could contribute to strengthening it.

2.2 Profiles of the Journals

2.2.1 Profile of the Journal of Media Economics

The *Journal of Media Economics*[3] publishes original research on the economics and policy of mediated communication with a broad focus on firms, markets and institutions. Reflecting the increasing diversity of analytical approaches employed in economics and recognising that policies promoting social and political objectives may have significant economic impacts on media, JME encourages submissions that reflect the insights of diverse disciplinary perspectives and research methodologies, both empirical and theoretical. All submissions undergo rigorous peer review, based on an initial screening by the editor and then double-blind refereeing by a minimum of two anonymous referees. The journal is published by Taylor & Francis in Philadelphia, USA.

The *Journal of Media Economics* was founded by Robert G. Picard (at the time of this writing, Director of Research for the Reuters Institute at Oxford University in the UK). The current editors are Nodir Adilov, who has posts at both Indiana University and Purdue University, and Hugh J. Martin from Ohio University. Past editors are Alan Albarran (University of North Texas), Benjamin M. Compaine (Northeastern University), Brendan M. Cunningham (US Naval Academy), Stephen Lacy (Michigan State University) and Steven Wildman (Michigan State University). All these editors (except for the founding editor) are located in the USA, and Picard is also an American, although he has lived and worked in Europe for more than two decades. North Americans are dominant in the current editorial board, which includes a number of government agencies and institutions as well as one scholar from Asia.[4]

The journal is abstracted and/or indexed in Cabell's Directory of Publishing Opportunities in Management, ComAbstracts, ComIndex, EBSCOhost Online Research Databases, Econlit, International Bibliography of the Social Sciences,

---

[3] Information retrieved from the journal's webpage.

[4] Full list of the editorial board members http://www.tandfonline.com/action/journalInformation?show=editorialBoard&journalCode=HMEC20#.U8YJuqie_uU

ISI: Current Contents/Social and Behavioral Sciences, Journal Citation Reports Social Science, LexisNexis, NORDICOM, RePEc, Social Sciences Citation Index and Social SciSearch.

Currently, there are signs that the journal's position might be deteriorating. Between 2011 and 2012, its 5-year impact factor dropped from 0.614 to 0.500. This factor indicates the average number of times articles from the journal published in the past 5 years have been cited in the Journal Citation Report (JCR). It is calculated by dividing the number of citations in the JCR for a particular year by the total number of articles published in the 5 previous years. An impact factor of 0.5 thus means that an article published in JME during the past 5 years has on average been cited 0.5 times during the current year. This drop in impact factor has an immediate effect on rankings within the disciplinary lists that sort journals. Thus, JME's ranking within communication dropped from rank 50 to rank 62 (out of 72 in total journals) and within economics dropped from rank 209 (of 320 total) to rank 290 (of 332 total the year after).[5] While this drop especially in economics appears dramatic at first sight, it is a sign of the large number of journals in the field having rather similar impact factors. For a journal in a niche discipline, like JME, it is very difficult to achieve a high impact factor, as this would require many citations by scholars outside of the media economics and management discipline.

2.2.2   Profile of the International Journal on Media Management

The *International Journal on Media Management*[6] aims to provide a global examination of the fields of media and telecommunications management, with a strong emphasis on management issues. The journal's goal is to publish original research that offers a close analysis of new industry structures, organisational forms and critical competencies in the changing media environment. It embraces a broad array of media-related issues and focuses on changes in this field caused by rapid technical developments and convergence. The journal explicitly includes communications in media management. JMM has a pronounced aim to serve as a forum that brings together academics and industry figures to explore the transition from 'classic' to 'new' media and to identify factors that might determine organisational and economic success in a fast-changing and converging environment.

The content is interdisciplinary (strategy, technology, marketing, finance, etc.) and multi-sectoral, exploring the interrelationship between developments in related industries. Editors expect every submission to be theoretically grounded, and the journal is open to all methodological approaches. The journal aims at a diverse

---

[5] All according to data from Thomson Reuters for 2012 versus 2013 and from Journal Citation Reports 2011 versus 2012, as stated on the journal's website in March 2013 and compared with June 2014.

[6] Information retrieved from the journal's website as well as one of its editors.

readership of academicians, researchers, students and managers with an interest in aspects of media management research, and policymakers in all sectors of the media industry. All papers published in JMM have undergone editorial screening and double-blind peer review, unless marked otherwise (in the case of invited submissions). The journal uses ScholarOne Manuscripts (previously Manuscript Central) to administer manuscript submissions and peer reviews. All submitted papers are screened for copied material using CrossCheck software. Papers published in JMM are rather short (maximum 5,000 words excluding tables and figures). The journal is published by Taylor & Francis in Philadelphia, USA.

The editors at this writing are Bozena I. Mierzejewska (Fordham University, USA) and Dan Shaver (Elon University, USA). There have been two previous editors. The founding editor was Beat F. Schmid, who established and ran the journal at the University of St. Gallen in Switzerland between 1999 and 2003. Alan B. Albarran (University of North Texas, USA) edited the journal between 2004 and 2008. The members of the editorial board reflect the international nature of the journal, and this covers not only North America and Europe but also Latin/South America and Australasia.[7]

The International Journal on Media Management is abstracted/indexed in Cabell's Directory of Publishing Opportunities in Marketing; CIOS: ComAbstracts/ComVista; EBSCOhost Online Research Databases; Scopus; IBZ—International Bibliography of Periodical Literature in the Humanities and Social Sciences; LexisNexis; OCLC: ArticleFirst, Electronic Collections Online; ProQuest: ABI/INFORM; PAIS International; and SAGE: Communication Abstracts.

The journal's impact factor is not yet included in Thomson Reuters' Social Sciences Citation Index (SSCI) and thus cannot be calculated. In consequence, direct comparison to the *Journal of Media Economics* is not possible. However, some national rankings list both journals; for example, the German Academic Association for Business Research lists JME as rank 80 and a 'B journal' and JMM as rank 384 and a 'C journal' (www.vhbonline.org, as of June 2014).

2.2.3 Profile of Journal of Media Business Studies

The *Journal of Media Business Studies* is devoted to research on business aspects of media including strategic, organisational, financial, marketing and entrepreneurial issues and practices. Its purpose is to convey research that develops, tests and applies theories and business analysis approaches to managerial and economic aspects of media enterprises and the issues confronted by media businesses.

---

[7] Full list of the editorial board members http://www.tandfonline.com/action/journalInformàtion?show=editorialBoard&journalCode=hijm20#.U8YKz6ie_uU

The journal has a particular focus on contemporary issues faced by media firms. Of special interest are topics like strategic problems of media in mature industries, growth strategies and management for emergent media operations, company renewal and rejuvenation processes, effectiveness of different types of corporate governance in media, best practices in organisational structures and operations of media firms, leadership in media enterprises and issues of small- and mid-sized media and family-owned media businesses.

Robert G. Picard founded this journal in 2004, and it has been published at the Media Management and Transformation Centre (MMTC) at Jönköping International Business School in Sweden. Picard was its editor until 2011 when Mary Alice Shaver took over. When she suddenly passed away in 2012, Picard returned as editor until 2014 when the new director of MMTC, Mart Ots, took over and, for this, joined forces with Patrik Wikström at the ARC Centre of Excellence for Creative Industries and Innovation in the Queensland University of Technology, Australia, and Greg Nyilasy at the University of Melbourne, Australia. In its 2014 annual general assembly, the European Media Management Association (emma) decided to accept JOMBS as its association journal. Details are still being negotiated, but it will likely be published and marketed by Taylor & Francis, Inc., in the future. Thus, all three journals discussed here would be in the same publisher's portfolio.

The editorial board reflects the journal's aim by consisting of professors in management with an interest in media, as well as media and communication professors with an interest in management issues. The majority of its members are European countries, but scholars from the USA and Canada are well represented.[8]

In terms of manuscript submissions, the journal considers manuscripts on relevant topics up to a maximum of 25 double-spaced pages in length. Authors submit their papers by e-mail as attachments in MS word (.doc) formats to the editor.

The journal is indexed in EBSCO Business Source Complete, CIOS and Communication Abstracts. It is the newest of the three journals and not yet listed in most rankings. However, the SCImago Journal Rank (www.scimagojr.com) lists JOMBS at rank 136 of 159 journals in Communication, rank 193 of 206 journals in Business and International Management and rank 179 of 184 journals in strategy and management.

2.2.4 Journal Comparison

A comparison of the editors and editorial boards of the three journals makes evident that some pronounced differences exist between the journals' strategic orientation. Scholars in the USA dominate the editorial board of the *Journal of Media Economics*. These 26 scholars are complemented with only nine from Europe

---

[8] Full list of the editorial board members: http://center.hj.se/mmtc/jombs/editorial-board.html

(representing five countries) and one from Asia. Given this picture, it is not surprising that all current and past editors have been US based to date. The *International Journal on Media Management* has a more international orientation as suggested by its name. There are 19 members of the editorial board from North America, and these are complemented with three colleagues from Latin and South America, 13 in Europe and four Asian/Australian scholars—in total representing 18 countries. The *Journal of Media Business Studies* has a clearly European focus, with 14 scholars active in Europe contributing to the editorial board, complemented by nine scholars from North America. Interestingly, a small group of media management scholars serves on the editorial boards of all three journals, namely, Sylvia Chan-Olmsted, Richard A. Gershon, Ann Hollifield, Angela Powers, George Sylvie and Hans van Kranenburg, with the latter being the only non-US representative.

Table 2.1 provides a summary comparison between the three journals. The *Journal of Media Economics* is the oldest, founded in 1988 and has therefore published the highest number of articles. Not surprisingly, it therefore has the highest number of articles with ten citations or more. The h-index refers to the number of published articles which have been cited at least the same number of times. Again, there is a clear pattern that is understandably keyed to the years each journal has been published. Only the percentage of articles not yet cited interrupts this pattern. Here, the *International Journal on Media Management* displays a lower percentage. This is suggestive of a rigorous policy of desktop rejections by the editors who concentrate on selecting articles of high potential interest for its readership.

2.2.4.1 The Most-Cited Articles in the Three Journals

It is clear that JME is the most-cited journal in the field of media management. However, the launch of JMM in 1999 led to a doubling of articles (cited ten times

Table 2.1 Comparison of the three academic journals

Journal	Year of foundation	Total number of articles published so far	Total number of articles with ten citations or more	h-index	% of published articles not yet cited
Journal of Media Economics	1988	480	169	38	27.5
International Journal on Media Management	1999	298	84	27	23.5
Journal of Media Business Studies	2004	119	23	8	38.7

Source: own analyses, based on data from 'Publish or Perish 4' (as of March 2013), available at www.harzing.com

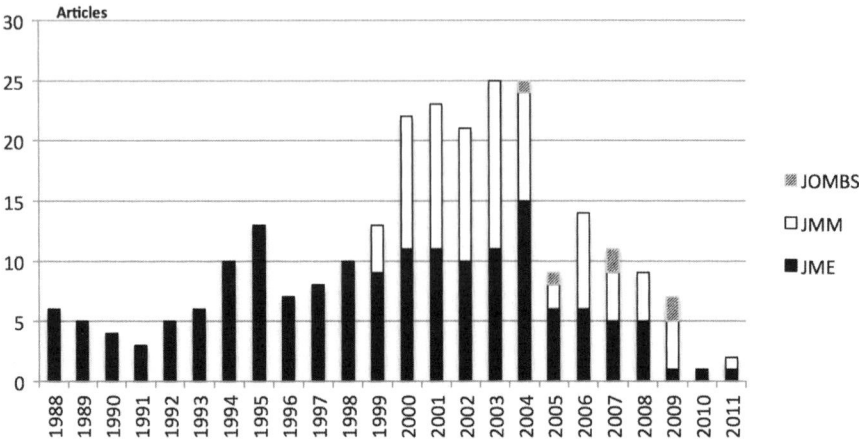

Fig. 2.1 Articles with more than ten citations in the three academic journals over time

or more), indicating a dramatic expansion of the number of articles that are relevant for the field (see Fig. 2.1). JMM has established itself as a journal of comparable relevance with JME for media management scholarship. Interestingly, the launch of JOMBS in 2004 did not have a similar impact. Its start coincided with the end of a 5-year period (2000–2004) that saw the highest number of articles cited ten times or more published by JME or JMM. During these years, the transformation and convergence of media industries were new phenomena, and insightful scholarly articles were of great interest and informed subsequent research.

Since 2004 research in media management has developed to match the diversity of the various media sectors and has increasingly addressed a plethora of research questions. This diversity and heterogeneity of the media sectors (cf. also Küng, 2007) is an additional challenge for the development of a systematic body of theory in the field. The broader range of research questions being addressed might necessarily imply fewer citations for each published article. The varied pattern of article citations for JOMBS could suggest that the journal's aim of focusing on business aspects of the media first needed to trigger a new wave of research projects addressing such topics.

When analysing the characteristics of the ten most-cited articles in the three journals, a number of observations can be made that will be discussed below. It is interesting to note that in JME and JMM, none of the most-cited articles are published after 2004. It certainly takes time for a published piece to become a most-cited article. In the two journals that have been in print longer and thus have published more articles in total, this might be an indicator that articles published during the last decade have not addressed topics that spurred much subsequent research efforts to further explore and build on their findings. If so, that would imply that cumulative knowledge development might not yet be an important issue in media management scholarship.

Table 2.2 The ten most-cited articles published in JME

Article title	Author(s)	Year	Total no. of cites
'Predicting financial success of motion pictures: the '80s experience'	Litman and Kohl	1989	206
'Competition between the Internet and traditional news media: the gratification-opportunities niche dimension'	Dimmick, Chen and Li	2004	177
'Predicting the performance of motion pictures'	Sochay	1994	168
'Concentration and economics of multiformity in the communication industries'	Albarran and Dimmick	1996	104
'Impact of moderate and ruinous competition on diversity: the Dutch television market'	Van der Wurff and van Cuilenburg	2001	95
'Diversification strategy of global media conglomerates: examining its patterns and determinants'	Chan-Olmsted and Chang	2003	89
'Competing with whom? where? and how? A structural analysis of the electronic newspaper market'	Chyi and Sylvie	1998	89
'Industrial organization theory and media industry analysis'	Wirth and Bloch	1995	81
'An explorative study on the market relation between online and print newspapers'	Chyi and Lasorsa	2002	75
'Exploring the characteristics of potential high-definition television adopters'	Dupagne	1999	70

Source: based on data from 'Publish or Perish 4', retrieved March 2013

Some of the most-cited articles in JME (see Table 2.2) focus on predicting performance, for example, of motion pictures (Litman & Kohl, 1989; Sochay, 1994). Changing competition is addressed, for example, by addressing its impact on TV programme diversity (van der Wurff & van Cuilenburg, 2001) but also industry concentration through mergers and acquisitions (Albarran & Dimmick, 1996), as well as product and international diversification (Chan-Olmsted & Chang, 2003). Three of the ten most-cited articles address the relation between online and printed newspapers (Chyi & Lasorsa, 2002; Chyi & Sylvie, 1998; Dimmick, Yan, & Zhan, 2004). The journal also offers some general, explorative articles that outline the logic and characteristics of how certain media sectors or phenomena work, as in Dupagne's (1999) article exploring the characteristics of potential high-definition TV adopters exemplify.

An interesting approach to advance the media management and economic literature is provided in the article by Wirth and Bloch (1995) who used industrial organisation (IO) literature to critically evaluate media economic literature, by first introducing basic IO concepts and then reviewing their (lack of) application to media economic studies. In conclusion, they strongly argued for more use of theory to facilitate rigorous analyses for media policymakers.

Not surprisingly, the most-cited articles published in JME generally take a quantitative approach and are (except for van der Wurff & van Cuilenburg, 2001) based on North American samples. Rather than taking their point of departure in a specific theory, a number of the articles build their study on previous research about a phenomenon (Chyi & Lasorsa, 2002; Chyi & Sylvie, 1998; Dupagne, 1999; Sochay, 1994). Surprisingly rare are explicit attempts to build media management and economics theory (examples of such attempts are Dimmick et al., 2004; Sochay, 1994), and these articles make a clear point of what is special about media in comparison to other industries.

For JMM (see Table 2.3), in line with the journal's aim, articles tend to have a more practitioner-oriented focus. This is evident in articles featuring hands-on concepts, such as business models (e.g. Bakker, 2002; Picard, 2000), as well as articles providing explicit recommendations for practice and/or policymakers (e.g. Picard, 2000; Vaccaro & Cohn, 2004).

The most-cited articles in JMM don't typically start out with the goal of helping to fill a gap in theory. They instead explore a practical challenge or issue that has been notable in one or several media sectors. While they are not firmly anchored in existing literature and/or theory, they contribute to building a possible foundation of media management theory by developing systems of categories, such as taxonomies and categorisations of polar types, thereby addressing the *what* and *how* of phenomena. For example, Picard (2000) identifies six typical business models for online content, Williams (2002) suggests five types of postures in the video game industry,

Table 2.3 The ten most-cited articles published in JMM

Article title	Author(s)	Year	Total no. of cites
'Changing business models of online content services: their implications for multimedia and other content producers'	Picard	2000	120
'Structure and competition in the US home video game industry'	Williams	2002	118
'Second generation net news: interactivity and information accessibility in the online environment'	Bucy	2004	68
'Entrepreneurial opportunities with toolkits for user innovation and design'	Franke and Schreier	2002	62
'Integrating new media and old media: seven observations of convergence as a strategy for best practices in media organizations'	Lawson-Borders	2003	57
'The evolution of business models and marketing strategies in the music industry'	Vaccaro and Cohn	2004	57
'Convergence processes, value constellations and integration strategies in the multimedia business'	Wirtz	1999	53
'Online newspapers in the US: perceptions of markets, products, revenue, and competition'	Chyi and Sylvie	2000	50
'Free daily newspapers-business models and strategies'	Bakker	2002	47
'New digital media and devices: an analysis for the media industry'	Rawolle and Hess	2000	45

Source: based on data from 'Publish or Perish 4', retrieved March 2013

Vaccaro and Cohn (2004) provide a taxonomy of three business models in the music industry and Rawolle and Hess (2000) outline attributes of digital contents. Through providing overviews of how different media sectors and phenomena work, a number of these most-cited articles lay groundwork for subsequent studies of these sectors, for example, Bucy (2004) by comparing news sites by local TV stations and newspapers on the Internet, Bakker (2002) on free dailies, and Chyi and Sylvie (2000) by exploring online news.

Given the more practical orientation of JMM, some articles focus on the potential of technological developments for media industries. For example, Franke and Schreier (2002) discuss opportunities of toolkits for user innovation and design for media companies, and Rawolle and Hess (2000) discuss how new technologies can be exploited by media companies. Given the explicit editorial focus for JMM on convergence, it is not surprising that convergence is thematic for a number of leading articles (e.g. Lawson-Borders, 2003; Picard, 2000; Wirtz, 1999). It's striking, however, that most of these ground breaking articles are either conceptual or draw on (limited) empirical study for illustration, rather than testing of the conceptualisation. Moreover, most of these articles do not explicitly build on or expand existing theory; at the most, they transfer an existing model or concept from general management theory or informatics to media settings, thereby introducing existing concepts from adjacent fields to media management. Franke and Schreier (2002) introduce toolkits for user innovation and design, Vaccaro and Cohn (2004) apply a service-marketing framework and Rawolle and Hess (2000) assess ICT technologies.

Some of the most-cited articles in JOMBS (Table 2.4) try to break new ground by conceptually defining the field of media management (Küng, 2007) and its intersection with adjacent fields, such as entrepreneurship (Hang & van Weezel, 2007), and by exploring certain aspects relevant to media management, such as the changing profession of journalists (Phillips, Singer, Vlad, & Becker, 2009; Witschge & Nygren, 2009), characteristics and business dynamics of media products (Picard, 2005) or the relevance of customer relationship management for public service broadcasters (Lowe, 2008). Similar to the most-cited articles in JMM, different articles propose taxonomies or patterns, for example, of digital strategies (Dennis, Warley, & Sheridan, 2006) or business models in mobile television (Prario, 2007). The most influential articles published in JOMBS are predominantly conceptual (e.g. Küng, 2007; Picard, 2005) or based on qualitative research, such as the case studies provided by Gershon and Suri (2004) and Tuomola (2004).

An Alternative Measure of Journal Comparisons

Comparing journals using one index for the three publications is not possible because only one is included in the bibliographical indexes of Journal Citation Reports (JCR) produced by Web of Science (Thompson Reuters). But an alternative way to compare journals' rank, citation records and other indicators of impact has

Table 2.4 The ten most-cited articles published in JOMBS

Article title	Author(s)	Year	Total no. of cites
'Journalism: a profession under pressure?'	Witschge and Nygren	2009	37
'Unique characteristics and business dynamics of media products'	Picard	2005	32
'Does media management matter? establishing the scope, rationale and future research agenda for the discipline'	Küng	2007	20
'Media and entrepreneurship: what do we know and where should we go?'	Hang and van Weezel	2007	13
'Implications of technological change for journalists' tasks and skills'	Phillips, Singer, Vlad and Becker	2009	12
'Disintermediation and reintermediation of the sound recording value chain: two case studies'	Tuomola	2004	11
'Mobile television in Italy: value chains and business models of telecommunications operators'	Prario	2007	10
'Customer differentiation and interaction for innovation: two CRM challenges for PSB'	Lowe	2008	10
Doing digital: an assessment of the top 25 US media companies and their digital strategies'	Dennis, Warley and Sheridan	2006	10
'Viacom Inc.: a case study in transnational media management'	Gershon and Suri	2004	10

Source: based on data from 'Publish or Perish 4', retrieved March 2013

recently been developed by their competitor Elsevier. A database under the trade name Scopus became available in 2004 and offers alternative indexes for a bigger range of publications than those included in the highly selective Web of Science. SJR (SCImago Journal Rank) is a measure of the scientific prestige of journals based on the idea that all citations are not created equal. It relies on methodology inspired by Google PageRank, which attributes different weight to citations depending on the 'prestige' of the citing journal without the influence of journal self-citations. In other words, citations coming from more important sources are more valuable and provide more prestige to the journals receiving them. The Scopus database provides computation of those factors for all three journals in our analysis. The graph below (Fig. 2.4) provides the latest available results calculated in June 2013.

Although comparison is possible only since 2009, it is evident that JME displays a relatively stable quality of citation sources, while JMM has shown 1 year (2012) of high growth, and JOMBS is still at the early stages of developing measured 'prestige' (see Fig. 2.2). These results are not surprising having in mind that JOMBS is the newest of the three journals, with the smallest number of articles published overall. In the long term this measure can be considered a good alternative for comparing and evaluating journals in media management. The emergent

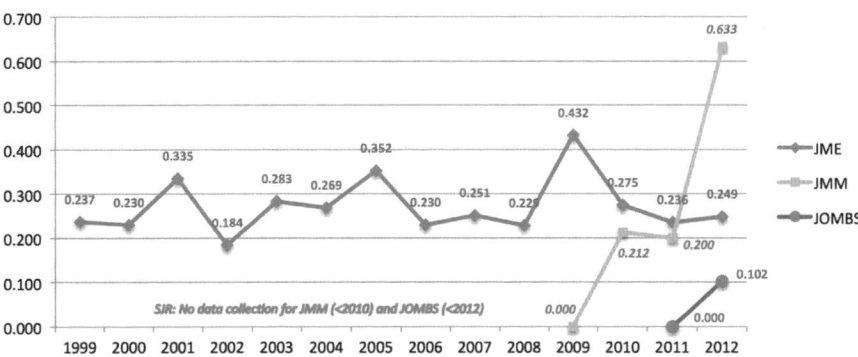

Fig. 2.2 Citation 'prestige' across the three journals

impact of new journals that could be alternative outlets for media management research can be more easily captured in this database.

Characteristics of Articles Cited in the Three Journals

When considering all articles published in the three journals, the defining characteristics are presented in Table 2.5.

In the 276 articles cited more than ten times that have been published in one of the three journals, the following patterns of topics specific for media management emerge:

- Exploring and mapping media sector characteristics and performance (including consumer/audience behaviour)
- Assessments of value chain and business model characteristics in specific media sectors
- Impact of technological trends
- Convergence
- Analysis of emerging media management trends

The different media sectors covered in the articles across the three journals are presented in Fig. 2.3. The largest category, representing slightly more than 30 % of the articles, is a 'residual category' of other media sectors, including publishing (book/magazines), radio, music, gaming and advertising. The second largest category comprises 24.3 % of the articles and addresses the media industries in general, i.e. no specific sector.

In terms of research methods employed, the following picture emerges (Fig. 2.4). It is evident that the large majority of papers take a quantitative approach to research (49.4 % of the articles). More than one-third of the articles published are conceptual, which can be interpreted as a sign of the academic field being still under development when conceptual discussion plays a major role in defining its contents,

Table 2.5 Characteristics of articles published in the three journals

	JME	JMM	JOMBS
Topics covered include	Predicting performance and profitability Industry characteristics and restructuring Competition and corporate/industry structure Government policies and (de)regulation Pricing Public service broadcasting Effects of globalisation	Convergence Communications Branding Business models Culture Consumer attitudes and behaviours Leadership Organisational change Media work Social media	Introducing new topics such as family businesses, entrepreneurship, consumption tax or joint ventures Business growth Strategy work Organisational learning and competencies (else similar to JMM)
Characteristics of published articles	Mainly quantitative methods, increasingly sophisticated methods and analyses	Empirically driven research questions based on practice-based phenomena, qualitative and quantitative research, some transfer of existing concepts	Conceptual and definitional articles, as well as qualitative and quantitative papers, clearer focus on business aspects than the other two journals

Fig. 2.3 Media sectors covered in media journal articles with more than ten citations

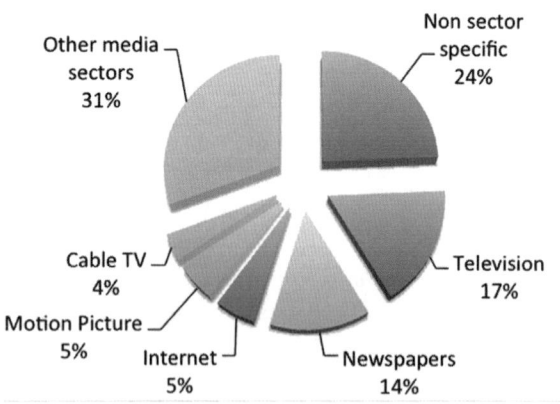

Split by Covered Media Sectors

contingencies and boundaries. However, these articles often illustrate the points made by providing examples of media companies in different contexts. Surprisingly, less than 15 % of articles use qualitative methods. A qualitative approach based on case studies, for example, could play an important role in exploring media phenomena for inductive theory building, such as by developing theoretical constructs and propositions (e.g. Eisenhardt & Graebner, 2007).

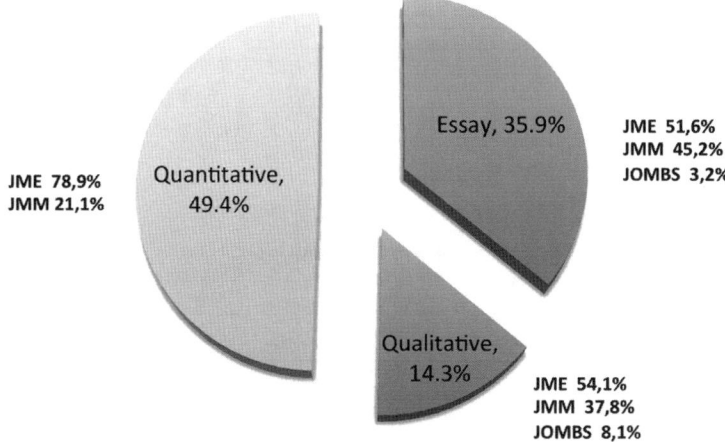

Fig. 2.4   Research methods employed in the 276 articles in our sample

2.2.5   Concluding Discussion

In this chapter, we assess the extent to which media management is an established academic field. Building on Bird et al. (2002), we confirmed two out of three prerequisites from the start, namely, the existence of (a) professional associations with communication sanctions, ethical codes and culture and (b) career opportunities. We therefore focused on assessing whether the third criterion of (c) a systematic theory and an established body of literature has emerged. While the numbers of publications as well as their citations indicate that an established body of literature exists, we found little evidence of anything systematic or, given the heterogeneity of the different media sectors, theor*ies* of media management emerging. We draw this conclusion based on the following observations.

Little explicit attempts at theory building have taken place. Building on Dubin (1978), Whetten (1989) proposed four building blocks of theory development. The first, the *what*, comprises which factors (such as variables, concepts and constructs) logically should be considered as part of the explanation of the phenomenon of interest. Two quality criteria can help to assess whether the 'right' factors have been identified, namely, comprehensiveness (i.e. whether all relevant factors are included) and parsimony (i.e. whether some factors should be deleted as they add little new insights). In media management scholarship we find quite a large number of articles providing vantage points for theory development by identifying categories and taxonomies, but many articles provide 'laundry lists' of such categories without theorising about them.

The second building block of theory development according to Whetten (1989) comprises the *how*, namely, how identified factors are related. Conceptually, this refers to connecting the factors by explicitly delineating patterns, and thereby introducing causality. Some articles in media management literature address the how, but relatively far less and especially in a number of more sophisticated quantitative studies where models outlining the causalities between different factors can be found. In short, this field is currently far more adept at handling questions of what than how, reflecting both its comparative newness and the continuing lack of theorisation in media management per se.

The third building block of theory development, the *why*, assesses the underlying psychological, economic and social dynamics that justify the selection of factors and their proposed causal relationships—the logic underlying the theory or model (Whetten, 1989). In the media management publications reviewed here, we found the majority of articles depart from empirical phenomena characteristic of one or several media sectors to mainly describe the what and to a lesser but developing degree also the how. There is so far relatively little evidence of work that provides robust explanation, or logic, of studied phenomena. Thus, a more explicit attempt at theorising explanations for the established characteristics of media management phenomena is mostly missing.

The fourth building block, the *who*, *where* and *when*, refers to conditions that place limitations on the propositions generated from a theory or model (Whetten, 1989). Different temporal and contextual factors set boundaries for how a theory, model or empirical findings can be generalised and thereby constitute the range to which a theory enjoys applicability. In many of the articles reviewed for the purpose of this chapter, we found little consideration of these contextual limits. Instead, articles often cite previous empirical studies on the same or similar phenomena without consideration of temporal and contextual factors, which would be prerequisite for developing more systematic theory.

What, then, is especially needed to develop more systematic theorisation about and for media management? Clearly, more focus is required on establishing and clarifying relationships between the different factors characterising the empirical phenomena under study. Whetten (1989: 493) aptly cites Poincaré (1983): 'Science is facts, just as houses are made of stone. . . . But a pile of stones is not a house, and a collection of facts is not necessarily science'. Theoretical insights come from demonstrating how the addition of a new variable alters our understanding of the empirical phenomenon. As already noted, a lot of the work so far published is about and that necessarily implies a lack of robust connections and relations that are essential for understanding how and explaining why. Beyond that, it is clear that there is great need for establishing the context of who, when and where issues.

As Küng (2007) pointed out, media management should concentrate on management issues. When reviewing articles for this chapter, we found surprisingly little focus on media *management* in many of the most-cited articles in the field's journals—and if considering the many articles which are cited less or not at all, this impression becomes even more pronounced. Küng (2007) also calls for the application of theories from management, rather than from adjacent relevant fields, such as media and communication studies. Many articles reviewed by us entirely lack theoretical grounding, or else they simply apply a theory or model without expanding on it or challenging it. As Whetten (1989: 493) points out: 'Conversely, applying an old model to a new setting and showing that it works as expected is not instructive by itself. This conclusion has theoretical merit only if something about the setting suggests the theory shouldn't work under those conditions'. Here, more focus should be put on pointing out the specificities of the media sectors in comparison to other industries—which would also contribute to building the case of the relevance of media management as a separate academic field.

Another aspect appears of utmost importance for developing systematic theory about media management and requires entering the *theoretical feedback loop*: 'Theorists need to learn something new about the theory itself as a result of working with it under different conditions. That is, different applications should improve the tool, not merely reaffirm its utility' (Whetten, 1989: 493). Such a feedback loop calls for improved communication with the general management and economic fields, building on relevant publications from those areas, as well as attempting to publish not only in media journals but also general management and economic journals (though we acknowledge that publication requirements at different universities might restrict such attempts in some countries). This communication could, for example, be enhanced by inviting general management scholars to media management conferences and events but also by setting editorial standards that require more explicit effort at theory building. A big step in developing more systematic media management theory could also be collaborative and longitudinal research projects within the community in order to circumvent some of the pressures especially younger scholars are facing, leading them to concentrate on empirically rather than theory-driven publications. The three journals discussed in this chapter could play an important role in supporting the development of more systematic theory in the field. Equally important, however, the journals need to maintain distinct editorial profiles. Possible ways to manage that are outlined in Table 2.6, although we understand that other options are just as possible and that our proposal needs discussion and development.

To conclude, for an academic field of study to become a discipline requires, among other things, a body of cumulative knowledge that expands understanding of that domain (cf., e.g. Bird et al., 2002) and some generally shared body of theory and foci for research, in short something that is systematic and distinctively relevant. The field of media management has grown from a group of isolated scholars with an interest in research on media management into an international community engaged with this area of study. However, knowledge production does not yet appear to be systematic and tightly enough interconnected; there is not yet nearly enough sharing and expanding on knowledge, theories and research methods to collaboratively advance the development of the field. Hambrick's (2007) advice for developing the field of management research seems equally relevant for media management: 'theory is critically important in our field, and we should remain committed to it'.

Table 2.6 Possible ways for the three journals to develop the academic field

	JME	JMM	JOMBS
Possible ways forward to build more systematic media management theory	Encourage theory-driven hypothesis development as well as a clear feedback loop for theory development	Maintain and strengthen focus on challenges and issues highly relevant for media managers and diverse methods for exploring those. For contributions based on qualitative research, encourage not only the development of practical implications but also the inductive development of propositions as a more explicit way of theory development, which could be tested in further research	Maintain and strengthen focus on business aspects, encouraging theorising about what is special about media management in comparison to other industries

References

Albarran, A. B. (2006). Historical trends and patterns in media management research. In A. B. Albarran, S. M. Chen-Olmsted, & M. O. Wirth (Eds.), *Handbook of media management and economics*. Mahwah, NJ: Lawrence-Erlbaum.

Albarran, A. B., & Dimmick, J. (1996). Concentration and economics of multiformity in the communication industries. *Journal of Media Economics, 9*(4), 41.

Bakker, P. (2002). Free daily newspapers—business models and strategies. *International Journal on Media Management, 4*(3), 180–187. doi:10.1080/14241270209389998.

Bird, B., Welsch, H., Astrachan, J. H., & Pistui, D. (2002). Family business research: The evolution of an academic field. *Family Business Review, 15*(4), 337–350.

Bucy, E. P. (2004). Second generation net news: Interactivity and information accessibility in the online environment. *International Journal on Media Management, 6*(1–2), 102–113. doi:10.1080/14241277.2004.9669386.

Chan-Olmsted, S. M., & Chang, B.-H. (2003). Diversification strategy of global media conglomerates: Examining its patterns and determinants. *Journal of Media Economics, 16*(4), 213.

Chyi, H. I., & Lasorsa, D. L. (2002). An explorative study on the market relation between online and print newspapers. *Journal of Media Economics, 15*(2), 91–106.

Chyi, H. I., & Sylvie, G. (1998). Competing with whom? where? and how? A structural analysis of the electronic newspaper market. *Journal of Media Economics, 11*(2), 1.

Chyi, H. I., & Sylvie, G. (2000). Online newspapers in the U.S.: Perceptions of markets, products, revenue, and competition. *International Journal on Media Management, 2*(2), 69–77. doi:10.1080/14241270009389924.

Dennis, E. E., Warley, E., & Sheridan, E. (2006). Doing digital: An assessment of the top 25 U.S. media companies and their digital strategies. *Journal of Media Business Studies, 3*(1), 33–51.

Dimmick, J., Yan, C., & Zhan, L. (2004). Competition between the internet and traditional news media: The gratification-opportunities niche dimension. *Journal of Media Economics, 17*(1), 19–33.

Dubin, R. (1978). *Theory development*. New York: Free Press.

Dupagne, M. (1999). Exploring the characteristics of potential high-definition television adopters. *Journal of Media Economics, 12*(1), 35.

Eisenhardt, K. M., & Graebner, M. A. (2007). Theory building from cases: Opportunities and challenges. *Academy of Management Journal, 50*(1), 25–32.

Franke, N., & Schreier, M. (2002). Entrepreneurial opportunities with toolkits for user innovation and design. *International Journal on Media Management, 4*(4), 225–234. doi:10.1080/14241270209390004.

Gershon, R. A., & Suri, A. (2004). Viacom Inc. A case study in transnational media management. *Journal of Media Business Studies, 1*(1), 47–69.

Greenwood, E. (1957). Attributes of a profession. *Social Work, 3*(2), 44–55.

Hall, R. H. (1968). Professionalization and bureaucratization. *American Sociological Review, 33*, 92–104.

Hambrick, D. (2007). The field of management's devotion to theory: Too much of a good thing? *Academy of Management Journal, 50*, 1364–1352.

Hang, M., & van Weezel, A. (2007). Media and entrepreneurship: What do we know and where should we go? *Journal of Media Business Studies, 4*(1), 51–70.

Hollifield, C. A. (2001). Crossing borders: Media management research in a transnational market environment. *The Journal of Media Economics, 14*(3), 133–146.

Küng, L. (2007). Does media management matter? Establishing the scope, rationale, and future research agenda for the discipline. *Journal of Media Business Studies, 4*(1), 21–39.

Lawson-Borders, G. (2003). Integrating new media and old media: Seven observations of convergence as a strategy for best practices in media organizations. *International Journal on Media Management, 5*(2), 91–99. doi:10.1080/14241270309390023.

Litman, B. R., & Kohl, L. S. (1989). Predicting financial success of motion pictures: The '80s experience. *Journal of Media Economics, 2*(2), 35–50.

Lowe, G. F. (2008). Customer differentiation and interaction: Two CRM challenges for public service broadcasters. *Journal of Media Business Studies, 5*(2), 1–22.

Mierzejewska, B. I. & Hollifield, C. A. (2006). Theoretical approaches in media management research. In A. B. Albarran. S. M. Chen-Olmsted, & M. O. Wirth (Eds.), *Handbook of media management and economics*. Mahwah, NJ: Lawrence-Erlbaum.

Phillips, T. M., Singer, J. B., Vlad, T., & Becker, L. B. (2009). Implications of technological change for journalists' tasks and skills. *Journal of Media Business Studies, 6*(1), 61–85.

Picard, R. G. (2000). Changing business models of online content services: Their implications for multimedia and other content producers. *International Journal on Media Management, 2*(2), 60–68. doi:10.1080/14241270009389923.

Picard, R. G. (2005). Unique characteristics and business dynamics of media products. *Journal of Media Business Studies, 2*(2), 61–69.

Prario, B. (2007). Mobile television in Italy: Value chains and business models of telecommunications operators. *Journal of Media Business Studies, 4*(1), 1–19.

Rawolle, J., & Hess, T. (2000). New digital media and devices: An analysis for the media industry. *International Journal on Media Management, 2*(2), 89–99. doi:10.1080/14241270009389926.

Sochay, S. (1994). Predicting the performance of motion pictures. *Journal of Media Economics, 7*(4), 1.

Sylvie, G., & Schmitz Weiss, A. (2012). Putting the management into innovation and media management studies: A meta-analysis. *The International Journal on Media Management, 14*(3), 183–206. doi:10.1080/14241277.2011.633584.

Tuomola, A. (2004). Disintermediation and reintermediation of the sound recording value chain: Two case studies. *Journal of Media Business Studies, 1*, 27–46.

Vaccaro, V. L., & Cohn, D. Y. (2004). The evolution of business models and marketing strategies in the music industry. *International Journal on Media Management, 6*(1–2), 46–58. doi:10. 1080/14241277.2004.9669381.

van der Wurff, R., & van Cuilenburg, J. (2001). Impact of moderate and ruinous competition on diversity: The Dutch television market. *Journal of Media Economics, 14*(4), 213–229.

Whetten, D. A. (1989). What constitutes a theoretical contribution? *Academy of Management Review, 14*(4), 490–495.

Wilensky, H. (1964). The professionalization of everyone? *The American Journal of Sociology, 70*, 137–158.

Williams, D. (2002). Structure and competition in the U.S. home video game industry. *International Journal on Media Management, 4*(1), 41–54. doi:10.1080/14241270209389979.

Wirth, M. O., & Bloch, H. (1995). Industrial organization theory and media industry analysis. *Journal of Media Economics, 8*(2), 15.

Wirtz, B. W. (1999). Convergence processes, value constellations and integration strategies in the multimedia business. *International Journal on Media Management, 1*(1), 14–22. doi:10.1080/ 14241279909384482.

Wirtz, B. W., Pistoia, A. A., & Mory, L. L. (2013). Current state and development perspectives of media economics/media management research. *Journal of Media Business Studies, 10*(2), 63–91.

Witschge, T., & Nygren, T. (2009). Journalistic work: A profession under pressure? *Journal of Media Business Studies, 6*(1), 37–59.

Competencies of Media Managers: Are They Special?

3

Juan Pablo Artero and Juan Luis Manfredi

3.1 Academic Thinking on the Functions of Business Managers

It is helpful to begin with a short historical perspective on the functions of business managers that is derived from twentieth-century management science. Our reasoning supposes it is necessary to identify how management science has understood what managers do in general in order to frame and ground the essential competencies we propose are needed by media managers today.

The founder of the 'scientific school' of management theory was Frederick Winslow Taylor (1911), an American. He was among the first thinkers to investigate and define the essential functions of business managers. His views were influential in the development of a highly rationalistic approach to business management, and thus establishing the roots of the field of management studies quite generally. His essential contribution is premised on the importance of developing a scientific mentality and methods as a best means for analysing, planning and implementing any business operation. The emphasis is almost completely restricted to maximising efficiency in production. In this perspective, design and implementation are radically separated. Managers must create a scientific system (based on measurable data rather than personal opinions) to run the company as professional managers while workers are expected do whatever their 'superiors' command. This traditional perspective relies on command-and-control techniques premised upon a separation between the 'brains' and the 'brawn'.

J.P. Artero (✉)
University of Zaragoza, Zaragoza, Spain
e-mail: jpartero@unizar.es

J.L. Manfredi
Facultad de Periodismo, University of Castilla-La Mancha, Albacete, Spain
e-mail: juan.manfredi@uclm.es

© Springer International Publishing Switzerland 2016
G.F. Lowe, C. Brown (eds.), *Managing Media Firms and Industries*, Media Business and Innovation, DOI 10.1007/978-3-319-08515-9_3

For Henri Fayol (1920s, 1984 edition), the great French thinker and founding father of the general theory of business administration, the core tasks for managers are forecasting, planning, organising and commanding. He framed these as managerial functions and considered them essential to the work (and responsibility) of co-ordinating and controlling an enterprise. His classic book was published in the 1950s, although he died in 1925, suggesting the increasing importance of his work over time, and thus its considerable influence. His perspective has been challenged for overemphasising a top-down process based on rationalistic practice in planning and the organisation of people, a typical general problem in much of the heritage literature in management science. His view is akin to Taylor's and prioritises planning, organisation, command, co-ordination and control as the five primary managerial tasks. In this, one finds support for a highly structured, even rigid, approach to organisation—all quite familiar to students of traditional military structures.

Chester Barnard (1930s, 1968 edition) was an early proponent of a more humanistic approach and merits mention when considering media management. Barnard proposed a theory of co-operation and organisation, an approach emphasising how organisations function in practice. He proposed that the basic functions of the executive facilitate people achieving what they could not achieve as individuals. In this view, short lines of communication are critical (i.e. avoiding bureaucratic and hierarchical arrangements). Employees and managers in an organisation are interconnected and interdependent. Executives should therefore nurture goals and values that are instrumental to collaborative work.

Mary Parker Follett (1941) was another early advocate of management as a fundamentally social process. In her perspective, relationships inside the company are of paramount importance and conflict (due to disagreements and internal competition) is a given. She believed there are three ways of dealing with conflict: domination, compromise or integration, with integration being the only 'positive' way forwards. In her view, the problems people have are not psychological, ethical and economic per se, but rather human problems that have psychological, ethical and economic aspects and consequences. Her work was an early humanist counter-perspective to the rationalist school of management theory. Not coincidentally given her approach, Parker Follett was one of the first management thinkers to pay attention to leadership. She proposed that a leader is able to see the whole rather than only pieces and details and that he or she organises the experiences of the group, offers a vision of the future and trains followers to become leaders as well. Her work marks a characteristic bifurcation in approaches to management theory, moving away from the command-and-control perspective to advocate a dialogue-and-direct approach.

Peter F. Drucker (1955) was perhaps the first to recognise (early in the 1950s) that management would become a profession of central importance in contemporary society largely because of its role in making key decisions that affect the economy. In this view, management is not simply a job but a motif. He proposed five functions for the managerial role: to set objectives, to organise, to motivate and communicate, to measure and to develop people. For Drucker, management implies an essential moral responsibility and must be driven by clear and stipulated objectives. To an important degree, his perspective bridges some of the differences accounting for the bifurcation in approaches to management theory. He sees the importance of measurement, setting goals and directing people, but also the need for exercising leadership and developing skills in motivating and communicating with people—and significantly in valuing their continual development in skills and capabilities.

Douglas McGregor (1960), another influential thinker in management science, proposed alternative, opposing models based on managerial assumptions about controlling people as the determinate factor to explain an organisation's character. He proposed neutral terms to describe the two essential approaches in order to avoid any implied normative bias. 'Theory X' assumes that workers are lazy and need to be closely supervised—this is essentially the command-and-control approach. The alternative is 'theory Y' that presumes people want and need to work and do that best under a collaborate-and-co-operate approach. In this approach, four kinds of learning are relevant for managers: intellectual knowledge, manual skills, problem-solving skills and social interaction. He prepared the way for future approaches that include employee empowerment and the 'learning organisation'.

Rensis Likert (1961) was a pioneer in studies about organisational leadership. He proposed a typology of four characteristic management styles: exploitative and authoritarian, benevolent autocracy, consultative and participative. Authoritarian management tends to produce dependent people and few leaders, fitting well with the rationalistic school of command-and-control, while participative management favours developing socially mature people who are capable of effectively taking initiative—fitting well with the humanistic school with its emphasis on collaborate and co-operate. Consequently, participative management was considered the best option, both for the business and in a personal sense based on the premise that an organisation can more reliably achieve outstanding performance if it has competent personnel, effective leadership and participatory practices in decision-making.

Robert R. Blake and Jane Mouton (1964) developed another management performance model, called 'the managerial grid' in which the critical dimensions are concern for productivity, concern for people and employee motivation. Combining these variables, they identified five key management styles that span from the 'do nothing manager' (poor performance in productivity and motivation) to 'managerial nirvana' (high performance in both productivity and motivation).

By this point, it is obvious that the developmental trend in management science is away from the command-and-control approach with its rigid hierarchies and heavy bureaucratic forms that were favoured in the first half of the twentieth century to a humanistic alternative that values workers and managers as fully human and capable of far more than Taylorist assumptions would accommodate, characteristic since the later half of that century. This trend accelerated in the 1970s as the era of heavy manufacturing drew to a close in the West. Given the kinds of enterprise media managers are required to handle, the humanistic approach is clearly more appropriate for success than the command-and-control approach.

Drucker (1969) is especially relevant for media management because so much of his later work focused on the manager as a knowledge worker, characterised by specialist expertise and working as a responsible individual who is paid for applying knowledge, exercising judgement and exercising leadership. Drucker forecasts a new economy that is not based primarily on labour, materials, energy or capital per se, but rather on knowledge and the capable application of those resources that depends primarily on expertise and knowledge. His predications have largely materialised because the knowledge-based 'information age' is highly dependent on educated middle-class professionals who are highly self-motivated and have a range of distinctive specialisations that must be co-ordinated and need to function collaboratively to ensure the success of an enterprise—certainly pertinent to media firms. His ideas anticipated today's emphasis on concepts and approaches such as 'knowledge management' and 'intellectual capital', also key concepts for media managers today.

Instead of thinking about what managers should do, i.e. normative prescriptions, Henry Mintzberg (1973) emphasised what managers actually do. He identified three key management roles: interpersonal, informational and decisional. The interpersonal aspect includes serving as a figurehead, leader and liaison. The informational function is based on being a monitor, disseminator and spokesperson. The decisional function is keyed to acting as entrepreneur, disturbance handler, resource allocator and negotiator. The prominence of each function will vary in different managerial jobs. Mintzberg's work is also evidently important for media managers because those roles are emphasised today in much of the training and development being conducted in media industries.

In all of this, one notes with interest an evident and growing emphasis on leadership principles and dynamics as a core interest of management science since the 1980s. This coincides with dramatic increases in competition, not only domestically but especially on a global basis. The focus is not as much on managing per se but rather on leading, although of course both aspects are critically important and one must be careful not to draw rigid lines. Moreover, a more nuanced understanding has emerged about the interdependence of workers and managers, with growing emphasis on the importance of worker participation and collaboration both in problem-solving and decision-making. For example, James M. Burns (1978) understood leadership as a structure for action that engages people. He identified two strands of leadership: transformational and transactional. Transformational leadership occurs when leaders and followers raise one another to higher levels of motivation and standards of professional practice, i.e. morality. Transactional leadership is built on reciprocity wherein leaders and followers exchange some reward. For Burns, effective leadership requires combining both elements so that targets, procedures and results are shared, but the former is emphasised as the developmental option.

Warren Bennis and Burt Nanus (1985) explained how and why leadership is open to everyone and not restricted to charismatic people. Consequently, a leader isn't only a formal role or management function but rather a skill (and talent) for motivating people to take appropriate action for themselves that benefit the firm.

Successful leaders develop a vision and communicate it effectively. They achieve their goals working through groups and are able to create an environment in which others can succeed. Bennis and Nanus identified four common abilities of such leaders: managing attention, meaning, trust and self.

We end this digest with Thomas Stewart (1998), who noted that although companies traditionally have relied on financial or physical capital to obtain competitive advantage, in today's business environments, intellectual capital is crucial. He divides this into three dimensions: human, customer and structural. Human capital is the employees; customer capital represents the value of the business relationship with clients; structural capital is the retained knowledge within the organisation. He concludes that value creation comes via capturing and deploying intellectual capital, which should be one of the main tasks for managers. In light of the growing emphasis on stimulating creativity, realising innovation and developing an entrepreneurial orientation, his work is of great importance for media firms today.

Attention devoted to elaborating specific competencies of media managers is scarce in academic literature. Alan Albarran (2013: 11–19) has integrated classical and modern perspectives and points out that management occurs in different levels (mainly, executives/middle managers/supervisors) and involves diverse skills, functions and roles. He proposes five types of skills (basic competencies): technical, human, conceptual, financial and marketing. Media managers from all levels need some knowledge in all five areas, even if not to the same extent for all. He further proposed seven basic functions (tasks they perform): planning, organising, motivating, controlling, facilitating, communicating and negotiating. Finally, media managers play three different roles while interacting with different constituencies: as leader (to their department or organisation), representative (to the public and local community) and liaison (to their parent company). This work is the exception, so far, rather than the rule. It points to the kind of scholarly work that is sorely needed in the field.

This digest of significant developments in management theory in the twentieth century makes it clear that the scientific school gave more importance to 'hard management skills' with emphasis on production per se, while the human relations school paid more attention to 'soft capabilities' with an emphasis on people. Even if from a theoretical point of view the second thesis is more advocated these days, reality confirms that examples inspired in both schools of conceptualisation are pertinent. Media organisations offer an especially good example of the importance of both, but with obvious priority on soft management competencies because these are critical for success in media as creative industries. This point will become clearer, we trust, as the thesis develops in what follows. Management science has been also moving from a rather restricted managerial perspective to broad consider-ations about leadership, as well as other more sophisticated concepts such as knowledge management, learning organisation and intellectual capital. These trends are indicated not only from the perspective of academic theory but also when taking a look at several key media leaders in the twentieth century.

Before moving on, we should clearly establish what is pertinent in this historical sketch for consideration of the thematic question that grounds this book: 'what's so special about media management?' We suggest that the humanistic turn in development of management theory is more fully aligned with characteristic realities in media industries than the earlier command-and-control approach that over-emphasised (arguably) rationalistic and rigidly structured designs. That is not to say that controlling a media organisation is unimportant today. Given the growing range of challenges and constraints on economic growth in this era of high uncertainty and general instability, control is arguably more important than earlier when competition was much less and profits were more secure. Neither is it to say that media as creative organisations producing talent goods don't have concerns about improving efficiency or ensuring that employees adhere to company policies. That certainly remains important. It is to say, however, that the kinds of work that professionals do in media companies, and the kinds of products that are produced, are comparatively unique both in their diverse and complex nature and in the potential for social impact. Development in management theory that prioritises people and emphasises the human dimension is highly reflective, we think, of the defining realities of a media enterprise. The next section strengthens this understanding.

3.2   Historical Perspective of Media Leaders

Although communication is as old and complex as human history, contemporary media industries are comparatively recent. From both a business and a managerial perspective, with the understanding that these are connected, three periods can be distinguished in recent decades. The first period can be dated from the early twentieth century and continued until the 1980s. The second phase was characteristic until the beginning of the twenty-first century, and the third phase is characteristic today. We put particular emphasis on news companies because of their prototypical importance for media industries more broadly and because a useful analysis requires narrowing to some manageable purview.

In the first phase, media firms were mostly organised around family businesses and these evidenced comparatively strong commitments to the city where an operation was based. This was of particular importance to developing democracies, as in the USA in the late-nineteenth century and in Spain, Italy and post-war Germany in the twentieth. This is not to say that there were no publicly quoted enterprises, but it is to say these were not characteristic but only emergent in the period. In addition, in some nations like the UK and France, the press had a strong national character from the early beginnings, mostly due to their capital centrism and, arguably, a colonial heritage. In both cases, and others of similar type, there is a strong sense of a patrician class in the press, whose contribution to the development of the public sphere often took priority over profits. The public sphere (in Habermasian terms) is highly co-related with political attitudes, and most newspapers hoisted some political flag, functioning largely as a partisan press that was evident in the editorial lines that governed each paper's perspectives.

The traditional business model was based on quasi-monopolistic control over distribution and advertising and focused on generating profits as a consequence of achieving a mass scale and character of product. This period coincides with rapid advances in industrialisation and enthusiasm for Fordist ideals about mass production. This clearly connects with Taylor's ideas about scientific management and rationalistic approaches to managing production and distribution. The newspaper is published 1 day after the event (in most cases) and is a physical medium that is distributed in a capillary network of outlets. Multiple revenue streams supported the enterprise, especially advertising (both display and classified) and subscription. This classical model is virtually the same in all countries, varying only in the design or quality of the newspaper in question and the degrees to which government has direct influence on content. It was a period when fabulous wealth could be realised from publishing newspapers and magazines, with consequential influences on social, political, cultural and economic life. It was also highly national (and often nationalistic) in orientation.

Development of the industry has always depended on various factors that especially include urbanisation, mass production and economies of scale, mass markets and a developing preference for brands, growth of leisure time and disposable income—and of course literacy (Steel, 1980). Interest in newspapers was almost always associated with the daily life of a home city. There have always been a few titles that are more national than local and all papers provided variable coverage of the wider world, but the newspaper industry was largely developed jointly with the importance and wealth of host cities. The Courier Journal (Louisville), Denver Post, Chicago Tribune, New York Times or Los Angeles Times are examples in the USA. The multiplication of local newspapers that need content about the wider world encouraged the development of wire services and large chains capable of cost-effectively handling that level of reporting as a supply chain for local papers that were subscribers. Examples include Knight Rider, Reuter's and the Associated Press.

Moreover, ideological journalism was characteristic in this period, evident, for example, in the reinterpretation of Manifest Destiny by William Randolph Hearst, who famously said: 'While others talk, the Journal acts'. Hearst created a new form of sensationalist journalism ('yellow journalism'). The business model was based on the strength and value of local advertising and an ability to influence the political agenda, which accounts for a 'hero' manager profile that remained stable for almost a century—and is still popular (if misplaced, according to Knee, Greenwald and Seave, 2009). Here also, the popular journalism pioneer Joseph Pulitzer and his New York World stands out (Swanberg, 1967). Pulitzer understood journalism as a mass product, not a medium limited to the elite. In this respect, continuous developments in mass production for printing and transportation systems for rapid, broad distribution of his newspapers are significant to its profitability, and so too the creation of a political agenda aimed at influencing a mass audience that ensured the profitability of Pulitzer's newspaper products. He boosted Sunday newspapers, such as Sunday World, which as early as 1897 sold 250,000 copies.

Pulitzer was in key respects the first great media entrepreneur because he realised that journalism is only meaningful when it becomes a social institution with the capacity to transform a sociopolitical environment. Unlike Hearst, Pulitzer wanted to combine popular journalism (human interest) with deep editorial analysis (public interest). His idea of the newspaper as a social institution (rather than mainly or only as an economic and political one) is evident in the reluctance of his paper to support presidential candidates or political causes. In Pulitzer's view, the mixture of money and journalistic activity was inconsistent with the larger social goal of serving democratic society. Another quite relevant aspect for scholarship is related to Pulitzer's commitment to the creation of the Columbia University School of Journalism. He linked journalistic success with a general requirement for professional training—i.e. with professional standards and ethics. Pulitzer (1904) believed that journalistic production is 'the battle for excellence' and that is only achieved with higher education to establish professionalism. Pulitzer pledged to not intervene in the appointment of the directors of the new school and bequeathed considerable funding in a perpetual trust for the creation of the awards for journalistic excellence that still bear his name—the Pulitzer Prize.

In these two early media moguls, we see the interests of media as business enterprise and political operative (Hearst), and the arm's length idea of serving the public interest as a social institution (Pulitzer). One can also identify an authoritarian command-oriented leadership style in Hearst, but a more humanistic counterpart in Pulitzer—as well as the latter's commitment journalism education. These two strands of management perspective and practice remain thematic to this day. Although the importance of realising profits is certainly as significant as ever, we see, for instance, in the Ochs and Schulzberger families who own The New York Times and the Grahams at the Washington Post that business profitability is not the only priority. Both papers are good examples of the continuity of surnames and editorial work at the head of major newspaper companies, and both have faced the challenges of succession within a family business, as well as industry diversification.

In her memoirs, Katherine Graham (1997), former publisher of the Washington Post, emphasised the point that business profitability was not her family's priority in owning and publishing the newspaper. During the strikes of 1974, for example, Graham noted that it was necessary to cut profitability to 15 % (compared to the 20 % or more of the Post's competitors) in order to facilitate the automation of workshops without costing jobs, although her employees at the time accused her of being greedy. During the Watergate scandal, Graham recalls how the newspaper suffered not only political attacks but also high economic pressure caused by the withdrawal of a significant share of advertising. A businesswoman with a very personal view of journalism ethics could 'afford' to lose readers if that was the price for resisting the untoward influence of self-interested politicians. Of course, this may be idealistic and one shouldn't discount the vested self-interest in her recollections, which make a good impression on the minds of readers. But the essential gist is undoubtedly true and well illustrates the point that this industry is not 'business as usual'.

In Europe, similar trends can be highlighted, although development dynamics were different because the role of the state in the development of media industries was much deeper, broader and more pivotal both in terms of media regulation and in generous public subsidies of various types. Here, radio and television started mostly as state-funded institutions after a brief initial period of early development by commercial manufacturers (e.g. Siemens, Phillips, etc.). In some parts of Europe, mainly the South, direct state control over content was an unfortunate consequence of dictatorships. Although commercialised from the start in the USA, in both regions, journalists and bourgeois families created new forms of news media linked to emerging political and economic demands. In the golden age of European journalism (1870–1914), this relationship was quite visible.

In Spain, the Godó family owned LaVanguardia, a leading newspaper in middle-class Catalonia that was launched in 1881. Two important families founded El País, the benchmark newspaper of Spain's centre-left: the Ortega family (from the intellectual world) and the Polanco family (in commercial publishing activities). El País inherited the tradition of an earlier newspaper, El Sol, that was the personal project of philosopher Ortega y Gasset. In Italy, Il Messaggero and Corriere della Sera share similar legacies and were associated with the process of unification, which was prioritised over private profits. In France, Le Petit Journal represented a focus on the common man while Le Figaro was equated with the conservative elite press. And in the UK, Lord Northcliffe (Pulitzer's contemporary) used technology to produce better journalism, modernise advertising and turn his newspapers into robust business organisations.

In the second period, from 1985 onwards (Picard, 2001), many media firms became global companies. This phase is characterised by the rise of transnational advertising (Halberstam, 1997), liberalisation of services, deregulation and the creation of a European audiovisual policy (Humphreys, 1996: 261), consolidation of mixed conglomerates and public trading in media corporation stocks (Cranberg, Bezanson, & Soloski, 2001). For media business, this constitutes a new information and communication structure that has become increasingly commercial, consolidated and transnational. The concatenation of changes in economic activity and the technology boom associated with digitalisation has in affect reconfigured what used to be a collection of small, mostly separated and comparatively modest industries (Álvarez, 2005). The importance of telecommunications in the growth cycle explains the arrival of new business leaders, such as Carlos Slim, the owner of Telmex in Mexico.

The global media company requires a new type of manager, especially as the trend coincides with digitalisation. A new media environment emerged in consequence to many and significant factors, including especially the impact of growing competition online, newsroom integration, mergers and acquisition of information companies (e.g. news agencies and newspaper titles), convergence between conventional media (press, radio and television), growth in specialist communication services (advertising agencies, public relations firms and independent content makers), a rapid expansion of entertainment holdings (e.g. sports clubs and theme parks) and even specialised outsourcing for training (like Kaplan).

Media executives have increasingly needed to develop skills and abilities in communication and leaned to deal effectively with politics. Some media managers come from showbiz and television. They generally understand the value of the projected image and the ability to influence through the screen. The Italianisation of European television (public and private) has its origin in this management method and style, especially characteristic of Silvio Berlusconi. As a media leader, Berlusconi introduced innovation and marketing into the daily management of his company, Mediaset. His 30 years at the helm were characterised as a far-sighted approach, anticipating trends such as vertical, diagonal and horizontal integration, internationalisation and dimensional growth (Balbi & Prario, 2010: 406). Whatever one thinks of his political rule and persona or character, he characterises one variant of a successful media manager—perhaps even a contemporary version of the moguls referred to earlier in discussion about period one.

A second variant of media manager in the second period are proponents of the transformation of information into a continuous spectacle, drawing on the yellow journalistic approach from period one but greatly developing the recipe. This approach pursues growing audiences as the top priority, even at the expense of the credibility and quality of news. Few media companies remain untouched by some degree of such commodification of information content, but Rupert Murdoch is the epitome of this approach. The Australian media proprietor has opted for invasive journalism and formulated editorial positions aligned with his variable best interest of the day, and evolving as these change, with evident explicit consequence for the front pages of the major newspapers and TV channels he owns. His support for conservative Prime Minister Margaret Thatcher and subsequent conversion to then labour opposition leader Tony Blair are a striking illustration, accounted for by his position on the deregulation of the television business in the UK. More recently, the phone-hacking scandal at now defunct News of the World revealed practices that have clearly not been one-off events but apparently a routine part of journalistic approaches at News Corp to news production within the media outlets he controls, which are all largely characterised by a focus on drama and sensationalism. Again, he is a contemporary version of earlier moguls who invented yellow journalism in phase one.

In a third category, we've seen an upsurge in star managers who have become global players and themselves part of news items, advertising actions and business decisions. The identification of a company with its CEO affects the stock market to degrees that either help or threaten the company's viability. A positive example would be Steve Jobs at Apple, although not strictly a media company in the traditional sense. On the negative side, we could consider the management style of Jean-Marie Messier at Vivendi, who undertook numerous changes including establishing a new corporate office and trying to change the internal rules of the game (corporate culture and brands) to overcome problems he inherited. Messier provided a clear corporate definition by restructuring the company into three main businesses where returns were higher. He acquired Havas publishing and media companies to promote content strategy and lead the mobile phone business with technological partners. In fact, however, the conglomerate created little value for the corporation because of an inability to use the resources and some business skills in other lines. Telecom, utilities, media and construction divisions share few keys to success. This did not matter to Messier, however, who was more interested in building a global empire and polishing his personal 'brand'. The international television business creates a sense of glamour for such managers, a potent attraction for some personality types.

The concept of the Principal-Agent Problem goes to the heart of what we are dealing with here. In a nutshell, the problem is one of separation of ownership and management, i.e. the shareholders (who own the firm) are usually not making (or even involved with) strategic and operating decisions. Decision-making authority is delegated to managers as Agents employed by the Principals (owners) to run increasingly large and diversified international media firms. In the Vivendi case, the main beneficiaries of Messier's diversification and growth strategy were apparently not shareholders but rather Messier himself.

The British newspaper entrepreneur, Robert Maxwell, has a similar profile. Journalism appears to be little more than a useful tool for achieving other business and also political aspirations. His ongoing (perhaps permanent) fight with Rupert Murdoch illustrates this, as does his investments in English football clubs. A certain type of executive makes such instrumental use of the media for largely self-serving interests. Richard Branson, owner of multi-business corporation Virgin, is a second example primarily thanks to his ability to align showmanship (advertising, airlines or F1 racing) with business. The type is also evident in German TV businessman Leo Kirch, who was able to professionalise entertainment (football) as the centrepiece of his television strategy, and Anna Wintour, the editor of Vogue, who managed to transform fashion into a global business and thereby globalised her publishing business.

Despite variation, all these managers understand the global dimension of media today—and the variable value that ownership and operation offer. They have used newspapers (and audiovisual companies) as levers for generating new business that is outside media, largely relegating their newspaper and other media businesses to an instrumental background endeavour. The value of this approach to management shows uneven results. Few could doubt their ability to capitalise assets or success in international expansion, but stock market earnings do not necessarily align neatly.

The third and current period started around 2004 and reached a crunch point in 2009. The economic recession caused by the severe contraction (some suggest even near collapse) of the financial sector in much of the West spurred trends that were already evident but not nearly as pronounced as in the aftermath. US print media lost 34 % of its readers and the figure in Britain was 22 %. Sales fell sharply in many cases, such as the Los Angeles Times (-14.7 %) and the Chicago Tribune (-9.8 %). The US model, which is based on almost monopolistic local papers funded by classified advertising plus local advertising, and with a comparatively small proportion derived from subscription fees, has been crippled by the emerging market in online digital advertising and by an evident unwillingness for many consumers to pay for news content online. According to data from the World Association of Newspapers, growth of newspaper sales is only strong in Latin America (+6.7 %) and Asia (+4.7 %). The fall in the West has highlighted the high dependence of the industry on advertising, the limited room for manoeuvre in sales of copies and poor management capabilities in too many cases.

The capacity to do business successfully today is based on the firm's ability to adapt to an increasingly digital environment, which is encouraging the emergence of a new type of media executive—a type that is more entrepreneurial than has been the case for decades (i.e. since period one). This orientation requires a range of competencies in analytical thinking and capability to lead in the achievement of business objectives, not (perhaps more simply) to understand and manage dynamic change in content production. The concern for stock exchange results has accelerated with the decline of founding families and a co-related connection of journalism with social responsibility for civil society. The new media executives and owners are increasingly 'digital natives'. For them, the Internet is not a by-product or sideshow to the main focus but increasingly the hub of media business activity.

For example, Jeff Bezos, owner of Amazon, acquired the Washington Post Company for $250 million after 7 years of losses by that company. His first public statements explained that the emphasis is now on developing a digital business for the new company, focused on three pillars: 'the first is the consumer; then invent; and have patience'. This formula gives priority to the customer market over the advertising market. He also explained that the purchase does not include buildings or other tangible assets, only the brand and content.

Arianna Huffington provides a second example. With her news website, The Huffington Post, she created a scalable model focused on exploiting new technologies. And it is producing profits. Huffington realised that the Internet is an entirely new medium that is not like the news*paper*. Her online news and information site doesn't try to replicate or imitate a paper format, but strives to create a viable service for a fundamentally different platform. In 2011, AOL purchased her company for $315 million US dollars.

Chris Hughes, one of the four founders of Facebook, the social media network, provides a third example. In January 2013, he was appointed editor of The New Republic, a long-running magazine and national reference in US journalism. In his blog for the magazine, Hughes recognised that the publication could not be just a print magazine but need also to become a live event organiser, a website for social conversations and mobile life, podcast versions of content, a tablet app, etc.

We are also seeing the emergence of a type of media manager who leads his or her own journalistic start-up. The transformation of journalists into entrepreneurs is a global phenomenon that is fuelled by the need to create new opportunities because the big legacy companies that were the historic employers are downsizing and struggling to regain viability. In technology, Rafat Ali, PaidContent blog creator, managed to distinguish himself with specialised content in the digital media sector. Gawker or FayerWayer provides a similar profile. In the political arena, Talking Points Memo, RealClearPolitics and Politico are start-up alternatives to the general news press. The situation is much the same in Spanish-speaking countries: Etiqueta

Negra (Peru), Revista Anfibia (Argentina), The Clinic (Chile) or El Confidencial (Spain) offer good examples.

Some key features of this model are important to underline. In most cases, these journalists are simultaneously owners, founders and shareholders, not simply workers. They are initiating projects that rely partly on the resources obtained from their layoffs. The basis of operation is consistently keyed to developments in digital media and efforts to create successful models for a new medium in a rapidly changing, complex environment. We see wide use of 'copyleft' licences and comprehensive agreements between owner-operators in other start-ups engaged in digital media. Journalists use their personal names as the primary brand for the business and as the key audience driver. Tweeting and blogs are typical elements in their strategies. Digital journalism is not simply a by-product of doing something else as the main focus, but rather the core business. In fact, the value proposition of such media outlets is substantially different from legacy companies and media. They rely not only on traditional advertising but also on 'freemium' options, subscription, community support and charitable donations. As a package, this suggests a different foundation for sustaining the media business in volatile, uncertain markets—one that still relies on a dual market (actually multiple markets) approach to funding, but constructed in new ways.

We also should note the development of such non-profit projects as ProPublica, which has already won several international journalism awards. Paul Steiger is the manager and editor and was previously editor for The Wall Street Journal. He convinced two philanthropists to invest a total of ten million US dollars over 3 years to create a digital news and information service that ensures long-term quality investigative journalism outside the corporate circuit. His business vision is clear: investigative journalism offers exclusive, public interest content with potential to influence the public affairs agenda.

Entrepreneurial journalism is a breath of fresh air in journalistic cultures and practices that have been steeped in traditional approaches and understandings that have grown stale and rigid. These companies are transforming the information environment by creating a new agenda, promoting critical journalism contents over infotainment and developing projects beyond traditional media groups. The approach depends strongly on building strong links and interdependencies with audiences as users and communities, not simply as 'consumers'. This development trend is particularly important because local newspapers are disappearing at a quickening rate in many media markets in the West. Change and development aren't easy, of course, and much of this requires new skill sets and different competencies for media managers. It certainly favours individuals who are adaptable, creative, good communicators and keenly interested not simply in 'the media' or 'the media business' but in the context that defines and enables that—whatever the forms or platforms.

There is a transversal theme in this short historical overview: the intersection of economic and business motives with more political and cultural aspects is a given in the media industries. This is arguably the most important distinguishing aspect regarding the specificity of the media enterprise overall. In addition, it is apparent that the nature of media managers has evolved over time from a 'founding father' construct (first phase) to a 'charismatic manager' model (second phase) to an 'entrepreneurial leader' today and probably even more the latter in the future.

3.3   Core Competencies and Specific Aspects of Media Managers

The OECD Core Competencies Framework summarises quite well the basic required skills for any type of manager these days. The framework combines skills that we earlier described as hard and soft. Competencies are understood as personal attributes or underlining characteristics in professional skills that enable the performance of a role and successful enactment of a body of work (i.e. a job). Factors such as personal values, motivation and type of work play a part in determining effectiveness in job performance. Core competencies are divided into three clusters: delivery, interpersonal and strategic, as show in Fig. 3.1.

It is generally accepted that all these competencies are important for any managerial position and have a bearing on management activities. This model recognises that technical skills are more related to particular jobs and within industries, and thus not as easily generalisable.

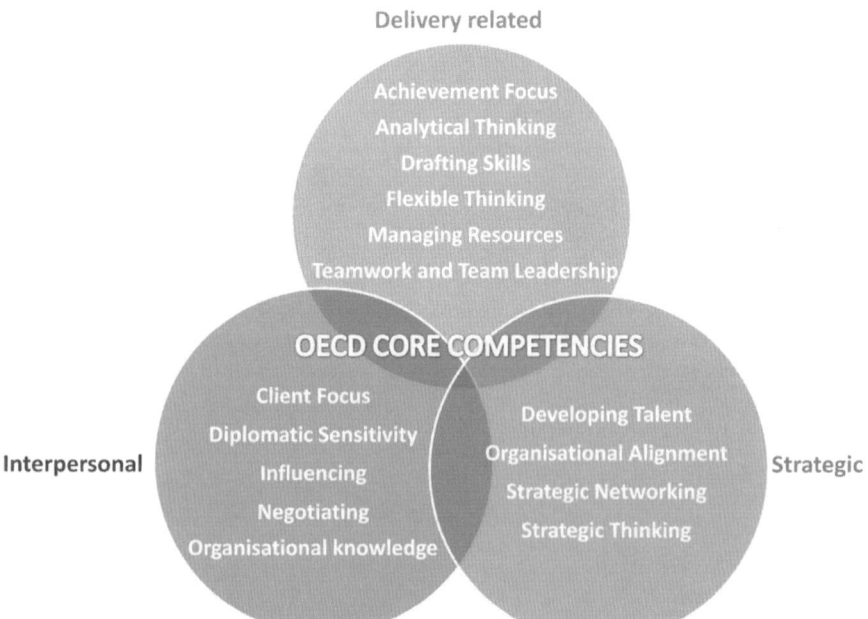

Fig. 3.1 OECD Core Competencies Framework (from OECD website)

What competencies seem especially important for media managers today? Henry Mintzberg (2004) suggested that a manager should not only deal with the managerial aspects of the company but also its leadership, and the examples offered surely suggest that media managers are doing much more than managing in a traditional sense. Today's media manager is increasingly required to be entrepreneurial in business orientation, to achieve innovation in the products on offer and to take responsibility for the company's brand and reputation as the core asset. Professionalism in media management is about creating value for the company through the exercise of leadership, which along with skills in negotiation and communication can be considered core competencies.

It is clearly true that different industry sectors in the media field (such as newspaper, television or the Internet) have unique characteristics despite important commonalities. Moreover, not all business functions within a media company have the same level of particularity. For instance, content/product management is probably the most specific functions within most media firms and these required variable skill sets related directly to the primary platform and essential genre (e.g. there are important differences between producing print news, drama TV, video games and animated films). The more generalisable attributes for management work are about the many tasks that are not industry-specific, such as marketing, operations, technology, finance, real estate and HR.

Although there are different sectors and business functions in media industries, being manager of a twenty-first-century firm requires more core competencies and higher mastery of them than in periods one or two. Arguably, it also requires a fourth cluster that isn't part of the OECD framework and is about industry-specific aspects that are critical success factors and vary by medium and market. A more general range of media-specific competencies can be derived from the previously analysed theoretical and historical patterns we observed. We propose ten that are evidently of critical importance today:

1. *Institutional Relations.* Media managers are responsible for handling businesses and institutions that have a strong public presence and are therefore routinely involved in, and targets for, negotiating complex relations with political, business and society leaders. This aspect is crucial for the success of senior managers especially, and competence to deal with this effectively has a strong bearing on the success of media companies. Media systems are always beholden to, engaged with and influential in political governance.
2. *Intellectual Leadership.* A media firm is usually a business, that's true, but it is also a cultural project—implicitly if not explicitly. It is especially the later for public service firms, if more often implicit (and frequently resisted) in the private sector. Regardless of the sector, however, today's media manager needs leadership competencies that are essentially intellectual in order to develop and represent the mission, vision and values of the company. And this is especially important in this era of high uncertainty given requirements for renewal and repositioning.

3. *Advanced Communication Skills.* A media manager must be able to communicate effectively in varied but routine media, including written texts, public speaking, making presentations, interpersonal interaction and so forth. Being persuasive and interactive is very important when bearing in mind the needs and expectations of diverse and sometimes conflicted stakeholders, e.g. customers, partners, employees, regulators, competitors and suppliers. A media manager that can't communicate effectively is in key respects 'a lame duck'.

4. *Creative Talent Management.* Media companies employ, contract and depend on a wide range of creative workers who are necessary to produce talent goods that succeed competitively. Skills related to the management of diverse and often complicated professionals who work not only for salaries or fees, but also for self-satisfaction and artistic expression, are clearly an aspect of vital importance that is industry-specific.

5. *Conflict Management.* Because media are complex social institutions, they are often the nexus for controversies with different publics and stakeholders, both within the firm and in the wider context. Time pressures, changing job conditions and competition for scarce resources easily provoke internal conflicts that must be managed and, however briefly, resolved. Being competent to manage conflict—and not reluctant to engage—is essential for a media leader today.

6. *Continuous Innovation.* Many industries depend on a production model that repeats the same pattern for long periods with only minor and largely cosmetic changes year to year. This is not as true for media products. Certainly, there is a degree of repetition that is evident in format and series production, but the content of each newspaper, magazine edition and television programme has to be different from the previous experience, despite format consistency. Media audiences are constantly looking for new and different books, films and music, which is precisely why the media are said to have a 'voracious appetite'. Continuous content supply, much of it profiled to fit channel-market strategic designs, means that product and format innovation is a continual challenge. Being able to manage for innovation is therefore an essential competency for media managers.

7. *Digital Technology Focus and Fluency.* The new media environment is increasingly digital and converges on a constantly expanding and diversifying Internet-based platform. Consequently, media operations must focus on digital technology in every link of the value chain: production, distribution and consumption. In addition, media companies are producing volumes of data these days, information with potential knowledge to enable deeper and more complex interaction with customers and higher loyalty. The need for managing this reality is necessary and requires media managers keep up with relevant technology, its uses and implications. Contemporary media management is a continual learning curve that is about developing skills as well as knowledge to use new media technologies. This will also increasingly involve competence to handle digital archives and content management systems.

8. *Social Monitoring.* Media activities impact societies, causing variable kinds and degrees of change. In turn, society impacts media requirements and performance, frequently requiring changes to adapt. All businesses need to monitor customer needs and wants, of course, but of keen importance for media management is the capability to understand diverse and always evolving lifestyles, values and social trends. Media managers need to understand how increasingly diverse, personalised and segmented populations use and perceive media.

9. *Entrepreneurial Skills.* Today's environment is characterised by upheaval, uncertainty and instability. That is in some ways a threat, especially for legacy media companies and their increasingly unviable systems for sustainability. But there is also tremendous opportunity for those with a capacity to recognise them and the skills and disposition to be entrepreneurial. This is an increasingly necessary orientation in such a volatile and fragmented industry. Being able to develop new projects, products, formats, services, business models and markets is already an essential competence for success as a media manager.

10. *Social Responsibility.* Production and distribution of media content is obviously a business, but this doesn't negate the fact that media are not business as usual. Mediation is a political, cultural and social activity that greatly impacts human communities and the character of social life. That requires a rather high degree of humanistic sensibility and maturity, suggesting these will remain core competencies for media managers in the future. Media managers are responsible for taking good care of a public trust and need to be conscious about their responsibilities and privileges as media operators. This applies as much to the private sector as the public, however unpopular the notion at present.

Thus, today's successful media managers need to develop not only general core competencies that apply to management in general (15 according to the OECD framework) but also media-specific competencies (at least the 10 proposed here). This is an ongoing debate, of course, both in academia and the industry. But we think it inarguable to note that media businesses share common managerial skills with other industries and sectors but also have particular requirements that are comparatively unique. This implies that both general and specific managerial competencies are crucial for a media company's success, not only in economic terms (if that to a large extent) but also in the varied political, social and cultural aspects than in effect determine economic success. This suggests the need to prioritise professional development among media managers at all levels. Specialised education, training and diverse experience in media management are important not only for professionals but equally for universities involved with media education and research.

References

Albarran, A. B. (2013). *Management of electronic and digital media* (5th ed.). Boston: Wadsworth.

Álvarez, J. T. (2005). *Gestión del poder diluido: La construcción de la sociedad mediática (1989-2004)*. Madrid: Pearson.

Balbi, G., & Prario, B. (2010). The history of Fininvest/Mediaset's media strategy: 30 years of politics, the market, technology and Italian society. *Media Culture and Society, 32*(3), 391–409.

Barnard, C. (1968). *The functions of the executive*. Boston: Harvard University Press.

Bennis, W., & Nanus, B. (1985). *Leaders: Strategies to taking charge*. New York: Harper & Row.

Blake, R., & Mouton, J. (1964). *The managerial grid*. Houston: Gulf.

Burns, J. M. G. (1978). *Leadership*. New York: Harper & Row.

Cranberg, G., Bezanson, R., & Soloski, J. (2001). *Taking stock: Journalism and the publicly traded newspaper company*. Ames, IA: Iowa State University Press.

Drucker, P. (1955). *The practice of management*. Oxford: Heinemann.

Drucker, P. (1969). *The age of discontinuity*. Oxford: Butterworth-Heinemann.

Fayol, H. (1984). *General and industrial management*. London: Pitman.

Graham, K. (1997). *Personal history*. New York: Vintage Books.

Halberstam, D. (1997). *Playing for keeps: Michael Jordan and the world he made*. New York: Random House.

Humphreys, P. (1996). *Mass media and media policy in Western Europe*. Manchester: Manchester University Press.

Knee, J. A., Greenwald, B. C., & Seave, A. (2009). *The curse of the Mogul: What's wrong with the world's leading media companies*. New York: Portfolio.

Likert, R. (1961). *New patterns of management*. New York: McGraw-Hill.

McGregor, D. (1960). *The human side of enterprise*. New York: McGraw-Hill.

Mintzberg, H. (1973). *The nature of managerial work*. New York: Harper & Row.

Mintzberg, H. (2004). *Managers not MBAs: A hard look at the soft practice of managing and management development*. San Francisco: Berret-Koehler.

Parker Follett, M. (1941). *Dynamic administration*. Management Publications Trust: Bath.

Picard, R. G. (2001). Relations among media economics, content, and diversity. *Nordicom Review, 20*, 65–70.

Pulitzer, J. (1904). Planning a school of journalism. *North American Review*, 5th May, 1904.

Steel, R. (1980). *Walter Lippmann and the American Century*. New Bruinswick: Little Brown & Co.

Stewart, T. (1998). *Intellectual capital: The new wealth of organizations*. London: Nicholas Brealey.

Swanberg, W. A. (1967). *Pulitzer*. New York: Scribner.

Taylor, F. W. (1911). *The principles of scientific management*. New York: Harper & Row.

Convergence, Similarities and Distinctions in Management Across Media Industries

4

Paulo Faustino and Luísa Ribeiro

4.1 Introduction

In the second half of the twentieth century, all types of media and media systems in Europe incorporated strengthening commercial characteristics and channels proliferated due to deregulation. This has required higher production levels and fuelled significant growth, resulting in part from heavy advertising investments and, in recent years, rapid expansion of pay and subscription services. Newspapers and magazines thrived, while radio and television became profitable businesses (in Europe most broadcasting operations were monopolies until the mid to late 1980s). This changed around the turn of the century and since 2008 has reached a nearly completely opposite situation. Due in large part to severe economic recession, in many information markets in Europe and the USA, media companies aren't as profitable as they were in the past, and traditional business models are no longer as valid. Today, there is great uncertainty. Also, the competition with Google and online streaming services has been increasing. This has changed the competitive situation for traditional media companies.

In the last 20 years, there has been considerable discussion about the transformation of the media industry and its relation with telecommunications, bringing these industries closer and making them more convergent—mostly in terms of content management and distribution. Thus, convergence (driven by digitalisation and deregulation, especially) can be seen as a characteristic trend undertaken

P. Faustino (✉)
Porto University, Porto, Portugal

Center of Investigation in Media and Journalism at Nova University, Lisbon, Portugal
e-mail: faustino.paulo@gmail.com

L. Ribeiro
Pathena SA - Private Equity, Porto, Portugal
e-mail: luisa.ribeiro@gmail.com

© Springer International Publishing Switzerland 2016
G.F. Lowe, C. Brown (eds.), *Managing Media Firms and Industries*, Media
Business and Innovation, DOI 10.1007/978-3-319-08515-9_4

towards the end of the twentieth century and increasingly powerful in the twenty-first century. This allows for, indeed it encourages, a confluence between platforms that were earlier treated in policy as separate entities and which did not as often compete directly as they do today when every kind of media company is rapidly developing online products and services.

The media industry is going through a period of accelerated transformation and is characterised by a comparatively radical disruption. This obviously has profound effects on management strategies and practices within and across media companies and industries. It is equally clear, however, that between media industries we find divergent characteristics that recommend practices and strategies for responding to the specificities of diverse media companies and kinds of products. Demands on management competencies regarding key media-related practices and strategies are different depending on whether we are referring to a regional newspaper or a transnational television company or a national telecommunications company.

Notwithstanding the fact that media industries are converging and companies are increasingly conglomerated, the two trends happening simultaneously, one can observe disaggregation of groups as well. We also note the entry of new players from the information technologies sector (e.g. Washington Post was acquired by Jeff Bezos from Amazon and Bertelsmann Group is selling some media businesses, namely, the book publishing activity).

According to Gershon (2009: 269), 'the clear lines and historical boundaries that once separated the fields of broadcasting, cable and telephony are becoming less distinct. A natural convergence of industries and information technologies is blurring those distinctions'. Thus, today's media managers face new industry players and more diverse issues compared with years past. That is not to imply, however, that everything has changed. As Borders (2006: 118) noted, 'convergence does not operate in a vacuum of the print, broadcast and online newsroom, marketing and promotion; convergence to the audience and advertisers is essential'.

Although one can identify different features within media industries compared with other types, at the level of business management, several analogies with other economic activities are evident. According to Deuze (2007: 63), 'It must be clear that media industries to some extent are faced with issues similar to those by any other commercial enterprise, such as global and local ('glocal') competition, and corporate concerns over sales, advertising revenue, and profits'. Albarran (2002) earlier observed that in the media, sector management is carried out at different levels and involves a variety of typical skills, functions and roles. Thus, management in the sector requires a combination of general managerial competencies, competencies that are characteristic within media as a whole, those that are specific to particular media industries and individual and unique talents. Clearly, there is great need at this point for developing more comprehensive and comparative understandings of what is perhaps too simplistically described as 'media management'.

According to some authors (Picard, 2002; Towse, 2008), media differ from other products and services due to differences in the mechanics of supply and demand.

On the one hand, media products are the result of creative, informative and artistic work; they therefore receive copyright production, which does not happen as often with other types of products and industries. Also, media companies are more visible to consumers because they are such an integral part of everyday life. Because of their cultural, political and social goals, media are more strongly influenced by public policies and regulations than many industries and operate in publicly condoned and 'owned' spaces.

As in other sectors that comprise the broader field of creative industries, the first stage of media production is always dependent on creativity, whether carried out at corporate or individual levels. Production cost is involved in the entire process, from the formation of an idea or concept to the production of what typically amounts to a cultural commodity. Much of the time, this is accomplished under conditions of high uncertainty because it is notoriously difficult to predict popular success. Strengthening economic pressures under conditions of higher uncertainty and growing competition account for contemporary trends in downsizing, outsourcing, a focus on maximising efficiency in the use of resources, promoting synergies, orientating towards marketing and branding and safeguarding profitability or revenue streams. Such vocabulary is common to all media firms and no longer unique to commercial operators (Picard, 2002). With increasingly fewer exceptions, the need to address financial performance conditions all media players.

A few important points should be noted before we proceed. First, we argue that media industries are in key respects unique when compared with other kinds of industry. At the same time, however, we highlight the fact that essential organisational and business-related functions are much the same as for any enterprise. Second, we argue that core competencies are in some aspects similar across media industries and types of firms, but that each media industry requires unique competencies. Third, we argue that operational and structural conditions have changed to a radical degree when compared with historic arrangements. These points are developed as we continue, and similarly important implications for the management of media firms. We begin with the changing conditions because that explains much about changes in required management competencies in terms both of what is distinctive and what is not across media industries.

4.2   The Impact of Technology on the Convergence of Media Business Models

In the past, economic sectors in media had limited relation to each other and operated in what amounted to separate markets. Newspaper companies, for example, did not compete directly with broadcasting and telecommunications had nothing to do with content. Nowadays, the trend is quite the opposite and emphasises convergent businesses. By the nature of their outputs, the economic sectors that have played a leading role in that convergence are computing power,

keyed to rapid development in hardware and software, and the increasing importance of communications and content production. With the advent of the Internet
and the globalisation capability it has empowered, the media industry (broadly
construed here) has been challenged to solve complex problems related to changes
in infrastructure and has needed to propose new solutions. Solutions have increasingly focused on the need to dematerialise content. The physical book, newspaper,
music CD or whatever becomes less viable as all types of content and services are
offered in digital form online. Media companies are increasingly developing their
capabilities for articulation with information technologies and across communication sectors, giving rise to a macro-sector we could designate as information
technology, media and telecommunications [TMT].

To understand convergence from the perspective of managing media firms, it is
necessary to comprehend the interdependence between actors in TMT and the three
platforms that are crucial to the process of making and distributing media goods:
print media (newspapers and magazines), electronic media (television and radio
channels, satellite and cable broadcasting) and telecommunications—mainly here
the Internet. As Killebrew (2005) suggests, from a technological perspective, the
goal of convergence is to allow for a combination of different platforms in order to
provide information to the public by sharing numerous technical resources. Conversely, in the information dimension, the goal of convergence is to guarantee a
relatively equal distribution to each available platform. Despite this, in practical
terms, the results can be the opposite with big operators using economies of scale to
fight and eliminate smaller, less popular players. Therefore, infrastructure networks
increasingly impose themselves as an important factor—an increasingly dominant
one. It is obvious that the media industry is going through a complicated and
sweeping process of change in which doubts and uncertainties about traditional
business models and management practices are multiplied.

Convergence produces a more complex media system that implies the need to
master new and different skills and may involve different risks for managers and
nonmanagement employees alike, namely, journalists. According to Killebrew
(2005), the art and the skills of managers of media companies are materialised in
the understandings they have, and in analyses of, organisations and these must take
into account a growing (and already vast) array of aspects. Print and audiovisual
media alike, as well as emerging new media, all face the challenge of transforming
the impacts of the digital revolution from threats into opportunities for new
products, services and business models. Information and knowledge are critical
production factors, and new virtual commodities—which respond to the needs of
consumers and industries—are entering the markets and building new business
areas in consulting, services and cross-media possibilities.

Mainly, our discussion so far applies to media firms that are comparatively big
and old, and hence traditional. But the impact of technology in the media is also
expressed in capacities for production, transfer and dissemination that are increasingly accessible to smaller companies, especially start-ups, with far less resources.
This facilitates a transfer of knowledge that allows small firms to adopt sophisticated best practice techniques for managing production and distribution across

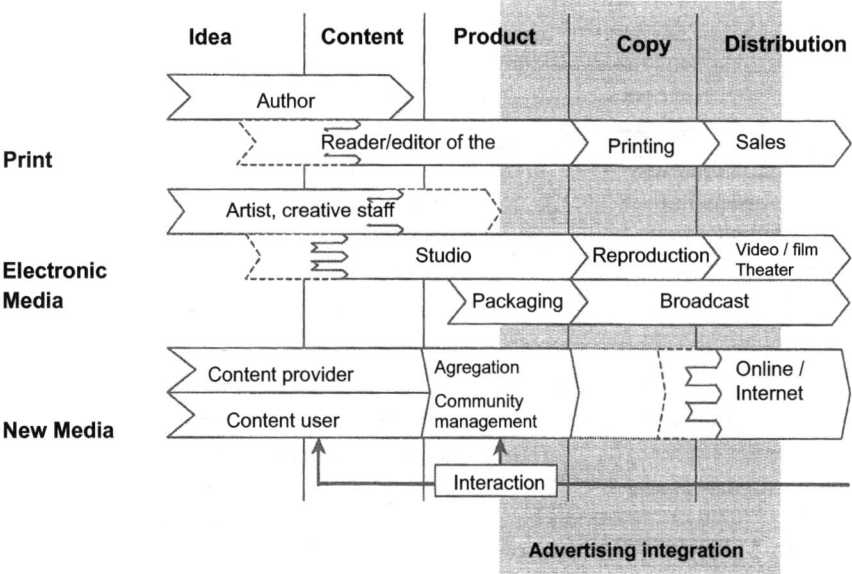

Fig. 4.1 Simplified value chain of different media formats. Source: Wossner (2003: 20)

types of media industry, regardless of the firm's size. Beyond management approaches, new technologies of information and communication have reduced entry barriers and blurred the boundaries of reachable potential market for large and small media companies alike. This has also created new challenges because audiences for digital media on the Internet can be local, national and international—even simultaneously.

Observing the specificity of the different formats and types of media, and the need to explore co-related competitive advantages, it is increasingly important to build highly specialised and structured value chains around those formats. This was illustrated by Wossner (2003) and is represented in Fig. 4.1.

Different media 'paths' indicate differences in the value chain and related business models, although the main characteristic is shared in that revenues are typically generated both by subscribers and advertisers. All media types compete among themselves for the same resources as, in principle, each receiver only has a budget of limited time for media consumption (either as advertising customers or as direct consumers of the media product).

All media content industries have similar value chain stages, as well: content creation (produced internally, externally or in a mixed way), content preparation (selection, organisation, packaging and processing), industrial production (transformation of contents into a presentable form), content distribution (logistics delivery process) and content promotion (marketing and advertising practices to attract consumers).

In fact, many functions and challenges are common to the different segments of media industry overall, although their forms of implementation may vary according to the strategy a firm or sector takes and to the type of media. For example, the film industry works according to project logic because each film is unique and tends to be discontinuous. Management practice depends on garnering sufficient investment (usually from multiple sources), hiring largely freelance or independent talent of many kinds and producing the product on a set schedule and within a stipulated budget.

With current technological advances, it is possible to observe a change in different parts of a business and the media value chain, but with a common trend in all the types of media that hinges on the importance of distribution via digital supports. With the increasing centrality of information technologies and the Internet, the value chains for media business between different media types are also converging and there is increasing effort to achieve synergies. This is most evident in cross-platform production, also called 360° commissioning (as at the BBC in Britain). Moreover, added value depends on achieving a joint approach rather than overreliance on the value of each media segment (Vizjak & Ringlstetter, 2003).

To understand the functioning of media companies and their management strategies in a convergence context, it is important to reckon with the network effects and the platforms used by the media companies. But one also should understand (i) the price structure—based on the financing model chosen, (ii) the price level (sale price in the content market and rate in the advertising market) and (iii) the ratio of advertising/content (in combination between both for a given service, which depends on the prices charged in the two markets). Key distinctions that help one to understand the business model of each media company and kind of media product are suggested in Table 4.1.

The construction of business models implies taking into consideration the value chains of the company because the two are inseparable. Business models reflect the systematic thinking that is so central to the comprehension and management of each type of media company. This tool facilitates understanding how a certain company develops its activities, as well as the features and specificities of the business and the necessary resources for its production and marketing.

Tassel and Poe-Howfield (2010: 346) looked into the relation of each medium with the consumer and systematised features that are always present in a media business regardless of the support or dimension considered (Table 4.2).

It is important to observe that the table demonstrates distinctions but also the increasing interdependence of media with new technologies and telecommunications. Moreover, the table demonstrates relative similarities between mass media platforms that aren't characteristic in newer media. From the business standpoint, one of the obvious and common aspects is that all types of media are engaged in a struggle for markets, customers and suppliers, competing in both direct and indirect ways that, in turn, require more sophisticated and also, arguably, aggressive management practices. This also accounts for the growing reliance on financial and economic rationality. At the same time, however, to remain competitive, media and telecommunications companies need to promote product innovation, which refers to

Table 4.1 Specificities within media types

Specificities	Online news	Newspapers	Radio	Television
Requirements for the consumer's access to content	Moderate	High	Low	Low
Limitations on content flow	Low	High	Moderate	High
Potential for audience participation and interaction	High	Low	Moderate	Low
Degree of content's geographic purview	High	Low	Moderate	Moderate
Degree of identification of sources	Low	High	Moderate	Moderate
Speed and timeliness of content delivery	High	Low	High	Moderate
Cost of content acquisition and production	Low	High	Low	High
Cost of infrastructure funding for media support	Low	High	Moderate	High
Requirements regarding the content's news value[a]	Low	High	Low	Moderate

Source: Constructed by the authors
[a]The lower requirements for the news value of content in online news are related to ethical and deontological issues. Although new technologies enabled value creation in journalistic production, one can question the destruction of some historical value, namely, as concerns the editing role and source validation

the complex process of bringing new products and services to the market, as well as to improving and increasing the market of the existing ones. This is not a characteristically low-risk pursuit due to high uncertainty, as earlier remarked.

In this section, we have expanded and illustrated what is unique not only about media management in key operational respects but also how media platforms compare. This has important implications with regard to core competencies for media managers, in both shared and comparatively distinctive terms across these industries. We address this in more detail next.

4.3   Central Aspects in Management, Functions and Skills in Media Companies

Our discussion so far makes evident that media and telecommunications managers face challenges that were not characteristic earlier. As suggested by Gershon (2009), media managers these days must be able to cultivate the tone and setting for the work environment, facilitating a positive and creative environment where content makers feel free to produce the best work possible within stipulated resource limitations. Being a successful media manager therefore involves six fundamental competencies: (1) planning, (2) organisation, (3) leadership, (4) staff management, (5) control and (6) communication. Of course, these are not unique to

Table 4.2 Characteristics of media firm operations

Core business/media support	Public and private television	Public and private radio	Newspapers and magazines	Web sites	Social media	E-mail instrument
Medium offers content	Content, advertising	Content, advertising	Content, advertising	Convenience, searchable and open access	Communication and user generated	Invitations, notices and reminders
Communication structure	One to many	One to many	One to many	One to many—one at time	One to many or one to one	One to many or one to one
Content appeal to viewer	Richness	Richness	Richness	Information, actionability	Immediacy, trust	Need or interest
Medium marketing element	Selling	Selling	Selling	Service	Recommendations	Addressability
Viewer and user reception behaviour	Passive	Passive	Passive	Active	Interactive	Active and interactive
Consumer cognitive response	Attention	Attention	Attention	Intension	Conversation	Attention and response
Maximal consumer response	Interest	Interest	Interest	Access and purchase	Engagement	Interaction
Element influence	Emotion	Emotion	Emotion	Actionability	Personal relationship	Target information

Source: Adapted from Tassel and Poe-Howfield (2010: 346)

media firms and that needs to be especially noted. What is distinctive, however, are the kinds of workers the media boss is managing. Creative talent and also journalists are not easy to manage in many cases. That implies that how the six competencies are applied, and particular features of them, will be somewhat different than generally reckoned.

Planning, for example, is essential but quite challenging in a context when so much within and related to the media enterprise is not stable these days. Organisations are complex in big companies, often with sharp differences between content makers in various professions and managers at diverse levels. Leadership is vital, but media workers are typically sceptical and not easy to lead or convince. The staff is diverse with a broad range of skill sets and personality types, often finding it difficult to work in required team-based contexts. Control is certainly important, but much of the success of a media firm depends on relatively high degrees of autonomy among workers. In fact, in some cases, media managers are questioning the productivity performance of journalists, partly to justify downsizing measures.

In general, media managers spend at least 80 % of their daily work communicating with others (Gershon, 2009). Communication permeates all the management work of a media organisation. The manager is constantly communicating with superiors and subordinates, either through face-to-face communication or through e-mail, television, calls or reports. At the same time, managers are responsible for communication with the company's external public. Marketing and branding is another key aspect that is increasingly important for managers of media and telecommunications companies. This goes hand in hand with product differentiation. Managing brands and branding is vital for keeping alive a certain range of expectations from the consumers' side in relation to a given product or service—and the company that is providing it (Gershon, 2009).

According to Herrick (2003: 57), 'there are three most critical skills that must be developed to succeed in running a company, namely: (i) management of cash flow through accounting and marketing; (ii) management of people through interpersonal skills, and (iii) management of time, both your own and your subordinates'. Again, these are not unique to media firms. But managing media employees is arguably more challenging than managing employees of many other types of businesses because reporters, editors, photographers, videographers, writers and designers all tend to be creative people with comparatively independent and 'strong-willed' personalities. Based on a study co-ordinated by Faustino (2009) with key findings presented in Table 4.3, the needs for training are intensely felt by media companies (in terms of management and editorial work) and linked to levels of required practical knowledge and the use of new technologies.

The authors of the book *Media Management: A Casebook Approach* (Sohn, Wicks, Lacy, & Sylvie, 1999) emphasise that teamwork is a very important activity in creating positive work strategies in media organisations. Along this same line of thought, they identify four major groups of factors that influence job satisfaction within the media company: (i) leadership factors, (ii) individual factors, (iii) market factors and (iv) organisational factors. Of all the factors identified, however, the issue of leadership seems to stand out: in newsrooms where new directors promote a

Table 4.3 Main needs of training in media companies (summary)

Managers	Management skills	Insight in anticipating the environment of future businesses
		Support innovative ideas and putting them into practice
		Provide an adequate training and motivation
	Behaviour skills	Negotiation skills
		Networking skills
		Demonstrate flexibility
	Personal skills	Problem-solving skills
		Constant updating towards the industry novelties
		Innovation and creativity skills
Editorial offices	Technical skills	Knowledge of new digital technologies
		Capacity to develop content on multiple platforms
		Knowledge of the propositions of the new media
	Behaviour skills	Demonstrate flexibility
		Professional empowering and continuous training
		Capacity to respect the ethical and deontological principles of the job
	Personal skills	Professional integrity
		Adaptation capacity
		Capacity to remain up to date

Source: Faustino et al., *Análise e Prospectiva dos Media: Tendências, Mercado e Emprego*, 2009

more humane approach and develop a more positive relationship, there is greater employee satisfaction at work. On the importance played by leadership, it is very important that leaders have a good level (which is easily perceived by the employees) of skills and knowledge about the media market and they have to be clear when manifesting their expectations and communicating with the collaborators.

Technology is causing changes not only in terms of content production but also in terms of content distribution. This offers managers and investors of the media industry the possibility to expand and diversify their investments across a range of media platforms. In this context, platform convergence—especially the interlinkage between traditional media and telecommunications—can also be seen, on one hand, as an aspect that influences professional profiles and the skills of employees and, on the other, as a generator of new challenges to management strategies and for the development of business models for media products, particularly in distribution and remuneration of the contents. A range of characteristic dimensions that are important to business approaches is illustrated in Table 4.4.

The table illustrates many aspects that may influence media management practices and strategies and should be taken into account. It is also important to remember that mature managers and employees of media companies have usually been trained to work on a particular platform (radio, television, magazines or newspapers) and rarely with an integrated view of the complementarities of different media. This approach is no longer very compatible with conditions in the

Table 4.4 Business approaches in the media and strategic and operational management

Types of platform/business management	Newspapers	Magazines	Television	Radio	Online	Cinema
Profile and dimension of the companies	A few large ones and several small ones	A few large ones and several small ones	A few large ones and some medium ones	A few large ones and several small ones	A few large ones and several small ones	A few large ones and several small ones
Stage of the product's life cycle	Decline trend	End of maturity	End of maturity	End of maturity	Moderate growth	Moderate growth
Management of distribution and logistics	High complexity	High complexity	Low complexity	Low complexity	Low complexity	High complexity
Market and competitive level	Oligopolistic structure	Oligopolistic structure	Oligopolistic structure	Duopolistic structure	Competitive structure	Oligopolistic structure
Target customers and markets	Readers and advertisers	Readers and advertisers	Viewers and advertisers	Listeners and advertisers	Users and advertisers	Mainly viewers
Business turnover	Tends to be low	Tends to be high	Tends to be stable	Tends to be stable	Tends to be moderate	Tends to be high
Investment on human capital	Frequently high	Frequently high	Frequently high	Frequently low	Frequently low	Frequently high
Business relation with the local culture	High dependence	Low dependence	Moderate dependence	Moderate dependence	Moderate dependence	Low dependence
Cost and investment structure	Tends to be high	Tends to be low	Tends to be high	Tends to be low	Tends to be low	Tends to be high
Activity and production seasonality	Tends to be continuous	Tends to be continuous				Tends to be unique
Scope of geographical coverage	Moderate	Moderate	Moderate	High	High	High

Source: Elaborated by the authors

current competitive context. Today, media management requires broader competencies as well as nuanced understandings about diverse platforms, flexibility and adaptability to accommodate different work processes and contexts and training initiatives that promote these skills. In this sense, one can say that present management practices of media companies require a broader vision and deeper knowledge about diverse distribution platforms and variable elements comprising the value chain. This professional and competitive demand is about business management in a multimedia perspective requiring not only new training but also the increasing introduction of related theories and practices, such as management models, business models and production and distribution models, that are influenced by the convergence of the information TMT.

So far, we have alluded to connections and also distinctions between telecommunications and media industries in the convergence context, but we've not directly addressed that. We do so next.

4.4   Management Characteristics in Media, Telecommunications and Other Industries

To identify the similarities and differences between media companies, including their relation with telecommunications companies, it is relevant to know the features of the different types of media companies with regard to their market, financial and operational and business dynamics. It therefore becomes increasingly important to analyse media products' interactions, to identify the various aspects regarding their creation and distribution and to comprehend their dependencies and vulnerabilities.

According to Picard (2002), several features influence the functioning, management models and the environment in which media and telecommunications companies operate. Although there are similarities, each has unique aspects that demand certain decisions be taken and affect market structures, opportunities and future development. Key aspects are presented in Table 4.5, which includes all media subsectors and describes particular aspects of media segments and supports.

Characteristics influence business dynamics for each media type that generates different strategies. Companies focused on unique creative products—such as books, computer games, music and movies—implement strategies where the profit from one product is used to cover the expenses of another product. In the 'hit model', successful products compensate investments in unsuccessful products and generate all the profits. Managers focus on marketing to fight the high risk of failure, which Picard calls 'management of failure'. Companies focused on continuous creative products—as newspapers, magazines and television series—can concentrate on improving the content over time through research on audience's preferences, renovating the creative staff, and through the replacement of products as some go stale and others pop up. Here, concentrating on branding strategies is

Table 4.5 Market characteristics of media industry

Newspapers	Magazines	Television	Radio	Cinema	Online media
– Strong connection to a particular geographical market	– Strong connection to special interests or topics	– Connection to geographical market	– Strong connection to geographical market	– National and global markets	– Low entry barriers
– Mature markets with a limited growth potential	– Mature markets with limited growth potential	– Product without durability, except when recorded	– Product without durability	– Strong secondary market (cable, video, TV)	– High level of direct competition
– Short duration products	– Products with a relatively short duration	– Regulated entry barriers	– Regulated entry barriers	– Moderate entry barriers	– Growing market
– Strong entry barriers	– Low entry barriers	– Other moderately high entry barriers	– High level of direct competition	– High level of direct competition	– Products with short to long durability
– Direct competition is relatively reduced in most markets	– Moderate level of direct competition	– Moderate level of direct competition	– Unstable audience	– High level of substitute products	– Unstable audience
– Circulation	– Growing number of titles	– Unstable audience	– High elasticity in the demand for advertising	– Genres and actors influence the demand	– Direct and free sale to the consumers
– Market penetration is declining	– Average circulation per title is decreasing	– High elasticity in the demand for advertising	– High participation of the public sector		– High elasticity in the demand for advertising
– Direct sales to the consumer through subscriptions and sales of single copies through retailers	– Moderate to high elasticity of the demand	– High participation of the public sector			– Weak participation of the public sector
– Low/inexistent elasticity of the demand	– Direct sales to the consumer through subscriptions and sales of single copies through retailers	– Moderate/high threats from new technologies			– Weak threats from new technologies
– Advertisers' preference for newspapers with higher circulation	– Moderate elasticity of the demand				
– Low/inexistent elasticity in the demand for advertising	– Moderate elasticity in the demand for advertising				
– Weak participation of the public sector (in developed countries)	– Weak participation of the public sector				
– Strong threats from new technologies	– Moderately high threats from new technologies				

Source: Adapted from Picard (2002: 12–16)

especially important. Competition in both types (single and serial) concerns the scope of the contents' selection and processing, and their longevity expectation.

Differences in media environments and the surrounding economic forces account for differences in production characteristics. The media differ when acting in production environments that rely on economies of unit costs and fixed costs. According to Towse (2008) and Throsby (2001), those that operate in economies of unit costs (books, magazines, newspapers, CDs and DVDs) feature activities based on an economy of scale: there is a decrease in the cost as consumption increases. In these industries, products depend on a physical process of production. The process involves high logistics that entail additional costs for storage, transportation and distribution. In fixed costs economies, additional production costs are not significant. The production costs of media such as cinema, television channels and the Internet tend to be based on product quality and branding. These industries rely especially on economics of scale and all the cost is in the first copy. Differences produced by these factors account for variation in the structure of costs and in the pressures experienced by business.

Since the twentieth century, the differentiation of media supports has increased significantly. The fundamental factors are the rapid expansion of the personal computing, the increase in broadband capacity, the exponential increase in computing power and the constant and progressive growth rate of the telecommunications industry. This has had drastic consequences for traditional media industries as a disruptive and destabilising effect, but also in opening new areas of business opportunity—even if so far complicated to monetise successfully.

In terms of business management, there is not much evidence that company size and platform create substantial differences in terms of management practices applied to different media companies. Much of the general principles in business management and strategy work are applied regardless of the platform, type of company or media product. However, we must consider that a company with activity in several types of media requires a greater effort in terms of managing its portfolio, particularly regarding the attempt to maximise possible synergies between the several businesses in its operations, and also in the need to clearly distinguish the forms of content distribution according to platform-specific characteristics.

The business dimension can generate a greater concern with the product's risk management, to the extent that it is necessary to mitigate the risks associated with projects that require large investments; and also, larger media companies tend to dispose of smaller assets (media products) that do not generate significant business volumes and margins, precisely because sometimes they require a business management work that is as demanding as in the largest media companies.

Now, we turn directly to the comparison of media and telecommunications companies with regard to some key similarities and differences in terms of their management (represented in Table 4.6).

In general, both sectors implement common management practices, particularly with regard to the importance of marketing management and the enhancement of

Table 4.6 Generic matrix approaches management in media and telecommunications

	General strategies	Risk business	Market orientation	Business organisation	People management
National newspapers	Concentration and product diversification	Low capacity to face business risks	Emphasis in marketing and in the consumer	Hierarchic models with little flexibility	Valuation of intellect and creativity
Magazines in general	Specialisation and service diversification	Good capacity to face business risks	Potentiating consumers' loyalty and maximising of the relationship with them	Fluid models and support to the collaborative work	Valuation of intellect and creativity
Paid television	Thematic segmentation and alliance with telecom companies	Business risk is mitigated by the thematic specialisation	Potentiating consumers' loyalty and maximising of the relationship with them	Fluid management models and moderate functional flexibility	Valuation of intellect and creativity
Free-to-air television	*Massification* and product diversification	Moderate capacity to risk and innovate formats	Emphasis in marketing and audience *massification*	Hierarchic models with little flexibility	Valuation of intellect and creativity
National radios	Concentration and alliances with regional and local radios	Moderate capacity to innovate and face risk	Emphasis in the interaction with the audience and in marketing	Hierarchic models with little flexibility	Valuation of intellect and creativity
Regional media	Thematic specialisation and geographical segmentation	Difficulties in facing business risk and in innovating	Incipient marketing and emphasis in the proximity—localism	Flexibility, voluntarism and functional versatility	Valuation of intellect and creativity
Online news	Segmentation and personalisation content	Low business risk and low structure costs	Strong possibility to interact with consumer	Fluid, flexible and informal organisation system	Valuation of technology and content creation talent
Telecommunications	Diversification of the services associated to the contents	Significant possibility of risk and product innovation	Valuation of the marketing and interaction with the consumer	Hierarchic models, typically rigid	Valuation of technology and technique

Source: Elaborated by the authors

intellectual and creative work. On the other hand, we note an exception for telecommunications where primacy is based on technical and technologic competence. There are differences in the organisational models, especially in the ability to innovate and to take risks and in the way of approaching the market—i.e. the client or customer. Here, we see key differences that are relatively proportional to the size of the organisations and to the business generated. Telecommunications companies generate high business volumes and are therefore able to generate more resources for venturing into new businesses and to innovate existent ones. This is similarly the case with larger media companies that also have more employees. These conditions explain the tendency to adopt more formal and hierarchical organisational models.

There is clear evidence of business management thinking in all of these organisations, however, regardless of size. In all cases, success depends not only on the greater or lesser qualification of their managers but also on the resource capacity to materialise the management thinking and strategies. A manager of a small media company can have a solid background in management—and even a keen strategic thinking—but may not have the human and financial resources required to implement the best overall strategy.

Conversely, the transfer and dissemination of knowledge is becoming faster not only because technologies allow it but also because the access is easier and less expensive through Internet searches, book acquisitions or attendance of online courses and other training activities. It is increasingly unlikely that the heads of media companies, regardless of their size, would be entirely unfamiliar with general principles of management and apply these in their companies. In the media industry, companies were born, in many cases, based on a social project of personal and cultural realisation—and even based on voluntarism at the expense of economic rationality. That is not true in telecommunications firms that emerged with a high orientation towards business and profit, even if required by regulations to provide some variable degree of universalism of access in connections.

Theoretically, public service media (PSM) could be excluded from the logic of market orientation, and during the monopoly era, PSB was largely excluded. But that has not been the case since the mid-1980s even in companies owned by the State. Everywhere and in every kind of media company in all sectors, there are growing concern about and pressure for adopting best management practices. This happens, among other factors, not only because the public media are under increasing pressure to compete with private media and with the leisure industry in general but also because citizens that finance public media with taxes or direct charges increasingly question the management of these resources and require greater rationality in their application. The modes of application of public funds tend to be increasingly monitored and transparent—accountability is a growing demand of the society across sectors (Lowe & Martin, 2014).

Despite generalisable traits, it is evident that there are distinct levels and characteristics in management approaches both for and across media. It is predictable that a company with larger dimensions and more resources will have more sophisticated politics in terms of talent management, business organisation, marketing management, etc. It is equally clear that smaller companies tend to have more fluid business structures and organisational models, not only because they privilege functional versatility but also because they use more subcontracted work and have less internal moving parts. They don't necessarily lack strategy or knowledge, but have less resource and opportunity risks are higher.

To systematise the differences and similarities between media companies, telecommunications and other industries, Table 4.7 observes some aspects that influence management and business models of each sector or subsector. The main idea is that notwithstanding specific characteristics of each business, the main functions traditionally associated with business management have a common application.

Despite some remarkable differences more specific to the media industry as a whole, such as the visibility and cultural and social impact, media are increasingly adopting management practices keyed to market logic. That is most evident in marketing, sales and financial profitability. This circumstance also reflects the tendency of media products to be increasingly perceived as a commodity. Thus, the management practices adopted by media companies increasingly approximate other industries' practices.

Table 4.7 Similarities and differences between the media, telecoms and other industries

Sectors/characteristics	Media	Telecommunications	Other[b]
Public visibility	High	Moderate	Low
Regulatory policies	High	Moderate	Low
Financing model[a]	Dual	Hybrid	Unique
Creativity and knowledge	Very intensive	Moderately intensive	Shortly intensive
Intellectual property	Very important	Very important	Important
Profit orientation	Low	High	Moderate
Social and public status	High	Moderate	Low
Influence on society	High	Moderate[c]	Low
Work precariousness	High	Low	Moderate
Impact of the digital	High	High	Moderate
Product perishability	High	Low	Low
State as owner	High (on public broadcasters)	Low and decreasing	Low
Competition level	Moderate	High	High
Work organisation	High autonomy	Moderate autonomy	Low autonomy
Product and marketing	Conflicting	Consensual	Consensual

Source: Elaborated by the authors
[a]The main exceptions to this dual financing model are the book and the film segments. However, we can also identify increasingly frequent situations of the financing application, via advertising, to the movie business, including through product placement. In the case of the book, the sales remain almost the only source of financing, although there are situations—very uncommon—of sponsorships
[b]Excluding sectors such as energy, water and other heavily regulated utility industries
[c]Although with convergence on TMT, telecommunications have increasing influence, namely, as content distributors

For its part, technology has contributed to the standardisation of management processes and operations by creating software and other models of business management support that are generally applicable. For example, many large companies use SAP software for enterprise management and the structure of the data system is geared to general management principles and practices. Media managers have a larger number of generic tools available to promote and manage their products than those that are especially created for media firms per se. Moreover, general areas of operation across sectors are largely the same. For example, promotional tools and financial management tools used by both media and telecommunications industries are similar if not actually identical.

It is possible to highlight some distinctive aspects of the media industry in comparison to the telecommunications, however, which may induce management approaches adapted to the context of media companies (although not *necessarily* different from general principles and theoretical assumptions). These would, namely, include:

- Economic irrationality in media industries is stronger than in other industries; key decisions are rather often based on noneconomic criteria (e.g. gaining political influence, the need for visibility, protecting cultural value, etc.). This is not characteristic of telecom firms.
- In media industries, many people produce content without remuneration for artistic reasons and intellectual satisfaction or in some cases due to the need of affirming themselves and to generate public visibility. That is far less characteristic in telecom firms.
- Media products involve autonomous professionals; thus, the organisational conflict is inherent to the media business since content creators may have diverging objectives comparing to managers. Telecom firms have not historically been involved with content production.
- The unpredictability of the media product's success tends to be high. Hence, the rate of failure is high for unique creative products. In telecom people pay for a connection and the factor to watch is the churn rate, which can be contradicted using retention techniques.
- Reuse and rotation practices of programmes and formats are common in media, but not in telecom.
- Functioning according to Pareto's logic (the 80-20 rule), the economic value of media products comes from a small number of 'hit' products or services and these few successes may compensate financially for many more failures. That is not characteristic of telecom companies where revenue depends on the number of customers and the average revenue per user (which, in turn, depends on minutes or band with consumption).

In Table 4.8, by way of general systematisation, we can observe some aspects that reflect characteristics associated with traditional media management versus a contemporary media management approach.

One differentiator of media industries from other industries is that content creators and media business managers work in comparatively quite independent

Table 4.8 Aspects associated with traditional and contemporary management of media

Traditional management approach	Contemporary management approach
Cultural products	Economic products
Monomedia products	Multimedia products
Lower technology-based products	Higher technology-based products
Products with a limited portfolio	Products with a large portfolios
Products with clear barriers or boundaries	Products without clear barriers or boundaries
Single-use products	Reusable products
Journalistic products	Journalistic and marketing products
Monomedia management: monomanagement	Multimedia management: multimanagement
Limited areas of required knowledge	Expansive areas of required knowledge

Source: Elaborated by the authors

ways and are quite often deliberately separated. This has long been evident in the separation of editorial and business management in news organisations. However, this idea—that advertising and news are separated activities and that print journalism companies and audiovisual journalism companies hold different businesses—has changed significantly due to increasing competition and higher uncertainty, and especially also declining margins.

4.5   Summary and Conclusions

In general terms, media markets are located in a confluent field determined by three key factors: (i) industry specificities, (ii) the legal and regulatory structure, and (iii) internal and external factors of success. Instability in the confluence of these factors is causing increasingly unpredictability and uncertainty. As a result, the routine behaviours, traditional skills and general resources of media companies have become insufficient and many practices that were tried and true are now largely obsolete. This requires new management approaches and adaptative capability in the search for new forms of production and distribution of content in order to build new markets and protect existing ones. This competitive environment has more or less forced media industries to acquire and develop skills, resources and management practices that are more market oriented than has been historically the case, arguably bringing the management of media industries closer to common practices in other industries.

Digitalisation in technology has encouraged convergence between media and telecommunications industries and that has fomented the emergence of greater similarities between them and higher standardisation in management practices and business strategies. Management practice in diverse media companies and across sectors, industries and contexts is increasingly similar due to a broad range of convergent aspects: (i) business models, (ii) distribution platforms, (iii) means of production, (iv) marketing tools and (v) interaction with the consumer. Finally, and regardless the type or dimension of the support, media are facing, with greater or lesser intensity, similar challenges in terms of management strategies and practices. This is evident in:

- Creation of new products and the drive for innovation
- Diversification of revenue streams and the drive for new business models
- Reorganisation of corporate structures and areas of work
- The rise of brand management
- Growing investment in new technology
- Co-operation with competitors and other companies in the ecosystem
- Demands for higher efficiency and productivity
- Project management
- Portfolio management
- Complications in attracting and keeping talent
- Cross-platform or multiplatform management and content
- Co-ordination between managers and makers
- The need for continuous training
- The focus on customer relations
- The emphasis on finding and creating synergies

The Internet is not only a distribution channel but an acceleration platform for the transition of media structures, activities and orientations in a new digital era. This circumstance reinforces the need for new knowledge and to raise professional profiles in media organisations, regardless of type or sector. This aspect is common to all media and telecommunications companies. The changes introduced by this flourishing of digital technology are felt intensely by the executives of media companies, who have been adapting gradually. The result is contributing to the dilution of historic boundaries between each type of media and also to standardisation in the practices of business management—again, regardless of the type or sector within media and telecommunications industries.

References

Albarran, A. (2002). *Management of electronic media*. Belmont, CA: Wadsworth.
Borders, G. L. (2006). *Media organizations and convergence*. Mahwah, NJ: Lawrence Erlbaum.
Deuze, M. (2007). *Media work: Digital media and society series*. Malden, MA: Polity.
Faustino, P. (2009). *Análise e Prospectiva dos Media em Portugal: Tendências, Mercado e Emprego*. Lisbon, Portugal: Media XXI.
Gershon, R. (2009). *Telecommunications and business strategy*. New York: Routledge, Taylor & Francis Group.
Herrick, D. F. (2003). *Media management in the age of giants: Business dynamics of journalism*. Ames, IA: Blackwell.
Killebrew, K. (2005). *Managing media convergence: Pathways to journalistic cooperation*. Ames, IA: Blackwell.
Lowe, G. F., & Martin, F. (2014). *The value of public service media, RIPE@2013*. Göteborg, Sweden: NORDICOM.

Picard, R. G. (2002). *The economics and financing media companies*. New York: Fordham University.

Sohn, A., Wicks, J., Lacy, S., & Sylvie, G. (1999). *Media management: A casebook approach* (2nd ed.). Mahwah, NJ: Lawrence Erlbaum.

Tassel, J., & Poe-Howfield, L. (2010). *Managing electronic media: Making, marketing, and moving digital content*. Burlington, MA: Focal Press.

Throsby, D. (2001). *Economics of culture*. Cambridge: Cambridge University Press.

Towse, R. (2008). *A textbook of cultural economics*. Cambridge: Cambridge University Press.

Vizjak, A., & Ringlstetter, M. (2003). *Media management—Leveraging content for profitable growth*. Munich, Germany: Springer.

Wossner, M. (2003). The media: An industry with tradition at the crossroads. In A. Vizjak & M. Ringlstetter (Eds.), *Media management—Leveraging content for profitable*. Heidelberg: Springer.

Media Management: A Critical Discipline?   5

Charles Brown

5.1   Introduction

From the outset, media management has been a hybrid discipline with roots in management science on one side and media and communication theory on the other. Each discipline has an intellectual and ideological heritage, particular assumptions and distinctive priorities and values. Typical of social science, there is an international dimension to many differences. National traditions and research cultures situate academic perspectives and practitioners work within the confines and liberties of national media policies and structures.

There is overlap between these disciplines, as well. Both social sciences have complex intellectual histories and contested epistemological foundations, with variations in preferred perspectives and subfields of specialised interest. Formed in response to intersecting and overlapping drivers, it would be wrong to see a simple opposition. Although there is a tension in the relationship between management studies and media studies, this is not necessarily unproductive. Neither would it be accurate to suggest that a critical research tradition is simplistically counterposed to a general practice that is essentially administrative in character.

Paddy Scannell has noted that the tension between critical and the administrative traditions was evident at the origin of modern media and communication studies. The 1930s saw collaboration between the émigré Frankfurt School where critical theory was characteristic and the Office of Radio Research where administrative interests were strong (Scannell, 2007: 13–23). The tension was enriching for Theodor Adorno and Paul Lazarsfeld (at Princeton and, later, Columbia University), who developed a quite personal working relationship. Certainly, they did not agree on many things. Although Lazarsfeld appreciated the critical nature of Adorno's approach towards mass culture, Adorno recoiled from the administrative

C. Brown (✉)
Media Management and Global Media Business, University of Westminster, Harrow, UK
e-mail: c.brown18@westminster.ac.uk

© Springer International Publishing Switzerland 2016   83
G.F. Lowe, C. Brown (eds.), *Managing Media Firms and Industries*, Media
Business and Innovation, DOI 10.1007/978-3-319-08515-9_5

research performed by Lazarsfeld and his colleagues, research that Lazarsfeld defined as a service to external public of private agencies (Scannell: 17). Indeed, it was called the Bureau of Applied Social Research.

It would be unfair to suggest that the work of Lazarsfeld and the Columbia School lacked a critical dimension. Projects such as the Princeton Radio Project (in particular, the study into the panic surrounding Orson Welles's dramatisation of *War of the Worlds*), the Mass Persuasion study and the Decatur Study (from which two-step flow theory emerged) reflected the concerns of policymakers in a country emerging from the Depression, into world war and, thereafter, Cold War. It is a period characterised by deep concern about the effects of propaganda and the cultivation of strong allegiances. This did not mean the researchers were lacking in concern about the potentially negative attributes and impacts of modern media. What Lazarsfeld's position did suggest, perhaps, was an unease with normative approaches that are concerned primarily with what media *should* be and do rather than developing a rich understanding of what they *are* and how they might be improved (however defined).

In this volume, Justin Schlosberg argues that media studies provide a critical counterweight to the goal-oriented focus of 'identifying the structures and practices which maximise a firm's capacity to survive and thrive under market conditions' (Schlosberg, 2015). Alan Albarran makes a similar point at the beginning of his survey of trends and patterns in media management research in the *Handbook of Media Management and Economics,* highlighting the unique social and cultural roles of the media (Albarran, 2006) although these are not examined in any depth.

There have been few systematic attempts to explicitly bridge, much less to integrate, the field of media management research with regard to the two separate foundational disciplines. At present, there is no evidence of metatheory. Rather, the two streams have existed, more often than not, in a state of friendly coexistence rather than engaging in productive discourse (i.e. dialogue and beyond). This disjuncture has been noted by leading figures in our field, most notably by Lucy Küng (2007) and Picard (2008). The issue has also been remarked upon in surveys of media management studies (Mierzjewska & Hollifield, 2006).

Bozena Mierzjewska and C. Ann Hollifield provide a useful inventory of media management scholarship. Relying on findings from a content analysis of two of the leading journals in field, the authors observe an eclectic and selective character in the emergent field of media management research roughly 10 years ago. The findings demonstrated a multidisciplinary approach in theory, ranging from sociology to management science and, more specifically, drawing on fields that especially include strategic management, structural contingency theory, organisational studies and studies about technology, innovation and creativity. Mierzjewska and Hollifield highlight the fact that there was a quite partial and limited conceptual toolkit for research about media management. In this volume, the chapter by Achtenhagen and Mierzjewska suggests the field is in a similar position still today, which should encourage this academic community to seriously consider what needs to be done to redress weaknesses and advance strengths. It may be fair to say, in light of these two studies conducted roughly 10 years apart, that we have not yet taken seriously enough the need to engage in a critical discourse about the nature of the field, the demands for maturing towards disciplinary status and the lack of a sufficiently robust development. We daresay this signals a fundamental issue of pivotal importance today.

Nonetheless, while unstated, the approach in both studies is essentially positivist. While Mierzjewska and Hollifield make reference to political economy and to normative theory, there is relatively little attempt to engage explicitly with those concerns. This is understandable for at least two reasons. First, there is an ad hoc character to the selection of methodologies and theory frameworks in the field. In some senses, this replicates the practice of management science. As Küng (2007: 24) noted, management is itself a fragmented and pluralist field of study and as such cannot be said to be a 'coherent science'. Second, the particular roots of media management as a social science are rooted in the earlier and largely positivist heritage of media economics. As discussed in the introductory chapter of this volume (by Lowe), many of the founders of this field are respected international authorities in media economics. As with economists quite generally, the dominant approaches are generally quantitative and epistemologically positivist. While that might be fine for media economics, it is quite uncertain how far this can take media management scholarship which is necessarily more often focused on micro and mezzo levels rather than at the macro level that is more characteristic of the former.

It seems reasonable to suggest that critical management studies (CMS) have much to offer in fuelling the needed discourse that can help redress the shortcomings identified. The first question is whether CMS provides sufficient resources and clues to enable that, and to especially clarify how we might bridge the gap between management science and communication science more effectively?

5.1.1 Critical Management Studies

The long gestation of CMS is usually thought to have reached a head in the late 1980s and eventually resulted in the 1992 volume from Mats Alvesson and Hugh Willmott that crystallised the field, *Critical Management Studies*. Not to minimise its importance, but in fact the origins of CMS can be found even earlier in adjacent fields that especially focus on labour process theory. In particular, one should note the work of Harry Braverman in his 1974 landmark book, *Labor and Monopoly Capital: The Degradation of Work in the Twentieth Century*. His work critically engaged the received tradition of classical scientific management, rooted in the theoretical perspectives of Frederick Taylor and the commercial practices of Henry Ford (amongst others).

The vein of scholarship is too deep and wide to provide a detailed account of the evolution of CMS, and it is not necessary for our purposes. It is sufficient to highlight some of the key themes and core debates that have a bearing on the field of media management in this stage of development. Anything more is not feasible in this context because, as others have suggested, 'it is probably fair to say that CMS is currently pluralistic' and explicitly resists any dominant or totalising approach (Alvesson, Bridgman, & Willmott, 2009: 8).

The antecedents for CMS are mainly in critical theory first articulated in the Frankfurt School of Marxist theory and later grounding the seminal work of Habermas with an abiding concern about the health and vitality of 'the public sphere'. It also derives from influences in sociology, especially the criticism of 'technocracy' located within C. Wright Mills's critique of *The Power Elite* and Loren Baritz's analysis of the subjugation of social research to industrial interests (*The Servants of Power*). Baritz echoed insights first offered by Adorno in arguing that management 'controlled the industrial social scientists in its employ' (Baritz in Grey & Willmott, 2005: 32). 'Managers did not make use of social science out of a sense of social responsibility, but rather out of a recognised need to attack age-old problems related to costs and worker loyalty with new weapons designed to fit the needs and problems of the twentieth century' (ibid).

The development of CMS is characterised by a proliferation of intellectual influences. Like other fields of social and political theory, it has also been shaped by the linguistic and cultural 'turns' in paradigmatic terms. Discourse theory, the influence of Michel Foucault and a more general popularity of postmodernist thought have all been significant influences, as have preoccupations with constructivist methodologies. Like much of the mainstream in management academia, media management has had (until recently) relatively little interest in epistemology and overarching theories. Although resistant to overarching narratives, CMS, by contrast, sees epistemological questions as fundamental. Shortcomings in management science generally are equally deserving of critique from CMS and certainly apply to media management science. We come to these aspects next.

But the point to be taken from discussion here is that CMS shares an intellectual heritage with sources that are equally important for critical studies in media and further that the richness of theoretical thought in political economy, cultural studies and postmodernist critique is vital for development of the media management field.

5.1.2 Thematic Aspects of CMS Scholarship

In this section, we consider six themes that are core concerns in CMS scholarship: (1) epistemological issues, (2) instrumental rationality, (3) denaturalising management, (4) performativity, (5) managerialism and (6) complexity and reflexivity. Each is treated briefly in turn, after which we provide some illustrations of the issues they raise. At the end, we summarise their importance for application in media management scholarship today.

5.1.2.1 Epistemological Issues

Although highly indebted to social theory (in particular, the work of Max Weber and Emile Durkheim), management science has largely been a positivistic discipline that generalises insights from empirical observation in often narrowly defined research projects. For an applied discipline, this tends to mean eschewing approaches that advocate any intrinsic merit in a particular course of action, especially if the underlying rationale is rooted in either value assumptions or normative theory. By contrast, the Frankfurt School—specifically, Horkheimer and Adorno—rejected the possibility of producing purely objective or value-free knowledge, at least in the social sciences. Taking a positivist stance too strongly in the social sciences creates troublesome blind spots that obscure underlying assumptions and values that are vital to grasp, whether these take the form of the rational, selfish agents of neoclassical economics or the maximisation of shareholder value as the cardinal aim of commercial enterprise.

5.1.2.2 Instrumental Rationality

Central to the work of the Frankfurt School is a critique of instrumental reason. The critique of instrumental rationality was most fully elaborated in 1944 in the *Dialectic of Enlightenment* (1944) by Max Horkheimer and Theodor Adorno and further developed in the *Eclipse of Reason* (1947) by Horkheimer. These leading members of the Frankfurt School saw their own work as part of the enlightenment project of subjecting superstition and received wisdom to rational criticism. Building on the earlier insights in Weber's notions about bureaucracy, they argued that modern rationality is not neutral or independent but highly subject to the interests of both business and the state. They observed that the 'features' of instrumental rationality 'can be summarised as the optimum adaptation of means to ends, thinking as an energy conserving operation. It is a pragmatic instrument oriented to expediency, cold and sober' (Horkheimer, 1941: 28).

Instrumental rationality is not reflective and assumes a 'given' nature in social phenomena. Enlightenment values are subverted from within and social science becomes lopsided. Frankfurt theorists rejected this conception of reasoning, seeing it as an exercise in domination over nature and human institutions. They described this as an 'efficient instrument of control for those who are in office and power' (Scherer, in Alvesson et al., 2009: 31). Moreover, by focusing exclusively on means (and efficiency), the perspective forestalls criticism of ends and ignores the values and interests that underpin decisions or the actions of leaders and ultimately therefore of the behaviour and actions of organisations. Indeed, positivist management research advances 'by default. . .the interests of the most powerful interest groups in society, as it provides the sociotechnical means to preserve existing relations of power' (Scherer, 2009: 38). As David Hesmondhalgh recently observed in an article about 'the menace of instrumentalism in media industries research and education' (Hesmondhalgh, 2014: 22):

> Most university research on media industries has not been of this instrumentalist kind. Much of it would claim to be critical: of concentration and conglomeration, of international inequality, of poor and unequal labour conditions, of organizational dynamics that lead to content that fails adequately to provide public knowledge or rich aesthetic experiences. However, the pressures towards instrumentalism are growing.

Work by later members of the Frankfurt School, notably Jürgen Habermas, takes a less pessimistic view, arguing that the possibility of critique and of undistorted communication (communicative rationality) is built into the structure of language. Nonetheless, he and others acknowledge the potential (the tendency, even) for communicative reason to be displaced by instrumental rationality.

The most notable rejection of the rationalist approach towards management amongst contemporary 'giants' in the management science field is found in the work of Henry Mintzberg, whose work focuses on the emergent nature of strategy and the skills and qualities of the manager in a rich social context. As observed elsewhere, Mintzberg's perspective (especially 1989) is 'academically rigorous while arguing that the assumptions and methods of much strategic management make little sense in understanding something that is more emergent and non-linear than it is often made out to be' (Phillips & Dar in Alevesson, Bridgman and Willmott: 419).

5.1.2.3 Denaturalising Management

Critical theory rejects 'given states' and instead sees social phenomena as historically constituted expressions of interactions of complex sets of economic, social and cultural forces. In their critical review of CMS, Valérie Fournier and Chris Grey take stock of the evolution of the field and seek to delineate what constitutes critical and uncritical work, although they acknowledge that the pluralism of the field and the breadth of theoretical influences make any simple demarcation impossible (Fournier & Grey, 2000: 180). Instead, they identify three key sets of issues: denaturalisation, performativity and reflexivity. We treat each in turn, beginning here with denaturalisation.

'Uncritical' approaches treat the object of study as natural, unchallengeable and, frequently, as something that is intrinsically desirable. This holds true whether the focus is on social relations, gender roles, organisational structures, managerial functions, entrepreneurialism, marketisation or hierarchies, etc. As Alvesson et al. (2009) argue, the role of CMS is, by contrast, working to denaturalise such functions and reveal the interests, power relations, ideological underpinnings and context dependencies that explain phenomena, thereby exposing their socially determined and unnatural or irrational character. As summarised by Fournier and Grey (2000: 181), 'Thus, whilst in mainstream management theories various 'imperatives' are invoked (e.g. globalization, competitiveness) to legitimize a proposed course of action and to suggest (implicitly or explicitly) that 'there is no alternative', CMS is committed to uncovering the alternatives that have been effaced by management knowledge and practice'.

The intellectual approaches to critiquing or denaturalising management processes and phenomena are wide ranging and include Marxist, structuralist and poststructuralist, realist, constructivist, cultural, linguistic, feminist and postmodernist approaches. This need not mean, to use Ann Cunliffe's words, 'criticising everything' but rather is about 'making the familiar strange and thinking about management differently as a means of opening up possibilities for developing more responsive, creative and ethical ways of managing organizations' (Cunliffe, 2009: 24).

5.1.2.4 Performativity

The question of performativity is a key differentiator between CMS and mainstream management studies. There is little consensus on the meaning of performativity. Significantly, the divisions that separate CMS researchers and theorists find a parallel within the field of media management and thereby highlight one of the ways in which a study of CMS may prove fruitful for our own discipline. Fournier and Grey cite Jean-François Lyotard, one of the founding figures in postmodernist philosophy, in defining performativity as 'the intent to develop and celebrate knowledge which contributes to the production of maximum output for minimum input; it involves inscribing knowledge within means-ends calculation' (Fournier and Grey: 180). Thus, they go on to say, 'management is taken as a given, and a desirable given at that, and is not interrogated except in so far as this will contribute to its improved effectiveness'. Alvesson, Bridgman and Wilmott agree (2009: 10), observing that the concept is frequently deployed 'in a somewhat technical sense to identify social relations in which the dominance of a means–ends calculus acts to exclude critical reflection on the question of ends'.

In the context of media industries, the critique of performativity would include such aims that may include overriding public interest concerns, the fostering of plurality (in its various forms) and calls for democratic control or intervention to encourage cultural breadth in content. On the other hand, anti-performativity may restrain scholars from dealing with recommendations for practice by restricting themselves to observing and analysing managerial practice. This divide is evident in media management papers at events such as the annual European Media Management Association conference and the biennial World Media Economics and Management Conference where papers tend to be either highly critical and prescriptive or instead largely supporting industry interests and mostly descriptive. Of course, there are plenty of papers removed from the extremes, but the fact that it is a noticeable divide merits mention.

5.1.2.5 Managerialism

More recent criticism of management examines the way instrumental rationality has been transformed into a set of beliefs, a way of seeing the world and 'a kind of systemic logic, a set of routine practices, and an ideology. . .a way of doing and being' in organizations which has the ultimate goal of enhancing efficiency through control' (Deetz, 1992 in Cunliffe, 2012: 17). Managerialism is championed as a solution to immediate problems and a set of values to which professionals should *aspire*. Managers are that because they possess status, skills and personal qualities that entitle them to *manage*.

Cunliffe identifies a number of assumptions within managerialism:

- Managers are skilled experts who have the right to act as agents for owners and shareholders.
- They have relative autonomy in making decisions and providing direction.
- Managers serve the common good and are the instruments and administrators of capitalism.
- Analytical and scientific management techniques should be used to resolve problems and increase efficiency (Cunliffe: 19).

The agents of managerialism are not simply managers themselves but also the system of actors and institutions into which they fit and by which the agenda is advanced and legitimised, i.e. business schools, management consultancies, legal firms and accounting firms. The cultural anthropologist, Georgina Born, highlights such factors in a detailed study of the BBC's changing internal managerial and creative cultures, pinpointing in particular the role played by the McKinsey consulting firm (Born, 2005: 212–253). Born traces an expansion of 'new model managerialism' at the BBC to the 1990s, while Carter and McKinlay (2013: 1229) trace the roots to the late 1960s. In a revealing historical paper, they argue that the 'calculative' practices that laid the groundwork for radical cultural transformation inside the British public broadcasting corporation first emerged from consulting work undertaken by McKinsey in 1968–71 (albeit to little *immediate* success).

As Carter and McKinlay go on to point out, the result of introducing the Producer Choice strategy was an organisational settlement involving a 'proliferation of agents producing measures', and, their penetration into daily organizational routines. . . legitimise(d) the principle of measurement and comparison, irrespective of the utility or ephemerality of specific calculations'. Thus, 'transparency moved from being a means to an end to an end in itself. Transparency had an appeal that reaches not just across the political spectrum, but also allowed a managerialist logic to penetrate new professional and creative domains' (ibid: 1239). As the Reithian mission was eroded, the authors argue, new spaces for managerialism were created.

Such critique resonates with the recent growing characterisation, levelled by commentators and policymakers at the BBC, that the institution has become top-heavy, overburdened with administrators, managers and strategists, a stratum that has grown at the expense of programme makers. In that light, Carter and McKinlay demonstrate how the critical and the mainstream are not hermetically sealed and that encouraging an intellectual, textual and terminological osmosis between the two approaches (CSM with media and communication studies) provides important insights that merit further development.

Managerialism has insinuated itself into almost every aspect of social, cultural and political life. 'Today, the ideology of managerialism has penetrated all key sections of society, thereby stabilising the managerial society' (Klikauer, 2013: 19).

5.1.2.6 Complexity and Reflexivity

Denaturalisation and its application to practices and ideologies (such as managerialism) highlight the inherently *complex* nature of the objects of study involved in the field of media management as social science. This is not to suggest that the management mainstream (or even media management) necessarily resists contextualisation or the consideration of externalities that accommodate complexity within systems. Cunliffe (2012) suggests, however, that the mainstream tends towards a certain reductionism and the downplaying of contradictions, tensions and conflicts. There is also a tendency to reframe complex challenges and phenomena in predominantly economic or operational terms, 'trying to simplify a complex, ideological, political and social process to a set of principles, roles and techniques justified by a supposed rationality' (ibid: 27).

Critical management epistemologies and methodologies are characterised by a reflexive character. The processes of denaturalisation and the critique of positivism as already discussed imply this quality, addressing the nature of research, the formation of research projects and the interests and social biases of the researcher or research institute. For social theorists like Pierre Bourdieu and Anthony Giddens, reflexivity addresses the socially situated nature of both the researcher and the socially constructed nature of knowledge, as well as the roles of social actors (Tsekeris & Katrivesis, 2008). In management research, reflexive approaches question objectivity and recognise that accounts of organisations are, by necessity, mediated (Alvesson et al.: 10).

Approaches that address the challenges of complexity and performativity have the potential not simply to provide more critical (or radical) analyses but, importantly—especially for management education—insights that can reflect the rich, multilayered character of business problems. That, in turn, has obvious implications for the quality and value of potential solutions. For example, some issues are not easily translated into the language of management science (such as the need to produce 'high-quality' content). One is forced to seek measurable proxies (e.g. range of output, plurality of voices, diversity of ownership) and at best to recognise that such issues remain stubbornly political and cultural in complexion.

To summarise, this section has highlighted six features of CSM that have something useful and needed to contribute to research and education in media management. All six suggest that a core problematic is failing to identify underlying assumptions and accepting as 'given' what is in fact constructed. Unless and until research in this field explicates the epistemology and interrogates assumptions rooted in instrumental rationality, performativity and managerialism, it will not be possible to denaturalise media management or deal properly with the complexity that is inherent in media management practice or the reflexivity that is characteristic of such practice. In short, we will likely still be more or less where we are today another 10 years down the road. That, we contend, is both unacceptable and unnecessary.

5.1.2.7 Application

How then might a critical media management research project differ from more traditional approaches, and what research questions might such an approach produce? We shall answer this by examining a number of relevant examples.

One example might be News Corporation's problems arising from the hacking scandal at the company's UK tabloids in 2011, principally its then largest circulation newspaper, the Sunday *News of the World*. For News Corporation, the crisis became almost a 'perfect storm', forcing not only the closure of the newspaper but also abandoning, for the time being at least, its bid to acquire the outstanding shares of the BSkyB pay-TV service.

That is a story that matters greatly to the management of media firms, but is hard to read in exclusively managerial terms.[1] In fact, it would not be nearly enough to read it in those terms if the goal is to understand the role of media as well as the responsibilities of management.

Moreover, it is a case study that cannot be fully understood outside of the power structures of the United Kingdom, the influence that News Corporation has wielded and the nature of the British political establishment as well as its newspaper industry. Certainly, proprietor Rupert Murdoch's interest in his UK publications is in large part commercial, but it is also explicitly political, in terms of the influence he wields. Meanwhile, the ensuing debate has dealt with press standards but also the wider function of the 'fourth estate'.

A more narrowly instrumental approach to the NOTW case might concentrate upon specific managerial challenges and problem—leadership, ethics, governance, strategy, the viability of traditional media business models and brand or crisis management—exploring how News Corporation may have responded more effectively, safeguarding its national and international interests.

A CMS approach, by contrast, might situate this within a wider context, questioning the assumptions underlying the UK news division's tactical response and attempting to understand the underlying drivers and motivations informing its

---

[1] Rupert Murdoch's son, James, was, until the phone-hacking crisis, chairman of News Corp. Europe ad Asia, where he ran its newspaper operations and much of the company's European TV assets.

actions and which framed the failings on its news desk. These might include declining news sales, a privileging of performance over other considerations, an overriding concern with celebrity culture and a relationship between Rupert Murdoch and his lieutenants and centres of power within British society (including both politicians and police) which at the very least suggested cause for concern on a number of levels. In reflexive terms, it would be important to address the relationship between the agency of protagonists—managers and leading media workers—and the structures within which they operate. Havens, Lotz and Tinic draw on Giddens' notion of structuration which 'emphasises the means by which the rules and discourses of social structures are internalized by social actors' (Havens, Lotz, & Tinic, 2009: 248).

The potential for denaturalisation is highlighted by the case of the embrace of marketisation and market-based solutions within conventional management research discourse, a preference taken almost as a given, at least until the financial crisis that began in 2008. The growth of the UK independent sector in the past 30 years has, for example, been portrayed within much of the industry and the academy in our field as an unalloyed good. Critical analyses have emerged, but generally from communication and media studies. Undoubtedly, in aggregate, the independent production industry has been a commercial success, but the complexion of the sector has changed considerably with a high degree of consolidation and the demise of many smaller 'indies' that was the intention in policy-driven initiatives to develop the sector (Chalaby, 2010). Instead, we remark the emergence of powerful 'super-indies' that have global stature and own most internationally popular formats and content brands.

The growth of the independent sector has been facilitated by changes in terms of trade, the development of sophisticated commissioning systems and a reduction in the role of in-house production and development. At the BBC, the legislatively mandate 25 % production quote was supplemented by the Window of Creative Competition, enabling independents eligible for up to half of the corporation's output. In a 2014 statement to the UK Parliament, the head of the independent representative body, PACT (the Producers Alliance for Cinema and Television), called for the BBC to drop all in-house guarantees and become a 'publisher-broadcaster' like Channel 4, abolishing BBC Productions (Kanter, 2014). Similarly, within the BBC, systems like Producer Choice, introduced in the 1990s by then director general, John Birt, also indicate how market-based systems have been incorporated into the inner workings of even publicly owned media organisations.[2]

Finally, a consciously reflexive example of media management research can be found in Tomas Müllern's contribution to *Leadership in the Media Industry* (2006). 'Middle Managers' Identity Work in a Media Context'. The chapter combines empirical research with an analysis of the roles and identity formation processes of middle managers while deconstructing popular myths and the authors own

---

[2] Not without considerable criticism from both within the organisation and opponents within both academic and policymaking circles.

preconceptions regarding media management. It argues that, more attention needs to be paid to the complex, emergent and contested nature of identity' (Müllern, 2006: 29).

5.1.3   Criticality and the Uniqueness of Media Management

All of which brings us to the question posed by this volume: what *is* so special about media management? Is the management of media firms qualitatively different to the management of other forms of organisation? If the field continues to largely accept the mainstream management perspective, then probably the answer is not much is all that different. Certainly, little that is all that distinctive for theory or practice is likely to emerge. But if we instead adopt a more critical, non-reductionist perspective that is focused on the specific nature of *ends* rather than mainly caring about the application of standardised tools (*means*), and if we evaluate relevant phenomena with a range of qualitative and quantitative measures not just calculative ones—in other words, if we accommodate a CMS perspective—then we are nudged towards the conclusion that, yes, media management *is* unique in a variety of ways. Indeed, implicit within such non-reductionist approaches is an assumption that all industries and spheres of management have some degree of specificity.

Of course, mainstream management research and practice acknowledge external factors. But that is not a typical emphasis. Critical media and management theory acknowledges not only the irreducibly *political* nature of media but also the central function that the Culture Industry performs in commodifying cultural works, creating demands which are 'evoked and manipulated' and integrating people as workers and consumers (Adorno & Horkheimer, 1997: 127).[3]

Critical management studies provide a route for improved treatments of the broader and deeper context for media industries, firms and systems. It offers great potential for constructing a more solid bridge with media and communication studies. This is a relatively undeveloped line of research and theoretical debate and thus holds promise for advancing the field if the opportunity is seized. It also suggests potential for new forms of critically informed media practice, which may prove to be in much higher demand than one might think as technological, behavioural and economic change continues to undermine the earlier certainties of traditional mass media. Everyone acknowledges that media industries are unstable and that a whirlwind of radical, rapid change is restructuring nearly every aspect as digitalisation develops. In that light, the turn to CSM in media management research and education provides a highly useful and a timely possibility to more fruitfully engage with new challenges, within North American and European markets—and much further afield.

---

[3] The Culture Industry first appears as a term in one of the chapters of the *Dialectic of Enlightenment*, 'The Culture Industry: Enlightenment as Mass Deception'.

Theoretically pluralistic, CMS has the potential to contribute to a shared interest in developing a distinctive set of theoretical foundations and to explore the insights that can emerge only by looking at the gaps and differences between disciplines, rather than simply borrowing and applying tools and concepts from mainstream management science. This does not suggest that one should throw away the tools that management science has developed—no more business models, no more value chains, no more resource-based view of the firm. Nor does it mean that the mainstream has been bereft of critical influence. Organisational research has been particularly influenced by elements of critical theory from Adorno to Foucault and Bourdieu. It is simply to say that our field has not been doing this nearly enough or well enough to reap the benefits entailed, and which are sorely needed at this point in the field's development as a discipline. That hopefully establishes the grounds for proposing a critical framework that should be useful for the work that is needed and lies ahead (Fig. 5.1).

While noting CMS scholars' warnings concerning performativity, media and cultural workers (and students *aspiring* to be media and cultural workers) are understandably concerned to acquire insights and tools that can be used to achieve organisational or creative objectives. Those objectives may be quite diverse and need not be purely about efficiency gains or profit maximisation (although some degree of efficiency may well ensure that their organisations survive to make a next

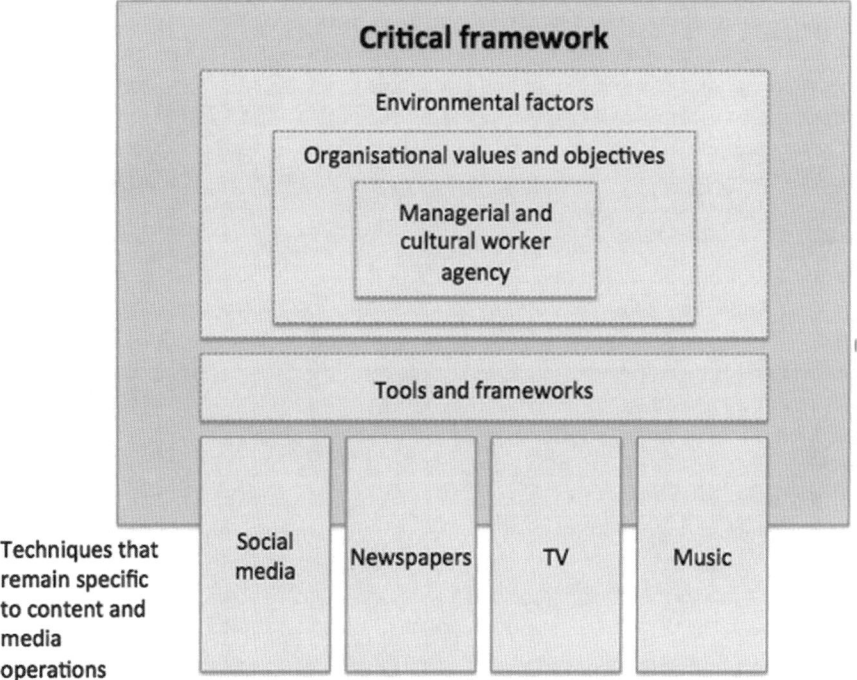

Fig. 5.1 A framework for critical media management research and practice

film or maintain an online campaign via a dedicated website or app). As we have seen, CMS scholars do not necessarily reject all forms of performativity and critical questioning does not translate into either passivity or contrariness. Rather, the focus is on developing forms of practice that are critically *situated* because that deepens and enriches insight.

Similarly, for media management scholars, this does not mean abandoning or rejecting empirical research. That is the foundation of science and we firmly support that. Neither does it mean dismissing as positivistic approaches because that perspective has produced a lot of highly relevant and valuable research. The problem is in the overwhelming character of its historic dominance to date, not its contributions per se. Taking a more critical approach means placing such research within a broader analytical framework and, ideally, using it to help develop more interesting research questions and more insightful research results.

Figure one outlines in schematic terms the proposed framework for critical media management studies. The framework accommodates familiar tools and methods but *situates* them within a broadly critical context. A scientist is supposed to be sceptical and thus must question *everything*. That is the core interest of the framework. One cannot and should not be prescriptive about the theoretical content that occupies this space. CMS has evolved considerably in the past two decades, engaging with new strands of critical thought and deploying a range of methodological approaches from realist and critical realist to the constructionist and ethnographic. There is no reason to think it won't continue to develop, and similarly, no good reason to think that critical media management studies can't contribute to that.

Perhaps the primary focus of media management research is the respective and interdependent organisation and the managers and media workers within that organisation. A non-reductionist approach recognises that such organisations and workers are influenced by external environmental factors and also their own values and further that there are contradictions as well as overlapping interests. In the critical view, these are not fixed and immutable but rather develop over time through reflexive interaction (hence the porous boundaries delineating these entities in the diagram). These agents, in turn, use generic tools derived from management science and other tools and techniques that are specific to particular disciplines (e.g. sociology, anthropology, political science, audience studies, production studies, etc.). It is rare, however, that such tools can be most usefully applied without a degree of adaptation.

Media management emerged as a new field at the very end of the era of mass media. That was a period of remarkable stability and certainty, as portrayed, for instance, in the television series *Mad Men*. Without question, that condition is no longer characteristic, and therefore it makes good sense to think that the status quo in our field must change to accommodate contemporary realities.

If the managerialism of the mass media era focused, as CMS scholars argue, upon *means* the destabilisation of established business models opens up the prospect of a rebalancing in favour of ends. A critical approach engages not simply with questions of efficiency and efficacy but larger questions about what media are *for* and why it matters, as well as to whom and how. This links the field with broader schools of philosophical thought and engages in social, cultural and political debates about the media's roles.

In questioning performativity, CMS does not exclude the possibility of impact. Indeed, CMS scholars may engage with a range of possible alternative approaches to management organisations, from the micro-emancipations and resistances identified by poststructuralist and postmodern authors to the creation or reinvigoration of alternative forms of organisations (e.g. co-operatives, collectives and mutual societies).

But of course, this begs a crucial question. Is the role of media management courses principally to nurture the next generation of media managers, or should we also be seeking to identify and cultivate those skills and attributes needed by a new and different type of critical practitioner, one more fully equipped with analytical and practical competencies and oriented towards outcomes beyond simple output (Moore, 1995) or the maximisation of shareholder value? We suggest it really ought to be the later.

5.1.4   Moving the Field Forward

In an important 2007 contribution to the *Journal of Media Business Studies*, Lucy Küng outlines some distinguishing features of media management—in her view, the inevitability of technological change, and the centrality of creativity—and argues for a new research agenda, away from rationalist approaches towards adaptive and interpretive ones. She also encourages a 'multi-lens' orientation that draws on insights from contextualist, constructivist, processual and pluralist perspectives (2007: 33). This is recommended because 'multi-lens analysis can accommodate the untidy, idiosyncratic and dynamic interrelatedness of organizations and their strategic activities. Indeed they do not simply accommodate, but build on the diversity and disorder of the organizational experience, and use these factors to increase understanding' (p. 36).

Küng's approach is not grounded in CMS; it is unapologetically instrumental. But interest in advancing the quality and value of research in the field is shared, and it's clear that her somewhat more traditional perspective dovetails with CMS to a useful degree. There are differences of opinion, perhaps. Rather than distancing (or denaturalising) media management science, Küng advocates closer proximity to industry. In this respect, her work perhaps follows in the footsteps of Lazarsfeld rather than Adorno. While that is fine, of course, it is problematic in our view that taking this position largely sidesteps the issue of reflexivity. For Küng, the way forward lies in 'greater application of theories from management rather than other media-related fields, and the application of a broader and more representative set of management theories and concepts' (ibid, 37). With that, we respectfully disagree. As Lowe also argues in the introductory chapter, the better way forward (in our view) lies in better connecting the two fields rather than privileging one at the expense of the other. Moreover, the problem in much of the media management scholarship to date is not in a lack of management science but in less incorporation of media studies and science. The better way forward is not in replication or application of already existing theories and tools, but in innovation and elaboration of such with particular importance for media management theory and practice.

It is important to note limitations and shortcomings of the CMS field. Some of these, such as its highly pluralistic nature, are strengths as well as weaknesses. CMS draws upon a wide range of theoretical influences, which is conducive to our interests in cross-disciplinary development. But it has meant the approach has been riven—sometimes to the point of inertia—by internal disputes and disagreements over where the boundaries of the discipline lie or even whether it is a distinctive field (much less a 'discipline'). The rivalry over different epistemo- logical and theoretical approaches can be fruitful and frankly speaking is probably unavoidable if a comparatively new field is to advance. Whether it is an example to be emulated, however, is another matter altogether.

An extension of this critique is that CMS is overly concerned with theoretical questions rather than engaging with study of concrete managerial activities. It is certainly true that much CMS research tends to focus on organisational research and analysis and that investigating the broad context and underlying normative assumptions is not cheap or easy. That is not to say it isn't possible or that the field doesn't need to do this. One needs a strong foundation upon which to build a sturdy structure. The scope of CSM research has broadened over the years to include many aspects of obvious importance for media management research: ethics, marketing, information systems, internationalisation, strategy, HR, commu- nication, project management and even accounting.

5.1.4.1 A Basis for Synthesis?

For many media management scholars and practitioners, the way ahead for the field is a conceptual broadening and a greater use of managerial science's theoretical toolkit, as Küng suggested. Certainly, media management scholarship needs to move beyond the relatively limited set of intellectual spanners, socket wrenches and screwdrivers the field has hitherto relied upon. The adoption of a wider range of methodological tools would be welcome. But welcome, too, would be a hearty dose of criticality of management science and drawing on insights derived from a long, rich and important heritage of media and communication science.

Situated within a critical framework, evaluation of the contributions made by management and communication studies, respectively, will facilitate identification of opportunities for synthesis and a much higher potential to generate new theories and develop fresh insights at the interstices between these disciplines. A reflexive approach holds the prospect of engaging with both the strengths and the limitations of current management theory, as well as contemporary media theory. What's special about media management scholarship depends a great deal on how expert the community becomes in mastering both fields and connecting them insightfully. Lacking that, there's no reason to think that management science can't do the job of research about media management at least as well if not better than most of the current community engaged with this area of study.

Finally, we need to adjust our thinking to incorporate theory, research and findings from a much wider arena than the mainly Western-centric perspectives that largely characterise the field today. Media management and the role of multinational organisations in the developing and postcolonial world are two areas where CMS may have particular benefit. CMS scholars are concerned with not only the globalisation of business but also the westernised and ethnocentric nature of management studies. Highlighting the work of Edward Said and Homi K Bhabha (on 'orientalism'), Cunliffe (2012: 27) argues that much international business teaching 'privileges the coloniser's (assumed to be more civilized) culture as the right worldview, the right rationality, set of values, way of behaving, etc., to the detriment of other experiences, other forms of knowledge and other voices'. Western models are of limited utility in transitional states (e.g. in China) where the state continues to play a pivotal role and where media management functions exist in a highly politicised environment.

In resisting reductionism, contextualising practice and countenancing the potential for alternatives, CMS provides a useful means of framing and bridging the two disciplines that gave birth to media management. We need not turn our backs upon the management *corpus*. That is not recommended here. But it is recommended that the field open itself to a more critical perspective because that will be conducive in answering questions about what is unique and *special* about media management as an academic field—and even, perhaps, advancing the specialisation as a distinctive cross-disciplinary discipline in its own right.

References

Adorno, T. W., & Horkheimer, M. (1997). *The dialectic of enlightenment, new edition*. London: Verso.

Albarran, A. B. (2006). Historical trends and patterns in media management research. In A. B. Albarran, S. Chan-Olmsted, & M. O. Wirth (Eds.), *Handbook of media management and economics*. Mahwah, NJ: Lawrence Erlbaum Associates.

Alvesson, M., Bridgman, T., & Willmott, H. (2009). *The Oxford handbook of critical management studies*. Oxford: Oxford University Press.

Alvesson, M., & Willmott, H. (1992). *Critical management studies*. London: Sage.

Born, G. (2005). *Uncertain vision: Birt, Dyke and the reinvention of the BBC*. London: Vintage.

Carter, C., & McKinlay, A. (2013). Cultures of strategy: Remaking the BBC, 1968–2003. *Business History, 55*(7), 1228–1246.

Chalaby, M. (2010). The rise of Britain's super-indies: Policy-making in the age of the global media market. *International Communication Gazette, 72*, 675.

Tsekeris, C., & Katrivesis, N. (2008). Reflexivity in Social Theory and Social Action. *Facta Universitasis (University of Nis) Series: Philosophy, Sociology, Psychology and History, 7*(1), 1–12.

Cunliffe, A. L. (2009). Management, managerialism and managers. In A. L. Cunliffe (Ed.), *Very short, fairly interesting & cheap books: A very short, fairly interesting and reasonably cheap book about management* (pp. 8–51). London: Sage.

Cunliffe, A. L. (2012). Managing, managerialism and managers. In: *A very short, fairly interesting and reasonably cheap book about management* (pp. 8–50). London: Sage.

Fournier, V., & Grey, G. (2000). At the critical moment: Conditions and prospects for critical management studies. *Human Relations, 53*(1), 7–32.

Grey, C., & Willmott, H. (Eds.). (2005). *Critical management studies: A reader.* Oxford: Oxford University Press.

Havens, T., Lotz, A. D., & Tinic, S. (2009). Critical media industry studies: A research approach. *Communication, Culture and Critique, 2,* 234–253.

Hesmondhalgh, D. (2014). The menace of instrumentalism in media industries research and education. *Media Industries, 1*(1), 21–26.

Horkheimer, M. (1941). The end of reason. In: Arato, A. & Gebhardt, E. (1978). The essential Frankfurt school reader. Oxford: Basil Blackwell.

Kanter, J. (2014). Pact: make the BBC a publisher broadcaster. *The Guardian,* 17 June 2014.

Klikauer, T. (2013). *Managerialism: A critique of an ideology.* Basingstoke: Palgrave Macmillan.

Küng, L. (2007). Does media management matter? Establishing the scope, rationale and future research agenda for the discipline. *Journal of Media Business Studies, 4*(1), 21–39.

Mierzjewska, B. I., & Hollifield, C. A. (2006). Theoretical approaches in media management research. In A. B. Albarran, S. Chan-Olmsted, & M. Wirth (Eds.), *Handbook of media management and economics.* Mahwah, NJ: Lawrence Erlbaum.

Mintzerg, H. (1989). *Mintzberg on management: Inside the strange world of organizations.* New York: Free Press.

Moore, M. H. (1995). *Creating public value: Strategic management in government.* Boston: Harvard University Press.

Müllern, T. (2006) *Middle managers' identity work in a media context.* In: Küng, L. (ed) *Leadership in the media industry,* Jonkoping International Business School Reports (pp. 29–40). Jonkoping: Media Management and Transformation Centre.

Phillips, N., & Dar, S. (2009). Strategy. In M. Alvesson, T. Bridgman, & H. Willmott (Eds.), *The Oxford handbook of critical management studies.* Oxford: Oxford University Press.

Picard, R. (2008). *Improving the harvest: Grafting media studies to management studies* Remarks to the seminar *media management as a new academic field: Reflections of the present and prospects for the future,* University of Tampere Finland, April 3–4 2008.

Scannell, P. (2007). *Media and communication.* London: Sage.

Scherer, A. G. (2009). Critical theory and its contribution to critical management studies. In: *The Oxford handbook of critical management studies* Online Publication Date, September, 2009.

Schlosberg, J. (2015). Resources and perspectives from media political economy. In G. F. Lowe & C. Brown (Eds.), *Managing media firms and industries: What's so special about media management?* Heidelberg: Springer.

Part II

Governance and Accountability

A Stakeholder Approach to Media Governance

6

Anker Brink Lund

6.1 Introduction

European media markets are diverse in terms of media policy and government regulation. In most political systems, privately owned newspapers, magazines and public broadcasters act under the arm's-length principles legitimised by norms related to freedom of speech. Other media systems are politically polarised, however, with less liberal or corporatist frameworks in government-media relations (Hallin & Mancini, 2004). Despite significant differences, most European media systems share common features regarding *procedures* related to media governance, and these are aligned with the guiding principles of EU law related to subsidiarity and proportionality (European Commission, 2001). Subsidiarity is the principle that the society level where regulation has the most direct impact ought to be where the rules and enforcement are mandated. Proportionality means that firms ought to have the resources necessary to fulfil mandates, but not significantly more as this would amount to 'waste'. The ideals of common market regulation are of particular importance for relatively small media markets (Berg, 2013; Salovaara-Moring, 2009). Co-regulated media market may bolster domestic players against imports, while European single market considerations may threaten this kind of media market structure, because EU member states must conform to the competition laws of the inner market. The impact of the EU regulatory regime is currently limited, but court cases are pending intended to harmonise the regulatory status of the European media markets.

This chapter does not go into detail with these specific regulatory decision-making processes. Instead, we shall explore formative tendencies in regulatory procedures influencing national regimes. The aim is to present readers interested in media management with a constructive framework suited for dealing with

A.B. Lund (✉)
Copenhagen Business School, Copenhagen, Denmark
e-mail: abl.dbp@cbs.dk

© Springer International Publishing Switzerland 2016   103
G.F. Lowe, C. Brown (eds.), *Managing Media Firms and Industries*, Media
Business and Innovation, DOI 10.1007/978-3-319-08515-9_6

government regulation and other external pressures in a proactive and strategic manner by creating shared value with stakeholders— rather than merely catering content for selected target groups. Research of this kind is hard to find, actually, and most publications are Anglo-American both in content and scope (e.g. Horwitz, 1991; McChesney, 2004; Porter & Kramer, 2011). This research-based work is valuable in its own context but must be treated with caution when attempting to apply the prescriptions to regulatory conditions outside the USA and possibly also the UK. The work grounding this chapter, of course, is also culturally and geographically situated, primarily based on a Scandinavian context and relying on data from Denmark, Norway and Sweden in particular (Berg, 2013; Lund, 2004, 2006, 2007; Lund & Berg, 2009; Lund & Lowe, 2013). To mitigate national bias, however, the chapter shall focus on the more generic levels of analyses, leaving the specifics to other authors (e.g. Kelly, Mazzoleni, & McQuail, 2004; Trappel et al., 2011).

The concept of 'media governance' employed here is derived from the work of Denis McQuail (2003: 91). He provides a common denominator for academic literature that addresses a range or related phenomena: media policy, government regulation, co-regulation and self-regulation. McQuail's conceptualisation serves as an umbrella term because it 'covers all means by which the mass media are limited, directed, encouraged, managed or called into account, ranging from the most binding law to the most resistible of pressure and self-chosen disciplines'. This perspective obviously includes the decision-making process leading towards specific standards, their implementation and more or less pervasive sanctions for non-compliance, our focus in this chapter. Here we limit our analysis to the first aspect because the main intention is to emphasise how the formative dimension of governance matters for media industries and firms.

Formative aspects of media governance are evaluated from a stakeholder perspective, which is not regarding the regulatory framework as a given externality but rather as an opportunity for demonstrating strategic leadership and changing management in differing alliances engaged with the policy-making process (Thomassen, 2009). The term 'stakeholder' was coined by R. Edward Freeman (1984) as a corrective to the traditional shareholder focus that has been characteristic in academic literature on strategic management. Freeman defined the term broadly to include any group or individual that can affect, or is affected by, the achievement of an organisation's objectives. For strategic action, however, the core holders of stakes must be mapped and evaluated in terms of power, legitimacy and urgency. When the key players have been identified, the characteristic process of negotiating the order of mutual and conflicting interest can unfold. This approach is of particular interest for media industries because companies and corporations in this field—private as well as publicly owned—are prone to scrutiny from a large and varied range of outside forces, inviting combinations of collaboration, mediation, coercion and subversion (Andriof et al., 2002).

Media governance includes restrictions (forbidden to do) as well as prescriptions (required to do), and both are fundamentally grounded, in the West at least, in the normative framework that prioritises freedom of speech traditions. This assures a relatively high degree of autonomy for media content provision and ensures that such autonomy is legally protected. By the same token civil society has other and wider norms that include demands for media organisations to take social responsibility for what they do and fail to do, within what amounts to a 'merited autonomy'. Consequently, media organisations are obliged to engage in dialogue, as well as debate and often disagreement, with varied stakeholders and typically required to institute regimes of self-regulation that are manifest in codes of conduct, mission statements and canons that inscribe the framework of a professional ethic.

Here we are mainly focusing on the European context to summarise regulatory regime shifts over time. It's really only possible to take a longer-term perspective when focusing on a particular context, as the challenge would otherwise be problematic given the space within which this work must be accomplished. Regulation is here understood as a challenge to and an opportunity for leadership that can make a difference in outcomes, especially important in lobbying for a better 'deal' and bargaining with varied stakeholders that typically have different priorities and self-interests. This perspective is aligned with the work of Des Freedman (2008: 1) who contends that 'media systems are purposefully created, their characters shaped by competing political interests that seek to inscribe their own values and objectives on the possibilities facilitated by a complex combination of technological, economic and social factors. . . .there is nothing predetermined [and this] is a deeply political phenomenon'.

How policy is formulated for media is well illustrated by one quite influential media manager in the late 1980s, Mr. Jan Stenbeck, who was acting through his investment firm *Modern Times Group*. He likened the conditions prevailing in media governance to a game of 'Rock-Paper-Scissors' (Andersson, 2002), where rock beats scissors, scissors beats paper and paper beats rock. The allegory suggests that media capital (the rock) has always been challenged, as evident in the fact that commercial interests are regularly trumped by government regulation (the paper), but that today's global technology and economic development (the scissors) has frequently overpowered national regulation. But because no media technology can develop in social application without capital, this takes one back to the rock and with new potentials for more paper.

In short, then, government regulation tends to be off tempo or out of kilter with business interests and to lag technology development, typically attempting to solve yesterday's problems and unwittingly contributing to the emerging disputes that come to characterise the issues tomorrow. Consequently, media governance cannot be regarded as a given set of commandments carved in stone, but should rather be understood as pieces of paper inviting participation in arriving at some negotiated order, prompting challenges not only to those being regulated but also to those doing the regulating. Any settlement is therefore best understood as always temporary, however long its duration. Changes in context and negotiations in technology as well as power relations, meanings and values, open new fields and cause fresh debate also over already settled issues that suddenly require policy revision—a highly politicised process.

Certainly many media managers regard this as a persistent nuisance, and very often as unwelcome intrusion, but in fact media are public and societal phenomena, and the ongoing nature of dispute is not surprising. And one is wiser to understand that policy debate and discourse invites participation and allows for stakeholder involvement in making the many and complex determinations needed to revise or renew a remit, which is a vital need not only to maintain but also to strengthen the firm's licence to operate. The fact that media governance must be regarded as a constantly renegotiated order also implies that effective media managers must be historically informed about the governance tradition of their industries and, especially, the policy heritage of their particular organisation. This point was well made by John Dimmick (2003) as a requirement for defending the firm's licence to operate in context that is always characterised both by competition and cooperation with key stakeholders. Thus, what we are talking about is not exclusive to Europe or only a topic of importance for 'progressive' theory; it is a characteristic of media policy everywhere short of authoritarian states and is a matter of real significance in the field of media economics.

6.2   Restrictive and Prescriptive Governance

The constitutions that ground governance in a liberal democracy accord news media a role in serving as a 'watch dog' on government, not the reverse. Censorship has been systematically criticised by journalists and pamphleteers, and resisted more generally, as an unacceptable practice that damages the interests of democracy and the broad civil society by creating unwarranted obstacles to freedom of speech and the press. At least in principle, most European governments herald political norms of noninterference and self-regulation of the press, requiring to varying degrees only that these firms be responsible to the courts after the fact and only in matters related to libel, slander and security of the realm. But in fact, news agency reporting was historically regarded as a matter of national security, and a global network of cartels was established along political demarcation lines (Cook, 1998).

Historically, as well, government regulation was integral to media policy in broadcasting and telecommunications and especially in the public service sector. The argument for state intervention was primarily linked to military needs and technical limits (spectrum scarcity), although commercial interests were quietly (for the most part) instrumental behind the scenes in decision-making. One should remember that Philips was important for the Netherlands, as Siemens was for Germany and RCA in the USA. In the aftermath of the very first regulatory conference on radio in Europe, held in 1903, Britain and Italy refused to sign an international treaty on radio communication that would pledge commitments to free trade and noninterference. Critics of the preference for self-governance characterised this position as 'Marconism' because the Marconi Company had a de facto monopoly and was based in Italy and Britain. In contrast, Germany and

France promoted national interests by protecting home markets and pushing for an international regime of government regulation in tandem with existing rules related to the national organisations for telegraph and the telephone communications (Spar, 2001).

After the First World War, radio was no longer strictly reserved for military purposes. In marked contrast to the USA where nonmilitary radio became quickly commercialised [see Barnouw (1966) and Lewis (1993)], 'the wireless' in Europe was usually regarded as a vehicle for nation-building and public education—the 'enlightenment mission'. Cross-border regulation was necessary to avoid inter-ference in a region with many nations and languages in close proximity and to prevent broadcasters from crowding the spectrum and interfering with military transmissions. Accordingly, each nation was given a limited number of radio frequencies and by 1927 even an initially reluctant government in the USA followed suit, due mainly to problems with frequency interference, and established a regulatory system (the FCC) in order to avoid congestion. In America, however, a supplementary aim of the regulation was to protect free trade and competition (McChesney, 1993), while most European nations explicitly sanctioned monopolies in public service broadcasting (Kelly et al., 2004).

The British Broadcasting Corporation (BBC) became the template for gover-nance, and philosophy, for broadcasting in Europe, placing the organisation not only outside the market but also outside of direct state control. Following suit, most European broadcasting services in the west of Europe became public service monopolies that were financed by government-sanctioned licence fees (originally a licence paid to own the radio receiving device). Argumentation that legitimated this was partly to spectrum scarcity of frequencies and partly to fears about market failure. Many agreed that only authoritative planning and mandated requirements would ensure that programming would provide the full range of desirable goods, construed as merit and public goods that were important for the common welfare of a general public (Scannell & Cardiff, 1991). Media goods were therefore peculiar in importance and in the potential effects of failure to supply—or to oversupply—a range that was considered desirable.

After the Second World War, the news agency cartels were largely deregulated, and cultural arguments became more prevalent in media policy both nationally and internationally (Curran, 2002). The emergence of television had no short-term impact on the well-established regulatory regime and public service approach in Europe. The established rules of radio governance were amended only slightly in most cases (Britain's ITV and Finland's MTV being exceptions and both beginning in 1957).

But over time, beginning in the 1980s, gradually a dual system of commercial players and public service players emerged. This dual system is comparatively unique to Europe, at least in terms of the characteristic size of each sector and the intensity of competition between them (Lund & Berg, 2009). Commercial players routinely called for less government regulation and advocated self-regulation along the lines of common practice in the USA. By the late 1980s, this was accomplished by political constellations that were increasingly in favour of neoliberal theory

(Ferguson, 1990; Freedman, 2008). State monopolies in telecommunications were privatised and public broadcasters were forced to contract out services to private companies on market conditions. New technologies offered more channels and lowered cost barriers for entry to the media business. New global media providers, with Rupert Murdoch's News Corp as the champion, aggressively built operations that crossed national borders, rendering previously important aspects of localised regulations at least irrelevant and in many css obsolete (Chenoweth, 2001).

In this situation, the EU, EFTA, the Council of Europe and other international agencies attempted to fill the regulatory gap (Hartcourt, 2005). The EU was especially persistent in pursuing transnational codes of governance to secure the interest in a competitive internal market. These attempts were encouraged by a desire to meet commercial challenges from the USA. In 1989 the *Television Without Frontiers* directive came into force, although the newspaper industry did not become EU regulated until the mid-2000s. Today, however, most media companies of all types are invested in online media, and at the same time newspaper companies are invested in TV and radio operations. Convergence and consolidation make platform-specific rules and regulations difficult to maintain—and in some aspects even to justify.

But the European Commission is pursuing conflicting targets in the commercial attempt to secure free trade and market harmonisation on the one hand and its normative aims to ensure media pluralism and diversity at the national level on the other. From the 1990s, the cultural grounds for regulation have been somewhat overshadowed by competition authorities acting more assertively. Content values, such as product variety, choice extension, new consumption opportunities and access, now define current political debates on media organisation and ownership regulation. According to research-based evaluations, hybrid combinations of private and public players in moderate competition are generating a relatively high degree of diversity in media output, in marked contrast to cut-throat competition that is reducing pluralism (Lund & Berg, 2009). Other aims of regulatory efforts in Europe are the protection of domestic programming and public service values, i.e. regulatory aspects that are currently being monitored more closely by transnational agencies—particularly within the EU. The increasingly interventionist policy in the media sector forces European managers to adapt to transnational precepts implemented across the board. In the decision-making process, however, Brussels has accepted that co-regulation may beat not only top-down but also self-regulation in the future (European Commission, 2001) (Fig. 6.1).

Today, EU member states with dual media systems consisting of private as well as public service providers are regulated under the principles of subsidiarity and proportionality, as earlier noted. Transnational regulation is being adapted and adopted as negotiated orders in different political cultures. Most European regulatory regimes also rest on the arm's-length principle between governments and media, also noted earlier, and enforced by public agencies similar to Britain's Office of Communication (Ofcom, created in 2003 as a conglomerate of former specialised regulatory agencies, e.g. the Independent Television Commission, the Broadcasting Standards Commission and the Radio Authority). Policy formation is

Prescriptive Media Regulation	**Restrictive Media Regulation**
Freedom of Speech	Limitation of Freedom of Speech:
	- slander & libel
	- national security
	- blasphemy
	- protection of minors
	- equal time during elections
	- prescription drugs advertising
	- tobacco advertising
	- alcohol advertising
	- hate speech
Copy Right Conventions	Copy Right Exemptions
Public Service Remit	Frequency Scarcity and Limitations
Government sanctioned Licence fees	Exemptions from licence fee payment
Press Subsidies	Targeted taxes
Must Carry Rules	Product Placement Rules
Property Rights	Cross-Ownership Limitations
Quotas for European Content	Commercial Time Limitations
Mandatory Digital Distribution	Termination of Analogue Distribution

Fig. 6.1   A selection of media regulation examples

usually carried out in incremental fashion to reach a negotiated order that secures parliamentary consensus and involves multilateral bargaining with a number of participating stakeholders.

Despite transnational convergence, most government regulators regard it as politically legitimate to treat public service media (PSM) and private commercial media (PCMs) differently. This is reflected also in EU policy because the main legal instrument for PSM is the Amsterdam Protocol on Public Service Broadcasting that was amended to the 1997 Treaty of Amsterdam, while the main legal instrument for PCM is Television Without Frontiers in 1989 (updated in 2009/2010 as the Audio-visual Media Services Directive). The persistent regulatory argument is that especially in relatively small media markets (the majority by number in Europe) with limited linguistic reach, an all-commercial media system would result in market failure (Doyle, 2002). Diversity of content would suffer and duplication of certain programme types would reduce collective welfare, resulting in a lowest common denominator type of output and a 'cultural discount' (Hoskins, McFadyen, & Finn, 2004). Media regulators negotiate compromises between public ownership and free market competition in attempts to avoid both market failure and regulatory failure. Both PSMs and PCMs are expected to offer a high-quality mix of information, education and entertainment. This may lead to cartel-like conduct, thus limiting consumer choice. Consequently, all European states have general antitrust laws prohibiting abuse of a dominant position. But all in all, specific media directives have been organised to leave room for self- and co-regulated action (Lund, 2007).

Content and process control currently consists of EU quotas, licensing procedures and prohibition of advertising directed specifically at children or for prescription medicines, alcohol, tobacco, etc. Furthermore, most national PSMs are obligated to air quotas of certain types of programming, primarily news, documentaries and cultural output. The main regulatory method is the so-called public service contract that defines programming requirements in considerable detail. Such contracts are usually negotiated, however, although in some media markets, these are one-sided demands from the government, and in more co-regulated media systems, they are based on self-assigned responsibilities (Svendsen, 2011).

All in all, then, commercial as well as public service media managers in Europe must consider their cultural and political roles in order to avoid rigid regulation. Here we adopt a pan-European perspective on these developments but find considerable variation in the degree to which commercial media managers are required to consider wider social responsibilities. Indeed, many focus their efforts mainly on minimising regulatory responsibilities in a post-scarcity environment and have an evident interest to end their public service status (most evident these days in the UK among the commercial PSB operators, like ITV and C4). Concomitantly, PSMs must deliver a broad market share and can't strictly cater to marginal types of content or audiences. Recently these considerations may be the impetus encouraging priorities that are more typically commercial. This, in turn, has stirred legitimacy problems regarding 'unfair competition' and 'state aid' in dual audiovisual markets, as voiced by private media owners and their lobbies and for the most part being backed by EU directives. Denmark's TV2, for instance, has been accused by commercial competitors of accepting unwarranted state aid. Furthermore, commercial players have complained about gatekeeper control in television distribution. These confrontations have increased due to the gradual switching off of analogue signals and the introduction of digital terrestrial television (DTT). In this respect, EU regulation takes the form of standards applied by regulatory authorities in all member states and those (as is the case in Norway) choosing to adhere without being EU members.

From the end of the nineteenth century, four phases of government intervention in European media matters may be detected: first, a period dominated by the print press with a high degree of self-regulation and controlled on a case-by-case basis by the courts and then a period of increasing government regulation, especially in relation to public service broadcasting, sanctioned not only by law but also by government authorised licence fee funding. From the 1980s, however, we have experienced a period of deregulation in the media business as a whole, especially in telecommunications and broadcasting. Finally, it may be argued, most European media systems are now working within a transnational EU regulatory regime based on co-regulation, which combines international conventions and national implementation within a negotiated order of re-regulation. This phase poses new challenges to media management and some of these are discussed next.

6.3   Media Managers Engaging Stakeholders

The current trend towards co- and re-regulation of the European media business influences not only national regimes of governance but also poses new challenges for media managers at the micro-level of stakeholder relations. The main challenge for media managers is not strictly cast in the form of autonomy versus compliance. Modern media governance is an invitation to demonstrate strategic leadership in collaboration with regulators, audiences, commercial competitors and other stakeholders. Government regulation is no longer an absolute given. If media managers engage stakeholders strategically in shifting alliances of negotiated order externalities, they may be proactively influenced (Lund, 2004).

Furthermore, cross-platform competition, prompted by digitalisation and de-regulation, increasingly renders media-specific, top-down regulation obsolete. The Internet, for instance, cannot be regulated in detail as was the case for radio or television in the last century. Accordingly, media managers may take advantage of differing regulatory regimes in print, broadcasting, telecommunications and on the World Wide Web in order to gain competitive advantages. In spite of growing international intervention in the media business, government regulation of the media in Western states is still primarily a national process grounded in ideals of representative democracy. These premises place the mass audience (and the mass media) as carriers of public opinion as a starting point for political decision-making. The decision-making route in Fig. 6.2. represents an ideal-typical parliamentary chain of command, originating among citizens offering voice, loyalty and exit for media regulation demands (Lund & Blach-Ørsten, 2013).

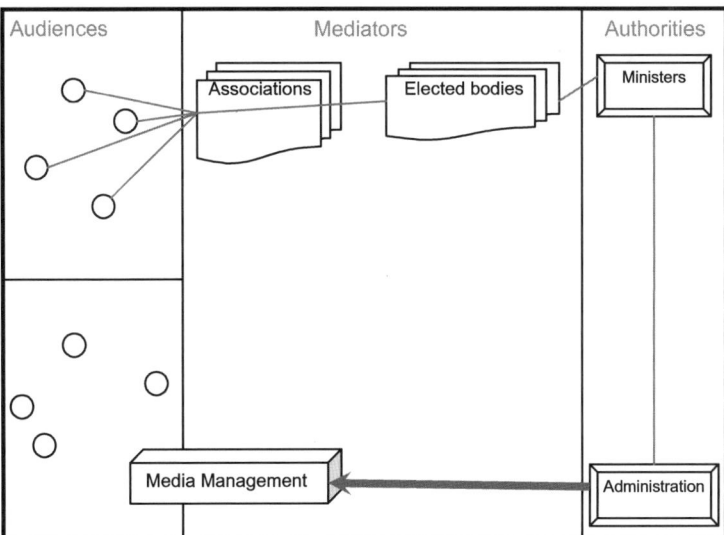

Fig. 6.2 Government regulation

These processes of governance can be illustrated by the concurrent efforts to ban certain types of advertisements on television (Federal Trade Commission, 2003). In order to gain support for claims of this sort, mediators and associations are mobilised, e.g. the National Cancer Society and Heart and Lung Associations, and opposed by others, e.g. Distillers' and Brewers' Associations. In tandem with elected representatives at the local, national and regional levels, stakeholder alliances woo governments for political action. If successful a bill or a directive will be prepared by the authorities, passed and amended by representative bodies, and forwarded to public administration to be more or less rigidly implemented. In the final event, the regulated media companies are expected to comply or they may risk sanctions of more or less severe kinds. The textbook example is tobacco advertising, now banned from television.

Before, during and after the regulatory process, if strategically apt, the targets of regulation may influence the decision-making process. This, we argue, can be done by various means, in priming, framing and lobbying the stakeholders involved. Proactive media managers are not limited to mobilising support or opposition through official channels. Consequently, the formal chain of command model rarely tells the full story about the making of media policy. In most instances, the mass audience, formally the subject of regulation processes, is situated on the sidelines of political decision-making and treated as passive bystanders (Schudson, 2003). If, however, lobbyists and other organisations can mobilise representatives of the concerned public, they may be mediated as key opinion leaders putting pressure on politicians and administrative authorities. The textbook example of this is alcohol advertising, which differs widely in Europe today.

Normatively, this may be regarded as unfortunate. Strategically, however, it may be interpreted as pluralistic opportunities for free speech in ongoing processes of stakeholder engagement and professional bargaining. Stakeholder engagement of this kind (Freeman, 1984) may be regarded as participatory governance among competing interests in order to create a sustainable compromise among conflicting interests. In these decision-making processes, media managers cannot realistically pay equal attention to all potential stakes and holders. One must choose the battles and prime potential opponents and lobbyists in order to frame political and administrative alliances related to future co-regulation (Fig. 6.3).

Compared to the one-way street of the government regulation model, the stakeholder governance model represents a web of interactions that crisscross formal chains of command. Regarding stakeholder relations as an integrated part of public opinion formation and media governance, we may define 'the public' as a conglomerate of interest-based holders of differing stakes (Lund & Blach-Ørsten, 2013). Freedom of speech and the associational ideal of mass participation constitute a social context for individual and collective action. In decision-making processes of this kind, bargaining most likely results in conflict and compromise, rarely satisfying any of the stakeholders in full.

Media managers opposing a regulatory measure, e.g. restrictions on advertising content, may attempt to mobilise stakeholders against the proposed rules in a

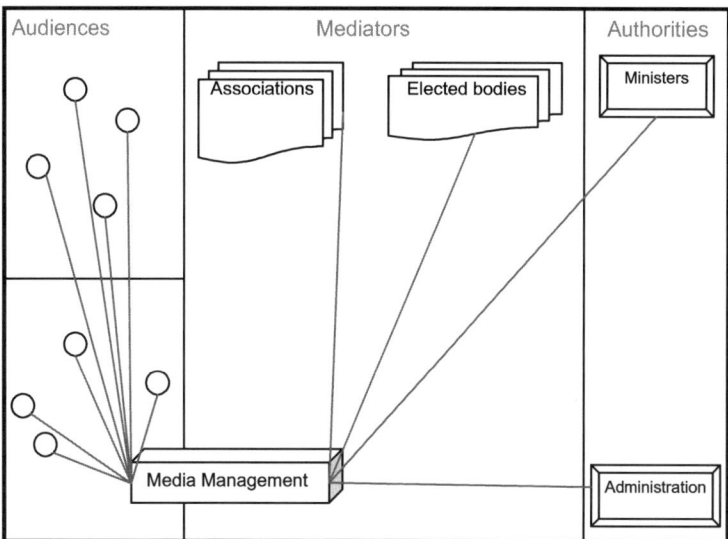

Fig. 6.3 Stakeholder governance

number of supplementary ways. In the final event, it requires priming the general public, e.g. threatening to reduce popular programming to the audience due to reduced advertising revenue. Another route to influencing the regulatory authorities is framing the restrictions as a threat to freedom of speech, i.e. endangering a higher principle of media governance. In so doing, new alliances can be formed that mobilise campaigns with strange bedfellows, even with competitors. Parallel to these measures, key opinion leaders, ministers and administrators may be lobbied. In the case of European limitations on advertising of alcoholic beverages, the net result of these processes has been rather different rules and implementations across the continent (O'Brien, Miller, Kolt, Martens, & Webber, 2011).

While some media systems accept commercial messages of this kind on television (some with the add-on that encourages the user to 'Drink Responsibly'), others have forbidden any form of advertising of this kind, while yet others allow for certain types of drinks (e.g. beer and/or wine, but not hard liquor). This may inspire European television networks to place their corporate headquarters within one political system, e.g. the UK where regulations are more liberal, while broadcasting into more regulated media markets, e.g. Scandinavian ones, as is the case with the MTG and SBS corporations. This, in turn, has prompted demands for harmonised, transnational EU regulation because the differing rules may impair inner market competition, opening up for yet more proactive processes of stakeholder involvement.

Even after an EU directive has been converted into national law, government regulation is not necessarily an absolute given. Strategically it may be regarded as a stake around which a number of competing and collaborating holders organise themselves. One way of influencing governance of this kind is to go directly to the minister from the national government under whom the regulative body is formally placed. This, however, is rarely effective, unless the minister is personally or politically engaged in the regulation at hand. Furthermore, media regulation need not be the business of one minister only, e.g. most European media are formally placed under a department of culture, but regulation of importation for the media business is often initiated by the ministry of finance or the ministry of taxation, i.e. the department of finance (collecting levies on beverages) may be less eager to limit advertising of this kind than the ministry of health, placing the ministry of culture under crossfire. This, in turn, invites lobbyism and compromise.

The individual media manager has limited influence on these issues. But working together within cross-national alliances has proven quite successful in curbing or modifying top-down regulation. For instance, the European public service broadcasters in concert have convinced the WTO that PSB should be recognised as a special case on cultural grounds, even within the general framework of free trade (Colling, 1994). In line with this, EU competition directives protect cultural interest when balancing merger control decision-making (Hartcourt, 2005). In this framework groups of media managers are more likely to influence national authorities that implement European directives. This can be done by offering to provide self-organised controls and reporting and promising minimal implementation costs. De facto repeal may also be possible by engaging political actors who share one's stake, preparing amendments or mitigation of negative effects from media policies. One way of doing so is to offer alternative self-regulation in a voluntary fashion rather than be subjected to external controls and sanctions.

Stresses and strains in relations between the private and public sectors have been further exacerbated by the economic recession since 2008. Many public service broadcasters have become increasingly involved in commercial practices, either via direct competition for scarcer advertising revenue (in much of Southern and Eastern Europe) or via commercial subsidiaries (like BBC Worldwide). Dating back to 1989 and the foundation of the Association of Commercial Television in Europe (ACTE), relations between commercial and public service stakeholders are not congenial. The dual system has become a duelling system (Alm & Lowe, 2001). National and international media regulation has become an important element in establishing competitive advantages and disadvantages. This, in turn, weakens efforts of co-regulation, limiting top-down pressure on the industry as a whole.

By regarding the formation of media governance as networks of interdependent stakeholders, the stakeholder approach invites a shift from traditional dichotomies of public versus private interests and from regulators versus the regulated. Instead, the managerial focus is on stakeholder networks and based on principles of mutual interdependency: Where power is exercised, opposing influences are simultaneously invoked. Media management is aptly described as being characterised by unstable relations between conflicting interests promoting self-serving ends in ongoing deliberation and bargaining processes. That constitutes the salience of issues that are relevant for government regulation and which stakes are left to self-regulation. In the long run, this kind of governance depends heavily on *framing*

(Reese, 2001). By shifting the frame of alcoholic advertising from a question of health and safety to a framework of commercial free speech, commercial media managers seek to mitigate negative connotations and thereby improve the legitimacy of their self-interests. Conflict frames make better media stories than consensus frames.

On the other hand, strategic use of stakeholder governance requires lip service to political consensus. If a stakeholder can convince the trendsetting news media that a particular framework is more 'politically correct' than opponents, then all things being equal such a frame will be more effective—even if not necessarily as spectacular as a controversial frame. Regarded from a stakeholder governance point of view, the strategic use of framing is an essential element in the constant struggle to promote special interests as common interests. Even more important is the effort to bury unfavourable demands for regulation in litigation and the so-called spirals of silence (Noelle-Neumann, 1984). This is not to say that stakes can be framed independently from frames promoted by competing stakeholders. On the contrary, framing efforts in media management are constantly being influenced by competing interests. With an almost unlimited supply of interests and stakes being framed and spun in political arenas, long-term *priming* of interests becomes a key to success. Just as a professional painter primes a surface before painting the portrait, the communications strategist must prepare the 'surface' (materiel and audience) before sketching the picture—at least if the goal is to have a message that covers and holds (Goidel, Shields, & Peffley, 1997). Priming defines premises that constitute the foundation for public affairs management (McCombs, Shaw, & Weaver, 2007). While lobbyists are busy spinning to political decision-makers, the professional primer is talking to key opinion leaders, e.g. academic researchers and administrators, to pave the ground for future persuasion efforts. To maintain a cooperative and effective working environment, it is critically important to monitor and anticipate the mood of public opinion (making) and political opposition.

In this way, effective stakeholder governance may hide a great deal by diverting attention away from unpleasant talk and action. Strategic combinations of priming and framing in media management are marked by paradox, and, consequently, engagement of stakeholders combined with co-regulation can hardly avoid becoming somewhat hypocritical (Brunsson, 2002). Frequently a media manager must say one thing while acting differently, engaging salient stakeholders in decision-making processes by promising to meet specific ends but only at some hazy time in the future. In strategic games of this kind, it is essential to engage relevant stakeholders in a long-term sustainable fashion. In doing so, professional stakeholder interaction may define which issues require political regulation and, conversely, what parts of the media business should remain unregulated. All in all, conflicting alliances of competing stakeholders create limits on government intervention. Professional stakeholder governance, however, rarely determines how the authorities should act. It is more likely that priming and framing stakes with salient holders may influence the authorities in terms of what they should not regulate because they risk facing fierce opposition.

One final challenge, often overlooked when discussing media regulation, is the ambiguities of competitors. In processes of co-regulation, competitors may become best allies, as clearly demonstrated by the actions and talk of trans-European trade organisations. Competitors may not share all stakes with each other, but quite frequently their mutual interests outweigh differences in opinion. On the other hand, a regulatory measure may damage the position of a competitor even more than one's own media company. So instead of working together in alliances, media managers may occasionally consider joining ranks with the government and/or the European Commission in confrontation with a competitor (Schoof & Brown, 1995).

For media managers brought up in the tradition of strategic thinking under cut-throat competition with 'Porter's Five' and similar zero-sum frameworks as guidelines for strategic thinking, the stakeholder perspective may be hard to stomach. But even Michael E. Porter himself has realised that win-win situations can be found by creating shared value with stakeholders rather than merely maximising profits for shareholders in the short run (Porter & Kramer, 2011). The creating shared value with stakeholder perspective calls for self-regulated corporation. Generally speaking, strategic management aiming at shared value creation is most effective when alliances based on common interests have *primed* regulatory decisions by *framing* talk and action in ways that balance legitimacy and efficiency while allowing room for trial and error.

In this fashion, principles of value-driven stakeholder involvement in the media business outperform the traditional target group thinking of competitive media management thinking (Lund, 2006). At the same time, the adjustments of regulatory orientation, advocated in this chapter, do not necessarily rule out the competitive tricks of the trade, e.g. strategic *lobbying* promoting rules and regulations for self-serving purposes. But it does warn against the old-fashioned hands-off media managers waiting passively for politicised regulation processes to be conducted and lobbied by outside forces. The latter shall increasingly be faced with 'no-go demands' reducing proactive media management to reactive choices between comply or complain.

Notably, you cannot engage all the stakeholders all of the time. A strategic sample of salient stakeholders, evaluated in terms of power, legitimacy and urgency (Andriof et al., 2002), must be selected specifically for situational decision-making processes. If successful in promoting relevant and cooperative stakeholder activities, the outcome strengthens the professional media manager's licence to operate by creating shared value with stakeholders. If unsuccessful, however, government regulation may seriously harm your market position turning salient stakeholders against you.

6.4   Conclusion

Once upon a time, stakeholder involvement, media policy and government regulation could be regarded as unwelcome externalities interfering negatively with day-to-day management of media firms. This chapter has made the argument that governance of media matters of the twenty-first century must be understood by media managers as an integrated negotiated order defined not only by official agencies and political actors but also by a number of non-authorised stakeholders. The implications of this analysis matter not only for those involved in old-fashioned mass communication but also for innovators in new media—especially for Internet service, currently regulated to a much lesser degree than radio and television.

For most media managers, the libertarian free riding times of deregulated markets are long gone. Nonetheless, most policymakers herald the arm's-length principle, questioning the regulatory regimes of media governance based on polarised majority rule, litigation and unconditional compliance. The current trends towards light-touch regulation, combined with long-standing traditions of parliamentary oversight of media content, invite media managers to engage stakeholders and move from a reactive single-media compliance towards a more proactive stance on multimedia governance. This is especially apparent when dealing with public service media, depending on government funding, and the so-called social media (e.g. Facebook and Twitter) where the traditional divide between producer and consumer is collapsed into *prosumer* relations.

Manifested as dual systems of commercial and public service players acting on inner market terms, most European governments tacitly accept the increasingly transnational framework for regulation of mediated content. But all media systems, including the Internet-based ones, operate under domesticated conditions that invite lobbying and involve engaging key stakeholders. According to the European Commission, co-regulation is currently the name of the game and regarded as particularly useful in situations where uniform rules must be implemented in a negotiated fashion that respects principles of arm's-length regulation as well as subsidiarity and proportionality. One size does not fit all, and the so-called open method of co-ordination may provide future inspiration for negotiated orders on media matters. In so doing, mutual trust and general credibility among stakeholders of co-regulatory regimes is hardly given. In marked contrast to the USA, most European media markets have maintained civil society traditions and domestic diversity with relatively strong public service media. Language and national regulation provide protective barriers of entry when regarded from the viewpoint of European inner market harmonisation. But it does not make national media immune to global competition at cut-rate prices, i.e. national regulation may actually be a competitive advantage.

These transnational conditions invite media managers to proactively engage not only national but also international stakeholders. Notably, this is a two-way street that can't usefully be reduced to lobbying, issue management or PR stunts. It becomes essential to understand stakeholder engagement as an ongoing bargaining process of long-term priming, middle range framing and short-term spinning of stakes and holders, including not only current friends but also former foes and future allies.

In other words, from a stakeholder framework point of view, top-down regulation is neither a given nor necessarily a threat to the corporation, but an occasion for rocking the boat and shaking things up—potentially to competitive advantage. The research-based advice we can offer media managers across Europe, and perhaps even occasionally far beyond, is quite simple: Never accept directives and government regulation as anything carved in stone. Political demands and administrative norms are significant externalities, but in the end, merely papers that can be cut into pieces by new technology and organisational innovations. It should, in short, be regarded as an invitation to constructive deliberation with salient stakeholders. In this respect, we can amend the anecdote presented at the beginning of this chapter: Senior managers would be wise indeed to think of media governance as a global game with local players where paper sometimes binds rock, but rock usually commands the scissors, if they are proactively primed to cut red tape of paper regimes and engage stakeholders.

References

Alm, A., & Lowe, G. F. (2001). Managing transformation in the public polymedia enterprise: Amalgamation and synergy in Finnish public broadcasting. *Journal of Broadcasting and Electronic Media, 45*(3), 367–390.

Andersson, P. (2002). *Stenbeck*. Stockholm: Pan Books.

Andriof, J., et al. (2002). *Unfolding stakeholder thinking. Theory, responsibility and engagement.* Sheffield: Greenleaf Publishing.

Barnouw, E. (1966). *A tower of Babel: A history of broadcasting in the United States.* New York: Oxford University Press.

Berg, C. E. (2013). *As a matter of size. The importance of critical mass for television markets.* Copenhagen: OpenAccess@CBS.

Brunsson, N. (2002). *The organization of hypocrisy: Talk, decisions and actions.* Copenhagen: Copenhagen Business School Press.

Chenoweth, N. (2001). *Virtual Murdoch. Reality wars on the information highway.* London: Secker & Warburg.

Colling, R. (1994). *Broadcasting and audio-visual policy in the European single market.* London: John Libbey.

Cook, T. E. (1998). *Governing with the news: The news media as a political institution.* Chicago: The University of Chicago Press.

Curran, J. (2002). *Media and power.* London: Routledge.

Dimmick, J. W. (2003). *Media competition and coexistence: The theory of the Niche.* Mahwah, NJ: Erlbaum.

Doyle, G. (2002). *Understanding media economics.* Thousand Oaks, CA: Sage.

European Commission. (2001). *European governance—A white paper.* Bruxelles: COM 428.

Federal Trade Commission. (2003). *Alcohol marketing and advertising: A report to Congress.* Washington, DC: Federal Trade Commission.

Ferguson, M. (1990). *Public communication: The new imperatives.* Thousand Oaks, CA: Sage.

Fleisher, C. S., & Bensoussan, B. (2003). *Strategic and competitive analysis: Methods and techniques for analyzing business competition.* Upper Saddle River, NJ: Prentice Hall.

Freedman, D. (2008). *The politics of media policy.* Cambridge: Polity Press.

Freeman, R. E. (1984). *Strategic management: A stakeholder approach.* Boston: Pitman.

Goidel, R. K., Shields, T. G., & Peffley, M. (1997). Priming theory and RAS models. *American Political Quarterly, 25*, 287–318.

Hallin, D. C., & Mancini, P. (2004). *Comparing media systems. Three models of media and politics.* Cambridge: Cambridge University Press.

Hartcourt, A. (2005). *The European Union and the regulation of media markets*. Manchester: Manchester University Press.

Horwitz, R. B. (1991). *The irony of regulatory reform: The deregulation of American telecommunications*. New York: Oxford University Press.

Hoskins, C., McFadyen, S., & Finn, A. (2004). *Media economics: Applying economics to new and traditional media*. Thousand Oaks, CA: Sage.

Kelly, M., Mazzoleni, G., & McQuail, D. (Eds.). (2004). *The media in Europe: The Euromedia handbook* (3rd ed.). Thousand Oaks, CA: Sage.

Lewis, T. (1993). *Empire of the air: The men who made radio*. New York: Harper Perennial.

Lund, A. B. (2004). Institutions of current affairs—Framework for comparative research in European public spheres. In F. Marcinokowski, W. A. Meier, & J. Trappel (Eds.), *Media and democracy—experiences from Europe* (pp. 127–140) Vienna: Haupt Verlag, 2006.

Lund, A. B. (2006). Domesticating the Simpsons—Four types of citizenship in monitorial democracy. *Politik, 9*(2), 15–25.

Lund, A. B. (2007). Media markets in Scandinavia: Political economy aspects of convergence and divergence. *Nordicom Review, 28*(1), 121–134.

Lund, A. B., & Berg, C. E. (2009). Denmark, Sweden and Norway: Television diversity by duopolistic competition and co-regulation. *The International Communication Gazette, 71*(1–2), 19–37.

Lund, A. B., & Blach-Ørsten, M. (2013). Media and politics. In B. Brincker (Ed.), *Introduction to political sociology* (pp. 155–172). Copenhagen: Reitzel.

Lund, A. B., & Lowe, G. F. (2013). Current challenges to public service broadcasting in the Nordic Countries. In U. Carlsson (Ed.), *Public service media: Politics, markets, programming and users* (pp. 51–73). Gothenburg: Nordicom.

McChesney, R. W. (1993). *Telecommunications, mass media, and democracy: The battle for the control of U.S. broadcasting, 1928–1935*. New York: Oxford University Press.

McChesney, R. W. (2004). *The problem of the media: U.S. communication politics in the twenty-first century*. New York: Monthly Review Press.

McCombs, M., Shaw, D. L., & Weaver, D. (2007). *Communication and democracy*. Mahway, NJ: Erlbaum.

McQuail, D. (2003). *Media accountability and freedom of publication*. New York: Oxford University Press.

Noelle-Neumann, E. (1984). *The spiral of silence: Public opinion—Our social skin*. Chicago: The University of Chicago Press.

O'Brien, K. S., Miller, P. G., Kolt, G. S., Martens, M. P., & Webber, A. (2011). Alcohol industry and non-alcohol industry sponsorship of sportspeople and drinking. *Alcohol and Alcoholism, 46*, 210–213.

Porter, M. E., & Kramer, M. R. (2011). *Creating shared value*. Boston: Harvard Business Review.

Reese, S. D. (2001). *Framing public life*. Mahwah, NJ: Erlbaum.

Salovaara-Moring, I. (2009). *Manufacturing Europe: Spaces of democracy, diversity and communication*. Gothenburg: Nordicom.

Scannell, P., & Cardiff, D. (1991). *A social history of British broadcasting: Volume 1, 1922–1939*. New York: Oxford University Press.

Schoof, J., & Brown, K. (1995). Information highways and media policies in the EU. *Telecommunications Policy, 19*(4), 325–338.

Schudson, M. (2003). *The sociology of news*. New York: Norton.

Spar, D. L. (2001). *Ruling the waves. From the compass to the internet*. New York: Harcourt.

Svendsen, E. N. (2011). From sovereignty to liberalisation: Media policy in small European countries. In G. F. Lowe & C. S. Nissen (Eds.), *Small among giants: Television broadcasting in smaller countries*. Nordicom: Gothenburg.

Thomassen, A. (2009). *Navigating in the landscape of ambiguity: A stakeholder approach to the governance and management of hybrid organizations*. Lund: Business Press.

Trappel, J., Meier, W. A., D'haenens, L., Steemers, J., & Thomass, B. (2011). *Media in Europe today*. Bristol: Intellect.

Obeying His Masters' Voices: Managing Independence and Accountability in Public Service Media Between Civil Society and State

7

Christian S. Nissen

7.1 Introduction

'After months of conflict with the government on the coverage of its foreign policy, the Director General resigned yesterday following a board meeting'. The history of public service media (PSM) contains numerous stories of such incidents. Another common dimension is the more or less automatic change of a PSM organisation's top management after a parliamentary election as a new government takes office. Despite broad domestic and international support of the 'arm's length principle' that is supposed to guard the independence of PSM from government interference, the principle isn't meticulously followed in many cases.

It should be noted that the balance between editorial independence and organisational accountability is not unique to PSM. Securing independence from potential meddling by corporate owners of media businesses and at the same time

C.S. Nissen (✉)
Copenhagen Business School, Center for Civil Society Studies, Copenhagen, Denmark
e-mail: csn@christiannissen.com; http://www.christiannissen.com

© Springer International Publishing Switzerland 2016
G.F. Lowe, C. Brown (eds.), *Managing Media Firms and Industries*, Media
Business and Innovation, DOI 10.1007/978-3-319-08515-9_7

being accountable to them is a common and difficult balance in any media business. But, as described in the following, it is far more difficult in public service media supposed not to refrain from exposing also their institutional 'owners' (parliament and government) to critical investigations and harsh commentary. Here we are confronted with a conflict of interest dilemma that goes to the heart of public service media as an institution established to serve civil society and regulated, financed and controlled by governments and parliaments in their role as representatives of their elective publics. Although sacking top management is an extreme and highly visible outcome, it is really only the tip of the iceberg. Beneath the surface one finds a broad range of ongoing power struggles over varied aspects, including programme policies and stipulations about the coverage of news and current affairs, conflicts that can be just as, if not more, detrimental to editorial independence.

Such problems seem to be widespread given the extensive general concern about political interference in media as evident in resolutions and recommendations, and in numerous reports, from international bodies that especially include UNESCO (2005, pp. 74–85), the Council of Europe (2006, 2012), the European Union (European Commission, 2012; European Parliament, 2011) and important NGOs (Deltenre, 2012; Open Society Foundation, 2005, 2008). In this light it is surprising that little has been documented and thoroughly analysed to explain the sources, dynamics and patterns of such conflicts and especially to describe how governmental interference takes place also in mature democracies with public service media institutions that are supposed to operate at arm's length from such interference.

One must however bear in mind that these are complex matters and that it is often difficult to draw a clear line of separation between heroes and villains. Media accounts and press conference pronouncements frequently oversimplify the causes of a fired DG. Efforts to 'spin control' the story is typical also by their supporters. The conflicting parties (PSM top management, other managers that work for and support or oppose them, the governing board, regulatory authorities and government agencies and parties) usually offer different interpretations. What from one side defined as a consequence of bravely defending institutional autonomy and editorial independence is described by another stakeholder as the deserved consequence of unsatisfactory management performance or inadequate accountability—which in this relation is usually discussed as lack of responsiveness or even loyalty.

Furthermore, it's not easy to collect trustworthy information in these situations. While sacking top management usually attracts considerable public attention, it doesn't have a strong bearing on daily life for most people and rather quickly disappears from the front pages of newspapers. It might not even survive long in the collective memories of PSM staff in the professional environment. Those who were directly involved on both sides don't want to open up about the details of what are often continuing conflicts or find it in their personal interests to provide a forthright explanation of the specific circumstances that determined their 'solutions'. Some have good reason to hide as much as possible due to culpability of varying degrees, while others refrain from blowing their whistles because they are afraid of retaliation. Most fired top managers want to get on with their lives, and there can be significant instrumental value in avoiding too much attention, as this would cause problems in finding a new job. Although some reveal their 'true story', doing so is rarely rewarded and is often seen as taking revenge causing lack of credibility that is only possible when taking a balanced approach, presenting both sides of the story.

This problem in obtaining reliable, neutral and balanced information has also been a challenge writing this chapter. The author was himself in the period 1994–2004 Director General of the Danish Broadcasting Corporation (DR) and was dismissed after a prolonged conflict with the DR Board of Governors. So part of the text can (at best) be considered to be based on personal observation and on close contacts with European colleagues, which on the one hand provides a comparatively unique window for observation but on the other of the very same reason must be weighed against the risk of bias and distortions.

With these analytical problems and reservations mentioned, it's the purpose of the chapter to bring some of the elements of this controversy out in the open. The following section will describe the importance of the two key concepts in public service media, *independence* and *accountability*, and their necessary and delicate coexistence. This is followed by a schematic description of channels and mechanisms of governance and public regulation and an account of their use in practice. At the end the chapter will conclude by addressing some broader questions on PSM governance with regard to the two definitive concepts.

7.2   Independence and Accountability Cannot Be Balanced on the Same Weight

Before taking a closer look at editorial independence and institutional accountability of public media organisations in their relation with governments, it should be noted that both concepts are fundamental to the general concept of *corporate governance*. Partly due to a growing separation between the ownership and the management of companies quite generally, more attention is typically devoted to the governance of their interrelations. As described by Robert Picard (2005, p. 2) with particular emphasis on media companies, 'Corporate governance is concerned with the owner and management relationships, distribution of power, and accountability in corporations ... [and] publicly traded firms typically have more significant corporate governance responsibilities under law and in regulations'. What goes for publicly traded firms is certainly even truer for public service media companies, both with regard to the reasons behind and the regulatory consequences of corporate governance. Following Hallvard Moe (2010), the 'governance' concept is used in its broadest sense, including not only legal regulation but of particular importance also a number of informal channels and processes used to exert influence.

A public media institution's degree of independence and accountability to the state and its government are often seen as codependent (Mendel, 2011, pp. 87–92). There is an apparent logic in that the more detailed the framework of legislative rules and executive government decisions governing PSM institutions, the more constrained they will be in freedom of action. As the number of commitments increases, to which they are held accountable, the degree of independence inherently decreases. It's also correct to assume that a free-flying PSM top management asserting institutional independence to a degree that ignores obligations towards all external stakeholders can only be justly criticised as acting unaccountable.

To fully understand the complexity of acting in a way that is both accountable and independent requires going beyond this surface logic, however, because the two terms are not necessarily opposite or inversely related principles; in fact, they don't balance on the same fulcrum and thus can't be fairly construed as a singular dimension. It can be argued that a public media management that refuses to support a government's foreign policy about an issue of public importance (such as war) in its news coverage is acting in a way that is very accountable to what should be the most relevant constituency—civic society. But most governments will regard this stance as acting in an unaccountable (and irresponsible) manner given their view of public service obligations to 'properly' align news coverage with 'the nation' or national interest in a time of crisis. In contrast, few would consider an amendment to a media law specifying that news and current affairs programming is a priority over entertainment to be undue political interference although, in fact, that would to some extent limit the independence of the public media firm.

7.2.1 Editorial Independence

In fact, then, the full or unlimited independence of public service media from political authorities is not the issue. The mere fact that there is a legal framework for PSM institutions with general operating rules and given that all or a considerable part of the funding is allocated by parliaments and governments leads rather naturally to a certain and unavoidable dependency that is not inherently unhealthy or problematic. The key issue, however, is to understand *why* editorial processes are vulnerable to governmental influence to a degree that merits setting up particular boundaries, as highlighted in the arm's length principle.

As mentioned earlier, the importance of editorial independence is not limited to public media. This is a well-established principle for any 'free press'. The editorial policy of a newspaper living up to journalistic ideals is not decided by outside forces and external pressures, whether they be politicians or economic interests. Historically, in the West at least, it has been generally agreed that the owners of a newspaper should limit their influence to the appointment and dismissal of the editor-in-chief and not interfere with the content of the daily paper. The reason behind this principle boils down to an issue of trustworthiness by and for the public and thus securing the media's special role in acting as an 'unfettered watchdog' for public interests and the healthy functioning of a democratic society. That is precisely the reason why media typically enjoy constitutional protections—unlike other 'industries'. External limitations on the editorial freedom of media, whether imposed by governments or any other self-interested constituency, are contrary to the basic principles of a free, open and pluralistic society. These general principles are even more important for a 'state-owned' and overseen public media firm, due to the inherent obligation to defend the interests of society and citizens against perceived wrongdoings carried out by the very same state and its political actors. This distinction between state and society is one recurring theme in governance disputes over editorial independence and also the reason why the accountability principle is not easily handled.

7.2.2 Accountability: To Whom and for What?

As hinted above, in dealing with accountability and governance for public service media, one sooner rather than later comes to the question of to whom the institution is accountable. It should be noted that accountability relations exist and function at many and different organisational levels (McQuail, 2010, pp. 206–220). In this discussion we are dealing with the issue at an institutional level, parallel to a publicly traded firm's accountability towards its owners, that is the shareholders. In the case of public service media, it is however less clear who the owner of the public media corporation is (the government, the parliament, the people, etc.) and, thus, to whom the institution is responsible. The fundamental tenet that legitimates public service media answers that question by positing that public media belong to a civil society and are accountable to its citizens.

This posited relationship between society and the public service corporation is rather unique. It could be conceived as a societal contract or 'pact' (Nissen, 2006a, pp. 19–20) typically containing ideological and normative clauses, quite commonly, for instance, to 'sustain national culture', to 'foster diversity and ensure media pluralism', to 'enhance social, political and cultural cohesion' and to 'support citizenship'. Demonstrating accountability for such abstract and overarching PSM obligations is much more difficult than what is required of the top management for a private, commercial enterprise. Here accountability towards shareholders is determined by relatively few criteria to evaluate (e.g. profit and loss) and there are well-established *accounting* procedures and quantitative measurements (Atkonson, 1997, pp. 63–72). Some of the higher complications for PSM provide useful illustrations.

Although broad and quite general PSM obligations are usually parsed into more focused operational goals with specific commitments, typically articulated in the text of media laws and 'public service contracts', neither these legal instruments are actually easy to use for demonstrating accountability. Because of the very complex governance environment principles, priorities and performance are all, and very often, interpreted differently and are subject to ongoing disagreements among diverse PSM stakeholders. That is evident, for example, when looking at the perspectives of different groups of organised viewers and listeners, private media competitors, political parties at diverse positions in the spectrum and certainly also diverse licence fee payers. Accommodating the interests and wishes of one group can often only be accomplished at some expense to one or several of the others and will almost always generate criticism whichever decision is taken.

Related to this problem is the question of how to operationalise the public ownership as the relevant addressee of accountability. Civil society can't act as a societal entity. It is a concept alluding to a physical being that is not specifically embodied or materially captured. That is why we elect members of parliament and governments to *represent* the interests of citizens in a civil society, which is supposed to be inherently diverse, often conflicted and constantly evolving. Because of this, regulatory and oversight authority is placed in the hands of parliament and administered by government and more or less independent regulators, who are supposed to act as the institutional addressees for a wider and more general public accountability.

This is perfectly aligned with principles of a representative and constitutional democracy but leads to another intricate problem, namely, the difficulty of differentiating public service media from 'state broadcasting' in which every activity can be decided in detail by the authorities of the state—i.e. dictated by various means of control (McQuail, 2010 pp. 42–44). Since the fall of communism, the notion of 'state radio and television' has disappeared from the official vocabulary in the Eastern European countries whose PSM institutions are however still burdened by features of that heritage. Also in other European countries, one often has difficulty in seeing a clear difference between PSM and state media, making it rather difficult to explain the distinctions to people from other continents who are eager to understand how the textbook ideals of European public service media are carried out in the real-life context of daily operations. It is also not easy—neither for governments nor for PSM institutions—to handle their sensitive interrelationships even in countries lacking an authoritarian legacy.

7.3   The Mechanisms of Public Regulation

This somewhat blurred picture is partly caused by the simple fact that the ideals of editorial independence and diffused accountability mechanisms, which are essential for and to PSM, are alien in the general political–administrative–regulatory system of any state bureaucracy. In the power struggles of daily politics, majority governments can usually, within the limits of a constitution, enforce their will through legislation and various supplementary cabinet decisions. In a hierarchical chain of command structure, the state bureaucracy transforms the results of such struggles (i.e. political decisions) into authoritative rules, executive decisions and numerous control and reporting procedures. Not distorting principles as broad, abstract and differently interpreted as independence and accountability in such a political–administrative culture is not easy. The typical mechanisms of parliamentary and governmental influence are illustrated in Fig. 7.1.

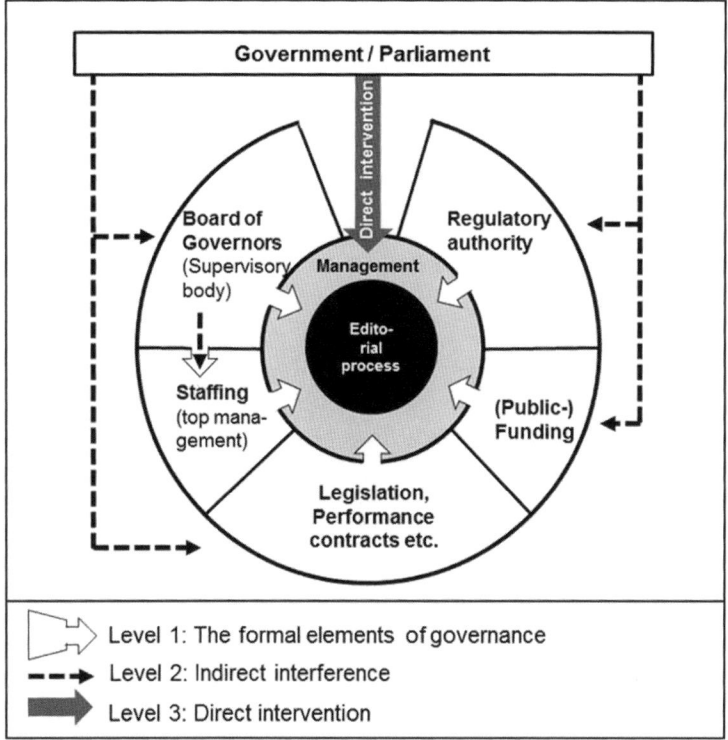

Fig. 7.1 Mechanisms of political influence on public service media

There are formal, constitutional procedures handled in legislation passed in parliament, which governments have responsibility to execute. Besides that governments exert influence by using both 'carrot and stick', exerting pressure by meting out punishment here and giving rewards there (Hanretty, 2011, pp. 25–29). Some of this takes place in transparent parliamentary procedures, but much happens by 'discrete' actions behind tightly closed doors. In the 'twilight zone' of power-play politics, governments—also in well-functioning and mature democracies—are only limited in pursuing their goals by their interpretation of 'the law of the land' and a variety of countervailing and contending forces such as opposing political parties, the judiciary, powerful lobbies, the civil society organisations and (hopefully!) an alert, independent and incorruptible press.

The model in Fig. 7.1 has three levels, beginning with the formal governance elements and processes in the outer circle and working inwards to indirect interference and direct interventions in editorial processes. The model is based on the ideal premise that although being subject to a fully legitimate external regulation and an obligation to act accountably, the responsibility for the editorial processes should rest with PSM top management. The organisational bodies, structures and processes described, and the terminology used, cover considerable variations in actual PSM governance from country to country, as no standard model exists that would be generally accepted. There are, however, sufficient common features in Western Europe, at least, to make some basic comparisons. The 'standard models' of PSM legislation (Rumphorst, 1999) and governance (Nissen, 2006a, pp. 37–40) can be used as reference points.

7.3.1   The Formal Elements of PSM Governance (Level 1)

Here we are dealing with the lawfully intended, formal governance elements of which the most important ones are illustrated by the five white cells in the outer circle (i.e. Regulatory authority, Public Funding, Legislation, Staffing, Board of Governors). These can be considered as the institutional channels for the interaction and exchange of political regulation and PSM accountability. Supervisory bodies and regulatory authorities are established to convey and enforce the influence of legal authority, either via ex ante (before the fact) and/or ex post (after the fact) procedures. Media laws and different kinds of more specific executive regulation determine PSM obligations, set priorities and establish boundaries. Public funding is followed up with careful critical audits that contain guiding conditions and come with strings attached.

All in all, these types of general regulatory oversight and authority are well established and supposed to entail different kinds of legitimate influences, which by inference may also influence programme policies and, to some extent, constrain editorial decisions. Further, it's worth noting that these formal governance elements also include possible legal sanctions (enforced by the courts and/or a regulatory authority with the power to levy fines, etc.) if the PSM institution does not live up to its obligations. These formal channels can however be misused and subvert editorial independence via illegitimate interference. That constitutes the battlefield of PSM governance quarrels. A few illustrative weak points and disputed areas are useful here.

The roles of the non-executive supervisory body or board of governors and the regulatory authority are crucial for establishing a presumed barrier between a PSM management group and the government. In spite of having no formal operational influence on the editorial processes, both of these bodies can—depending on circumstances—have a substantial influence at a general level. How robust the barrier is in practice depends, for instance, on how much influence the government has on *appointing the members* of these two bodies. That varies from country to country, with different combinations of appointment by government, parliament and civil society representatives, but even though in formal terms the members are not directly appointed by a government, it anyway often has considerable influence on the process and its result.

Besides that, the *formal power* of the two bodies to influence programme issues and editorial decisions is certainly crucial. A rather extreme case of using a regulatory authority for what amounts to governmental control over media is seen in the Hungarian media law from 2011, so extreme that it caused the EU to react (European Parliament, 2011). The case is significant because the EU rarely interferes in this sort of issue and because the text of the specific Hungarian law, as argued by the Hungarian government, was not very different from similar regulations in other European countries. A neutral external evaluation by the Centre for Media and Communication Studies (CMCS, 2012) confirmed some of the claimed similarities but based its critique of the Hungarian law on a broader scope.

Another area of dispute is in how *the governing boards* administer their supervisory role. By typically having the formal authority to decide and control PSM corporate strategy, general programme policy and operational budgets, a governing board is empowered to set and to adjust the course of the corporation. It is generally considered ideal that governing boards limit themselves to overarching tasks, but those lines often become hazy in practice and it seems quite difficult to live up to the 'standards' in practice. Board members are usually tempted to meddle for their own reasons or—as discussed below—pressured by their hinterland (the appointing source) to intervene in specific programmes that have aroused public attention and are drawing criticism. If an occasional 'lapse' develops into a general habit, it can't help but influence top management to a significant degree and risks trickling down to programme departments where priorities are accordingly distorted and where creeping self-censorship becomes a problem. In summary, the formal governance elements described as level 1 play a complex dual role in both protecting the PSM institutions from direct government interference and providing channels for political steering and control. Adding to this complexity they also function as the main channels for *documenting and reporting on accountability* to PSM stakeholders, which entails two further problems we will consider next.

The first is the knock-on effect of two decades of a prevailing pattern of public steering and control described as the 'New Public Management' (NPM) paradigm (Dunn & Miller, 2007). The contentious character of NPM is related to its alleged instrumental rationality that legitimates a top-downward managed control system stressing performance contracts, quantifiable outcome indicators and detailed reporting obligations. Although NPM contains a lot of common sense in many areas of decentralised public service production (hospitals, schools, social security, etc.), it doesn't fit very well with the overarching and rather vague societal obligations and goals of public service media, especially because they are difficult to operationalise in an environment with such conflicting interests—as already discussed.

Taking into account that the PSM audience, the politicians and the competing private sector are primarily focused on what is broadcast, this growing detail in regulations is ultimately directed towards programme policy and the media services provided for the audience. Regulations that limit, constrain or otherwise create boundaries in the PSM remit, such as specific quota obligations, service contracts and the ex ante evaluation (public value tests), are—practised with national variations (Moe, 2010)—examples of the dense grid of gradually accumulating restrictions that are curtailing PSM independence. Although executed at a macro level, this has also a knock-on effect on editorial freedom (Coppens, 2005; Nissen, 2006a, pp. 35–40).

The second problem of the predominance of accountability through the formal channels of state administration is that such procedures tend to overshadow the broader and equally important accountability relations towards the principle stakeholder, i.e. civil society. To put it simply, radio listeners and television viewers do not read annual reports and performance accounts, and few participate in meetings where they can (in principle, at least) hold PSM management accountable. They have another and quite formidable means of influence, however, which they exercise daily—the remote control, which facilitates the power of market competition. This causes a difficult, unsolvable dilemma for PSM management that must manoeuvre between 'the Scylla of populism and the Charybdis of elitism' (Nissen, 2006b, pp. 74–77). On the one side, PSM management is held accountable for its obligations (stated in public regulation and contracts and supported by an influential cultural elite) to provide content of an alternative kind not delivered by the commercial market. On the other side, they will desert their fundamental civic obligation if, by neglecting to accommodate a mass audience, they are marginalised in the market. This is worth bearing in mind as we move on to the more informal and less transparent channels of PSM–government relations taking place outside popular access and insight.

7.3.2   The Twilight Zone of Indirect Interference (Level 2)

Although the formal, 'constitutional' channels of influence (level 1) also contain some problematic unintended side effects, as discussed, they are certainly a lesser if necessary evil. The problems are more pronounced in the twilight zone of level 2 where government influence is indirect and efforts are taken to conceal government interference. This aspect—illustrated by the dotted black arrows in Fig. 7.1— takes place via proxies and by misusing the formal channels of legislation and fiscal budget procedures in order to serve the specific political purposes of one group or another for interests that are not premised on media laws or any part of the 'pact' between society and the PSM institution.

It is easy to understand how detrimental this can be to the editorial independence of a PSM institution when, for instance, a government during negotiations over a multiyear agreement on activities and funding explicitly threatens or even obliquely hints that the institution will 'take a hit' of some kind if they don't acquiesce to the government's wishes. The state representative need only allude to dissatisfaction within the government over unfavourable media coverage of its policies and performance to make the point—and to have some effect, even if the 'threat' is resisted. PSM top managers are however often rather responsive to such signals and need only the risk of pressures like these to be concerned enough to take some steps in a direction that can lead to growing and self-imposed limitations on editorial freedom.

As alarming as that scenario, which is not uncommon, it is even more serious when government interference takes place through the back door of the boardroom. The histories of PSM as an institution are riddled with incidents where a government has instructed top management, or at least exerted formative pressure on board members with oversight authority, to intervene in programme policy—and in the worst cases even to cancel the broadcast of a specific scheduled programme. To use a rather infamous example, in 1985 when the conflict in Northern Ireland was at one of its heights, it became publicly known that the BBC planned to broadcast a television interview with a leading figure in the IRA. In a letter dated 29th of July 1985 to the Chairman of the Board of BBC governors, the Home Secretary urged the board not to broadcast the programme. The phrasing is of particular interest and not atypical in such cases:

> May I first make it quite clear that I unhesitatingly accept that the decision to broadcast or refrain from broadcasting this programme must rest exclusively with the Corporation. It is no part of my task as Minister with responsibility for broadcasting policy generally to attempt to impose an act of censorship on what should be broadcast in particular programmes. To do so would rightly be inconsistent with the constitutional independence of the BBC, which is a crucial part of our broadcasting arrangements. I do, on the other hand, also have a Ministerial responsibility for the fight against the ever present threat of terrorism, and I would be failing in my duty if I did not let you and your colleagues have my considered views on the impact of this programme in that context . . . . I cannot believe that the BBC would wish to give succour to terrorist organisations; and it is for this reason that I hope that you and your colleagues will agree on reflection that the Real Lives programme should not be broadcast. (Copy of the original letter published by The Guardian, 2005)

In his memoires the then BBC Director General, Alasdair Milne, describes the painful decision process and makes a pertinent comment about the letter from the Minister:

> . . .A formal letter from the BBC's sponsoring Minister (the Home Secretary) asking that a programme should not be shown (even though he had not, of course, seen it and could have used his powers to ban it, if he so wished) could not easily be shrugged off. (Milne, 1988, p. 142)

The BBC board followed the urging request from the Minister and decided that the programme should not be broadcast, a decision which, by the way, was reversed by the same board 3 months later. The conflict over this specific programme was only one in a long row of battles between the Thatcher government and the BBC that was also related to its broadcasts about the Falklands War and the miner's strike. In 1986 a new Chairman of the Board was appointed and shortly after Milne was forced to resign.

It is interesting to note that the 'power to ban it', which Milne refers to in his memoires, is still today rooted in the BBC agreement with the government under the heading Defence and Emergency Arrangements, with the following wording: 'The Secretary of State may give the BBC a direction in writing that the BBC must not broadcast or otherwise distribute any matter, or class of matter, specified in the direction, whether at a time or times so specified or at any time' (BBC, 2006, article 81, 4).

Such disagreements on programme policy and even about particular programmes between a government and a PSM institution are neither unusual nor unhealthy in constitutional terms. The two parties have different and equally important positions and should often take opposing roles. That is especially the case when dealing with policy issues that are dividing 'the nation' in popular opinion and causing rifts and complications in the political arena, where public media is obliged to deal impartially with both sides of any divide. Doing that well and properly is almost impossible without being considered biased by either the one or the other side. Striking an appropriate balance during wartime can be particularly challenging. But it is precisely during such times, as already illustrated, that the balancing problem and potential interference become severest.

In the weeks leading up to the second Iraq War in 2003, the News Director of the Danish Broadcasting Corporation, DR, anticipating a Danish participation in the intervening forces, drilled her staff on which vocabulary to use in news casts about the situation. Should an American-led intervention in Iraq be described as an '*attack*', an '*invasion*' or a '*liberation*'? Should the intervening forces be called 'the *attackers*', 'the *allied*' or 'the *coalition*'? Words and expressions were balanced on a finely tuned weight. Little did it help; however, on the 25th of March 2003, 5 days after the beginning of the war, the conservative Danish Minister of Culture, Mr. Brian Mikkelsen, confidentially e-mailed the Chairman of the DR Board of Governors, Mr. Jørgen Kleener, the following report from a cabinet meeting (author's translation):

> Dear Jørgen, Purely for your information, the DR's coverage of the government and especially the Iraq war was discussed at the cabinet meeting today, first at breakfast by many ministers and then during the formal meeting. There is a very great dissatisfaction with DR's coverage, which is very one-sided—they are specifically annoyed with a few female hosts and Ole Sippel* (whom many referred to as extreme in his expression against the coalition). It came as far as to the Foreign Minister suggesting that we should not privatize TV-2** which was considered fair in its coverage, but rather DR. This very fact is the strongest argument among liberal-conservatives against privatization of TV-2. Many believe that we should privatize DR, which is anti-government, while they do not understand that we are privatizing TV-2, which is positive toward the government. I know it's hard for you—this morning I was the one in the line of fire because it was suddenly seen as my responsibility—but you should be informed about the government's position. I mentioned to the Prime Minister that I continually have a confidential dialogue with you about the situation. Also that I had the impression that the Board of Governors and Nissen took it very seriously, but the problem lay with Lisbeth Knudsen***. Yours sincerely Brian
>
> --
>
> * DR's Middle East correspondent
> ** TV2 is the second of the two Danish public service broadcasters. It was at that time on the liberal-conservative government's agenda to privatise TV2.
> *** Lisbeth Knudsen was DR Director of News from 1998–2006 and a member of the managing board.

Four years later, the e-mail was published by the author of this chapter as one of the several illustrations of government interference (Nissen, 2007), and it has since been used in another book (Hanretty, 2011 pp. 174–175). The initial publication created some furore and was the subject of debate in the Danish Parliament. Having been dismissed 3 years earlier from the DG position, the author was met with two opposite reactions, representing two very different organisational cultures. From the one side, top civil servants confided that publishing a confidential e-mail from a minister was a serious and unforgivable breach of norms considered fundamental by the top of the civil services. From the other side, experienced journalists blamed the author for breaching a key journalist norm by cowardly keeping the e-mail hidden while serving as DG.

Securing PSM independence during wartime and other 'national emergencies' can be a challenge even in well-functioning, stable democracies and societies with relative high degrees of economic, social and political stability. How much more difficult then in societies ravaged with social unrest, ethnic division and less mature political systems, where emergency situations tend to be the norm and everyday occurrences. This is worth bearing in mind when contrasting editorial independence and measuring the arm's length principle in comparative contexts. The crucial difference might not be sought solely in the PSM governance system itself and the way it is handled, but as much in the society in which it's embedded.

If pressure through the back door of the boardroom on the top management of a PSM organisation fails to produce the intended results, i.e. to make the managers fall in line, governments can choose another method to exerting pressure; they can urge the governing board members (together or as individuals) to dismiss the Director General. Certainly there can be fully acceptable and completely legitimate reasons for a governing board to fire the executive manager. If the initiative for doing so, however, originates from outside the boardroom, that is quite another situation. The crude way to do this is to initiate a dismissal as a punishment for a specific piece of a news or programme considered unfavourable to the government. As this will often create unpleasant public attention, a more 'discrete' way of handling the dismissal is to postpone it for a while and make the governing board do this under some other pretence more acceptable due to typical reasons of managerial misconduct and lack of confidence.

If the board can't be persuaded to use one or the other of these two methods, then it might help to replace the Chairman—which was probably what happened in the above-mentioned case when the Thatcher government in 1986 appointed a new BBC Chairman, who shortly after forced DG Alasdair Milne to resign. An even smoother way to get rid of 'inflexible' directors general—and if necessary also stubborn chairmen—is to synchronise, more or less formally, such shifts to coincide with changes in government.

This phenomenon has been studied by Chris Hanretty (2011) in his book *Public Broadcasting and Political Interference*, by using a proxy measure of independence based on two sets of data: (a) the rate of turnover of chief executives (directors general) and (b) the percentages of government changes which within 6 months were followed by a change in the chief executive. Although the method—as also mentioned by Hanretty—has some deficiencies, it results in an 'interference index' ordering the 47 analysed cases (PSM corporations) in a sequence (Hanretty, 2011, pp. 11–15). Among the 27 European PSM organisations included in the analysis, eight of the ten with the lowest score on government interference are situated in the north-western corner of Europe (the two remaining are Switzerland and Austria). At the other end the seven out of ten PSM organisations with the highest interference score are situated in Eastern European, former communist countries (the remaining three are Italy, Spain and Portugal).

This clear geographical division corresponds with the picture of media independence in general and especially suggesting public service media being at stake in several Eastern European countries (Dragomir, 2009). Here directors general, heads of news, editorial managers and even individual critical journalists are fired more or less automatically following changes in government offices, in the wake of a critical broadcast, or due to their reluctance to follow the line of the ruling political parties. The methods used in countries including Poland, Slovakia, Romania and Croatia generally fall under the above-described categories but often take place in very opaque processes, which makes it especially difficult for outsiders to clearly distinguish between 'the good and the bad guys' (see, for instance, Bacisin, 1998; Czwitkovics, 2011; Karpinski, 1996).

As a somewhat balancing comment to this rather rude mapping of political interference related to dismissals of top PSM executives, one could imagine that governments that are seldom criticised for interfering in the hiring or firing of PSM top management are simply more adept at handling the practice in ways that are discrete and subtle. That would be the case, for instance, in patiently waiting for some time-lag between changes of government and directors general. Take, for example, the Nordic countries, reputed for their immaculate political culture and governance. While their directors general are rarely fired at short notice due to disagreements with government, or automatically dismissed after changes of government, few hold their positions for extended periods or get reappointed for a new term if they are not 'in tune' with the government of the day.

7.3.3 Direct Government Intervention (Level 3)

Direct intervention can take place in the open in various ways, for instance, in published comments in newspapers or in public speeches in which PSM management is criticised for an alleged lack of accountability (read 'loyalty') or more specifically in relation to some critical broadcast that was not appreciated (so to say). Such public statements are not necessarily in conflict with the arm's length principle unless they are followed up by threats of retaliation. Anyhow it is clearly preferable to go this route compared to the covert direct personal contacts which take place behind closed doors outside reach of public attention. Most directors general and their heads of news and current affairs departments can recall ministers making angry phone calls or drag them into a corner during one meeting or another to scold them about a special broadcast or demand 'equal airtime' to correct reports about perceived misdeeds—often followed up by threats with various kinds of retaliation. Very few such incidents are however substantially recorded or documented.

A well-known case combining open criticism and more covert pressure is the battle between the British Prime Minister's office at Downing Street 10 and the BBC in 2003 concerning its reporting and commenting on the government's reasons for participation in the Iraq War. In May 2003, the BBC Defence Correspondent, Andrew Gilligan, quoted an unnamed source who alleged that Downing Street wanted the government's dossier on Iraq 'sexed up' with a reference to Saddam Hussein's ability to launch a biological or chemical attack within 45 min. Although the UK government fiercely denied the allegation and publicly accused the BBC of lying, the BBC's top management stood firm and was backed by the Board of Governors. When Gilligan's source, a Ministry of Defence microbiologist named David Kelly, was found dead, it triggered a public enquiry led by Lord Hutton. In January 2004 the Hutton Report was published and it included serious allegations against BBC. The British government was more or less acquitted, a verdict that has been heavily debated (Cowling, 2004; Dyke, 2005, pp. 250–330; *The Economist,* 2004; *The Guardian,* 2004). The BBC Chairman, Gavin Davis, resigned on the day of publication, and the next day the Director General, Greg Dyke, was forced to follow.

What makes this case exceptional is not so much the end result but rather the process that led to that result, with frequent exchanges of letters between a very offensive government and a BBC top management defending its editorial independence. One might add that compared with many other such conflicts between governments and broadcasters, the BBC case was also extraordinary both because the top management didn't silently give in and due to the fact that the BBC was eventually exonerated and came out of the conflict with the public considering it more trustworthy and accountable than its political adversary. Compared to such conflicts in other countries, the BBC–government conflict over the Iraq War was also an exception because a public enquiry was indeed conducted.

7.4 General Patterns and Trends of PSM Independence and Accountability

Specific cases have illustrated the twilight zone between the formal independence of public service media and the more 'brutal' examples of direct government interference, even manipulation, in controlled 'state radios'. This background contextualises a couple of more general questions related to the independence and accountability issue of the primarily European PSM landscape.

7.4.1 Government Interference Going from Bad to Worse

Measured by the many statements, resolutions and alarming reports highlighted in the introduction to this chapter, there would seem to be a general tendency of increasing government interference in the editorial work of public media corporations. The subtitle of the Open Society Institute/Foundation report from 2008, *More Channels, Less Independence*, following up on a previous analysis 3 years earlier (Open Society Foundation, 2005, 2008), confirms this general feeling of things going from bad to worse. Assessing the general trend in the nine—primarily Eastern European—countries reassessed, the Open Society Institute report states:

> Another feature revealed by this monitoring is a worrying determination on the part of political elites to reaffirm their influence over broadcasting. Many of the regulators are still subject to blatant political interference. There are clear signs that the inclusion of civil society representatives—introduced over the past 10 to 15 years—has not had much impact on regulators' partisan behaviour. Political elites have proven quite capable of manipulating these representatives . . . . In our sample, the re-politicisation of public service media is clearest in Poland, Romania and Slovakia, though it is evident too in Lithuania and elsewhere. (Open Society Foundation, 2008, p. 20)

This apparent trend could be a misconception caused by the growing concern in itself and the many studies carried out to substantiate it. But there are other and plausible explanations providing a sufficient basis for increasing awareness. One key fact is that the honeymoon days of liberation from totalitarian regimes in Central and Eastern Europe in the early 1990s are over and done. Converting 'state radio and television' into 'public services' of an open society was quite rightly conceived as a key ingredient of democratisation and also by the way as one of the conditions—although a rather soft one—for joining the European Union. Such a conversion is however not done overnight by changing the corporate name and the clauses of media law. Engaged in severe conflicts over deep societal divides, politicians revert to familiar patterns and old habits, and ('their') PSM top management is inclined, if not forced, to follow.

Another explanation, also covering the development in the rest of Europe, and closer to the governance theme of this chapter, is the new challenge stemming from a changing communicative political culture. Political communication has in recent decades been thoroughly professionalised because the battleground over public opinion has become increasingly important to political success and social processes. The timing and substance of political initiatives are pretested in focus groups and tracked by opinion polls. The back offices of ministries are staffed with media consultants and communication officers employed to influence—both defensively and offensively—the press in order to create a favourable media environment. This development has made the position of public service media especially difficult. While media in general is often considered an adversary by many governments, they seem particularly tempted to look upon and treat 'their own' PSM institutions as a potential part of their communicative arsenal.

This development can be illustrated by comparing two of the examples mentioned above. In 1985 the attempt by the Thatcher government to stop the BBC from broadcasting a specific programme related to the conflict in Northern Ireland was handled in a personal letter from the Home Secretary to the BBC Chairman. Two decades later, during the Iraq War, government pressure on the BBC was exerted via a virtual bombardment over a long period 'on land, at sea and in the air', which was administered by a professional communication officer (Alasdair Campbell) and his team in Downing Street 10.

7.4.2 The Notion of Profound Differences in Media Systems Might Be Somewhat Superficial

Choosing the United Kingdom to illustrate serious political interference begs an intriguing question: is it possible that the general conception of PSM governance in the north-western corner of Europe—especially the United Kingdom and Scandinavian countries—considered close to the ideal of the arm's length principle is based on an ethnocentric prejudice? And then another series of questions arises: is referencing this region a basis for bias? Can it be argued that this whole discourse is to some extent based on the fact that the idea and the principles of public service media were developed in Britain and more or less 'wholeheartedly inherited' in the rest of Europe? And when measuring editorial independence, are we unconsciously using the 'genuine UK' model as the normative yardstick? This is certainly a line of argument often raised by those accused of editorial interference.

The repeatedly reported pattern on government interference in the editorial domain of public service media is probably quite correct in general. The central, eastern and southern parts of Europe—not to speak of countries in Asia, Africa and South America—are troublesome areas in this respect, whereas the countries in the north-western corner of Europe seem to be less plagued by these problems, yet more open about them when interference occurs. Not only is this observation supported by the many worried citizens and media professionals in the countries of concern but also by the way protesters, daring to highlight the abusiveness, are often treated. This view also conforms to the more analytically based picture drawn by Hallin and Mancini in their book, *Comparing Media Systems* (Hallin & Mancini, 2004).

On the other hand, crucial differences might be sought and better understood in a broader societal context than solely focusing on the media systems and the way PSM governance is handled. It seems reasonable to suggest that all governments want to influence media coverage, especially when they are in difficult situations and under extreme pressure. Also it is reasonable to expect that they will aim their interventions especially at media institutions that are constitutionally, so to speak, within easier regulatory reach, and that implies the public service institutions. If so, it would be an obvious hypothesis that any government—regardless of country and media system—will try to circumvent or limit editorial independence of its public media institution if the hazards are considered to be at a certain 'national emergency' level.

In the peaceful north-western corner of Europe, this level of emergency only occurs in the comparatively rare situations when 'the nation goes to war', whether against other countries or against terrorism within its own borders. In less fortunate countries, marred with social unrest, profound economic crisis, ethnic division and unstable political systems, governments find themselves in emergency situations as a routine fact of social life. If accepted, then it is not unreasonable to argue that—all other things being equal, i.e. dealing with crisis at a level being considered equal by the ruling politicians—European governments are treating their public media institutions and handling the principle of editorial independence very much the same way.

7.5   Conclusion

Although by no means pretending to be based on a representative sample of countries or on a thorough analysis of single cases, this chapter describes some of the most important governance elements by which public service media organisations are politically controlled and held accountable. It substantiates the widespread concerns over threats to editorial independence of PSM institutions and the ways their accountability obligations are handled, overtly and covertly. Not only are the editorial processes subjected to all manner of government pressure, but also the increasingly zealous and detailed institutionalisation of regulation entails a risk of dominating and distorting the more diffuse and less manageable responsibilities that are important for PSM relations to and with civil society, the principle addressee of public service media accountability in ideal terms.

The most daring assertion of the chapter is that all governments—including those usually considered generally to observe the arm's length principle—intervene if and when the stakes are considered high enough to warrant that. And when this happens, all PSM top managers either submit or are removed. This calls into question whether government interference can be reduced by establishing stronger barriers in media legislation or by refining internal PSM editorial guidelines, as argued by Chris Hanretty (2011, pp. 193–195). Nor is it reasonable to assume that any significant improvement will come by simply 'encouraging' PSM management to stand bravely firm against governmental pressure.

The reasoning behind this rather pessimistic view is that we are dealing with basic societal conditions and power relations that are of a more general and complex nature than those usually found in corporate governance relations between owners and managers of private enterprises in any industry. The atypical dual stakeholder composition (civil society and government) in public service media is one of the strongest reasons validating this argument. Here real editorial independence and adequate accountability are not two balancing extremes of a single continuum. On the contrary, they are better understood as two sides of a coin.

Few things are helping PSM institutions secure independence from governments as much as being conceived accountable by their real owners: civil society. Supported by international institutions and NGOs, this might be the *only* factor capable of exerting the necessary continuous counterpressure needed to improve editorial independence from government interference. This is essential to grasp because one especially important implication is that the trend to develop ex ante evaluation instruments may not guarantee the kinds of accountability that are most important for PSM to have or to the most important addressees of accountability. This trend might be considered even more worrisome as it also threatens the more fundamental and essential demand for editorial independence.

As a final point, the focus on public service media independence ought briefly to be extended to media in general because, as mentioned at the beginning of the chapter, editorial independence from owners and specific external interests is crucial for all media companies living up to basic publicist principles. It's worth noting that, firstly, governments eager to optimise their media coverage usually don't limit their attempts to interfere to public media. General media legislation, regulatory authorities, discriminatory placement of official advertising and licensing of the broadcast spectrum are a few of the ways that governments influence all media companies, private and public alike. In passing it should be mentioned, however, that sometimes governments are met with such powerful adversaries and media as agents of influence and that very close links between government and industry result in pressure and interference being exerted in the opposite direction, as revealed by hearings on Murdoch's media empire in the *News of the World* phone-hacking scandal (Kellner, 2012).

Secondly, we should remember that private media companies are also subject to tight editorial control from their corporate owners. The aforementioned Rupert Murdoch is together with Silvio Berlusconi, probably some of the best known examples of owners exerting an editorial influence over their media corporations that goes far beyond what is possible for any government. Finally, one should not forget the strong indirect influence that large advertisers have on the media by virtue of deciding where they place their ads.

All in all, then, we can conclude that editorial independence is always at risk regardless of whether we are dealing with a public or private media firm. From a governance perspective, the crucial difference is the more complex stakeholder constellation for public media as a sector. Not only is the formal owner (the state) often characterised by strong, conflicting interests between different political parties, one also has to consider the unique role of civil society—ideally very different from that of consumers—as the genuine addressee of PSM accountability.

References

Atkonson, D. (1997). Public service television in the age of competition. In D. Atkonson, & M. Raboy, et al. (Eds.), *Public service broadcasting: The challenge of the twenty-first century*

(UNESCO 1997). Accessed January 2013, from http://unesdoc.unesco.org/images/0010/001097/109746eb.pdf

Bacisin, V. (1998). *Attacks on the press in 1998—Slovakia*. Refworld, UNCHR. Accessed March 2013, from http://www.unhcr.org/refworld/country,,CPJ,,SVK,4562d8b62,47c56585c,0.html

BBC. (2006). *Broadcasting, an agreement between her majesty's secretary of state for culture, media and sport and the British Broadcasting Corporation 2006*, article 81, 4. Accessed April 2013, from http://downloads.bbc.co.uk/bbctrust/assets/files/pdf/about/how_we_govern/agreement.pdf

Centre for Media and Communication Studies (CMCS). (2012). Hungarian media laws in Europe—An assessment of the consistency of Hungary's media laws with European practices and norms. Accessed February 2013, from http://www.eui.eu/Documents/General/DebatingtheHungarianConstitution/HungarianMediaLawsinEurope.pdf

Coppens, T. (2005). Fine-tuned or out-of-key? Critical reflections on frameworks for assessing PSB performance. In G. F. Lowe, & P. Jauert (Eds.), *Cultural dilemmas in public service broadcasting*. RIPE 2005, Gothenburg University: NORDICOM

Council of Europe. (2006). *Declaration of the Committee of Ministers on the guarantee of the independence of public service broadcasting in the member states. Adopted by the Committee of Ministers on 27 September 2006*. Accessed February 2013, from https://wcd.coe.int/ViewDoc.jsp?Ref=Decl-27.09.2006&Sector=secCM&Language=lanEnglish&Ver=original&BackColorInternet=9999CC&BackColorIntranet=FFBB55&BackColorLogged=FFAC75#

Council of Europe. (2012). *The state of media freedom in Europe*. Accessed February 2013, from http://www.assembly.coe.int/Communication/26062012_HorsleyReport_E.pdf

Cowling, J. (2004). *How should BBC be regulated?*, Open Democracy 5 February 2004. Accessed March 2013, http://www.opendemocracy.net/media-journalismwar/article_1718.jsp

Czwitkovics,T. (2011). *The former head of the Slovak Radio prepares for RTS project"*. Mediálne. sk. Accessed March 2013, from http://medialne.etrend.sk/televizia-spravy/rts-docasne-povedie-zemkova-niznansky-skoncil.html

Deltenre, I. (Director General of the EBU). (2012). *Political interference in public service broadcasting growing*. PublicServiceEurope. Accessed February 2013, from http://www.publicserviceeurope.com/article/2447/political-interference-in-public-service-broadcasting

Dragomir, M. (2009). *Politics as usual*. EuropeanVoice.com 2009. Accessed March 2013, from http://www.europeanvoice.com/article/2009/03/politics-as-usual/64159.aspx

Dunn, W. N., & Miller, D. Y. (2007). A critique of the new public management and the Neo-Weberian State: Advancing a critical theory of administrative reform. *Public Organizational Review, 2007*, 345–358.

Dyke, G. (2005). *Inside story*. London: Harper Perennial.

European Commission. (2012). *A free and pluralistic media to sustain European democracy, The report of the high level group on media freedom and pluralism*. Accessed February 2013, from http://ec.europa.eu/information_society/media_taskforce/doc/pluralism/hlg/hlg_final_report.pdf

European Parliament. (2011). *Resolution of 10 March 2011 on media law in Hungary*. Accessed February 2013, from http://www.europarl.europa.eu/sides/getDoc.do?pubRef=-//EP//TEXT+TA+P7-TA-2011-0094+0+DOC+XML+V0//EN

Hallin, D. C., & Mancini, P. (2004). *Comparing media systems, three models of media and politics*. Cambridge: Cambridge University Press.

Hanretty, C. (2011). *Public broadcasting and political interference*. London: Routledge.

Karpinski, J. (1996). *Another battle over Polish Public TV won by the ruling coalition*. The Open Society Archives (OSA). Accessed March 2013, from http://fa.osaarchivum.org/ft?col=210&i=318

Kellner, D. (2012). The Murdoch media empire and the spectacle of scandal. *International Journal of Communication, 6*(2012), 1169–1200.

McQuail, D. (2010). *McQuail's mass communication theory* (10th ed.). London: Sage.

Mendel, T. (2011). *Public service broadcasting: A comparative legal survey*. Kuala Lumpur: UNESCO.

Milne, A. (1988). *DG: The memoires of a British broadcaster*. London: Hodder and Stroughton.

Moe, H. (2010). Governing public service broadcasting: Public value tests in different national contexts. *Communication, Culture and Critique, 3*, 207–223.

Nissen, C. S. (2006a). *Public service media in the information society*. Report prepared for the Council of Europe's Group of Specialists on Public Service Broadcasting in the Information Society (MC-S-PSB). Accessed January 2013, from http://www.coe.int/t/dghl/standardsetting/media/Doc/H-Inf(2006)003_en.pdf

Nissen, C. S. (2006b). No public service without both Public and Service—Content provision between the Scylla of populism and the Charybdis of elitism. In C. S. Nissen (Ed.), *Making a difference—Public service broadcasting in the European media landscape*. Eastleigh: John Libbey Publishing.

Nissen, C. S. (2007). *Generalens veje og vildveje, 10 år i Danmarks Radio [Roads and detours of the General, 10 years in the Danish Broadcasting Corporation]*. Copenhagen: Gyldendal.

Open Society Foundation. (2005). *Television across Europe: Regulation, policy and independence*. Budapest: Open Society Institute/Foundation.

Open Society Foundation. (2008). *Television across Europe—More channels, less independence*. Budapest: Open Society Institute/Foundation.

Picard, R. G.(2005). Corporate governance: Issues and challenges. In R. G. Picard (Ed.), *Corporate governance of media companies* (JIBS Research Report Series No. 2005-1)

Rumphorst, W. (1999). Model—Public service broadcasting law. Geneva: ITU and UNESCO. Accessed February 2013, from http://portal.unesco.org/ci/en/files/5630/10353894120Model_public_service_broadcasting_law.pdf/Model%2Bpublic%2Bservice%2Bbroadcasting%2Blaw.pdf

The Economist. (2004, January 29). Not guilty, How Lord Hutton cleared the government of "sexing up" its dossier on Iraq's WMD. *The Economist*. Accessed March 2013, from http://www.economist.com/node/2388579

The Guardian. (2004). *BBC boosted by increase in public support*. Accessed March 2013, from http://www.guardian.co.uk/media/2004/mar/24/broadcasting.huttoninquiry

The Guardian. (2005). *Home secretary's letter to the BBC chairman July 29 1985*. Accessed February 2013, from http://image.guardian.co.uk/sys-files/Media/documents/2005/12/12/July29A.pdf

UNESCO. (2005). *Public Service Broadcasting: A best practice sourcebook*. Accessed February 2013, from http://unesdoc.unesco.org/images/0014/001415/141584e.pdf

Christian S. Nissen (M.A. in political science 1975) began his career as Associate Professor in international politics at the University of Copenhagen and later held different management positions in the Danish public administration before joining DR, the Danish Broadcasting Corporation, as Director General (1994–2004). He is currently Adjunct Professor at the Copenhagen Business School and member of the Editorial Commission of the Open Society/Soros Foundations project *Mapping Digital Media: Journalism, Democracy and Values*. He has authored and edited articles and books about international politics, public administration and media.

Corporate Social Responsibility and Media Management: A Necessary Symbiosis

8

George Tsourvakas

8.1 Evolution of the "Corporate Social Responsibility" Concept

In many respects, the arrival of explicit conceptions of corporate responsibility coincided with the Industrial Revolution. Before that time, the vast majority of companies had neither the desire nor saw a need to address social issues. Industry was generally dominated by small, family firms working within a relatively stable external environment, with the human factor manifested in specific forms of craft and commercial expertise.

The advent of Industrial Revolution and the consequent rapid growth of firms totally transformed this situation. Furthermore, the transformation of companies' legal status through incorporation brought about by limited liability ownership enabled the scale of resources needed for mass production and markets. This also had the unfortunate consequence of encouraging an unequal distribution of wealth and brought significant changes in the way that companies behaved and took decisions. Such changes prompted an increasingly thorough reconsideration about the nature of business activities and relationships. It is from this conjuncture that we can gauge the emergence of "corporate social responsibility" [CSR] at the earliest stage in its development (Carroll, 1979, 1999, 2000; Carroll & Shabana, 2010).

In key respects, CSR counters the notion that the obligations of businesses are restricted to a limited number of stakeholders—principally shareholders—and extend solely to the maximization of profits. This perspective on shareholder value inhibits the cultivation of CSR. In the name of maximizing profits, firms

I gratefully acknowledge the helpful comments of Charles Brown, Gregory F. Lowe, and Zoi-Charis Belenioti.

G. Tsourvakas (✉)
School of Economic and Political Studies, Aristotle University of Thessaloniki, Thessaloniki, Greece
e-mail: gtsourv@auth.gr

© Springer International Publishing Switzerland 2016
G.F. Lowe, C. Brown (eds.), *Managing Media Firms and Industries*, Media Business and Innovation, DOI 10.1007/978-3-319-08515-9_8

have too often ignored the significant aspect of proper alignment with principles of mutual respect that are vital for long-term sustainability. The overexploitation of resources arising from the previous and in many respects "mainstream" business logic is now generally realized by individuals and institutions and even by some progressive entrepreneurs who have at least informally introduced the concept of CSR in their thinking and to steer decision-making.

During the nineteenth century, charitable giving and the endowment of trusts served as a precursor of elements that eventually were taken over by the designs of a modern welfare state. Arguably such initiatives were as much defensive in nature as they were examples of the embryonic CSR strategies of good corporate citizens because they were undertaken as a counterweight to the increasing organization of labor, manifested in strong unions and a general unrest that produced waves of strike action that seemed to threaten capitalism. In the longer term, CSR became part of the public relations strategy of companies and a means of building public goodwill, which is not the same but is partly rooted in a similar vein of defensive calculation (Blowfield & Murray, 2008).

During this period, in many emerging, modern capitalist economies, the media sector was comprised of small print media firms concentrated on narrow rather than mass audiences. Most of their clients and customers were members of elite political and social groups. The print media were expensive and depended largely on revenue from circulation, which wasn't cheap. In some countries, actually quite a few, newspapers were either directly or indirectly owned by political parties or trade unions and formed part of the ideological armory of contending movements. Since there were few newspapers, magazines, and books, their responsibilities were largely limited to economic performance (Picard, 2010).

The expansion of manufacturing and service industries in the first half of the twentieth century saw the extension of media's economic, social, and *institutional* power. From the 1950s onwards—and particularly in the sixties and seventies—such power drew attention not only from policy makers but also from public social movements, often countercultural in nature and intentions, bringing increasing pressure upon businesses to become more responsible members of a wider community. Moreover, the importance of business philanthropy was significantly higher with the enhancement of corporate donations to health, education, and culture—essentially following in footsteps of earlier industrialists like Andrew Carnegie, John Hopkins, and Joseph Rowntree.

Research interest in CSR accelerated in the 1980s with a keen interest in more developed and interrelated theories in pursuit of a systematic approach (Amir & Amir, 2010; Lee, 2008). One increasingly influential approach was stakeholder theory, according to which a socially responsible company endeavors to balance a variety of widely drawn contending interests. Instead of being overly driven by the incentive to realize profits and grow shareholder returns, a "responsible" enterprise also takes into account the needs and interests of employees, suppliers, distributers, local communities, and, ultimately, a nation as a whole—perhaps even a group of nations for a transnational enterprise. During this period, new terms emerged for describing the actions of socially oriented enterprises, such as social response, corporate social performance, and CSR itself.

Exploring the dimensions of such concepts generated deeper insight into the nature of social responsibility in the corporate context. For example, social performance integrates three dimensions: a firm's social obligation (corporate behavior in response to market forces); its social responsibility, which is normative; and social response, defined as the adaptation of corporate behavior to the needs of a host society (Carroll, 1999, 2008). Noteworthy is the fact that during the 1980s, the first empirical investigations explored business philosophy to specify actions and practices that are in line with a CSR framework. The majority of those studies aimed to provide a record of companies' performance in fulfilling social and cultural objectives in diverse dimensions: respecting the rights of minorities; meeting environmental targets; and, more generally, supporting education, the arts, urban regeneration, and human rights. However, despite a greater focus on defining CSR in more scientific terms and using such insights to improve monitoring, there was less focus on the nature and application of constituent practices and objectives (Carroll, 1999, 2008).

From the 1990s, management research in this area became increasingly preoccupied with empirical studies intended to extend the range of issues embraced by CSR and theorizing about potential corporate responses. The period was also characterized by a further period of growth in the global economy, particularly within the banking and financial sectors that encouraged an increasing focus on theoretical models of corporate social performance and business ethics (Garriga & Mele, 2004). The concepts of "sustainability" and "corporate citizenship" were, for the first time, subsumed under the conceptual umbrella of CSR with an emphasis on comparing social performance with financial performance (Carroll, 2008; Moura-Leite & Padgett, 2011).

Perhaps most importantly, the advent of the globalization has transformed the international economy. For multinational companies, increasingly characteristic in commercial media industries, globalization has encouraged the international adoption of best practice in CSR and prioritized the management of public and community issues. In this light, CSR is seen as a coherent framework for linking policies, practices, and programs as an integrated "package" that informs the running of a business and as a cornerstone in decision-making.

In the early twenty-first century, and especially in the aftermath of financial calamity since 2008, evolution in the development of CSR has reached the point where discussion about the social role and responsibilities of large corporations and their ethical priorities has moved to center stage (Bonn & Fisher, 2005; Carroll & Buchholtz, 2006; Gentile, 2001; Kotler & Leee, 2005; Porter & Kramer, 2006).

8.2   CSR and Media

The emergence of formalized approaches to CSR coincided with significant developments in the character of mass media. Newspapers and other mass media outlets progressively added more entertainment content in the latter half of the nineteenth century, in the case of newspapers tripling the average number of pages. Cover prices were lowered (i.e., the penny press) and greater emphasis was placed upon attracting advertising revenues. This was especially pronounced in the USA but also evident elsewhere if not usually as extreme. The number of broadcasting outlets also grew, most of them state or public operators in the first half of the twentieth century in Europe, which by definition were more socially oriented and typically mandated to cater for a wide range of needs. There were strongly regulated mechanisms for the allocation and utilization of spectrum and national airwaves (Picard, 2008).

The evolution of mass media during the twentieth century was characterized by an inherent tension between public interest and public service concerns on one side and commercial drivers on the other—a condition that was institutionalized beginning in the mid-1980s with the licensing of commercial broadcasters and the creation of a dual media system in Europe. For much of this period, regulation and strong public service institutions provided a counterweight to the attributed value-neutral profit maximizing tendencies described earlier.

The 1980s and 1990s saw the liberalization of most national media markets. This encouraged extensive consolidation and an increasingly significant role for major international media conglomerates, notably AOL Time Warner, Viacom, News Corporation, Bertelsmann, Sony, and Vivendi Universal. There was significant growth in multichannel, cable, satellite and pay television companies. The regulating mechanism that has been more or less national in orientation and author was becoming less effective and media markets were very profitable, although still at a lower degree in comparison some other economic sectors (Barwise & Picard, 2012).

In certain respects, the pattern of development within the media industries would seem to be the opposite of that seen in the commercial sphere as a whole. While management studies and corporate practice have embraced—to greater or less degrees—CSR principles and methods, many national media markets have seen, at varying rates, a high degree of dismantling of externally levied regulations and also internally imposed codes and regimes of best conduct. Such processes have been uneven, in some cases slower and in others rapid, but often with troubling outcomes when considering the social responsibility of media operators historically.

In the digital sphere, where regulation and best practices race to keep up with the pace of technological change and the proliferation of internet and mobile products and services, the challenges are even more profound. Audiences vary in size from small to extremely large, and they are more powerful than ever as they can interact directly with one another, create their own content, and, significantly, highlight instances of poor or unethical journalism. This also encourages media managers to be more aware of, and concerned with, CSR as a vital aspect of the firm in practice.

The growth of social and user-generated media has been paralleled by a number of notable failures of governance and professionalism and in the standards of behavior and duties of care expected from media organizations and their leading employees. Examples range from Jayson Blair's acts of journalistic fraud when working for the New York Times to the phone-hacking scandal at News International. There are signs that this might lead to a new dialogue on the policy issues, media pluralism, and independent professionalism (Doyle & Schlesinger, 2012).

Hitherto, public interest and public service values, as well as strong industrial and professional codes of conduct, helped limit such ethical failures while stable industry models and predictable revenue streams meant fewer pressures to cut corners. In an environment characterized by deregulation and increasing financial pressures, however, some wonder if it is realistic (or practicable) for media organizations to reconcile commercial imperatives with wider ethical and social obligations. In the remainder of this chapter, we shall explore what media can learn from the managerial mainstream and whether a CSR adapted to the unique character and needs of the media enterprise (whether public or private) can provide a counterweight to mitigate against ethical lapses and malpractice. We begin with an encapsulation of theoretical view of CSR in application to media firms and industries.

8.3   Carroll's Model of Corporate Social Responsibility

As we have seen, CSR has gone through several phases of evolution. There remains little consensus on its precise definition. We can say that all the theoretical constructions developed after the 1950s agree that companies committed to CSR demonstrate corporate motivations that go beyond profit-making and formal legal obligations to involve a wider set of social and ethical concerns. Such principally include protection of the environment, fostering an improved society, supporting economic development, and sustaining good corporate relationships (Dahlsrud, 2008).

The social responsibilities of media companies are arguably more extensive and intensive than for most other industries because media are so central to cultural production and play such an important role in educating citizens and equipping them to participate in the democratic process. Moreover, media firms are able to influence others by shaping public opinion, cultivating social perspectives, and inculcating systemic values (not ignoring the fact that such is contentious, of course, and always fractured). It is clearly true that media industries have, or should have, significant responsibilities.

Carroll's model synthesizes a range of theories and models summarized in four kinds of social obligations that together constitute CSR:

- Economic responsibilities are fundamental. Without the foundation of profitability, none of the other responsibilities are feasible or deliverable.
- Moving up one step, legal responsibilities are the next most important and reflect the way that society's ethical principles are codified and applied.
- Ethical or moral responsibilities form a higher set of internalized obligations that encourage workers, managers, and firms to do what is right and avoid doing harm.
- Philanthropic obligations reside at the apex of Carroll's pyramid of corporate social responsibility, obliging the corporation to act as a good corporate citizen to promote a generalized social welfare that is crucial to shared quality of life (Carroll, 1991).

These levels are not independent. Carroll sees them as tightly interrelated with a high degree of interdependence.

Carroll's model is useful because it allows us to map the theories that have been developed to analyze CSR activities in application to media organizations. Media industry theory typically prioritizes the economic dimension of media's social responsibilities. The second group can be summarized as media ethics theories and corresponds to the second level in Carroll's hierarchy. The third category can be related to media shareholder theories. Finally, I will argue that the ultimate category—that of the philanthropic or the good corporate citizen—can be at least partially identified in the work of sustainability media theorists like Garriga and Mele (2004). In what follows we treat each level in turn.

The first level of theorization focuses on socially responsible activities as *tools for wealth creation*. Of course this is significant for any commercial enterprise, but one needs to understand that even not-for-profit public corporations are nonetheless financial organizations. Lacking the resources to operate effectively inherently means that no other aspect of social responsibility is possible for a media firm. The problem, however, is that too often (and increasingly) this is considered as the *only* social obligation of media companies. If that were indeed valid, then it would strongly suggest that the management of media firms is no different from any kind of firm.

This approach traces its origins to the work of Milton Friedman and his seminal New York Times article, "The social responsibility of business is to increase its profits" (Friedman, 1970). For Friedman, the only responsibility for any firm—and thus by extension any media firm—is to maximize shareholder value within the regulatory framework and without violating the most general morals of a (national) society. Apart from achieving the financial targets, media companies have no further obligation other than avoiding outright breeches of ethics that are endemic to an industry in the public's expectations for its performance. The key task, then, is to secure economic benefits. Also, it is generally accepted that the requirement to maximize shareholder value is not incompatible with taking into account the interests of other media stakeholders. Obviously wealthy media companies have more resources to produce quality and diverse content, although that is not to say they will do that if a less expensive alternative produces better margins.

Therefore, the conclusion drawn from the theory is that the social contribution of media firms is not the issue at all and that media enterprise and entrepreneurial actions are clearly financial in prioritization. This theory is subject to extensive criticism mainly given the increased risk that media face by focusing only in the economic field and the overly restrictive approach it implies for long-term planning. In fact the "bottom line" for a media firm is strongly determined by the perceptions it has of higher ethical standards, such as integrity in journalism and fairness in the portrayal and representation of diverse peoples. A media firm that ignores the general standards of public expectations for these industries courts disaster, as the News Corp phone-hacking scandal illustrates all too well. But one could make the same claim, if too a lesser degree, of the recent controversies about the salaries and benefits awarded to BBC managers.

Thus, adherents and critics alike generally agreed that it is important to broaden CSR in media beyond the purely economic approach, if for no better reason than the importance this has for marketing and public relations. Working on the assumption that reputation and brand name are important drivers of profitability, media companies feel compelled to forge a more intimate relationship with their audiences. For adherents, therefore, investment in public relations is a key element in bolstering the financial foundations of effective CSR—other aspects bolster the bottom line and are critical to success in that pursuit. The latest development here is about how media achieve measurable social targets and how those targets are related to corporate financial performance (Burchell, 2008; Hawkins, 2006; Schwartz & Salla, 2012).

The second layer of theories terms as *media ethics theories* highlight the firm's relationship with society and the influence that each company can have in the political sphere. Because the basic assumption is that growth depends on the enterprise's harmonious engagement with society, it is necessary to take ethical social requirements into account as a priority. The ethical complexion of CSR encourages greater sensitivity regarding the actions of each media company in relation to the host community. In short, ethical theories acknowledge the relationship between media business and society as a relationship with deeply rooted moral values. Media is not, in short, "business as usual."

To usefully analyze the ethical dimension of CSR requires understanding the complex, collective character of responsibility. Groups of social actors—shareholders, employees (journalists and content producers), and volunteers—have individual responsibility to act ethically and ensure the socially responsible character of the enterprise. An ethical breach or lapse by an associated individual can have profound consequences for the entire corporation. Regarding the collective aspect, we need to realize that the enterprise as a whole is a social actor in its own right and will be judged for its actions—both good and ill.

In media industries particularly, professional ethics and continually strengthening a moral "center" are core components of CSR because these provide the internal impetus for media companies to go beyond self-interest to meaningfully respond to social as well as economic drivers. The argument I advance is that CSR should be understood not only as a means to improve the functioning of the media business but that managers are wise to remember that in this business, they are responsible on a moral basis.

In this light, the concept of media ethics is an integral part of CSR for these industries and functions as a benchmark to establish the degrees to which media companies fulfill social expectations and, moreover, that financial incentive is a practical reality. The management challenge for media companies is how to achieve the best "ethical fit" between legal macroethics, organizational middle ethics, and individual micro-ethics (Appelbaum, Vigneault, Walker, & Shapiro, 2009; Schwartz & Carroll, 2003).

8.4   Stakeholder Theory and CSR

Stakeholder theory provides a useful means of engaging with CSR issues in media firms and acts as a bridge between the ethical and philanthropic levels of Carroll's CSR pyramid. For a media company to be consistent with sound ethical principles, it must firstly take into account the groups that have a legitimate interest in its activities and their consequences. These are stakeholders who either benefit or suffer from the actions taken by a media companies and thus ultimately from the decisions made by its managers. Managers therefore need to pay attention to and embrace issues that matter to the host community and not just those parties that directly associated with its financial interests, i.e., shareholders. Media managers will often struggle to balance the rival interests and concerns of diverse stakeholders that include owners, advertisers, audiences, shareholders, and politicians (to name but a few). Environmental protection is another important concern today, and this raises the question of whether media organizations also have obligations to fairly consider the interests of nonhuman stakeholders (other species, wilderness preservation, habitat diversity, etc.). Culture, technology, and the physical environment all pose challenging questions for society and commerce and have always had a strong bearing on media industries.

Carroll's model and the stakeholder approach converge in the pursuit of maximizing shareholder value, which has a conceptual foundation in the ideals of democracy as well as the proper functioning of a free market economy. But the important difference is that in stakeholder theory, the media company is required to overcome an often complicated, always complex, and constantly evolving set of conflicting interests (Jonker & de Witte, 2006; Werther & Chandler, 2006). While all industries and types of companies must deal with this to varying degrees, the complexity and intensity of the challenge is arguably much higher for media firms than many others.

In one of its most far-reaching manifestations, media firms are beginning to embrace concepts of sustainable development and "green media" as an important dimension of CSR policy. The intention is to ensure that companies (and industries) can grow and develop without compromising the interests of future generations and the environmental legacy passed down to them (Bansal & Roth, 2000; Saha &

Darnton, 2005). Such notions are closely tied to those dealing with the improvement of general welfare and quality of life. The pursuit has financial and practical benefits, as well. For example, Yleisradio in Finland is now encouraging employees to work several days per week at home, providing them with laptops and smartphones to facilitate this. That is good for the environment but also means the firm doesn't need as much physical space and facility as in the past. It is thus possible to lease or even sell some Yle properties to other investors, lowering the fixed costs of the firm.[1]

Some media firms now vaunt their green agendas. For example, BSkyB announced in 2009 that it had invested £233 million to develop "Europe's most sustainable broadcasting facility." The company has also led the way in developing energy-saving set-top box technologies (BskyB, 2009).

Sustainable development theory prioritizes forms of development that serve long-term and generalizable human needs and contribute to the improvement of quality of life (Haddock-Fraser, 2012). Such outcomes are only possible with popular support for conservation and the responsible use of scarce resources that are the "property" or sphere of societies as a whole, whether natural, human, or *financial*. Of course one of the main limiting factors is the increasing dominance of multinational media corporations that are less beholden to, and often less intimately linked with, local interests or geographic communities.

Notions of corporate citizenship underpin what is perhaps the most activist and interventionist of all the forms of CSR identified by Carroll. The philanthropic organization and professionals working for them actively donate to causes as a form of investment in the production of social goods. In fact media companies were among the earliest proponents and are historically evident in the first stage of development. Corporate citizenship, as we would now call it, was associated with the involvement of media businesses in charitable activities and donations as illustrated by Pulitzer's commitment to social life and education in journalism and various endowments that benefit media research and development (such as the Rockefeller Foundation and the Open Society Foundation). For Carroll, social solidarity is one of the fundamental aims of such programs (1991). For all firms—including media firms—corporate citizenship and philanthropy can take a variety of forms from ad hoc and discrete donations to ongoing support for "third sector" entities (charities, cultural institutions) and investment in community projects and social enterprises.

Another important contextual factor in many countries is the downsizing and even withdrawal of the state from former areas of social and cultural provision in which states previously had a key role. Private organizations not only have the opportunity to work more closely with citizens and communities to meet obligations formerly addressed by national and local governments but increasingly are rather expected to do that. This is evident in frequent claims that the private sector can do much of what has been historically handled by the public sector in

---

[1] Personal communication with Gregory F. Lowe, 21 May 2014.

ways that are more efficient and effective. While not always true, but there is cause for renewed consideration of where and how that argument has merit. Media companies can identify which specific social actions can influence people and societies for the better and complement their strategic intentions (Heikkurinen & Ketola, 2012; Jamali & Mirshak, 2007; Kramer & Kania, 2006). For example, it is clear in the newspaper industry's best interests to support literacy and civic engagement. That has a bearing on the health of their business and on the welfare of society.

The theories we have considered support that argument that media companies should be more actively engaged in helping solve social problems, including pressing environmental concerns. CSR is a positive way to complement existing public interest models and potentially offset both the seemingly inherit weaknesses (e.g., bureaucratic and slow) and their overall diminution. The CSR approach takes a different view from traditional public interest approaches because there is not a third party (state intervention or independent authorities) to decide what is good for people and how to fit with the social interests ex post but rather is about making decisions by the managers themselves (a self-regulated mechanism) in ex ante fashion. Of course CSR is not a panacea for all failures of either the free market or governmental provision. Nor should we underestimate either the contradictory impulses within organizations employing CSR strategies or ignore criticisms leveled at CSR from within academia or political and social movements. There is much truth in the general critique. But this doesn't invalidate the contemporary importance of, even social necessity for, CSR as a core dimension of principle and practice in media industries.

8.5   Challenges for Media Companies in the Framework of CSR

I am arguing the importance of CSR theory and principals for media companies. This is particularly important for media industries because they are distinguished in having a dual role as both market and social actors. Media firms contribute significantly to the overall quality of social life when practicing corporate social responsible behaviors and being committed to sustainable development. This matters, as well, because they face mounting challenges for improvement in accountability and transparency. The media sector is less regulated today than in the past, and that suggests the crucial need for thinking more precisely about how they gather information, what responsibilities they have in choices about content, and how to act responsibly as corporate citizens in an increasingly globalized world. In this section, we want to better understand what I'll call media CSR practices (MCSR).

As discussed, media mangers are influenced by different stakeholders and face a number of dilemmas (McManus, 1997; Stern, 2008). The first and a fundamental decision for media managers is how to balance the offering of a public good with the economic interests of a business with costs and the need for profits. The difficulty is evident in decisions about what kind of content managers chose to produce, as this reflects the rationale as well as priorities. Media content is important because it affects everyone in the many daily decisions about political, cultural, and social issues. Certainly the commercial aspect is significant because of the cost of production and the need for revenue (Achtenhagen & Raviola, 2009; Tsourvakas, 2003). As already mentioned, the first duty of any company is to ensure its continuation with sufficient resource to fulfill the mandate. Media managers face challenges to make their media companies profitable, but also with a sufficient quality content and (across operators and sectors) for all types of audiences, not only segments that are highly profitable (Lowe, 2009; Picard, 2005).

A related dilemma has to do with the priority media managers assign to their main source of revenue because commercial operators typically must serve the (often) divergent interest of two markets at the same time: audiences and advertisers. According to Ots (2009), managers weigh and filter what to prioritize in the light of their firms' self-interested needs. Will the focus privilege journalistic values or care more about the desires of advertisers when advertisers want specific thematic content or angles of coverage to appeal to particular audience profiles? Here is the risk of ignoring issues relevant to minority audiences or an audience with lower purchasing power or indeed even the overall interests of society at large in some instances. A large readership or viewership is usually the first reason for an advertiser to choose a medium and media firm. Media managers experience strong cross-pressures and must develop ample competence to handle this. Although our example here is focused on commercial firms, it is worthwhile to note that public sector companies also have dual markets to satisfy—governments and regulators on the one side and audiences and users on the other. These interests also frequently diverge. Governments affect media manager's decision-making via regulation, subsidies, and offers of loans or tax relief (Doyle, 2000; Loomis, 2008).

Thus, a constant and characteristic dilemma that media managers encounter is being able to effectively manage the interests of diverse stakeholders with varying incentives. Staff working within media companies—journalists, producers, artists, technicians, and administrative staff—often pursue both economic and noneconomic incentives. They like to work within their chosen medium and to wield influence. Professional identity is a core feature of personal identity and self-worth. Many choices in media industries are based on noneconomic considerations. As Picard (2010) has noted, many people will do media work for free. There aren't many industries where that happens.

The potential for ethical problems becomes pronounced where conventional workplace rewards (principally salaries) are very low or there are no clear or agreed professional standards. Financial pressures, or the allure of fast money, can encourage corrupt relationships with politicians or business people, or the use of inappropriate methods to collect news in manner that risks violating human dignity or producing low quality content (Clifford & Nordenstreng, 2004; Tsoukamoto, 2006). Competitors influence, as well, when the intensity encourages short-term thinking or prioritizes low-cost strategies (Van der Wurff & van Cuilenburg, 2001).

Media managers cope with direct and indirect efforts to influence the selection or shaping of content to support their own opinions or to slow or constrain the free exchange of information. They face problems with the entertainment programs that have language or images that some find offensive, that have a sensationalistic character, that rely on social stereotypes, and that promote sexism or racist attitudes (Beam, 2001; Lacy, 1992). When media companies are managed in an opportunistic and irresponsible way, they are far away from an MCSR business model (Breit, 2010; Kaye & Sapdsky, 2009; Li, 2012). In many European media markets, public media organizations do a better job, overall, than private sector counterparts, according to Ingenhoff and Koelling (2012). The authors attribute this to the probability that public media feel more accountable to audiences because of their public service obligations and funding.

Gulyas's (2009) research suggests that the giant communications agencies and broadcast industry in UK have far more developed processes of regulating and self-regulating social responsibility than longer-established newspapers and small-sized media organizations. The author attributed this to the fact that the broadcast industry was for many years more regulated than the print industry and that large organizations are more exposed to the public eye since most of them are listed firms on stock markets. Finally, a small number of UK media companies announce yearly reports on corporate social responsible results, although a sense of best practices is so far elusive.

For Han, Lee, and Khang (2007) who compared only print media, the main reason that some newspapers are more socially responsible in their content than other is explained mainly by an organization's work culture. It's also important to consider the role of general editorial policy. Adams-Bloom and Cleary (2009) studied the degree of social responsibility of the morning news segment of major US TV channels and concluded that channels with appropriate policy gave equal weight to economic objectives in relation to shareholders and the journalistic values for independence and professionalism. The researchers proposed clear and distinct roles to distinguish the products advertised from the news production. Napoli (2001) conducted research about the degree to which American TV outlets are concerned with the public interest and found that all private television channels have reduced the number of public interest programming such as news that supports democratic procedures but does not attract large audiences and is expensive to produce.

For Kung (2008) and Agas, Georgakarakou, Antonopoulou, and Tsourvakas (2011), MCSR is mainly about diminishing the potential negative effects of content, such as reducing the level of violent content, declining pornographic aspects, and encouraging respect for human dignity and concern about life for minorities and the disadvantaged.

All the empirical evidence suggests that there are unique peculiarities of MCSR that are characteristic of challenges managers constantly face in media companies. These peculiarities are mainly caused by fundamental conflicts between public interest obligations and private financial interests, resulting in various ethical dilemmas and continually requiring a complicated process of balancing the contending interests of different stakeholders. Thus, media managers are required to strike a fair and useful balance between social mission and ensuring the necessary financial resources to produce quality content that is also competitive in an ethical manner (Chong, 2010; Worth, 2009).

8.6   Recommendations for Media Social Responsible Practices

With all of that in view, I suggest that corporate social responsibility should be a mandatory competence for media managers. I would go so far as to argue that some set of best practices should be developed and adopted internationally. A social responsible index for all media should include variables that are more important for media industries in comparison with other industrial organizations or service providers, as argued in this chapter. I propose four variables to start:

1. *Content quality measure*. Content is the core focus and purpose for media companies and its consumption influences everyone in a society. Therefore, content policy should be transparent regarding editorial practices for collecting and producing news, the freedom to express opinions, and should include a plurality of types and styles of programs for diverse social groups and heterogeneity of news, featuring the widest possible range of voices including activists, subcultures, and minorities or regional groups. Broadcasters should be serious about children programs, especially, and all operators should be respectful of human rights and careful in the production of all types of programs and contents.
2. *Healthy media business practices*. Best practices will include policies to ensure fair labor relations and proper care for employees' life balance. Managers should have transparent relationships with shareholders, independent producers, distributers, financial institutions, advertisers, and others. MCSR means, in practice, developing a different way of thinking. It's important to treat workers, both those on staff and those contracted as freelance or other temporary labor, as fully *human* resources. This requires supporting sufficient social activities of employees, organizing leisure activities systematically, and working to solve organizational problems that cause unnecessary and hurtful stress.
3. *Social solidarity report*. Media companies could be required to make annual investments at some reasonable and (varying, we suppose) proportionate level to contribute in resolving persistent social problems. Some will be media related, such as education and cultural issues, and others more general, such as concern with supporting the development of tolerance for pluralism and diversity. Those investments could include economic support (philanthropy or donations) or know-how support for a period of time.
4. *Environmental improvement measures*. These could be defined as the percentages of shift to achieving green media companies. This would include direct support of staff members in voluntary activities to improve the company's

internal effectiveness in sustainability and in working with citizens to solve environmental problems (deforestation, threats to endangered species, cleaning beaches, etc.). It would certainly include ongoing support for efforts to reduce negative influences and support beneficial influences in content.

After the 2008 economic crisis, there is no doubt that regulations, free market, or other hybrid models do not guarantee a stable and sustainable economic and physical environment. MCSR strategy for media companies will validate investment to balance social service and public interest functions with financial self-interest.

References

Achtenhagen, L., & Raviola, E. (2009). Balancing tensions during convergence: Duality management in a newspaper company. *The International Journal on Media Management, 11*, 32–41.

Adams-Bloom, T., & Cleary, J. (2009). Staking a claim for social responsibility: An argument for the dual responsibility model. *The International Journal on Media Management, 11*(1), 1–8.

Agas, K., Georgakarakou, C., Antonopoulou, V., & Tsourvakas, G. (2011). Corporate socially responsibility practices for internal and external stakeholders differences between print and electronic media. In Z. Vukanovic & P. Faustino (Eds.), *Managing media economy, media content and technology in the age of digital convergence* (pp. 160–190). Montenegro: Media XXI, Narodua Knjiga.

Amir, A., & Amir, R. (2010). Corporate social responsibility as a conflict between shareholders. *Journal of Business Ethics, 97*, 71–86.

Appelbaum, S., Vigneault, L., Walker, E., & Shapiro, B. (2009). Good corporate governance and the strategic integration of meso ethics. *Social Responsibility Journal, 5*(4), 525–539.

Bansal, P., & Roth, K. (2000). Why companies go green: A model of ecological responsiveness. *The Academy of Management Journal, 43*(4), 717–736.

Barwise, P., & Picard, R. (2012). *The economics of television in a digital world what economics tells us for future policy debates*. Oxford: Oxford Reuters Institute for the Study of Journalism.

Beam, R. (2001). Does it pay to be market oriented daily newspaper? *Journalism and Mass Communication Quarterly, 78*(3), 466–483.

Blowfield, M., & Murray, A. (2008). *Corporate responsibility: a critical introduction*. Oxford: Oxford University Press.

Bonn, I., & Fisher, J. (2005). Corporate governance and business ethics: Insights from the strategic planning experience. *Corporate Governance, 13*(6), 730–738.

Breit, E. (2010). On the (re)construction of corruption in the media: A critical discursive approach. *Journal of Business Ethics, 92*, 619–635.

BskyB. (2009). *Sky steps up green broadcasting,* 9 January 2009 [Press release] Accessed May 6, 2014, from https://corporate.sky.com/media/press_releases/2009/green_broadcasting

Burchell, J. (Ed.). (2008). *Corporate social responsibility reader: Context and perspectives*. London: Routledge.

Carroll, A. B. (1979). A three-dimensional conceptual model of corporate performance. *The Academy of Management Review, 4*(4), 497–505.

Carroll, A. B. (1991). The pyramid of corporate social responsibility: Toward the moral management. *Business Horizons, 34*, 39–48.

Carroll, A. B. (1999). Corporate social responsibility: Evolution of a definitional construct. *Business and Society, 38*(3), 268–295.

Carroll, A. B. (2000). A commentary and an overview of key questions on corporate social performance measurement. *Business and Society, 39*(4), 466–478.

Carroll, A. B. (2008). A history of corporate social responsibility: Concepts and practices. In A. Crane, A. McWilliams, D. Matteu, J. Moon, & D. S. Siegel (Eds.), *Oxford handbook of corporate social responsibility* (pp. 19–46). Oxford: Oxford University Press.

Carroll, A. B., & Buchholtz, A. K. (2006). *Business and society: Ethics and stakeholder management* (6th ed.). Mason, OH: Thomson South-West.

Carroll, A. B., & Shabana, K. M. (2010). The business case for corporate social responsibility: A review of concepts, research and practice. *International Journal of Management Review, 12*(1), 85–104.

Chong, D. (2010). *Arts management* (2nd ed.). London: Routledge.

Clifford, C., & Nordenstreng, K. (2004). Social responsibility worldwide. *Journal of Mass Media Ethics: Exploring Questions of Media Morality, 19*(1), 3–28.

Dahlsrud, A. (2008). How corporate social responsibility is defined: An analysis of 37 definitions. *Corporate Social Responsibility and Environmental Management, 5*, 1–13.

Doyle, G. (2000). The economics of monomedia and cross-media expansion: A study of the case favouring deregulation of TV and newspaper ownership in the U.K. *Journal of Cultural Economics, 24*, 1–26.

Doyle, G., & Schlesinger, P. (2012). *Quality, diversity and innovation: Their role in the economic functioning of the media industries*. Glasgow: CCPR University of Glasgow. Accessed April 10, 2012, from http://www.gla.ac.uk/media/media_246977_en.pdf

Friedman, M. (1970). The Social Responsibility of Business is to increase its profits. *New York Times. Magazine*, September 13.

Garriga, E., & Mele, D. (2004). Corporate social responsibility theories: Mapping the territory. *Journal of Business Ethics, 53*, 51–71.

Gentile, M. (2001). Preparing business leaders to manage social impacts: Lessons from the field. *Journal of Human Values, 7*(2), 107–115.

Gulyas, A. (2009). Corporate social responsibility in the British media industries. Preliminary findings. *Media Culture and Society, 31*(4), 657–668.

Haddock-Fraser, J. (2012). The role of news media in influencing corporate environmental sustainable development: An alternative methodology to assess stakeholder engagement. *Corporate Social Responsibility and Environmental Management, 19*, 327–342.

Han, E.-K., Lee, D.-H., & Khang, H. (2007). Influential factors of the social responsibility of newspaper corporations in South Korea. *Journal of Business Ethics, 82*(3), 667–680.

Hawkins, D. E. (2006). *Corporate social responsibility: Balancing tomorrow's sustainability and today's profitability*. London: Palgrave MacMillan.

Heikkurinen, P., & Ketola, T. (2012). Corporate Responsibility and identity: From a stakeholder to an awareness approach. *Business Strategy and the Environment, 21*, 326–337.

Ingenhoff, D., & Koelling, M. (2012). Media governance and corporate social responsibility of media organizations: An international comparison. *Business Ethics: A European Review, 21* (2), 326–337.

Jamali, D., & Mirshak, R. (2007). Corporate social responsibility theory and practice in a developing country context. *Journal of Business Ethics, 72*, 243–262.

Jonker, J., & de Witte, M. (2006). *Management models for corporate social responsibility*. Berlin, Heidelberg: Springer.

Kaye, B., & Sapdsky, B. (2009). Taboo or not taboo? That is the question: Offensive language in prime-time broadcast and cable programming. *Journal of Broadcasting and Electronic Media, 53*(1), 22–37.

Kotler, P., & Leee, N. (2005). *Corporate social responsibility: Doing the most good for your company and your cause*. Hoboken, NJ: Wiley.

Kramer, M., & Kania, J. (2006). Changing the game: Leading corporations switch from defense to offense in solving global problems. *Stanford Social Innovation Review, Spring*, 20–27.

Kung, L. (2008). *Strategic management in the media from theory to practice*. London: Sage.

Lacy, S. (1992). The financial commitment approach to news media competition. *Journal of Media Economics, 5*(2), 5–21.

Lee, M. (2008). A review of the theories of corporate social responsibility: Its evolutionary path and the road ahead. *International Journal on Management Reviews, 10*(1), 53–73.

Li, R. (2012). Media corruption: A Chinese characteristic. *Journal of Business Ethics.* doi:10. 1007/S 10551-012-1464-6.

Loomis, K. (2008). The FCC and indecency local television general managers' perceptions. *The International Journal on Media Management, 10,* 47–63.

Lowe, G. F. (2009). The meaning of money: Models and implications for funding PMS. In *Proceedings of the European Media Management Association EMMA Annual Conference,* Paris, February 13–14.

McManus, J. (1997). Who's responsible for journalism? *Journal of Mass Media Ethics: Exploring Questions for Media Morality, 12*(1), 5–17.

Moura-Leite, R. C., & Padgett, R. (2011). Historical background of corporate social responsibility. *Social Responsibility Journal, 7*(4), 538–539.

Napoli, P. (2001). Social responsibility and commercial broadcast television: An assessment of public affairs programming. *International Journal on Media Management, 3*(IV), 226–233.

Ots, M. (2009). Who is the customer in the 'customer value?' Inherent problems in the marketing of advertising. *International Journal on Media Management, 11*(3–4), 124–134.

Picard, R. (2005). Money, media and the public interest. In G. Overholser & K. Jamieson (Eds.), *The Pres* (pp. 337–350). Oxford: Oxford University Press.

Picard, R. (2008). The challenges of public functions and commercialized media. In D. Gaber, D. McQuail, & P. Norris (Eds.), *The politics of new the news of politics* (2nd ed., pp. 211–229). Washington, D.C.: CQ Press.

Picard, R. (2010). The future of the news industry. In J. Curran (Ed.), *Media and society* (pp. 365–379). London: Bloomsbury Academic.

Porter, M., & Kramer, M. (2006). Strategy and society: The link between competitive advantage and social responsibility. *Harvard Business Review, 84*(12), 78–92.

Saha, M., & Darnton, G. (2005). Green companies or green con-panies: Are companies really green, or they pretending to be. *Business and Society Review, 110*(2), 117–157.

Schwartz, M. S., & Carroll, A. B. (2003). Corporate social responsibility: A three domain approach. *Business Ethics Quarterly, 13,* 503–530.

Schwartz, M., & Salla, D. (2012). Should firms go beyond profits? Milton Friedman versus broad CSR. *Business and Society Review, 117*(1), 1–31.

Stern, R. (2008). Stakeholder theory and media management: Ethical framework for news company executives. *Journal of Mass Media Ethics: Exploring Questions of Media Morality, 23*(1), 51–65.

Tsoukamoto, S. (2006). Social responsibility theory and the study of journalism ethics in Japan. *Journal of Mass Media Ethics: Exploring Questions of Media Morality, 21*(1), 55–69.

Tsourvakas, G. (2003). Techniques to enhance the transmission of quality programs by private television channels in Europe. *European Journal of Law and Economics, 16*(2), 233–245.

Van der Wurff, R., & van Cuilenburg, J. (2001). Impact of moderate and ruinous competition on diversity: The Dutch television market. *Journal of Media Economics, 14*(4), 213–229.

Werther, J., & Chandler, D. (2006). *Strategic corporate social responsibility: Stakeholders in a global environment.* London: Sage.

Worth, M. (2009). *Nonprofit management principles and practice.* London: Sage.

Resources and Perspectives from Media Political Economy

Justin Schlosberg

9.1 Introduction

The existence of media management studies as a delineated field of scholarly inquiry rests on an inherent conceptual tension. Management studies have traditionally been goal oriented towards identifying the structures and practices that maximise a firm's capacity to survive and thrive under market conditions. Within this context, empirical research has been chiefly concerned with variables that affect related indicators of efficiency, productivity, competitiveness and profitability. Within the broader scholarship of media and communication studies, however, it is the social and public value of media outputs that carry the most weight. This calls attention to an altogether different set of performance indicators regarding things like an informed citizenry, the circulation of diverse viewpoints and ideas, the representation of minorities and the subjection of powerful interests and institutions to proper scrutiny and accountability.

Of course, the social and public value of media output may not always be in conflict with the profit-oriented goals of media firms. Indeed, media organisations that are self-sustaining within the market and produce positive social externalities may be inherently desirable because:

1. They are not compromised by a dependence on state or philanthropic sources of funds.
2. They can provide an effective counterweight to state or public broadcasting in those countries where it is dominant.

Nor does the tension discredit media management studies that do not take the societal impact of media output as their starting point. There are certainly core

J. Schlosberg (✉)
Birkbeck College, University of London, London, UK
e-mail: j.schlosberg@bbk.ac.uk

© Springer International Publishing Switzerland 2016
G.F. Lowe, C. Brown (eds.), *Managing Media Firms and Industries*, Media
Business and Innovation, DOI 10.1007/978-3-319-08515-9_9

characteristics of media products—or symbolic goods—that make conventional management studies inadequate to the task of understanding how media organisations can optimally function in the marketplace. For instance, attention to the value of novelty attached to media products (and the inherent risks associated with it) tells us much about the acute need of media firms to achieve economies of both scale and scope and the incessant drive towards concentration and consolidation within and across media markets (Garnham, 2000). This in turn underlines justifications for policy interventions and regulation that are particularly sensitive issues for media companies, not least because of the perceived association between media independence and free speech rights.

Even studies that are centred on questions about market performance of media firms are therefore always linked—at least tacitly—to broader concerns to do with policy, democracy and freedom. For this reason, the impact of media management variables on media output (as opposed to market performance) is considered by some to be the most pertinent line of inquiry and 'the raison d'etre of the field' (Mierzjewska & Hollifield, 2006: 40).

Seen from this perspective, the central question underlying media management scholarship has to some extent been reframed from that which underlies management studies more broadly. In particular, the articulated goal is to address not simply how media firms can optimally survive and thrive under various market conditions but how they can optimally survive and *fulfil their social role* under various market (and indeed nonmarket) conditions.

This intrinsically links the study of internal management structures and processes to the social externalities of media output, both positive and negative. But if media management scholarship is intimately concerned with social externalities rather than just market performance, we might well question whether it constitutes a distinctive field at all. Much of critical media theory, for instance, is concerned precisely with what we might consider to be media management variables and their effects on media output and society at large. This is most clearly the case with respect to the political economy literature, which takes the ownership structures of media firms and their entrenchment within the market as the basis for explanations of media output. This is used to develop a broader understanding of the relationship between media systems and structures of power in society.

Given its central concern with internal production processes and characteristics of media firms, media management scholarship may complement, underpin and extend political economic accounts and help to fill in some crucial gaps. In particular, political economic accounts have tended to be very effective in probing the nature and extent of the problem, but much less effective in determining the precise causes, and perhaps partly as a result of this, there has been relatively scant attention to possible alternatives and solutions.

At the same time, media management scholarship would be emboldened by attention to not just the social value and cultural characteristics of media output but more acutely to its (often presumed) ideological features and its purported role in challenging or reproducing relations of power. It is the core contention of this chapter that if political economists have intrinsically linked market dynamics with ideology and power, media management studies are best placed to probe, question and define that link.

As such, broader media theory—and critical media theory in particular—can offer useful conceptual starting points for media management research. In turn, media management research may offer important contributions to the development of critical media theory. In order to illustrate this, we will first sketch an overview of key studies in the political economy of the media, addressing some of the central critiques that have been levelled against them. We will then consider how media management research may help to answer some of these critiques in ways that may be especially fruitful amidst current market conditions and the age of 'crisis'.

The focus here is on the provision of news and current affairs. This is not to disregard the importance to democracy in respect of the wider cultural contribution of the media industries, nor the increasingly blurred boundaries of news in a converged media environment. But the conventional liberal narrative of the media reserves a special place for journalists as agents of democracy, holding power to account and fostering an informed citizenry. The extent to which they can or do live up to this role is a core concern shared by political economists and media management scholars alike.

9.2   Political Economy Roots

Political economy is the study of the relationship between economic structures and processes on the one hand and the production of values and power in society on the other. When applied to the media, political economic accounts tend to examine the impact on media output of industry structure and ownership or the various elements of the commodity cycle (production, distribution, exchange, consumption). They are rooted in theories of historical materialism, though not all are explicitly Marxist. Some are closer to the historical materialism advanced by Harold Innis through his conception of 'knowledge monopolies' as the by-product of media technologies. According to this view, it is the determining effects of media technology that both structure and nurture the development of civilisation—and imperial conquest (Innis, 1950). Nor are all political economic accounts of the media unequivocally critical. Some (e.g. Mosco, 2004) acknowledge that processes of commodification and control in the media industries are not flawless or unchecked but subject to various obstacles, including political conflict and resistance.

In the main, however, media political economy tends to be grounded in Marxist analyses of power and the reproduction of social and economic relations. These assert that the 'function' of the mass media is to propagate the legitimating ideology of the ruling class and that this is achieved by virtue of its control over the 'means of mental production', or the 'ideological apparatus of the state' (Althusser, 2008; Marx & Engels, 1976; Poulantzas, 1978).

Not surprisingly, the development of mass media in the twentieth century—particularly television and radio—was seen by Marxist political economists as a consolidation of elite ideological control. More acutely, the mass media were seen as the primary means by which late capitalist societies endured the tremors of foundation-rattling crises. They provided the glue or 'social cement' (Thompson, 1990) to preserve a dominant systemic order, engineering just enough consensus to avoid popular revolt. This was despite a growing concentration of wealth and income inequality, particularly since the Second World War.

One of the earliest and most explicit invocations of these ideas was offered by Adorno and Horkheimer in their *Dialectic of Enlightenment* (Adorno & Horkheimer, 1933 [1944]). Focussing on patterns of standardisation and rationalisation that accompany the commodification of cultural forms, they painted a dystopian picture of late capitalist societies becoming increasingly unified and conformist, with the mass media serving to normalise, exclude or co-opt deviance and individuality.

In the 1970s and 1980s, more empirically based studies influenced by political economy became adept at demonstrating ideological bias in the news. In both public and commercial broadcasting, they found persistent patterns of bias in the coverage of crime, terrorism, industrial conflict and the Cold War, among other topics (Chibnall, 1980; Glasgow University Media Group, 1976; McNair, 1988; Schlesinger, Murdock, & Elliott, 1983).

9.3   Critiques and Counter-Critiques

The most vociferous challenge to these accounts has centred on their (often) embedded assumptions about media effects (e.g. Klaehn, 2002). Critics have rightly pointed out that audience studies beginning in post-War America have consistently demonstrated 'minimal' media influence on the audience's political views and dispositions. Marx's notion of a 'camera obscura' or false consciousness—according to which the proletariat come to perceive their own social reality in ways that legitimise the status quo—began to look somewhat detached from the reality of complex and heterogeneous post-industrial societies.

Radicals countered that the most potent media effects were beyond the scope of experimental, survey-based or even anthropological studies. They were held to consist not so much in persuasion but reinforcement, the 'drip, drip, drip' which characterises subtle and long-term mobilisation of bias and is a function of the mass media's pervasive presence in people's lives (Downing, 1980; Silverstone, 1999). Others suggested that ideological effects consisted not in the media's 'message' but rather in what was left unsaid (Curran, 2002; Hall, 1982). It is, after all, difficult to study audience responses to content they have never consumed.

In any case, the presence of ideological bias in the media is undesirable irrespective of whether it has mobilising effects on audiences. Access to diverse viewpoints is considered a foundation of the media's liberal democratic function, and as such, critical media studies in the political economy tradition have been right to focus their attention on processes of production over and above consumption.

Whilst the latter has been a particular point of focus for cultural studies, political economists place greater weight on the former in view of its poll position within the 'integrated circuit' of mass communication.

In effect, however, the political economy tradition has been concerned with the first two of what Stuart Hall (1973) considered the three key 'moments' in the flow of mass communications—production, content and reception. It is when asserting the influence of production—both instrumental and structural—over content that political economists have more to answer for. It is one thing to observe that the media are controlled and operated by an elite or privileged group, but it is another to assert that ownership, or the media's entrenchment within the market system, somehow *determines* the nature of its output. Just as Marx himself was unclear as to what the ideological apparatus of the state consists in (and much less how it functions), critical media theorists have been accused of falling victim to the 'fallacy of internalism' (Thompson, 1990)—making assumptions about the causes and effects of media output based only on patterns observed within the output itself.

A related charge is that political economists have generally failed to explain the relationship between structures and processes on the one hand and social behaviour and norms within the journalism profession that give rise to systemic ideological bias on the other. Equally, there has been scant attention to how agency or instrumentalism might impact on structures in turn (Manning, 2001). In a convincing critical review, Michael Schudson dubbed this gap a 'black box' that political economists have shown little interest in examining (Schudson, 1989).

None of this negates the important contribution of political economy to critical media theory, however. In particular, we have at our disposal various contentious models that attempt to explain and predict the behaviour and performance of media firms in Western democracies (at least). If nothing else, these can be empirically 'tested' with a view to rejecting, accepting or refining them.

9.4   Models of Dominance

Perhaps the best known and controversial of these is the Propaganda Model which attempts to link patterns of systemic bias in the media to strategic priorities consistent with the global expansion and consolidation of capital (Herman & Chomsky, 2002). It is a useful focus for the purposes here because it draws on, as we shall see, a range of other models that position journalists in a dependency role vis-a-vis media owners, advertisers and elite sources. The absence of journalist autonomy is perhaps the common defining feature of political economy explanations of the media.

The controversy that continues to surround the Propaganda Model stems in part from its name. Given its intimate association with Nazism and other violent dictatorships of the twentieth century, it's not surprising that the term 'propaganda' might be inherently contentious when applied to the media in liberal democracies. The distinctive features of propaganda in autocratic regimes are that a) it is centrally and consciously directed by the state and b) it is 'total' insofar as media output outside of the state-sanctioned framework is prohibited.

This is clearly not an accurate picture of the media landscape in Western democracies. But the literal meaning of the word propaganda, based on its Latin derivation, is simply 'that which ought to be propagated'. Its use in the Propaganda Model therefore reflects no more than the observed, or assumed, *functionalist* role of the media in capitalist democracies. That function—as Marx asserted—is to protect, serve and advance the interests of capital above all else. The social democratic value attached to the media in liberal democracies is therefore no more than a convenient fiction, underpinned by what are occasional, exceptional or marginal departures from the consensus framework (Chomsky, 1989).

In explaining how the news media come to play this essentially functionalist role, the Propaganda Model is predicated on five 'filters' that condition and shape media output. These filters consist of the various influences and pressures that operate on the media stemming from (1) advertisers, (2) media owners, (3) official sources (both in terms of 'subsidy' and 'flak') and (4) the overarching ideological paradigm (e.g. 'anticommunism' in the model's original formulation).

The third of these sources of influence warrants particular attention in view of its strong connection to the way news organisations are bureaucratically organised and structurally constrained—a theme that intersects with media management studies. The two 'filters' at issue here concern the capacity of elite sources to offer both a carrot and a stick to journalists that resonate with their institutional norms, professional values and careerist goals. According to the Propaganda Model, these are used to encourage conformity and deter deviation from the official line.

The carrot or 'subsidy' consists in the provision of a steady diet of newsworthy source material—regular press conferences, statements, interviews, etc. It is the regularity and predictability of these often pre-scheduled news 'events' that help media firms cope with the endemic risks and uncertainties associated with news as a commodity. Accreditation and access to official sources are therefore extremely valuable to journalists and news media firms, and official sources are able to equally exploit this in the form of 'flak'—punishing overly critical individual journalists or firms by denying or limiting their access. Sanction may take the form of accreditation or licence withdrawal or the threat of libel suits. The key point is that the conditioning power of both subsidy and flak is predicated on the intrinsic value of exclusives, which drive the business of news making. Scoops are dependent on journalists' access to authoritative sources—the bigger the scoop, the greater the dependency on that access.

This aspect of the Propaganda Model traces its roots to the structural model of Primary Definition that emerged in the 1970s, which posited that the perceived reliability and authority of officials provided them with a default advantage in defining the news agenda (Gans, 1979; Hall, 1978; Sigal, 1973). There are at least two conditions that determine this privilege. First, the activities of leading political figures and other elites are intrinsically newsworthy in virtue of their widespread consequences and hence their suitability to dramatic news narratives (Galtung & Ruge, 1965; Tuchman, 1978). Second, they are often the 'key holders' to public information (Golding & Elliott, 1979; Miller, 1994) meaning that their accounts carry authoritative weight, absolving journalists of the need to source additional evidence or engage further in the often difficult and resource intensive task of fact-checking.

As a consequence of these conditions, news media firms tend to be bureaucratically organised in such a way as to exploit official source subsidy as far as possible. The so-called Westminster lobby—exemplified by the BBC's dedicated news desk at Milbank—is one example. According to the model of Primary Definition, the way that media firms are organised to take full advantage of accreditation and access to elite sources further enhances their dependence on them.

Primary Definition has also underpinned several other model variants collectively known as 'indexing', according to which dissent in the media is triggered all but exclusively in response to a split within elite ranks (Hallin, 1994; Livingston & Bennett, 2003). Their common standpoint is that inter-elite conflict provides the benchmark according to which journalists will respond—and crucially *legitimate*— any given controversy. But the important distinction of the indexing model is its conception of a relatively dynamic and fluid process, with the degree of consensus among elites liable to shifts over time and subject to a range of variables and influences. It went some way to addressing a central charge against radical functionalist accounts (such as the Propaganda Model) for their overattention to static and determinist structures. This came at the expense of examining dynamic and fluid conditions that shape both the scope and limits of journalist autonomy in any given context, at any given time (Schlesinger & Tumber, 1994).

An even more nuanced depiction of journalists' adherence to elite source definitions offers a 'cascading activation' model of news framing (Entman, 2004). According to this model, whilst elite conflict may trigger public debate through the media, the content of that debate is further modified by interventions at various stages in the news filtering process. Such interventions may stem from so-called 'mid-level' sources, journalists themselves or public opinion. The opportunities for challenging elite definitions were, according to this model, given considerably greater force by the decline of the Cold War ideological paradigm.

9.5 Political Economy at a Crossroads

The decline of this paradigm coincided with the rise of digital communications and an associated dismantling of information control (McNair, 2006). Digital utopianists place emphasis on the exponential growth of decentralised and de-territorialised networks of communication, the spread of multiway and micro media news flows and the emergence of new forms of resistance such as culture jamming and hacktivism, all of which undermine political economy approaches based on the centrality of mass media power.

But political economists countered that processes of commodification in the digital sphere were erecting new barriers to specialist or in-depth information

(Bagdikian, 2004), creating 'artificial scarcities' (Mansell & Jarvery, 2004) and replicating patterns of consumption around the 'legacy' media brands (Curran, Fenton, & Freedman, 2012). A major study by Pew Research in 2011 found that of the top 25 most visited news websites in the USA, 17 were those of legacy media organisations (Pew Research Centre, 2012). Meanwhile, television viewing in the UK and elsewhere has actually increased in tandem with Internet growth (albeit at a slower rate), and it remains overwhelmingly the dominant source of news and information for most people in both the developed and developing world (Open Society Foundations, 2012). And despite the structural and terminal decline in print media sales and advertising revenue in the UK, most of the major national newspapers are collectively reaching a wider audience than ever before, courtesy of their online editions.

So where does all this leave the study of media political economy and what, if anything, can media management studies contribute to its enduring relevance? We have seen that political economists have offered robust responses to their critics in respect of empirical concerns including evidence of 'minimal' media effects, instances of journalist autonomy and the 'cultural chaos' and transparency characteristic of the digital age. With regard to more theoretical critiques based on the relationship between structures and output, and between structures and agency, various models have been advanced which provide a useful basis for testing and refinement through empirical research.

But there is one problem area that has not been satisfactorily addressed and which carries increasing weight and urgency amidst an apparent and enveloping market failure in news making. The crux of the problem is this: if systemic ideological bias is a function of the media's entrenchment within the market system, how does this compute with markets that are increasingly unable to support professional news making? Indeed, radical media accounts must confront the reality that much of the mainstream news media, at least in the UK, has long been the product of nonmarket systems such as public service broadcasting. Even within strictly commercial news markets such as print newspapers, leading agenda-setting titles—including the papers like the UK's *Guardian* and *The Times*—have long functioned as loss leaders propped up by philanthropy, foundation funding or cross-subsidy.

Where political economists have compared the output of public service with commercial broadcasting, they have found little difference in patterns of ideological bias (Glasgow University Media Group, 1976; Lewis, 2006). Explanations of such similarity have tended to rest on the assumed entrapment of public service broadcasters within the logic of markets, both in terms of production and competition for ratings (Murdock, 1982). There is also clear alignment in the bureaucratic organisation and culture of public service and commercial newsrooms, such that the former are equally vulnerable to the structural power of elite sources identified in the Propaganda Model and Primary Definition.

But this seems at best an insufficient explanation given the profound distinctions in organisational goals, structure and operation between public service and commercial broadcasters. Similarly, journalists and editors working at broadsheet newspapers clearly work within a different set of priorities and pressures compared to those at the tabloids. It is one thing to show that the ideological function of the media transcends distinctions in the type of news organisation, but the question of why very different institutional structures and cultures can produce essentially the same end result demands more scrutiny.

Likewise, as a wider array of alternatives to the market framework of journalism begin to surface, we need more attention to the crucial question of which organisational structures can or could produce a *different* end result, one that better lives up to the promise of adversarial journalism without fear or favour.

These questions carry profound implications for the study of media management as much as media political economy. Both fields have adopted the age of crisis in the media industries as a focal point in recent studies. For political economists, the crisis has been considered variously in terms of its impact on journalist-source relations (Franklin & Carlson, 2011), its implications for media policy-making (McChesney & Pickard, 2011) and its consequences for news quality (Fenton, 2010). Much of this work has offered a sobering counterweight to more celebratory accounts of the rise of citizen media (e.g. Allan & Thorsen, 2009). But there is still comparatively little attention paid to the implications of nonmarket alternatives for *professional* journalism. Emergent media management studies, on the other hand, have tended to focus on the implications of crisis for those working within media industries, examining, for instance, the impact on labour conditions (e.g. Deuze, 2011) and the creative value chain (e.g. Aris, 2009). But with the focus thus restricted, we gain little insight into the implications for citizens and democracy at large and the media's role in shaping and reproducing relations of power.

9.6   Towards Synthesis

In regard to journalism specifically, despite a burgeoning literature revolving around the notion of crisis, there has been comparatively little empirical work on the actual causes, nature, extent and consequences of that crisis. It is at this point that a synthesis between media management and political economy approaches may prove especially useful in uncovering the 'why' and 'how' questions of structural decline and the funding crisis currently gripping journalism in many parts of the world. Most urgently, we need research that scrutinises and evaluates how processes of consolidation and tabloidisation affect both the market and social value of news media output. Studies embedded in the tradition of political economy would do well to factor in a focus on the strategic responses of firms to structural pressures, rather than just the conditions which shape and determine output. On the other hand, media management studies in this area would benefit from attention to broader dynamics characteristic of critical political economy that impact on both news output and audiences. These include media ownership, journalist-source relations, as well as policy and regulation.

In short, both disciplines would benefit from a more holistic approach to assessing media economics in light of normative, descriptive and critical accounts of the media's democratic and social role. Such research should be driven not just by the need to understand the nature of the problem but also by a goal to identify effective solutions both in the context of management strategies and public policy. Political economy critiques have tended to eschew the notion that the market could—under any conditions—meaningfully support the kind of media that underpin theories of liberal democracy. But this may well turn out to be an oversimplification. If declining audiences are at least partly a function of errant market strategies, this suggests the possibility that different strategies under different market conditions might well produce more sustainable, democratic and accountable media capable of fulfilling their expected social role.

There are certainly cogent examples of such alternatives. Cooperative news firms in such diverse regions as Camden in North London (*Camden New Journal*) and the West Highlands of Scotland (*West Highland Free Press*) have demonstrated that local news markets *can* support independent titles at least under certain conditions. In a compelling argument on behalf of the cooperative movement, Dave Boyle (2012) draws a connection between the ownership structure of a local news organisation and the essential ingredient of its survival: trust. This is understood both in the context of trust among workers within a cooperatively owned title and the trust of readers placed in that title. Indeed, the two may be mutually reinforcing.

But whilst political economy approaches have all too summarily dismissed alternative possibilities for sustaining public interest news within the market system, emergent media management studies have so far neglected to articulate the problem explicitly as a crisis for democracy and to apply their distinct methodological approaches to this wider context. In particular, we need attention to the feasibility and sustainability of nonmarket and hybrid models of professional journalism outside of the state-corporate framework. Here too, recent years have seen encouraging developments. There is an emerging sector in foundation-funded initiatives of investigative journalism in a broad range of countries—with some indications that they have been given added momentum by the development of digital media (Open Society, 2012). Examples such as ProPublica in the USA and the Bureau for Investigative Journalism in the UK demonstrate the potential for hybrid models of both funding and dissemination to breathe new life into the sector.

In sum, we need attention to the sustainability of cooperative, foundation-funded and cross-subsidised news media. Such attention should be directed towards *critical* research questions such as:

- To what extent are foundation-funded models sustainable in the long term?
- Are cross-subsidies helping to ensure the survival of the quality news sector or simply enhancing the political influence and leverage of owners?
- To what extent can cooperatively owned media firms function outside of particular local market contexts?

Underpinning these questions is a need to gather data on new and developing models of news provision in different regions and at both the national and local level, to conduct in-depth feasibility studies aimed at identifying which structures of ownership/funding work best under different state and market conditions and to identify ways in which hybrid organisations can extract maximum value and cost-efficiencies through digital tools and networks and multiplatform strategies of dissemination.

There is an equally pressing need to broaden the scope of such inquiry beyond a Western media focus. Much of this work is already being done in the study of global journalism (e.g. Curran & Park, 2000; Thussu, 2009). But greater attention specifically to the nature of crisis as well as new and emerging models of 'third sector' journalism in different regional contexts around the world would substantially enrich the field.

9.7 Conclusion

The key question of whether, or to what extent, autonomous, public interest journalism can be sustained by the market remains deeply unresolved and more pertinent than ever. At a time when the professional news media are facing an unprecedented crisis of legitimacy as well as funding, political economy and media management scholarship is best placed to examine this critical question. Research can be bolstered by approaches that draw on both. This in turn might help to shed light on broader and more theoretical questions at the heart of critical media theory, which remain equally unresolved. At their core, these questions concern the capacity of the media in post-industrial societies to support pluralism and diversity, hold powerful interests to account, and to serve citizens through the provision of both informative news and a platform for engagement and voice. It is a concern that both media management and media political economy studies ultimately share in common and are both goal oriented to addressing.

This chapter has contended and attempted to show that their distinctive areas of focus may yet yield far-reaching insights in combination and synthesis. It began by suggesting that the central and distinctive feature of media management scholarship concerns not just how media firms can function optimally in the marketplace but how they can optimally survive and fulfil their social role under various conditions—both within and outside of the market. As such, it is well suited to complementing traditional scholarship in the field of media political economy insofar as it appears better placed to consider alternatives and solutions rather than simply dissect the nature of the problem. But I have argued that studies starting from a media management theoretical standpoint could benefit from attention to some of the broader themes characteristic of media political economy, including its explicitly critical dimension and intimate concern with power. Finally, both fields ought to take more account of professional news provision outside of the state-market framework and the possibility that marketisation may itself be a potent cause of market failure in the news industries.

Such harmonisation between the respective approaches may prove not only fruitful but essential in order to sustain the relevance and theoretical force of media political economy in the digital age, to justify media management studies as a growing and distinctive subsector of the field, to enable media studies as a whole to adequately address the crisis of funding and legitimacy which has enveloped news industries around the globe and to provide the basis for meaningful alternatives at the level of both strategic agency and public policy.

References

Adorno, T., & Horkheimer, M. (1933 [1944]). *The dialectic of enlightenment.* New York: Continuum.

Allan, S., & Thorsen, E. (2009). *Citizen journalism: Global perspectives.* New York: Peter Lang.

Althusser, L. (2008). *On ideology.* London: Verso.

Aris, A. (2009). *Managing media companies: Harnessing creative value.* Hoboken, NJ: Wiley; Chichester : John Wiley [distributor].

Bagdikian, B. H. (2004). *The new media monopoly.* Boston, MA: Beacon.

Boyle, D. (2012). *Good news: A co-operative solution to the media crisis.* Accessed March 2013, from http://www.uk.coop/sites/storage/public/downloads/good_news_-_fresh_ideas_2.pdf

Chibnall, S. J. (1980). *Crime reporting in the British press: A sociological examination of its historical development and current practice* [Electronic resource].

Chomsky, N. (1989). *Necessary illusions: Thought control in democratic societies.* Boston, MA: South End Press.

Curran, J. (2002). *Media and power.* London: Routledge.

Curran, J., Fenton, N., & Freedman, D. (2012). *Misunderstanding the internet.* London, New York: Routledge.

Curran, J., & Park, M. J. (2000). *De-Westernizing media studies.* London: Routledge.

Deuze, M. (2011). *Managing media work.* London: Sage.

Downing, J. (1980). *The media machine.* London: Pluto Press.

Entman, R. M. (2004). *Projections of power: Framing news, public opinion, and U.S. foreign policy. Chicago, Ill.* London: University of Chicago Press.

Fenton, N. (2010). *New media, old news: Journalism and democracy in the digital age.* London: Sage.

Franklin, B., & Carlson, M. (2011). *Journalists, sources and credibility: New perspectives.* London: Routledge.

Galtung, J., & Ruge, M. H. (1965). The structure of foreign news. *Journal of Peace Research, 2*(1), 17.

Gans, H. J. (1979). *Deciding what's news: A study of CBS evening news, NBC nightly news, newsweek, and time.* New York: Pantheon Books.

Garnham, N. (2000). *Emancipation, the media, and modernity: Arguments about the media and social theory.* Oxford: Oxford University Press.

Glasgow University Media Group. (1976). *Bad news.* London: Routledge and Kegan Paul.

Golding, P., & Elliott, P. (1979). *Making the news.* London: Longman.

Hall, S. (1973). *Encoding and decoding in the television discourse [S.l.].* Birmingham: The University of Birmingham.

Hall, S. (1978). *Policing the crisis: Mugging, the state, and law and order [S.l.].* London: Macmillan.

Hall, S. (1982). The rediscovery of ideology: Return of the repressed in media studies. In T. Bennett, J. Curran, M. Gurevitch, & J. Wollacott (Eds.), *Culture, media and society*. London: Routledge.

Hallin, D. C. (1994). *We keep America on top of the world: Journalism and the public sphere*. London: Routledge.

Herman, E. S., & Chomsky, N. (2002). *Manufacturing consent: The political economy of the mass media*. New York: Pantheon Books.

Innis, H. A. (1950). *Empire and communications*. Oxford: Clarendon Press.

Klaehn, J. (2002). A critical review and assessment of Herman and Chomsky's 'Propaganda Model'. *European Journal of Communication, 17*(2), 147–182.

Lewis, J. (2006). *Shoot first and ask questions later: Media coverage of the 2003 Iraq War*. New York: Peter Lang.

Livingston, S., & Bennett, W. L. (2003). Gatekeeping, indexing, and live-event news: Is technology altering the construction of news? *Political Communication, 20*, 17.

Manning, P. (2001). *News and news sources: A critical introduction*. London: Sage.

Mansell, R., & Jarvery, M. (2004). New media and the forces of capitalism. In A. Calbrese & C. Sparks (Eds.), *Toward a political economy of culture—Capitalism and communication in the twenty-first century*. Oxford: Rowman and Littlefield.

Marx, K., & Engels, F. (1976). *The German ideology [S.l.]*. Moscow: Progress Pubs.

McChesney, R. W., & Pickard, V. W. (2011). *Will the last reporter please turn out the lights: The collapse of journalism and what can be done to fix it*. New York: New Press. Distributed by Perseus Distribution.

McNair, B. (1988). *Images of the enemy: Reporting the new Cold War*. London: Routledge.

McNair, B. (2006). *Cultural chaos: Journalism, news and power in a globalised world*. London: Routledge.

Mierzjewska, B. I., & Hollifield, C. A. (2006). Theoretical approaches in media management research. In A. B. Albarran et al. (Eds.), *Handbook of media management and economics*. London: Routledge.

Miller, D. (1994). *Don't mention the war: Northern Ireland, propaganda and the media*. London: Pluto Press.

Mosco, V. (2004). Capitalism's Chernobyl? From ground zero to cyberspace and back again. In A. Calbrese & C. Sparks (Eds.), *Toward a political economy of culture—Capitalism and communication in the twenty-first century*. Oxford: Rowman and Littlefield.

Murdock, G. (1982). Large corporations and control and the communications industries. In T. Bennett, J. Curran, et al. (Eds.), *Culture, media and society*. London: Routledge.

Open Society Foundations. (2012). *Mapping digital media: Journalism in a changing world*. Accessed July 12, 2013, from http://www.opensocietyfoundations.org/projects/mapping-digital-media.

Pew Research Center. (2012). *The state of the News Media in 2012. Project for excellence in journalism*. Accessed March 2013, from http://stateofthemedia.org.

Poulantzas, N. (1978). *Political power and social classes*. London(7 Carlisle St., W.1): Verso Editions.

Schlesinger, P., Murdock, G., & Elliott, P. (1983). *Televising 'terrorism': Political violence in popular culture*. London: Comedia.

Schlesinger, P., & Tumber, H. (1994). *Reporting crime: The media politics of criminal justice*. Oxford: Clarendon Press.

Schudson, M. (1989). The sociology of news production. *Media, Culture and Society, 11*, 19.

Sigal, L. V. (1973). *Reporters and officials. The organization and politics of news making*. Lexington, MA: D. C. Heath & Co.

Silverstone, R. (1999). *Why study the media?* London: Sage.

Thompson, J. B. (1990). *Ideology and modern culture: Critical social theory in the era of mass communication*. Cambridge: Polity.

Thussu, D. K. (2009). *Internationalizing media studies*. London, New York: Routledge.

Tuchman, G. (1978). *Making news: A study in the construction of reality*. New York; London: Free Press; Collier Macmillan.

Part III

Business and Economics

Managing in the Distinctive Economic Context of Media

10

Gillian Doyle

10.1 Introduction

Anyone interested in media management will be aware that the number of scholars working in this subject area and in the related area of media economics has expanded dramatically over the recent years. Growth of this subject area has been fuelled by many factors including increased recognition within mainstream media studies of the relevance and value of the analytical tools provided by business, management and economics as disciplines. More academic research and an expansion of teaching in the area of media management also reflect the demands of industry and of policymakers who share a burgeoning need for a better understanding of the many complex forces that bear upon an ever-changing media landscape.

The challenges for media executives and strategists concerned with how best to manage and use their resources span a broad range of factors including how to ameliorate risk and uncertainty, manage creative personnel, maximise the value of intellectual property at a time of unprecedented piracy, adjust to a globalised competitive environment, negotiate powerful new gateway monopolies, sustain and build markets and harness the opportunities created by digitisation. Growing scholarly interest in such themes is central to media management studies and comes at a good time. For researchers who want to develop knowledge and shape the analytic concepts of this emerging field of enquiry, opportunities are abundant.

Professor Gillian Doyle (Gillian.Doyle@glasgow.ac.uk) is the director of the Masters programme in Media Management at the Centre for Cultural Policy Research (CCPR), University of Glasgow, and is a visiting professor (II) at the Institute for Media and Communication (IMK), University of Oslo.

G. Doyle (✉)
Professor of Media Economics and Director of the Centre for Cultural Policy Research (CCPR), University of Glasgow, Glasgow, Scotland, UK
e-mail: Gillian.Doyle@Glasgow.ac.uk

© Springer International Publishing Switzerland 2016
G.F. Lowe, C. Brown (eds.), *Managing Media Firms and Industries*, Media Business and Innovation, DOI 10.1007/978-3-319-08515-9_10

The field of media management is diverse but the management practices and strategies that are prevalent often reflect the distinctive nature and characteristics of this industry, including the distinctive economic features of media. An unusual but crucial economic attribute for media content industries is that the essential quality that consumers get value from resides in meanings, which are not, in themselves, material objects. Despite the many challenges for media firms associated with adjusting to persistent technological change and advancement, this very core economic attribute of media gives rise to a distinctive and ongoing set of issues and opportunities for managers in this industry.

This chapter provides an introduction to some of the key distinctive economic attributes of media outputs and markets and assesses what this implies for the organisational, business and corporate strategies that suppliers of media output need to deploy. Focusing on network formation, corporate expansion and diversification and risk spreading, it provides an overview of the relationship between the distinctive economic characteristics of media, changing market conditions and some of the main business strategies that enable media firms to manage their resources effectively.

10.2   What Is Distinctive About Media Economics?

The media industry is unique on a number of counts. One characteristic that distinguishes it from other areas is that media firms often operate in 'two-sided' markets (Rochet & Tirole, 2003) or what have sometimes been termed 'dual product' markets (Picard, 1989, pp. 17–19). Media markets are two sided because, in many instances, media firms simultaneously produce two different commodities that, in turn, can be sold to two distinct and separate groups. The two sorts of commodities generated are, first, content (e.g. television programmes, news stories, etc., arranged into a schedule or, usually, some bundled product, e.g. a newspaper or magazine) and, second, audience attention. The latter is routinely packaged, traded and sold to advertisers. The commercial income it generates is substantial, for example, accounting for some 50 % of the revenues of the global television industry (OFCOM, 2012, p. 131). The features of media as a commodity that are especially distinctive generally relate to the first sort of output: media content.

Collins, Garnham, and Locksley (1988) were amongst the first to shed light on the economic peculiarities of media content as a form of output. Focusing on the attributes of television programmes and other broadcasts, they noted that 'the essential quality from which their use-value derives is immaterial' (p. 7). Many cultural goods share this common characteristic that their value for consumers is tied up in the messages or meanings they convey, rather than with the material carrier of that information (e.g. the radio spectrum, a CD or the digital file, etc.). It follows that media content is not truly 'consumable' in the purest sense of this term (Albarran, 1996, p. 28). Messages can be enjoyed by audiences without being depleted in any way in the process and so, like other 'information' goods, media content has the so-called public good characteristic that the act of consumption by one individual does not reduce its supply to others (Withers, 2006, p. 5). Broadcast material and other content outputs exhibit the peculiarity that they can be supplied over and over again at zero or quite marginal cost. If one person watches a television broadcast or listens to a song, it does not diminish anyone else's opportunity to view or listen. In this respect, media seems to defy one of the very basic premises on which the laws of economics are based—scarcity (Doyle, 2013).

Given that the main value residing in media content is generally to do with attributes which are immaterial, it follows that once the 'first copy' of, say, a video or a news feature has been created, it then costs little or nothing to reproduce and supply it to additional customers. Increasing marginal returns will be enjoyed as more and more customers for an item of content are added. As a result, the industry is strongly characterised by economies of scale. Firms in this sector tend to enjoy increasing marginal returns as consumption of their output expands. 'First-copy' production costs are usually high but then marginal reproduction or distribution costs are low and, for some media suppliers, zero (ibid).

Another feature that is commonly characteristic of media industries is the prevalence of economies of scope. Economies of scope are generally defined as the savings available to firms from multiproduct production or distribution. They are common again because of the public good nature of media content output and the fact that a product created for one market can, at little or no extra cost, be reformatted and sold through another. Because the essence of what we value about media content is contained in ideas and messages that are intangible and therefore do not get used up, the product is still available to the supplier after it has been sold to one set of consumers to then sell over and over again. For example, an interview with a celebrity can potentially be packaged into a television documentary, a news item, a radio transmission, etc. The reformatting or altering of the scope of a product intended for one audience into a 'new' one that extends consumption of it releases savings for the firm and therefore generates economies of scope (ibid).

The challenges for media managers that derive from the distinctive economic attributes of media are varied and considerable. One such is the difficulty of measuring or evaluating the impacts that arise from a decision to allocate resources in one fashion rather than another. Communicating with mass audiences, as an economic activity, is inextricably tied up with welfare impacts. And as a field, media economics seeks to play a role in showing how to minimise the welfare losses associated with any policy choices surrounding media provision. And yet, as prominent economist Alan Peacock observed some years ago, welfare impacts are and still remain very difficult to measure convincingly (Peacock, 1989, pp. 3–4). As a corollary, performing outcome-based assessments in efforts to assist managerial decision-making is often far from straightforward.

Another problem is that whereas notions of economic 'efficiency' and assessments of whether efficiency is being achieved or not depend upon clarity about objectives, the circumstances surrounding cultural provision, of which media is a subset, often militate against such clarity. The perceived objectives associated with media provision are multifaceted and at times contradictory, with some organisations operating in the nonmarket sector (Doyle, 2013; Wirth & Bloch, 1995). So, managers in the media are apt to find themselves subject to a diverse and complex array of expectations on the part of differing constituencies and stakeholders. And when it comes to using the tools of economics to analyse media markets and industries, whereas paradigms suited to the peculiarities of this particular industry are still very much in development, few if any all-embracing models based in conventional economic theory can fully match that challenge.

Other special difficulties that media managers in the media are faced with stem from, for example, the uncertainties, risks and irrationalities associated with producing creative output or from seeking to analyse production, distribution and consumption in an ever-changing technological environment for mass media (Doyle & Frith, 2006). The presence of risk, such as uncertainty of demand, and incentives and motivations guiding artistic and creative 'talent', is a particularly noteworthy aspect of media and other creative industries (Caves, 2000). The process of creating the initial copy of, for example, an edition of a magazine or a television programme is often highly expensive while suppliers have little certainty about which content properties will be a hit with popular taste—itself unpredictable. So a key objective for content creation businesses is to establish operating conditions that are conducive to the production of regular hits and that enable effective management of failure (Picard, 2005, p. 63). As discussed below, the economic imperative of counteracting risk is another feature that is strongly impressed upon the sorts of managerial and corporate strategies that are prevalent in the media industry.

However, the presence of economies of scale and scope has had and continues to have a major and determining influence over production practices, managerial strategies and market behaviours in the media sector. The spread of digital technology in the twenty-first century had a transformative impact on the industry (Küng, 2008; Napoli, 2011). Fragmentation of mass audiences and progressive empowerment of individuals to express preferences via the digital return path have fundamentally altered modes of interaction between the forces of demand and supply. Notwithstanding the ways that digitisation has reshaped the media landscape, the presence and availability of economies of scale and scope remain a dominant feature of the sector, and as discussed further below, this has major implications for the operational and corporate strategies that make sense in this distinctive industrial context.

10.3 Networks

On account of the high initial production costs that typify production of many forms of media content and the low marginal costs associated with facilitating additional consumption of that content, a strong incentive exists to extend consumption of any given content property as far and widely as possible. The urge to increase profits in this way is reflected in numerous different sorts of managerial strategies in the media industry, the fundamental aim of which is to spread per-consumer production costs across an extended audience base. The formation of networks, for example, in radio and television, is a prime example. A broadcasting network usually consists of a group of players located in distinct geographic regions who have entered into a strategic alliance in order to create and then exploit some mutual advantages, usually centred around shared use of content.

The media industry is not a 'typical' network industry because the array of economic structures and activities it encompasses extends beyond the systems of interconnections and links typically associated with network industries such as transport. Nonetheless, networks are a well-established and distinctive feature of traditional media industries. Moreover, as the spread of digital technology has brought media, communications and IT industries closer together, the role of networks has assumed far greater prominence in the converged order (Doyle, 2013). Therefore the ability to manage effectively in media industries has become increasingly dependent on understanding the distinctive economic features of networks and the different sorts of economic rationales that underlie the formation of networks.

Other types of networks have traditionally been characteristic in the media industry. In magazine publishing, networks of international players working in partnership to produce different local editions of a magazine under a contract-based arrangement are common (Doyle, 2006). An important feature of most magazine networks, and other such conventional media networks, is that they involve a unidirectional flow of content to consumers. Content flows from the centre to regional hubs and, from there, on to audiences. The main advantage of forming a conventional media network is that it allows shared use of content, brands and management expertise. Again, the formation of a geographically dispersed network of media outlets provides an effective means of spreading the high initial fixed costs involved in content creation across additional audience groups and constituencies that share an interest in that content and are situated in other localities. So the key economic incentive that lies behind the formation of a media network of this sort is predicated on supply-side economies of scale.

Setting aside media for a moment, most 'standard' network industries such as electricity supply, railways or telecommunications are constructed to facilitate traffic flow to and from all nodes in a reciprocal manner (Shy, 2003). When traffic is multidirectional rather than unidirectional, different sorts of benefits arise. Multidirectional networks are prone to 'network effects', sometimes called positive network externalities, and based on the idea that the value of a network will increase when others share it (Katz & Shapiro, 1985). Telecommunications is a good example: the more people that are signed up to participate in the service, the more valuable that service becomes. Network effects refer to the ways that higher or wider usage of certain products or services confer greater value for *all* users (Shapiro & Varian, 1999). For instance, when an extra member joins a business-related or professional online network such as LinkedIn, this confers a benefit on all other subscribers that have registered to use it. Likewise, beneficial network effects accrue to online social and communication networks such as Facebook and Twitter because the more people that use these services, the greater the utility for each network participant.

Metcalfe's law, named after computing engineer Robert Metcalfe, suggests a way of quantifying this benefit by proposing that the total value of, say, a telecommunications network is proportional to the square of the number of users connected to the system (Shapiro & Varian, 1999). Whether the value of individual users is actually as high as Metcalfe proposed is questionable, however. Recent work on applied network effect theory has suggested that this is an exaggeration (Odlyzko & Tilly, 2005). But there is no disputing the basic notion that extra participants add value to a communications network. And network benefits are not only based on opportunities for reciprocal communication; they often stem from technological compatibility. If many people have the equipment needed to be part of one sort of system, then others, in order to synchronise with the dominant technology, will want to invest in it too. Thus, network effects are especially endemic to computing and electronic industries.

A crucial point for media managers to take on board is that whereas supplying media to mass audiences has traditionally involved unidirectional traffic flows, network benefits are generally predicated on facilitating multidirectional traffic. As digital infrastructure supercedes analogue distribution, a return path is increasingly present and available to facilitate multidirectional flows of communication and content. In fact, digitisation has introduced new and successful players into the converged realms of media and communications whose *raison d'etre* is harnessing the benefits and advantages that stem from facilitating multidirectional flows. The rise of online social networking services such as Facebook, LinkedIn and Twitter demonstrates how the Internet can play a huge role in facilitating networks of users who want to engage in multiple conversations with each other.

It is important to observe that the economics of operating an online social network are different from running a conventional media network (Doyle, 2013). Online social networks are centred around sites (e.g. Facebook and China's Renren) where members are encouraged to generate individual personal profiles by uploading content such as videos and photos and posting text about themselves and their interests and opinions. Thus, a major difference between traditional media networks and online social networks is that in the latter the clear distinction between suppliers and consumers of content is blurred. While traditional media networks have to invest in creating or acquiring compelling original content, in social networking sites, members serve the role of both producers *and* consumers of content. Although audience attention can be monetised by the online social network owner, no cost burden stemming from the need to originate content will arise.

The business of running a social networking site is different from a conventional media network, but in both cases, growth of the network will generally bring significant benefits. Even though introducing extra traffic to digital networks adds marginally to distribution costs and on occasions may give rise to capacity problems, a range of incentives will propel network owners towards expansion (Doyle, 2013, p. 57). However, the nature of the economic incentives to expand the network is different for conventional one-to-many versus digitally interactive many-to-many networks. Social network sites benefit from 'network effects' in that the more people who join a social network, the greater its usefulness to each member because each will be able to communicate and interact with more people. For conventional media networks, the value of the service does not change simply because new audience members sign up, but instead, the chief advantage of wider participation is that it enables the high fixed costs involved in content production to be spread across more individual consumers. Of course, it is possible that bigger audiences can legitimate higher prices to advertisers.

As more and more traditional media companies—broadcasters and magazine publishers—respond to digital convergence by migrating towards strategies of content delivery that involve multiple delivery platforms including digital, a significant challenge is identifying how best to use two-way connectivity to their advantage, how to use return path data 'intelligently' (Gershon, 2011), and how best to capitalise on network effects as is the case for social networking sites.

10.4   Corporate Expansion and Diversification

The high initial investment and low marginal costs associated with facilitating additional consumption that typify the process of supplying media are strongly reflected in the corporate expansion and diversification strategies that managers in and across media industries are apt to deploy. Of course, propensities towards expansion may be motivated by alternative factors that have little to do with economics or profit maximisation. This is true of all sectors of industry—the desire to build empires may reflect personal or managerial agendas. But it is obviously a particularly relevant consideration in the context of media where control over the main channels for public communication is accompanied by significant political and cultural influence. Sánchez-Tabernero and Carvajal (2002, p. 83) have identified a variety of not only economic but also noneconomic factors which fuel an 'obsession' with enlarging company size, especially including political and psychological motives and pressure from investors. Expansion in the media sector is not always fuelled by economic motives and nor does it offer an assured route to increased profits.

That said, profit maximisation is frequently present as a fundamental motive guiding corporate strategy (Griffiths & Wall, 2007, p. 81). And in the media industry, the prevalence of economies of scale and scope has a major bearing on what sorts of corporate configurations make sense (Doyle, 2002). The imperative of exploiting the public good characteristics within media content and the need to spread per-consumer production costs across an extended audience base are reflected in a natural and persistent gravitation in media industries towards oligopoly and monopolisation. As numerous empirical studies have shown, a tendency towards highly concentrated levels of ownership is a widespread and common feature of media industries internationally (Noam, 2013).

The ongoing globalisation of media markets and the effects of convergence in blurring the boundaries between media and other industries have caused many firms to adapt their business and corporate strategies accordingly (Doyle, 2013). The logic of exploiting economies of scale—a natural feature of media industries as already discussed—creates an incentive to expand product sales into secondary, external or overseas markets. As market structures become more competitive and international in outlook, opportunities to exploit such economies have become increasingly alluring. Globalisation and convergence have created additional possibilities and incentives to repackage or to 'repurpose' media content into as many different formats as is technically and commercially feasible and to sell that product through as many distribution channels in as many geographic markets and to as many paying consumers as possible.

Sánchez-Tabernero and Carvajal also argued that the financial and managerial challenges associated with enlargement sometimes cause serious problems for media firms who, in the process, lose their focus and momentum (2002, pp. 84–87). Nonetheless, strategies of enlargement and diversification in the media often make a great deal of economic sense. Highly concentrated firms can spread production costs across wider product and geographic markets to benefit from natural economies of scale. Enlarged, diversified and vertically integrated groups appear well suited to exploit technological and other market changes sweeping across the media and communications industries.

Strategies of corporate growth can be divided into at least three different categories: horizontal, vertical and diagonal expansion. A 'horizontal' merger occurs when two firms who are in the same product market or engaged in the same activity combine forces. This allows firms to expand their market share and, usually, rationalise resources and gain economies of scale. Companies doing business in the same area can benefit from joining forces in a number of ways including, for example, by applying common managerial techniques or through greater opportunities for specialisation of labour as the firm increases in size (Griffiths & Wall, 2007, p. 79). In the media industry, the prevalence of economies of scale makes horizontal expansion a very popular and attractive strategy.

Vertical growth involves expanding either 'forward' into succeeding stages in the distribution chain or 'backward' into preceding stages in the supply chain. Vertically integrated media firms may have activities that span from creation of media output (which brings ownership of copyright) through to distribution or retail of that output in various guises. Vertical expansion generally results in reduced transaction costs for the enlarged firm (Lipsey & Chrystal, 2007, p. 116). But gaining more control over their operating environment and better guarding against losing market access in important 'upstream' or 'downstream' phases are also benefits that vertical integration provides firms, and these are generally of particular significance for media managers. A television production company that is vertically integrated into distribution has assured access to audiences. Likewise, a media distributor that expands upstream into production is assured of having a secure supply of content to disseminate via that infrastructure (Doyle, 2013).

Diagonal or 'conglomerate' expansion occurs when firms diversify into new business areas, often adjacent. For example, a merger between a telecommunications operator and a television company might generate efficiency gains as both sorts of services—audiovisual and telephony—are distributed jointly across the same distribution network. Newspaper publishers may expand diagonally into television broadcasting, or radio companies may diversify into magazine publishing. A myriad of possibilities exists for diagonal expansion across media and related industries. Such strategies often create economic gains and synergies, but not necessarily so. One possible benefit is that such expansion helps to spread risk. Large diversified media firms are, to some extent, cushioned against any damaging movements that may affect a single sector in which they are involved. More fundamentally however, the widespread availability of economies of scale and scope in the media means that strategies of diagonal expansion are generally apt to deliver very significant cost efficiencies.

In addition, many media firms have become transnational entities in recent years—i.e. corporations with a presence in many countries and (in some cases) an increasingly decentralised management structure. Globalisation has encouraged media operators to look beyond the local or home market as a way of expanding their consumer base horizontally and of extending their economies of scale. UK media conglomerate EMAP, for example, acquired several magazine publishing operations in France in the mid-1990s to become the second largest player in that market, before itself being taken over by German publisher Bauer in 2007. US publisher Hearst acquired the substantial magazine publishing interests of French media conglomerate Lagardère in 2011 and is pursuing further opportunities for international expansion in emerging economies such as China, Latin America and India (Gelles, 2011).

A desire to exploit the public good characteristics within media content drives all of these enlargement strategies. Diversified and large-scale media organisations are in a good position to squeeze additional value out of content assets and other common resources across different product and geographic markets. This is not to deny the potentially numerous difficulties and challenges associated with management of enlarged and multifaceted enterprises (Sánchez-Tabernero & Carvajal, 2002, pp. 84–87). In terms of profit performance, the financial pitfalls and managerial complexities associated with expansion and diversification may sometimes outweigh the benefits that might be realised through economies of scale and scope (Kolo & Vogt, 2003), at least in the short term. Even so, large, diversified and transnational entities are at least potentially better able to reap the economies of scale and scope that are naturally present in the media industry and which, thanks to globalisation and convergence, have become even more pronounced.

10.5   Management of Risk

Creation of media products and services typically requires sizeable initial investments in production. At the same time, processes of media content creation involve elements of novelty and risk and, therefore, uncertainty about likely demand for an as-yet-unproduced item of content. That is a fact of life that managers in media content production industries live with daily. Because a creative product is an 'experience good', the extent to which it will please and satisfy is a subjective matter and 'nobody knows' how consumers will respond or what will work (Caves, 2000, p. 3). Publishers, television production companies and filmmakers are obliged to take on major risks. So, on account of uncertainty about demand, managers in the media industry must routinely deploy a number of strategies aimed at reducing risks.

Of course content production does not necessarily have to be expensive. The spread of digital technology has made it feasible to produce and distribute media content at a much lower cost than in the past. The Internet is a repository for vast amounts of user-generated digital content, most of which has been created at extremely low cost. Because digitisation has reduced content production costs, some have argued that publishing no longer entails the same high levels of risk and uncertainty as in the past (Shirky, 2010). It is suggested that low production costs and free copying of digital files mean that virtually anyone can publish anything, and in consequence, quality-based decisions about what should or should not be produced are now unnecessary.

Although it is true that the Internet has made publishing of low-cost and less popular content items for micro-audiences much more feasible than in the past (Aris & Bughin, 2009, p. 101) and moreover that some conventional suppliers have clearly suffered from the rise of online alternatives—especially in news, it would appear that overall patterns of media consumption continue to strongly favour expensive professionally crafted content. We see this in popular television shows such as *Mad Men* and *The Big Bang Theory* that succeed more readily than most low-cost user-produced alternatives. So the conventional model of publishing which is based on high initial investment and hopes of wide distribution to yield economies of scale still predominates in the digital era, and thus the pressure on media managers to use strategies which counteract risk is as great as ever.

In other industries such as an investment where uncertainty is endemic, an approach commonly used by managers looking to spread risk involves a portfolio strategy. The same approach can be found for example in television and radio, where broadcasters routinely offer audiences a range of products (elements of programming), with some parts of the schedule designed to appeal to some audiences and others to a different group of individuals (Blumler & Nossiter, 1991, pp. 12–13; Collins et al., 1988, p. 11). The use of portfolio strategies by broadcasters has grown in recent years as digital compression techniques have multiplied the number of distribution channels available to them and facilitated new strategies based on more extensive diversification and targeted development of content. For instance, the range of channels offered by ITV (ITV1, ITV2, ITV3 and ITV4) provides an example whereby each somewhat differentiated service is designed to extend exposure of ITV content to a different set of individuals. Since uncertainty exists about which channels, strands or items of content will perform better than others, a portfolio approach enables the broadcaster to disseminate an array of elements based on the expectation that the success of a few will subsidise the provision of all—and generate a suitable profit. The strength of individual elements—the ones that happen to hit with popular taste—spreads risk and equalises costs across a range of total output that is designed to generate the greatest possible audience value or appeal.

The use of content portfolio strategies is widespread across the media and, for example, most major magazine publishers such as IPC, Bauer, Time Inc. and Hachette Filipacchi offer not just one or two but rather an extensive range of different titles. The more risky the business, the more compelling the case for reliance on portfolios. Such strategies are common, for example, in book and music publishing where commercial prospects are often subject to the vagaries of fashion or to fads that are difficult to predict and impossible to control. Management of the portfolio is not simply about countering risk by developing as wide an array of products as possible, but rather the manager's function is to intervene—to discriminate and filter—so those innovations and product ideas which are most likely to succeed will receive an appropriate level of backing and attention (Aris & Bughin, 2009, p. 97).

Thus, the hit-or-miss nature of the business of supplying a product such as a feature film or a television programme requires risk mitigation. Hoskins, McFadyen and Finn (1997) explained how risks and uncertainties associated with generating high-cost audiovisual content could be offset through such tactics as using sequels. The use of sequels and series that build on successful formats, as well as the use of the 'star' system, helps build brand loyalty amongst audiences and thereby promote higher and more stable revenue streams (Bielby & Bielby, 1994; Caves, 2005). Another strategy that enables the risk involved in developing new products to be managed and mitigated is to lease the rights for a programme format that is already successfully established elsewhere for domestic production (Esser, 2010; Kretschmer and Singh, 2009).

The film industry is characterised by both high costs and extreme uncertainty about the revenue prospects for any new production. Many scholars have focused on effective management of risk as being key to the success of the Hollywood majors in dominating international trade (De Vany, 2004). The key to the risk reduction strategies of Hollywood is control over distribution plus the ability to supply a copious well-funded product. The ability of the majors to support and replenish a large portfolio of film output depends on being able to fully exploit new and old hits, as with the music industry. This is now potentially under threat from growth of the Internet and—associated with this—growth in illegal copying.

10.6 Conclusions

The question of what is 'special' about the management of media can be addressed from a number of angles, but an essential starting point is to recognise that media, as a primary vector for our thoughts, ideas and understanding of the wider world, is inherently different from other sectors. Central to the complexity of managing media is that, whether willingly foregrounded by media businesses or not, decisions about how best to allocate the resources involved in supplying media to mass audiences may be imbued with significant sociocultural and welfare implications. But even so, with that as a given, the issues that are distinctive to management of media also clearly stem from specific *economic* attributes of media outputs and markets that mark this sector out as comparatively unique. The purpose of this chapter has been to introduce some of the key economic characteristics and peculiarities that underlie operational realities, an understanding of which helps to make sense of business and corporate strategies that are prevalent in media industries.

Differing sectors of the media of course have their own special attributes but, in general, reliance on technology is a widely shared feature. As industries, the media are strongly affected by new advances in how content may be produced, distributed and consumed. Each major evolutionary step—from the invention of the printing press, to the arrival of broadcasting, to the spread of the Internet—has brought both upheaval and opportunity for market incumbents. The spread of digital technologies is significant today and has brought with it a host of commercial and creative possibilities and created a variety of new challenges and problems for media managers. Despite changing technology and widening market access, however, many aspects of the economics of content provision remain both distinctive and unchanged.

While the struggle to discover how to make the most of advances in technology is a perpetual challenge for media industries, it is evident that the structure of markets and the interactions and behaviours of organisations in this sector are frequently shaped by a core set of economic issues with characteristic features. This chapter has focused attention on some of the most important: the prevalence of high initial or 'first-run' production costs and, on account of the public good characteristics of media content, relatively low marginal distribution costs which, in turn, give rise to economies of scale and scope. Despite changing patterns of media usage, the presence of these particular economic attributes can be discerned and attributed as the basis for many typical operational, business and corporate strategies deployed in and across media industries. The examples discussed in this chapter—network formation, corporate expansion and risk-spreading—while not exhaustive are intended to highlight the inescapable relationship between decisions about how to manage media resources effectively and awareness of their distinctive economic characteristics.

References

Albarran, A. (1996). *Media economics: Understanding markets, industries and concepts.* Iowa: Iowa State University Press.

Aris, A., & Bughin, J. (2009). *Managing media companies: Harnessing creative value* (2nd ed.). Chichester: Wiley.

Bielby, W., & Bielby, D. (1994). All hits are flukes: Institutionalized decision making and the rhetoric of prime-time program development. *American Journal of Sociology, 99*(5), 1287–1313.

Blumler, J., & Nossiter, T. (Eds.). (1991). *Broadcasting finance in transition: A comparative handbook*. Oxford: Oxford University Press.

Caves, R. (2000). *Creative industries: Contracts between art and commerce*. Cambridge, MA: Harvard University Press.

Caves, R. (2005). *Switching channels: Organization and change in TV broadcasting*. Cambridge, MA: Harvard University Press.

Collins, R., Garnham, N., & Locksley, G. (1988). *The economics of television: The UK case*. London: Sage.

De Vany, A. (2004). *Hollywood economics: How extreme uncertainty shapes the film industry*. London: Routledge.

Doyle, G. (2002). *Media ownership: The economics and politics of convergence and concentration in the UK and european media*. London: Sage.

Doyle, G. (2006). Managing global expansion of media products and brands: A case study of FHM. *International Journal on Media Management, 8*(3), 105–115.

Doyle, G. (2013). *Understanding media economics* (2nd ed.). London: Sage Publications.

Doyle, G., & Frith, S. (2006). Methodological approaches in media management and media economics research. In A. Albarran, S. Chan-Olmsted, & M. Wirth (Eds.), *Handbook of media management and economics* (pp. 553–572). Mahwah, NJ: Lawrence Erlbaum Associates.

Esser, A. (2010). Television formats: Primetime staple, global market. *Popular Communication, 8*(4), 273–292.

Gelles, D. (2011, October 24). Hearst to diversify revenues with emerging market push. *Financial Times,* 17.

Gershon, R. (2011). Intelligent networks and international business communication: A systems theory interpretation, Issue 12, *Media Markets Monographs*. Pamplona: Servicio de Publicaciones de la Universidad de Navarra.

Griffiths, A., & Wall, S. (Eds.). (2007). *Applied economics* (11th ed.). London: Pearson.

Hoskins, C., McFadyen, S., & Finn, A. (1997). *Global television and film: An introduction to the economics of the business*. Oxford: Oxford University Press.

Katz, M., & Shapiro, C. (1985). Network externalities, competition, and compatibility. *American Economic Review, 75*, 424–440.

Kolo, C., & Vogt, P. (2003). Strategies for growth in the media and communication industry: Does size really matter? *International Journal on Media Management, 5*(4), 251–261.

Kretschmer, M., & Singh, S. (2009). The paradox of TV formats. Why pay for something that is free? In: *1st Annual Workshop of International Society for the History and Theory of Intellectual Property*, Milan, Italy, 26–27 June 2009

Küng, L. (2008). *Strategic management in the media: Theory to practice*. London: Sage.

Lipsey, R., & Chrystal, A. (2007). *Positive economics* (11th ed.). Oxford: Oxford University Press.

Napoli, P. (2011). *Audience evolution: New technologies and the transformation of media audiences*. New York, NY: Columbia University Press.

Noam, E. (Ed.) (2013, Forthcoming). *Media concentrations around the world*. Oxford: Oxford University Press.

Odlyzko, A., & Tilly, B. (2005). *A refutation of Metcalfe's Law and a better estimate for the value of networks and network interconnections*. http://www.dtc.umn.edu/odlyzko/doc/networks.html.

OFCOM. (2012, December 13). *International Communications Market Report*. London: Ofcom.

Peacock, A. (1989). Introduction. In G. Hughes, & D. Vines (Eds.), *Deregulation and the Future of Commercial Television*. (pp. 1–8) (David Hume Institute Paper No. 12). Aberdeen: Aberdeen University Press.

Picard, R. (1989). *Media economics: Concepts and issues*. London: Sage.

Picard, R. (2005). Unique characteristics and business dynamics of media products. *Journal of Media Business Studies, 2*(2), 61–69.

Rochet, J., & Tirole, J. (2003). Platform competition in two-sided markets. *Journal of the European Economic Association, 1*(4), 990–1029.

Sánchez-Tabernero, A., & Carvajal, M. (2002). *Media concentrations in the European market, new trends and challenges* (Media Markets Monograph). Pamplona, Spain: Servicio de Publiciones de la Universidad de Navarra.

Shapiro, C., & Varian, H. (1999). *Information rules: A strategic guide to the network economy.* Cambridge: Harvard Business School Press.

Shirky, C. (2010). *Cognitive surplus: Creativity and generosity in a connected age.* New York, NY: Penguin Press.

Shy, O. (2003). *The economics of network industries.* Cambridge: Cambridge University Press.

Wirth, M., & Bloch, H. (1995). Industrial organization theory and media industry analysis. *Journal of Media Economics, 8*(2), 15–26.

Withers, K. (2006). *Intellectual property and the knowledge economy.* London: Institute for Public Policy Research.

Entrepreneurial Venturing and Media Management

11

Andreas Will, Dennis Brüntje, and Britta Gossel

> *If nature has made any one thing less susceptible than all other of exclusive property, it is the action of the thinking power called an idea, which an individual may exclusively possess as long as he keeps it to himself; but the moment it is divulged, it forces itself into the possession of everyone, and the receiver cannot dispossess himself of it. [. . .]*
> Thomas Jefferson, *1813 in Quah, 2003, p. 14.*

11.1 Introduction

Recent developments in the media industries—foremost those caused by progress in information and communication technologies (McKelvie & Picard, 2008)—create increasing opportunities for the market entry of innovative media ventures even in established media industries. These ventures might be start-ups like Spotify (2012) with its "freemium" streaming model for online music listening or Readmill (2012) that connects e-books and digital social networks. Media ventures might be spin-offs of existing units or new business units launched by large, established media companies, as the examples of Hulu (2013) (Disney, News Corp. and NBC Universal) and Watchever (2013) (Vivendi) illustrate. These firms and business units might threaten the business models of other established media firms, which in turn will have to answer the challenge. Novel business models would have been hardly imaginable for media industries some years ago and are fuelled by the dramatically rising speed of innovation in the media industries overall. We contend that entrepreneurial venturing is a suitable mean of acting in highly innovative environments and this is one significant area that makes the practice of media management comparatively unique today.

Undoubtedly, media management practice and entrepreneurship are drawing closer and are more interconnected—in short, the practice of media management is becoming entrepreneurial. Thus, the question arises: What is special about *entrepreneurial* media management? The answers are situated in the context of

A. Will (✉) • D. Brüntje • B. Gossel
Institute for Media and Communication Science, University of Technology Ilmenau, Ilmenau, Germany
e-mail: andreas.will@tu-ilmenau.de; dennis.bruentje@tu-ilmenau.de; britta.gossel@tu-ilmenau.de

© Springer International Publishing Switzerland 2016
G.F. Lowe, C. Brown (eds.), *Managing Media Firms and Industries*, Media Business and Innovation, DOI 10.1007/978-3-319-08515-9_11

highly innovative and fast-changing media markets. It is useful to think more deeply about the interconnections between media management and entrepreneurship research and see what can be learned from these interconnections that matters for improved understandings, description and analysis of novel media ventures in the digital era. That is the focus of this chapter.

Media management research is still dominated by a focus on existing (and mostly large) enterprises operating in (assumed) discrete media markets and industries, most notably books, TV, radio and various new media platforms. This division of the media by sectors and as discrete industries has proven useful for describing the historic structure of media markets and is a good starting point for explaining key challenges the traditional media industries face. However, when media management research strives to analyse the creation of innovative media ventures, an industry-sector focus is too narrow. Traditional boundaries between industry sectors no longer determine or restrict the formation of new media ventures. For example, an online news platform operated by a TV or radio station, by a print publisher or by any other operator contains text, picture, video and audio content, but is not a newspaper, a television channel or a radio station. Thus, the question arises as to how we can better describe and explain those new ventures.

As new media ventures are vitally important for both start-up media enterprises and established media firms, the approach taken in this chapter holds promise for the field as a whole in thinking through and about industry development. Based upon a detailed literature review, we aim to identify crucial characteristics of entrepreneurial media ventures and to provide a conceptual framework for describing and explaining the creation of new media ventures in the digital era.

We start by an examination of current research about the interconnections between media management and entrepreneurship. We then discuss our perspective on entrepreneurship with a keen focus on entrepreneurial opportunities. In Sect. 11.4 we introduce our perspective on media management with emphasis on digital media products. In Sect. 11.5 we connect both perspectives and offer recommendations for future research, before drawing conclusions.

11.2 Media Management and Entrepreneurship: Two Fields of Research that Need Integration

In Schumpeterian terms (1943), start-ups feature an entrepreneurial, innovative spirit with considerable potential for creative destruction in the media industries. van Weezel (2010, p. 47) supports this presumption: "creative destruction is the reason why we see traditional business models of media companies crumbling". While accepting that historic success often limits the will of larger and older media firms to think in new ways because of perceived threats and also accepting that these firms are often complicated and that makes entrepreneurial efforts difficult, all kinds and sizes of media firms are nevertheless required to redevelop in the digital environment.

Obviously, this argument holds true for businesses other than in media, but we believe that for media industries the requirements for change are very high, arguably to a unique degree. For most industries their products are essentially the same even when production and delivery are coordinated by software and even if a customer can configure his or her dream model digitally. But in the media industry, the product itself is becoming digital and *dematerialised* to a degree that is unusual. Of course some media products have been nonmaterial when consumed, such as TV signals, but most have depended on some physical basis (a film, a tape, a book, a newspaper, etc).

Due to instability, fast-changing environments and much greater difficulty in achieving a mass media situation, the media across sectors are now faced with the need to become entrepreneurial. Larger and older media companies that find this impossible should be concerned about dooming themselves to decline. Thus, they need to succeed at entrepreneurial activities, and in our view they can. Our examination of entrepreneurial activities is limited to two stages, the concept-formation stage and the market entry stage, because we are interested here in new media ventures. Nor do we highlight the role of the individual entrepreneur or the motivational aspects for starting a business or identifying and exploiting opportunities. That would require more space than we have to work with, and would obscure the focus we intend. Here the entrepreneurial organisation is the essential point of focus.

The first major efforts to introduce research on entrepreneurship into the field of media management were achieved by Hang and van Weezel (2007) and by Achtenhagen (2008). Achtenhagen (2008) conceptualised and explored the phenomenon in traditional media industries and showed that nowadays it is still possible that sustainable entrepreneurial ventures can emerge in traditional media firms. The study by Hang and van Weezel (2007) remains the most thorough and systematic overview of the media entrepreneurship literature published from 1971 to 2005. They found that two-thirds of the 78 relevant studies appeared in the latter part of the period, between 2000 and 2005, which means that research about the link between media and entrepreneurship is recent but increasing. The strong relevance of entrepreneurship research for media management studies should not be surprising because "the essential characteristics of the entrepreneurial activities such as creation, innovation and novel ways of thinking are critical in building media business success" (Hang & van Weezel, 2007, p. 51). But their research limited "its scope to the traditional forms of media, leaving out the Internet as a medium" (Hang & van Weezel, 2007, p. 54). Therefore, entrepreneurial media management in the digital era is underdeveloped.

Hang and van Weezel (2007) concluded that entrepreneurship research in media industries is unevenly distributed. From the media management perspective, certain media industries including newspapers, film and music have been investigated more frequently than others (e.g. radio). From the entrepreneurship research perspective, specific phenomena have been preferred (e.g. innovation, creativity, the role of the entrepreneur), while others are only rarely and insufficiently examined (e.g. entrepreneurial opportunities, entrepreneurial orientation, the financing of entrepreneurs). "This uneven distribution might [...] be caused by the nature of media industry and entrepreneurship (e.g. family business is a frequent topic in newspapers, while financing entrepreneurs is likely to be a common issue in the film industry)" (Hang & van Weezel, 2007, p. 62f). Although important, this means that insight about the peculiarities of the creation of innovative media ventures in the digital era is lacking.

Hoag (2008) concluded that existing entrepreneurship studies of media are mostly either micro level or industry level. The earlier study by Hoag and Compaine (2007) underlines this observation: with respect to the products and services offered, media entrepreneurs are subdivided into categories according to the historic pattern of differentiating between media industries. Even earlier, Hoag and Seo (2005) found that big media corporations may be innovative organisations but are not entrepreneurial on an individual level. Hass (2011) countered this, however. But although disruptive technologies like the Internet provide additional opportunities for new entrants in the media industries, the majority of entrepreneurial activities still take place within established firms. The emergence of new media ventures like Spotify (2012) and Readmill (2012) are kicking up dust in the media industry with their innovative business models, and that merits research as well.

Recently Compaine and Hoag (2012) analysed 30 media entrepreneurs, focusing on factors affecting entry in media markets. Other than noting the importance of few existing barriers, they emphasised two outstanding factors of support: "the effects of technological innovation and so-called 'big media', which far from erecting barriers can be a major source of opportunity" (Compaine & Hoag, 2012, p. 27). These examples show the controversy in scientific discussion about new ventures entering the media industries.

Furthermore, van Weezel (2010) sought explanations about why research in media management mainly focuses on big companies in the media sector instead of nascent ventures and small firms. He suggested that, first, large organisations seem more exciting for researchers who presume that such study leads to more important implications. Second, data on large firms are more easily available, a fact that is especially important for the prevalent quantitative approaches in media management and economics research. Third, the influence of established theories in media economics (especially industrial organisation) has shaped the way researchers approach media firms and the industries in which they compete. van Weezel (2010) recommended conducting studies about small media firms and applying consistent research methods, including qualitative and mixed methods (i.e. triangulation). The authors discussed in so far several interconnections between the research fields of media management and entrepreneurship, but a conceptual framework connecting the two perspectives on a theoretical level does not yet exist.

Our conceptual framework adopts a broad understanding of media and media ventures, encompassing not only start-ups operating in the traditional media sectors but also in new media. In emphasising the *creation of innovative media ventures*, we want to distinguish media ventures from other types of ventures in order to more usefully characterise the terms of innovation and to focus on the creation aspect. For this reason, our assumption is based on the key definitions of (a) media economics and (b) innovation.

Following Picard (1989, p. 9f), "media economics is concerned with how the media industries allocate resources to create information and entertainment contents to meet the needs of audiences, advertisers, and other societal institutions". In our argumentation we emphasise specialties of digital media products and their consequences for new media firms. But in classical definitions of media ventures, a consideration of the digital value chain is missing. For example, according to Wirtz (2006, p. 11, own translation), a media venture is defined as a "methodically organised economic unit [. . .], packaging made or bought editorial content (informational or entertainment content), transforming those contents to a storage-capable carrier medium, and directly or indirectly distributing it". However, the distinctive aspects of an entirely digital value chain and business creation process are not in focus.

Thus, our understanding of a digital media venture follows the definition of an "e-venture" outlined by Kollmann (2011, p. 11, own translation): "An 'e-venture' can be assumed as a new venture originating within the Net Economy based upon an innovative business idea, which offers its products and/or services by utilising an entirely digital value chain delivered via electronic platforms and on data networks, presenting an offer enabled by the development of information technology". As regards "innovation", we employ a broad definition within parameters defined by Schumpeter (1964) and Barnett (1953). Both assume that innovation is a recombination of previously existing elements. While Schumpeter describes innovation as the new combination of existing resources, Barnett emphasises cognitive configurations: "An innovation is here defined as any thought, behaviour, or thing that is new because it is qualitatively different from existing forms" (Barnett, 1953 quoted in Röpke, 1977, p. 102). Thus, our argumentation does not focus (only) on technological innovation.

As current literature focuses on certain media industries or special entrepreneurial phenomena rather than exploring the interrelation between media and entrepreneurship in general, and having our initial assumptions of our introduction (see Sect. 11.1) in mind, a discrete observation of both fields seems promising. We start with a focused aspect of consideration in the entrepreneurship perspective.

11.3 The Entrepreneurship Perspective: Focusing Opportunities

Caught in crossfire of several influences from various disciplines, entrepreneurship research is not yet agreed on the key conceptualisation of the field. However, the most highly regarded definition of entrepreneurship was given by Shane and Venkataraman (2000): "Organization scholars are fundamentally concerned with three sets of research questions about entrepreneurship: (1) why, when, and how opportunities for the creation of goods and services come into existence; (2) why, when, and how some people and not others discover and exploit these opportunities; and (3) why, when, and how different modes of action are used to exploit entrepreneurial opportunities" (Shane & Venkataraman, 2000, p. 218).

Recently, Shane (2012, p. 12) noted that this definition—criticised as well as supported—is tending to become a consensus and pointed out that current research focuses especially on the "nexus of opportunities and individuals", as well as questions about "new combinations" (ibid, p. 18f). This leads to the concept of opportunities as a focal field of interest in entrepreneurship research. In their systematic literature review on the subject of "opportunity", one central problem identified by Frank and Mitterer (2009, p. 400) was that "the construct of opportunity with its complexity is not yet described in an appropriate way" (own translation). Nevertheless, two threads of discussion can be identified within the literature, which are in some sense alternatives: (1) the idea of pre-existing opportunities (discovery) and (2) the concept of opportunities as a result of entrepreneurial action (creation) (e.g. Alvarez & Barney, 2007; Berglund, 2007).

11.3.1 The Opportunity-Discovery Perspective

The assumption of pre-existing opportunities is an essential feature of the Austrian economic tradition. As one of the main representatives, Kirzner (1997) introduced the entrepreneurial discovery approach based on key elements first proposed by Mises (1949) and Hayek (1948). "From Mises the modern Austrians learned to see the market as an entrepreneurially driven process. From Hayek they learned to appreciate the role of knowledge and its enhancement through market interaction, for the equilibrative process" (Kirzner, 1997, p. 67).

The opportunity-discovery perspective covers both active and passive search. The assumption of a passive search was introduced in Kirzner's framework by the attribute of "alertness". Following his theoretical assumptions, he "focuses attention on the entrepreneur not as a creator, but as being merely alert" (Kirzner, 2009, p. 148). In this view, the entrepreneur "simply had to be alert to price differentials that others had not yet noticed" (Kirzner, 2009, p. 147). As well as being "merely alert", the entrepreneur is further assumed to have some presumably innate ability to identify opportunities without search (Kirzner, 1979).

Most of the research in the alertness perspective has been conducted on the basis of these characteristic assumptions. One example is the study of Gaglio and Katz (2001), who provided "a new translation of the concept of entrepreneurial alertness into its appropriate cognitive and psychological properties" (Gaglio & Katz, 2001, p. 96). A second example is the work of Kaish and Gilad (1991), who focused on the differences between managers and entrepreneurs in relation to their alertness and information-seeking behaviour. They suggest one broad conclusion: "Entrepreneurs do seem to expose themselves to more information and their alertness takes them to the less obvious places" (Kaish & Gilad, 1991, p. 59).

Active search in the opportunity-discovery framework is represented by the systematic search approach. Pre-existing opportunities are assumed here as well, but the systematic search approach is far from any assumption of surprise. Based on Stigler (1961), "in the case of systematic search, prospective entrepreneurs intentionally seek out entrepreneurial opportunities to the extent that the marginal benefits (information) gained by the search exceed the marginal costs (time) of conducting the search" (Smith, Matthews, & Schenkel, 2005). According to these assumptions, the search for opportunities is assumed to be strategic and deliberate. Several authors have conducted relevant empirical and theoretical work. Fiet (2007) developed a prescriptive model of entrepreneurial search and discovery. Patel and Fiet (2009) found a positive relationship between the use of systematic search and success in new venture creation. The difference between both approaches can be described by the following: "In fact, it should be possible to consider alertness and systematic search as they are practiced as being at opposite ends of a continuum, depending on how deliberate and systematic were the actions of the entrepreneur" (Patel & Fiet, 2009, p. 504).

11.3.2 The Opportunity-Creation Perspective

As introduced by Berglund (2007) and by Alvarez and Barney (2007), the -opportunity-creation perspective follows a radical subjectivist tradition and is contrary to the realistic view of the discovery perspective. The key difference lies in their assumptions about the nature of opportunity. The discovery perspective assumes that opportunities pre-exist and are awaiting discovery (opportunity is independent of the entrepreneur), whereas the creation perspective assumes that opportunities do not exist without the entrepreneur—the entrepreneur actually creates opportunity. "Search implies entrepreneurs attempting to discover opportunities—like mountains—that already exist. In creation theory, entrepreneurs do not search—for there are no mountains to find—they act, and observe how consumers and markets respond to their actions" (Alvarez & Barney, 2007, p. 131). The works of Dimov (2007, 2010) and Sarasvathy (2001, 2008) are leading sources in creation theory. Sarasvathy concluded that "these opportunities are a result of the efforts of particular entrepreneurs striving to construct stable economic and sociological institutions, including the organizations and markets we see in the world"

(Sarasvathy, 2008, p. 178). Dimov (2007) suggested an elaboration of the opportunity concept as a creative product, seeing opportunity development in a creative context as a social learning process.

Focusing our key question on the creation of new media ventures with respect to these theoretical perspectives on opportunities, the aspect of information seems to be of enduring concern (e.g. Grichnick, 2006, p. 1308). The results of Shane (2000) can be seen as one example from the discovery perspective: "differences in prior information influence who discovers entrepreneurial opportunities" (Shane, 2000, p. 467). In this view, media entrepreneurs are engaged in a search for opportunities that exist but have not yet been discovered, and do so either as a function of trained alertness or by a systematic method (or some combination). While that certainly has merit in many respects, one could ask: "If these opportunities exist, and could be exploited right away, why have they not already been exploited?" (Casson & Wadeson, 2007, p. 286). These authors answer the question from a cost-oriented viewpoint: "The misunderstanding arises because the costs of discovery have been ignored. More opportunities could be discovered if more resources were devoted to their discovery. But diminishing returns are liable to set in" (Casson & Wadeson, 2007, p. 286). All of this clearly has relevance to the "search for weak signals" school of thought (e.g. Day & Schoemaker, 2006).

Clearly it is important to recognise that entrepreneurs do not always or only discover opportunities, but are actively engaged in the creative work of making opportunities in the first place. The question that is most pertinent for media managers is the extent to which companies are, in the first instance, actively searching out opportunities as a routine practice and, in the second, actively engaged in creating opportunities as well. The answer to that question goes to the heart of where and how scholarship on media management and entrepreneurship connect, and suggests why the integration of the two fields matters for practice. Keeping these assumptions in mind, a deeper analysis of the media management perspective is requested.

11.4   The Media Management Perspective: Digital Media Products

Turning to the media management perspective, the focus of this section is on digital media products and their characteristics, providing a link to the discovery and creation perspective of entrepreneurial opportunities discussed above. Undoubtedly, the market will see novel media products and new media ventures based upon traditional production processes, distribution channels or carriers. Nevertheless, it can be assumed that the vast majority and the most important and sustainable innovations will be digital media products based upon a digital value chain. Thus, it is important to understand the distinctive characteristics of digital media products. For the purpose of a clear analysis, we assume a completely digital value chain, and we do not take into consideration any obstacles that media firms face while transiting from the analogue to the digital world.

The constituting characteristic of a digital product is its representation by a digitally stored bit string; moreover, the product itself is "a payoff-relevant bit string, i.e. a sequence of binary digits, 0 s and 1 s, that affect the utility of or payoff to some individual in the economy" (Quah, 2003, p. 6). Thinking of a simplified three-step chain of creating, producing/bundling and distributing digital products, the digital representation starts at the very beginning of creation and continues through the value chain to the crossroads of digital or "traditional" delivery (the latter not to be examined in this chapter).

With respect to entrepreneurial opportunities, digital products play a double role as input and output of entrepreneurial venturing (cf. Quah, 2003, p. 7ff). (1) On the input side of the value chain, they represent—on a quite general level—(new) ideas, technical concepts or human knowledge. They arrive as, e.g. patent specifications, technical standards, scientific journal articles and software codes. As inputs to the production function, they "feed" the process of value creation in the economy. They especially provide means and tools operationalised by encoding and decoding software, which allow bit strings to be consumed by end users on the demand side of the economy. Given this, digital products can be seen as pre-existing opportunities which can be searched after, discovered and combined by entrepreneurs. And with the same arguments, they represent the result of the entrepreneurial creation of opportunities: condensed ideas as blueprints for new media ventures. (2) On the opposite side, at the output end of the value chain, digital (media) products represent, e.g. video games, movies, poems or symphonies, which can be played, viewed, read or heard, thereby meeting the information and/or entertainment needs of recipients—what traditionally (in the predigital era) would be associated with a willingness to pay for the ownership or usage of these products.

In the remainder of this section—following Quah (2003)—the characteristics of digital products are discussed, which can be derived from their representation as bit strings. These characteristics apply to, and affect, innovation and value creation on the input side and the consumers' utility on the output side. The representation as bit strings implies that "digital goods are non-rival, infinitely expansible, discrete, a-spatial, and recombinant" (Quah, 2003, p. 13).

11.4.1 Infinite Expansibility and A-Spatiality

At the end of the path of digitalisation, we can assume an *ideal* digital product which can be reproduced at zero time and zero cost (i.e. it has infinite expansibility); copies can be made available to everyone everywhere instantaneously (indicating a-spatiality). Obviously, a *real* digital product might have above zero, but very low time and costs of copying. The copy cannot be distinguished from the original product, meaning it is identical. In many cases, reality comes close to this ideal: copies of a product can reach millions of users worldwide without any relevant lack of quality within seconds (e.g. tweets) or hours (e.g. music files).[1] We concentrate on the ideal product, thereby contributing to a clear line of the following argumentation.

The characteristics cause a market equilibrium price of zero because at any place and instantaneously the product can be reproduced and made available at zero marginal cost. This means that making an additional unit (copy) does not cause an increase in the original cost of production. Under this condition the market is threatened by failure due to the nonrival aspect (treated below). The good is not diminished by consumption. For the ideal digital media product, the non-existence of a *perfect* competition market (industrial organisation theory) may imply that such a product will not be produced at all. To keep it simple, there is no market for uncovered, unprotected bit strings. Traditional answers to this problem have tried to restrict access to digital media products, for example, by means of digital rights management, encryption and paywalls (changing a public good into a club good) without dismissing the old idea of the now digitally represented product as the good to be sold. The observable weakness of such solutions (e.g. in the newspaper or recording industry) leaves media management with the great and still open challenge of finding business models beyond selling digital bit strings. In this sense and following the discovery perspective of entrepreneurship, "free" media products could not be seen as a problem, but as easily available inputs used in novel business models, as entrepreneurial opportunities for new media ventures.

11.4.2 Nonrivalry

The use of a copy of an infinitely expansible digital media product (reproduced at zero marginal cost) does not affect the use of any other copy of the product. As Kollock pointed out in a technical argument: "one person's use of the information in no way diminishes what is available for someone else" (Kollock, 1999, p. 4). For the input side of the value chain, it can be concluded that using an idea or any freely available digital product as input to value creation cannot prevent any other entrepreneur from using the same idea for the same or another purpose. We do not state that literally every idea will become a nonrival digital product (e.g. it might be secured behind the boundary of a firm). But once an idea has entered the public domain as a digital good, nonrivalry conditions rule and any firm could use the idea for their respective purposes.

On the output side of the value chain, the same argumentation holds true: consuming a digital media product will not affect the satisfaction of another consumer's need. An additional reader of an online newspaper or an additional user of a search engine does not affect the usage of any other consumer. More

---

[1] A major restriction of free distribution is governmental prohibition of access—and punishment when prohibition is bypassed.

strongly stated, we know that due to network effects the value of information for one person can even increase with the number of persons having received (a copy of) the same information. In other words, information is sometimes more valuable when shared than when exclusive. Obviously, nonrivalry applies to traditional analogue broadcast media. But while in the analogue era it was restricted to the output of a limited number of TV and radio channels with their specific characteristics, in the digital era nonrivalry is predominant for every single digital media product.[2] Again, media management faces the challenge of finding business models dealing with the problem of nonrivalry. And again, we presume that entrepreneurship may help find solutions to this challenge, namely, by the creation of novel and individual media services which can be built upon the last characteristic of digital products, the ease of recombination.

11.4.3 Recombination

Digital products are easy to recombine and the recombination creates products of new or different quality. The larger the number of input products, the larger the number of possible recombined products. Thus, infinite expansibility and a-spatiality of digital products favour a broadening of range, number and speed for novel recombined products in media industries. Again, this characteristic applies to both digital products as inputs and outputs of the value chain. With respect to inputs, Weitzman (1998) described this as a process by which "knowledge can build upon itself in a combinatoric feedback process" (Weitzman, 1998, p. 331), suggesting "that the ultimate limits to growth may lie not so much in our abilities to generate new ideas, as in our abilities to process to fruition an ever increasing abundance of potentially fruitful ideas" (Weitzman, 1998, p. 359). This goes directly to the heart of innovation and entrepreneurship. With respect to digital media products, the broad span of recombination opportunities is obvious: from "copy and paste" plagiarism to novel business models built on recombination of content (e.g. music) with individual preferences generating immediately and ubiquitously a unique content stream or bundle, completely built upon pre-existing elements.

Consequently, we come to the key aspect that makes digital media products distinctive from non-media products: the product itself is digital and therefore dematerialised. Once having entered the public, it is unsaleable: a pure bit string can be made available everywhere and instantaneously at (nearly) zero costs. Thus, one conclusion is that media management under these conditions is closer to *service* management than to traditional *product* management. To lock the bit string behind

---

[2] By the nonrivalry argument, we do not state that digital distribution systems are per se cost-efficient, however. For example: in terms of costs, broadcasting might often enjoy superior advantages to peer-to-peer networks with their high infrastructure costs.

a paywall will not guarantee economic success. If only one identical copy is "free", the willingness to pay the entrance fee is greatly diminished. But an entrance fee to a superior service experience of personalised, convenient media usage can be an attractive offer for consumers, especially if time limitations constrain the will to search after and combine media products on their own. This may go along with a "digital revival" of the traditional editorial function as a service offering emphasising on selecting, sorting and bundling digital information. In a broader sense, a service offering will be valued if it is supporting consumers in constructing the "meaning behind the message", e.g. by building on revealed personal preferences concerning usage habits, genres, etc.

To summarise and connect the discussion so far, we elaborated the non-existence of a conceptual framework connecting the perspectives of media management and entrepreneurship on a theoretical level. This is the initial point of our argumentation: there is too little said about specialties of new media ventures, the specialties of their products and its consequences for the creation of new ventures in media industries. If we assume that media ventures are characterised by those specialties that make a difference in market position and performance, there is a need to highlight and segment those specialties of digital media products and their consequences for new media firms. According to our observation, constructs of an entirely digital value chain and business creation are missing in classical definitions of media ventures.

We next elaborated four distinctive characteristics of digital media products: An ideal digital product theoretically can be reproduced at zero time and zero cost (infinite expansibility). Copies can be made available to everyone everywhere instantaneously (a-spatiality). Furthermore, the use of any copy does not affect the use of any other copy of the products (nonrivalry). Finally, digital products are easy to recombine and the recombination creates products of new or different quality (recombination). We complemented these observations with discussion about two perspectives in entrepreneurship research related to the discovery or creation of new business opportunities. In the following section we will connect these perspectives on entrepreneurship with the media management perspective.

11.5 Connecting the Perspectives

As explained earlier, the constituting characteristic of a digital media product is its representation as a digitally stored bit string that applies and also affects innovation as well as value creation, and does so on both the input side where production happens and on the output side with respect to consumers' utility. This is pertinent to any discussion of a digital media economy. The discussed characteristics of digital media products indicate increased opportunities for innovative media ventures and suggest the following presumptions: (1) Infinite expansibility and a-spatiality make it comparatively easy for anybody with reasonable intelligence and experience to be aware of, search after, find and use ideas and concepts that offer opportunities for media business development. (2) Infinite expansibility also implies nonrivalry, and thus, using an idea as input to one firms' production function does not prevent another firm from using the same idea[3] for the same or another purpose. Of course there are copyright and intellectual property issues, which create barriers, but there are limits in that as well (e.g. a title cannot be copyrighted, and a format can be used after appropriate modification). (3) Finally, the infinite expansibility and a-spatiality of digital products also favour the range, number and speed of novel recombined products. Hence, the infinite expansibility and a-spatiality affect both nonrivalry and recombination so that the four characteristics of digital media products are inherently integrated. Looking at current developments in media industry development, we observe that new media ventures are virtually built on this construct, as evident, for example, in Spotify (2012) with their freemium streaming model for online music listening and Readmill (2012), which brings together e-books and digital social networks.

This is suggestive for how media management can affect the opportunities for entrepreneurialism in media industries and offers a good starting point for introducing media management into the field of entrepreneurship research. But what can media management learn from entrepreneurship research that is especially important? We presented the two central perspectives that dominate the scientific discussion in this field. The opportunity-discovery perspective assumes that opportunities already exist independently from the entrepreneur and have to be discovered, ascribing to the entrepreneur two ends of a continuum: the attributes of better alertness and strategies for systematic search. The opportunity-creation perspective instead assumes that entrepreneurs create opportunities. We adhere to the second perspective and propose that the alertness and systematic search of an entrepreneur is not enough, although it is required as one important element. The entrepreneur should be understood as a "composer" and a "creator" of business ideas, here typified as recombination of self-created opportunities and, we suggest, are empowered by the highlighted characteristics of digital media products.

This brings us back to the quoted statement from Thomas Jefferson at the beginning of this chapter. Jefferson believed that as soon as an idea is published or professed, it forces itself into the possession of everyone. Although the degree to which incorporation of the idea is actually "forced" versus "adapted" is arguable, the essential notion is useful. In our view, ideas and concepts represented as and in digital media products are observable and recombinable and therefore offer more than ample opportunities for entrepreneurs to create (see also Gossel & Will, 2012, p. 321ff). Obviously, these increasing opportunities do not directly lead to success in media venture creation. Recognised opportunities might not be pursued because the perceived risks are too large. Moreover, timing is an essential element in

---

[3] Ideas are naturally not capable of being protected (e.g. business ideas, format ideas). In contrast a concept (e.g. technological method, industrial design) can be patented or copyrighted. Apple and Samsung are proof of that, and earlier the legal battle over graphic interfacing between Apple and Microsoft. To protect format ideas, media companies draft the so-called production bibles that are copyrighted and cannot be infringed without courting penalty.

deciding when an opportunity is worth pursuing. Last but not least, other entrepreneurial success factors (e.g. entrepreneurial skills, motivation, flexibility, market knowledge) influence the probability of successfully starting a business. Nevertheless, the potential of recombination offers potentially more lucrative possibilities for creating business ideas, and these can increase exponentially, which seems especially true within media industries, for the creation of new business units as well as for spin-offs in large media companies.

The classic example from corporate media entrepreneurship is iTunes complementing the iPod. Apple did not invent legitimate digital music services from scratch. The components were already in existence in a variety of devices, music download services, early music industry initiatives and digital rights management experiments. However, Apple was able to bring all the elements together as an integrated business model, as a service offering with a viable user proposition. Importantly, that means Apple was able to make entrepreneurial decisions and do the deals required to make the business happen.

Furthermore, without these increased possibilities in observing and recombining digital media products, particularly new media ventures such as Spotify (2012) or Readmill (2012) would not have been imaginable even several years ago. Both start-ups were keen enough to face big challenges of their respective media industry, e.g. piracy in the music business and lacking innovation in the e-book market, by developing new and innovative business models and services. Music catalogues, playlists, social media, sharing options and streaming technologies were not invented by Spotify, but this start-up succeeded in observing and recombining these components to create an innovative business model, whose core is the use of streaming as distribution model and reliance on a freemium pricing model. Free access to the main features accounts for a fast-growing user base. A large number of users create network effects and an active community. Incentives encourage users to subscribe to the premium features, e.g. offline listening. Thus, premium users pay for a superior service and user experience (but not for "bit strings" per se—in other words, they pay for the well-prepared meal, not for the immaterial ingredients).

Books, libraries, social media, recommendation systems, cloud technology, e-reading technology and usability were not novel concepts for *Readmill*. But combining these elements under the umbrella of reading, discovering and sharing book contents created a unique entrepreneurial business idea: to service as an intermediary between authors, publishers, e-book stores and readers. The service is completely free of charge to users. The revenue model is based on an affiliate programme for bookstores and publishers, enabling publishers to learn much more about the interests of their readers (Wohlert, 2011). Due to the competitive situation on the e-book market today, it remains to be seen if this model will be successful (e.g. Amazon, further social reading platforms, etc.), but that does not detract from the example's relevance.

11.6   Recommendations

As a conclusion, we want to give final recommendations for research as well as for practice in media management and entrepreneurship.

Media management research and entrepreneurship research need to explore and develop the interrelation between the fields. Both research communities should engage much more in reciprocal learning processes. On a conceptual level, media management research should focus more on the emergence of new media ventures—in start-ups as well as established media firms. Entrepreneurship research should do more to address media products and services and to investigate relevant phenomena in media industries. The Internet has fuelled an astonishing number and variety of new media ventures in the last decade. Research in entrepreneurship and media management would mutually benefit from investigating media venture creation.

Of course we have only addressed the first two stages of idea and market entry for new media ventures because our focus has been on encouraging more attention to starting ventures. In further research later stages in the entrepreneurial process have to be considered as well. Certainly, more empirical research is needed using various methods, qualitative as well as quantitative. Furthermore, observations by many scholars of media and management indicate a blurring of boundaries that merits in-depth investigations.

Our work in this chapter also has implications for how media ventures ought to be managed in order to realise entrepreneurial intentions. Media managers need to be open-minded and to resist defensive logic; keen to observe apparently unconnected concepts, ideas and technologies; and active in developing connections. They can benefit from entrepreneurial thinking by developing their skills in the ability to recombine elements to create new and integrated business models: innovative bundles (such as creating superior service or user experience), novel forms of distribution or pricing models beyond selling bit strings (such as selling services, setting incentives to convert free users to paying customers or building upon a business-to-business pricing model).

This process of composing in the sense of recombining existing elements is precisely in line with assumptions in the opportunity-creation perspective: "Clearly, the creation of a new combination can be interpreted as the creation of an entrepreneurial opportunity" (Buenstorf, 2007, p. 325). It all starts with the "*seed of a new opportunity*" (Luksha, 2008, p. 275) represented by new ideas, beliefs or framings (Sarasvathy et al., 2003). Thereafter, "the organization, entrepreneur, or group thereof, frames or reframes an issue so that a potential new construct (new beliefs and new ideas) emerges" (Luksha, 2008, p. 275). Although the ingredients already exist, what is most important is figuring out to recombine them successfully, as our examples illustrate. "In opportunity creation neither the supply nor demand exists prior [. . .] instead the individual through their actions develops both the opportunity and the market" (Alvarez, Barney, & Young 2010, p. 30). This opens a wide field not only for the practice of media management but also for research in both media management and entrepreneurship.

What is recommended for media management, then, is learning to compose business ideas as an everyday practice and the ability to this as recombinant approach in pursuit of new self-created opportunities. This has not been sufficiently in the focus of media management, which is still strongly influenced by perspectives inculcated in the era of mass media. In short, then, what is special about media management is not only in its comparison with other industries (perhaps dominating media management research so far) but crucially lies in comparisons within this increasingly complex and complicated industry overall.

References

Achtenhagen, L. (2008). Understanding entrepreneurship in traditional media. *Journal of Media Business Studies, 5*(1), 123–142.

Alvarez, S. A., & Barney, J. B. (2007). Discovery and creation: Alternative theories of entrepreneurial action. *Organizações em context, 3*(6), 123–152.

Alvarez, S. A., Barney, J. B., & Young, S. L. (2010). Debates in entrepreneurship: Opportunity formation and implications for the field of entrepreneurship research. In Z. J. Acs & D. B. Audretsch (Eds.), *Handbook of entrepreneurship research: An interdisciplinary survey and introduction* (pp. 23–45). New York: Springer.

Barnett, H. G. (1953). *Innovation: The basis of cultural change.* New York: McGraw-Hill.

Berglund, H. (2007). Opportunities as existing and created: A study of entrepreneurs in the Swedish mobile internet industry. *Journal of Enterprising Culture, 15*(3), 243–273.

Buenstorf, G. (2007). Creation and pursuit of entrepreneurial opportunities: An evolutionary economic perspective. *Small Business Economics, 28*, 323–337.

Casson, M., & Wadeson, N. (2007). The discovery of opportunities: Extending the economic theory of the entrepreneur. *Small Business Economics, 28*, 285–300.

Compaine, B., & Hoag, A. (2012). Factors supporting and hindering new entry in media markets: A study of media entrepreneurs. *International Journal on Media Management, 14*(1), 27–49.

Day, G. S., & Schoemaker, P. J. H. (2006). *Peripheral vision: Detecting the weak signals that will make or break your company.* Boston, MA: Harvard Business School Press.

Dimov, D. (2007). Beyond the single-person, single-insight attribution in understanding entrepreneurial opportunities. *Entrepreneurship Theory and Practice, 31*(5), 713–731.

Dimov, D. (2010). Grappling with the unbearable elusiveness of entrepreneurial opportunities. *Entrepreneurship Theory and Practice, 35*(1), 57–81.

Fiet, J. (2007). A prescriptive analysis of search and discovery. *Journal of Management Studies, 44* (4), 592–611.

Frank, H., & Mitterer, G. (2009). Opportunity recognition. State of the art und Forschungsperspektiven [Opportunity recognition. State of the art and research perspectives]. *Zeitschrift für Betriebswirtschaft, 79*, 367–406.

Gaglio, C. M., & Katz, J. A. (2001). The psychological basis of opportunity identification: Entrepreneurial Alertness. *Small Business Economics, 16*, 95–111.

Gossel, B. M., & Will, A. (2012). Neue Medien—neue Wertschöpfung—neue Unternehmen? Eine theoretische Betrachtung medialer Potenziale für den Entrepreneurship-Prozess [New media—new value creation—new ventures? A theoretical examination of media-based potentials in the entrepreneurship process]. In C. Kolo, T. Döbler, & L. Rademacher (Eds.), *Wertschöpfung durch Medien im Wandel [Value creation by changing media]* (pp. 321–336). Baden-Baden: Nomos.

Grichnick, D. (2006). Die opportunity map der internationalen Entrepreneurshipforschung: Zum Kern des interdisziplinären Forschungsprogramms [The opportunity map of international entrepreneurship research: about core elements of the interdisciplinary research programme]. *Zeitschrift für Betriebswirtschaft, 76*(12), 1303–1333.

Hang, M., & van Weezel, A. (2007). Media and entrepreneurship: What do we know and where should we go? *Journal of Business Studies, 4*(1), 51–70.

Hass, B. H. (2011). Intrapreneurship and corporate venturing in the media business: A theoretical framework and examples from the German publishing industry. *Business, 8*(1), 47–68.

Hayek, F. (1948). *Individualism and economic order*. London: University of Chicago Press.

Hoag, A. (2008). Measuring media entrepreneurship. *International Journal on Media Management, 10*(2), 74–80.

Hoag, A., & Compaine, B. (2007). *Media entrepreneurship: Missionaries and merchants.* Paper presented at the Media Management and Economics Section of AEJMC conference 2007, Washington, DC, August 9–11, 2007. Retrieved December 4, 2012, from http://compaine. bcompany.com/articles/hoag_compaine_AEJMC2007eship.pdf.

Hoag, A., & Seo, S. (2005). *Media entrepreneurship: Definition, theory and context.* Paper presented at the NCTA Academic Seminar, San Francisco, April 2, 2005. Retrieved February 7, 2012, from http://www.smeal.psu.edu/research/fcfe/more/white/mediaentre.pdf.

Hulu. (2013). Company website. Retrieved May 22, 2013, from http://www.hulu.com.

Kaish, S., & Gilad, B. (1991). Characteristics of opportunities search of entrepreneurs vs. executives: Sources, interests, general alertness. *Journal of Business Venturing, 6*, 45–61.

Kirzner, I. (1979). *Wettbewerb und Unternehmertum [Competition and Entrepreneurship].* Tübingen: Mohr Siebeck.

Kirzner, I. (1997). Entrepreneurial discovery and the competitive market process: An Austrian approach. *Journal of Economic Literature, 35*, 60–85.

Kirzner, I. (2009). The alert and creative entrepreneur: A clarification. *Small Business Economics, 32*, 145–152.

Kollmann, T. (2011). *E-Entrepreneurship: Grundlagen der Unternehmensgründung in der Net Economy [E-Entrepreneurship: Basic principles of founding enterprises in the net economy].* Wiesbaden: Gabler.

Kollock, P. (1999). *The economies of online cooperation: Gifts and public goods in cyberspace.* Retrieved December 12, 2012, from https://wiki.cc.gatech.edu/scqualifier/images/b/b0/ Kollock-Economies_of_online_cooperation.pdf.

Luksha, P. (2008). Niche construction: The process of opportunity creation in the environment. *Strategic Entrepreneurship Journal, 2*(4), 269–283.

McKelvie, A., & Picard, R. G. (2008). The growth and development of new and young media firms. *Journal of Media Business Studies, 5*(1), 1–8.

Mises, L. V. (1949). *Human action*. New Haven: Yale.

Patel, P., & Fiet, J. (2009). Systematic search and its relationship to firm founding. *Entrepreneurship Theory and Practice, 34*, 501–526.

Picard, R. (1989). *Media economics: Concepts and issues*. Newbury Park: Sage Publications.

Quah, D. (2003). Digital goods and the new economy. In D. Jones (Ed.), *New economy handbook* (pp. 289–321). San Diego, Amsterdam: Academic Press, Elsevier Science.

Readmill. (2012). Company website. Retrieved December 17, 2012, from http://www.readmill. com.

Röpke, J. (1977). *Die Strategie der Innovation: Eine systemtheoretische Untersuchung der Interaktion von Individuum, Organisation und Markt im Neuerungsprozess [The strategy of Innovation: a systems-theoretical examination of interaction of individuals, organization and market in the innovation process].* Tübingen: Mohr Siebeck.

Sarasvathy, S. D. (2001). Causation and effectuation: Toward a theoretical shift from economic inevitability to entrepreneurial contingency. *Academy of Management Review, 26*(2), 243–263.

Sarasvathy, S. D., Dew, N., Velamuri, S. R., & Venkataraman, S. (2003). Three views of entrepreneurial opportunity. In Z. J. Acs & D. B. Audretsch (Eds.), *Handbook of entrepreneurship research: An interdisciplinary survey and introduction* (pp. 141–160). New York: Springer.

Sarasvathy, S. D. (2008). *Effectuation. Elements of entrepreneurial expertise.* Cheltenham: Edward Elgar Publishing.

Schumpeter, J. A. (1943). *Capitalism, socialism, and democracy.* London: George Allen and Unwin.

Schumpeter, J. A. (1964). *Theorie der Wirtschaftlichen Entwicklung: eine Untersuchung über Unternehmergewinn, Kapital, Kredit, Zins und den Konjunkturzyklus [Theory of economic development: An examination of entrepreneurial profit, capital, loan, interest and economic cycle].* Berlin: Duncker & Humblot.

Shane, S. (2000). Prior knowledge and the discovery of entrepreneurial opportunities. *Organization Science, 11*(4), 448–469.

Shane, S. (2012). Reflections on the 2010 AMR decade award: Delivering on the promise of entrepreneurship as a field of research. *Academy of Management Review, 37*(1), 10–20.

Shane, S., & Venkataraman, S. (2000). The promise of entrepreneurship as field of research. *Academy of Management Review, 25*(1), 217–226.

Smith, B. R., Matthews, C. H., & Schenkel, M. T. (2005). *The search for and discovery of different types of entrepreneurial opportunities: The effects of tacitness and codification.* Paper presented at Babson College Entrepreneurship Research Conference (BCERC) 2005. Retrieved February 7, 2012, from http://fusionmx.babson.edu/entrep/fer/2005FER/chapter_xii/paperfr_xii4.html.

Spotify. (2012). Company website. Retrieved December 17, 2012, from http://www.spotify.com.

Stigler, G. (1961). The economics of information. *The Journal of Political Economy, 69*(3), 213–225.

van Weezel, A. (2010). Creative destruction: Why not researching entrepreneurial media? *International Journal on Media Management, 12*(1), 47–49.

Watchever. (2013). Company website. Retrieved May 22, 2013, from http://www.watchever.com.

Weitzman, M. L. (1998). Recombinant growth. *The Quarterly Journal of Economics, 113*(2), 331–360.

Wirtz, B. (2006). *Medien- und Internetmanagement [Media and internet management].* Wiesbaden: Gabler.

Wohlert, N.-V. (2011). *Berliner startup launcht [Berlin start-up Readmill launches]: "We wanted to create something fucking cool".* Retrieved May 22, 2013, from http://www.gruenderszene.de/news/readmill-launch?utm_source=rss&utm_medium=rss&utm_campaign=rss&utm_source=rss&utm_medium=rss&utm_campaign=readmill-launch.

Business Models of Media Industries: Describing and Promoting Commodification

12

M. Bjørn von Rimscha

12.1   Introduction

For legacy media, questions of branding and business model often lack explicit recognition. Organisations may *possess* both, but their nature and existence often go unacknowledged (Gerth, 2012). By contrast, in discussions about new and social media, they come to the fore. The term business model became fashionable with the emergence of the Internet economy—first in the jargon of consultants and trade papers but later also in the academic literature. However, there is still no consensus about what a business model actually is and what it comprises (Morris, Schindehutte, & Allen, 2005; Zott, Amit, & Massa, 2011). The origin of the term can be traced back to business informatics where all business processes shall be captured in the IT architecture (Stähler, 2002). In everyday speech, a business model is often reduced to the revenue model that is the question how a venture derives its cash flow for its operations. Another popular perspective equals business models to strategy. And indeed, the concept of business models builds on theoretical groundwork in strategic management. There are references to the value chain (Porter, 1985), to strategic positioning (Porter, 1996) and to the resource-based view (Barney, 2001).

Since the advent of the Internet in the 1990s, the use of the term has proliferated (Ghaziani & Ventresca, 2005; Zott et al., 2011). With every new wave of start-ups and Internet-based services, the concept of business models returns to the public and academic attention, often with the implicit suggestion of a fundamental change with completely new business models for media companies. This of course is not the case, as the following chapter shall demonstrate. For the most part, changes are limited to the service offer, which might entail some new or accentuated

M.B. von Rimscha (✉)
Institute of Mass Communication and Media Research, University of Zurich, Zurich, Switzerland
e-mail: b.vonrimscha@ipmz.uzh.ch

© Springer International Publishing Switzerland 2016   207
G.F. Lowe, C. Brown (eds.), *Managing Media Firms and Industries*, Media
Business and Innovation, DOI 10.1007/978-3-319-08515-9_12

possibilities in other elements of the business model. However, the public focus on business models highlights a tendency to regard media solely as commercial enterprises and downplay the societal aspects of media. This goes in line with a general tendency of media companies to focus on the publishing part of the industry and pull out of the production. The business model approach by and large neglects externalities of the media industry such as culture or public sphere.[1] Thus, a withdrawal from production and a focus on business models can be understood as an effort to turn the management of media companies more akin to general management circumventing some of the challenges the characteristics of the media product pose to managers.

This chapter is structured as follows: First, a short overview of the literature on business models in general and on media business model in particular will be provided. The defining elements of a media business model will be identified, and it will be discussed how, to what extent and why social media may be any different from legacy media in terms of their business models. For reasons of clarity, social and legacy media will be used as the two ends of a continuum. The term legacy media shall describe traditional offline media such as a newspaper or a broadcast channel; the term social media shall describe online platforms that focus on the interactions between their users as defined by Ellison and Boyd (2013) and Bechmann and Lomborg (2013).[2] It will be pointed out that the business model approach fails to address externalities which are a defining aspect of the media business. Thus, the conclusion argues that business models are a useful but not sufficient means of media management possibly fostering commodification.

12.2   Business Models

The business model concept evolved from a popular term to a key concept in management (McGrath, 2010). In a basic sense, the business model describes how a company is set up to sustain itself. The term is used in a multitude of disciplines including entrepreneurship, strategy, organisation, finance, marketing and operations management and information systems. In a recent approach, business models are defined as the choices (in terms of deployed resources and competences, value propositions and internal/external organisation) made by a firm to operate (Demil & Lecocq, 2010). In a changing industry such as the media industry, the dynamic aspects of resources and thus business models (Teece, 2010) become important. If media companies want to stay in business in

---

[1] While in principle it might be possible to describe public service business models, usually proponents of this approach restrict themselves to models that allow for profit rather than utility.

[2] In doing so, this chapter neglects in-between media such as online newspapers that allow user comments.

a changing industry, they have to continuously adapt and renew their business models, redesigning or updating the logic or mechanisms of how they create and capture value (Achtenhagen, Melin, & Naldi, 2013). Not all media businesses want to and have to turn themselves into Internet-based social media. But still their business model needs to be adapted according to changes in the market. Before the question how social media business models differ from those of legacy media can be addressed, we will have a look on what is generally understood as a business model, how is it defined in the literature.

12.2.1 Definitions

Zott et al. (2011) have shown that business models are often studied in lack of an explicit definition of the term. If the concept is defined at all comparisons between different research results is hampered by the fact that a great number of definitions are used which at times have little overlap. Key elements in numerous definitions compiled by Zott et al. include such divergent terms as 'statement' (Stewart & Zhao, 2000), 'description' (Applegate, 2001; Weill & Vitale, 2001), 'representation' (Morris et al., 2005; Shafer, Smith, & Linder, 2005), 'architecture' (Timmers, 1998, p. 2; Dubosson-Torbay, Osterwalder, & Pigneur, 2002), 'conceptual tool or model' (Osterwalder, 2004; Teece, 2010), 'structural template' (Amit & Zott, 2001, p. 511), 'method' (Afuah & Tucci, 2001), 'framework' (Afuah, 2004), 'pattern' (Brousseau & Penard, 2007), 'set' (Seelos & Mair, 2007; Johnson, Christensen, & Kagermann, 2008, p. 52), 'system' (Zott & Amit, 2010, p. 216), 'reflection' (Casadesus-Masanell & Ricart, 2010), 'heuristic logic' (Chesbrough & Rosenbloom, 2002, p. 529) and 'stories' (Magretta, 2002, p. 4).

Thus, depending on the perspective, a business model can be either very concrete or very vague. It can be a sales as well as a planning tool or no intended tool at all but an ex post description of business proceedings. Zott et al. conclude that 'the literature is developing largely in silos, according to the phenomena of interest to the respective researchers' (Zott et al., 2011, p. 1019) or organisational roles. Despite this dissension in terms of definition, they also identify a common ground between the authors where, among other things, business models shall explain how firms do business by analysing both value creation and value capturing.

In this regard, it is widely agreed that a business model consists of several elements that either contribute to value creation and capturing or provide a measurement category. One promising approach to a generalisable concept of business models thus would be to compare the elements used in different studies that are said to constitute a business model. Morris et al. (2005) have conducted a literature review to identify the core elements. The 18 articles on business models they include in their review feature 24 different elements in total. There are several overlaps; however, there is not a single element that is present in all studies analysed. The most mentioned elements are value offering, economic model, customer interface/relationship, partner network/roles, internal infrastructure/ connected activities and target markets. Again, despite a lot of dissent in details, there is a certain consent about what is needed to describe a business model. The concept itself is generic; however, it is not particularly suitable to capture positive externalities of media for society, since in any case the value offering in question is individual rather than societal. A business model requires a business case, but especially the societal functions of media regularly do not constitute a business case. Some (news) media content can be considered as merit good and thus per definition not as a business case but as a public remit.

12.2.2 Media Business Models

The ambition of this paper is not to reconcile divergent perspectives on business models; thus, for the following, the focus will be narrowed to concepts of business models discussed in the media business context. According to Picard (2002), business models describe the basic characteristics of companies to have sustainable success in the media business. Business models in this sense are not about the everyday operations but about the basic layout of the business, its interfaces with other industries and which (financial) interactions potentially render it successful. Business models are the structure of the relevant streams of information, services and products. Thus, they provide an overview of the necessary operations and their respective relative importance. Wirtz (2011) takes this concept further when he differentiates these operations into six partial models of a media business model.

12.3   Elements of a Media Business Model

Following a heuristic put forward by Wirtz (2011, p. 68), a business model comprises six partial models that are necessary to describe all aspects of a business model. While all partial models are necessary, they are not equally important in all cases. Each media business has its own business model where the partial models are in a characteristic balance (Fig. 12.1).

In the following, the partial models will be described in more detail. For each partial model of a business model, differences between legacy media and social media will be identified. The focus will be on social media since the operations of legacy media are well documented in the literature.

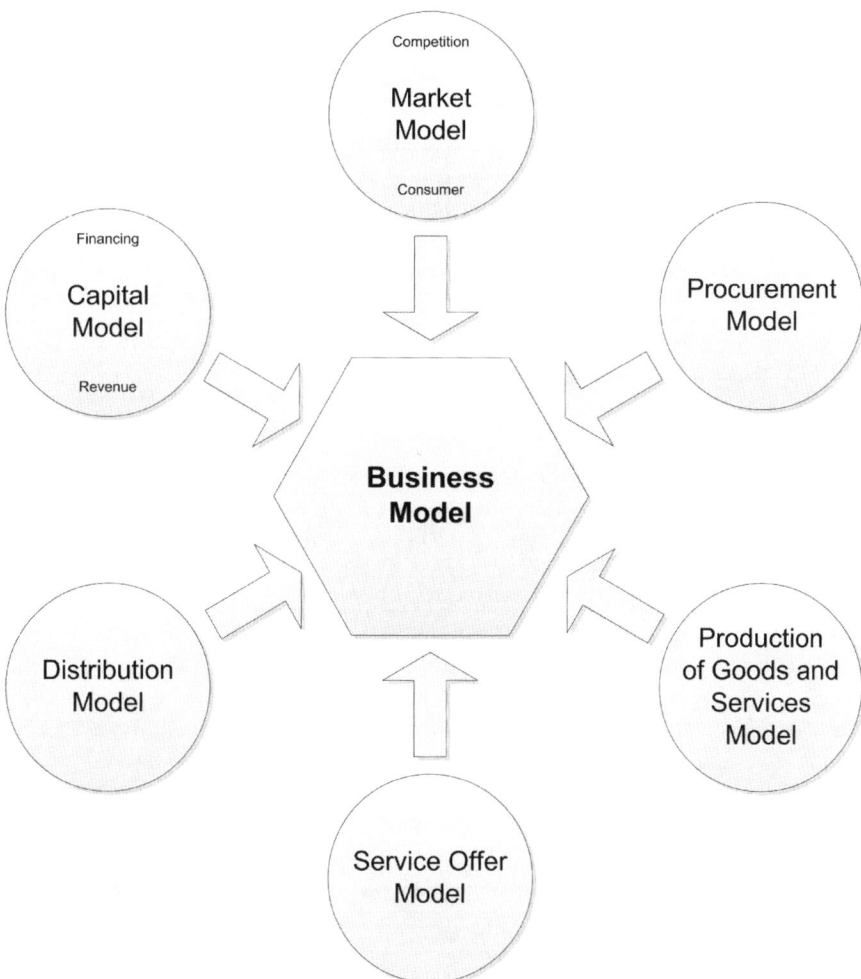

Fig. 12.1 Partial models of a business model (*Source*: Wirtz (2011, p. 70))

12.3.1 Market Model

The market model clearly lays out the markets in which the company interacts with which other actors, be they buyers or competitors. Accordingly, Wirtz (2011, p. 69) distinguishes between a consumer and a competition model.

The consumer model describes the extent and nature of the demand and the associated willingness to pay: Who wants what at what price point? The potential customers can be distinguished in submarkets based on their respective properties. For example, one can differentiate customers with a high willingness to pay from those with no or minimal willingness to pay. It seems sensible to address and serve these two groups differently according to their respective needs.

The competitive model describes the competitive environment of the company. Therefore, the structure of the sales market as well as the market behaviour of existing and potential competitors needs to be analysed. For Internet services that are available globally, it is necessary to take into account the respective national legal and economic framework in each market served. Legal regulations concerning the protection of minors or health may require adjustments to the business or to the permitted means of advertising.

12.3.2 Procurement Model

The procurement model describes the other side of the market: Which input factors must be obtained in order to serve the market? This part of the business model deals with products and services that are purchased from external parties. In the last decades, procurement has become more important for legacy media as they have reduced the share of content they produce themselves. Tunstall (1993) has illustrated this shift from producer to publisher using TV as an example; however, the trend is evident in other legacy media as well, for instance, when newspapers lay off editors and procure complete segment from news agencies. Other legacy media have experimented more or less successfully with user-generated content, turning the idea of citizen journalism into a low-cost content procurement model. Social media have taken that idea even further. They have pulled out of editorial production altogether and limit their procurement on infrastructure that is necessary to provide the service (servers, Internet connectivity, user interface, etc.). An exception from this rule can be found in offers that are not based on user-generated content but only allow users to comment on professional content to generate recommendations for other users from the aggregated user behaviour and comments. In these cases, the procurement is about licensing existing professional media content similar as for legacy media. An example in this context would be music streaming services like Spotify or simfy.[3]

12.3.3 Production of Goods and Service Model

The production and processing of input factors within the company is represented in this partial model. Legacy media used to produce their own content; however, today

---

[3] However, in this category of services, the social networking aspect is less prominent. The paramount objective is to use recommendations and chats to increase session length and thus drive advertising revenue or to turn occasional users of the free offer to paid subscribers.

they restrict themselves largely to selecting and (re)arranging ready-made content they have procured. Social media providers usually neither procure nor create their own content. YouTube does not pay directors to shoot short films, and Facebook has no journalists writing on 'how things are going'. Both companies mainly provide a platform for the self-portrayal of its users. That said, YouTube has commissioned original content to boost the quality of the content and compete with platforms run by legacy media corporations such as Hulu (Halliday, 2011). With a further decline of advertising revenues for legacy media, social media might take over as commissioners of content, but this depends on their market model: do they consider themselves in the entertainment market (like a cable channel) or in the socialising market (like the local pub)? For the time being, the vast majority of the content on the platform stems from users, professionals as well as amateurs. Even Wikipedia does not pay employees to write and amend articles. The platform character of social media means that no in-house staff have to be employed to create original content and only few might feel a need to hire commissioners. The production of goods and service model primarily is about software programming in order to enable users to create their own content, be it comments, reviews, status messages or even advertisements. Furthermore, the provision of services implies the creation of software that stores, sorts and links the user-generated content (Lorenz & Hess, 2010). This can be automated in the software, for example, when a music recommendation service like Last.fm distils its recommendations from the evaluation of the aggregated preferences of its registered users. The generation of links between content elements can also be delegated to the users themselves, for example, when users tag familiar faces in pictures on Facebook. In principle, the software programming is a one-time effort, but in reality constant updates are necessary to ensure both the data integrity and security. Furthermore, improved usability and new features are necessary to stand up to the competition for new users and retain existing ones. The main difference between social and legacy media in this context is that with social media the selection and arrangement of content are mostly automated. There are no editors or commissioners who rate content using criteria such as news values or measures of relevance and normative quality which determine the societal and cultural value of a media content. The paramount criteria for a social media publisher—that is, most of the time an algorithm—are popularity and supposed individual relevance. In other words, most of the aspects that render legacy media companies and their management special are excluded from the business model of social media.

12.3.4 Service Offer Model

In the service offer model, it is laid out which potential customers are offered what services. Most media companies are at least partially advertising funded and thus operate in two-sided markets (Dewenter, 2004). This means different user needs must be met and the aggregate and qualified demand of recipients has to be processed for advertising customers. Ideally, different groups of users and advertisers are offered specific services according to the segmentation of the market, in order to address their respective needs and skim their willingness to pay. Thus, for the service model, there are two basic offers. On the one hand, the recipient is provided information, entertainment or a platform for self-expression and communication; on the other hand, advertisers are offered the users' attention. In this context, social media is not fundamentally different from legacy media. However, there are important differences in details: Social media users are usually forced to create a user profile and in doing so reveal their (consumer) preferences. Furthermore, they document these preferences by their behaviour on the platform which can be easily monitored unlike the behaviour of a newspaper reader or a TV spectator. This allows the proprietor of a social media platform to segment their users in a considerably higher resolution. Target groups of advertisers can thus be represented accurately, at least if the potential customers use that specific social media platform.

Also on the user side, there is an important difference between offline legacy and online social media. The social media offer can be easily adapted to the respective willingness to pay. A newspaper must determine the copy price once and for all and decide on the desired proportion of the advertising revenue. A reader cannot decide to pay £5 for a Sunday Times instead of the regular £2.5 and then demand to get it printed without the advertising. Not so with online offerings, user regularly can choose between a free, ad-supported version and an ad-free version that comes at a fee. The attractiveness of the payable version is enhanced by additional features. The peculiarity for social media is that it is visible to other users, whether someone pays or not. The premium paid-up membership is therefore an element of the profile and the self-expression that can be regarded as a signal to other users. The users' willingness to pay works as a signal that the network and thus the contacts that are made and maintained there are value for money.

12.3.5 Distribution Model

The distribution model describes how the goods and services produced by the company reach its customers. The most important question in the context is whether a media product is tied to a physical carrier medium (newspaper) or not (TV, radio, social media). Thus, social media again is not fundamentally different from (electronic) legacy media. However, the distribution model also includes ensuring the availability of the service for the users. Notwithstanding net neutrality, this could mean that the provider of a video sharing platform has to pay for the preferred handling of its data packets. Furthermore, the distribution model includes the relationship with intermediaries. For social media providers, this implies the integration of recommendations and links in as large a number of other Internet sites as possible.

An important characteristic of media products, both legacy and social, is the existence of network effects that influence the value of a media offering beyond the individual use. A network effect occurs if the value of a product or service increases with the number of users. A single phone is worthless; however, if connected to a second phone, two households can communicate, and between five phones the number of possible connections already equals ten. According to Metcalfe's law, the value of a network increases in proportion to the square of its participants (Shapiro & Varian, 1999). At some point in time, a situation is reached when no one can afford not to be connected to the phone network. In a market with network effects, a company with a small competitive advantage can expand its market share to gain a dominant position, while a company with a small disadvantage will lose market share and will possibly be driven out of the market. The Internet industry is particularly affected by network effects and thus has been referred to as 'winner-takes-all market' (Kelly, 1998; Shapiro & Varian, 1999). In some sense, there are network effects at work also in legacy media markets, for instance, if we think of consumption capital in the context of follow-up communication. If a user follows a popular TV show instead of one with a mediocre rating, he or she will have more potential communication partners, with whom he or she can chat about the latest episode. Thus, an additional user increases the attractiveness of the show to others. Likewise, in politics, newspapers with a reputation for investigative stories may set the public agenda and thus exert influence beyond their paid circulation.

However, in social media services, network effects are much more evident. A social media platform, with a lone user, is worthless. With an increasing number of participants, the probability to meet like-minded people on the platform rises. At the same time also, the attractiveness of the platform for developers who provide applications and for advertisers who want to reach narrowly defined target groups increases. This means there are multiple positive feedbacks to a rising number of participants since the value of the network synchronously increases for multiple stakeholders. This explains why newly established social media services emphasise a growing user figure over monetisation of the users. Prior to the dotcom crisis, many Internet start-ups pursued a 'get-big-fast strategy' in which they tried to maximise the number of users without generating any significant revenue (Liebowitz, 2002). The same can still be observed today at many social media platforms, where the number of participants is increasing much faster than their revenue. It is difficult to put a price on an offer that was offered initially for free to maximise the number of participants. The obvious result could be the exodus of the majority of users to a new competitor. Providers try to lock in participants in order to impede the migration to potentially better or cheaper networks—for example, when Facebook prevents the transfer of user contacts to Google+. 'As a result, there will probably be no cross-community services with transferable user profiles for the foreseeable future, since hardly any community has an interest in sharing their data with competitors' (Berge & Buesching, 2008, p. 32). Therefore, the aim of the major social media platforms is to offer their once established reach to the advertising industry. Thus, indirect network effects lead to a dominance of the advertising revenue model (see below). From a media management perspective, externalities of the network are limited to the marketability neglecting the societal value of media.

However, social media is only partly to be described as a winner-takes-all market. Besides Facebook as the current top dog and all-purpose provider, specialist providers can hold their ground if they offer a better functionality for a certain thematic realm (Cusumano, 2011, p. 33) or if clustering in a network means that contacts in close proximity are more valuable than distant ones (Lee, Lee, & Lee, 2006). This might be a reason why the social network Orkut prevailed in Brazil. Portuguese is not a world language, so the exchange within the country was more important than with foreign language users around the globe. In addition, maximising the number of participants does not necessarily mean maximising returns. An offer that charges a fee, as several business contact platforms do, can turn profitable with a much smaller number of participants than a solely ad-funded platform [for a sample calculation, see Berge and Buesching (2008, p. 44)].

A rather new trend is that specialised networks such as SoundCloud for musicians allow users to log in using their Facebook account. In doing so, they lower the barriers to entry for their users and avoid being pushed out of the market. The big network allows smaller ones to coexist in exchange of the user data they receive from these deals.

Overall network effects lead to concentration in both legacy and social media markets; however, in social media markets, concentration is less of a market entry barrier for media managers than in legacy media markets.

12.3.6 Capital Model

Finally, the capital model presents the financial resources of a company and the opportunities available to refinance its operations. The capital model can be differentiated in the financing model, that is, the description of the sources from which the capital to finance the company is derived, and the revenue model, that is, the question of where and how revenues can be realised for refinancing the operations. It also includes questions about the optimal volume, the desired margin and flexibility of prices.

In the context of the capital model, there are only minor differences between legacy media and social media. Concerning the financing model, there is a difference in terms of who are the investors in the business. In most European countries, new outlets of legacy media are usually founded and financed by existing publishers. An alternative might be a group of frustrated laid off journalists who come together for a content-driven rather than a commercially driven project. Thus, the market usually evolves through activities of existing players. However, similar to the IT industry, start-up companies in the social media context are mostly financed by venture capital and later either taken public or purchased by an established media corporation. The on-going popularity of social media offerings among investors represents a distinct business model for entrepreneurs in this context. A social web service with high reach is set up quickly with the help of venture capitalists and sold or taken public even before the operating break-even is reached (or at least it is clear that it can ever be reached). StudiVZ, a once popular German social network, was bought in 2007 by the publishing group Holtzbrinck for 85 million euros. In 2011—still not profitable—Holtzbrinck failed to find a buyer. Eventually, in 2013 they sold to an investment group at an undisclosed price. While the founders and venture capitalists were able to sell with a high profit, the later investors have suffered significant losses. At the same time, the example shows the impact of network effects in winner-takes-all markets. StudiVZ suffered from the appeal of Facebook because users are not willing to maintain multiple profiles with different services and if in doubt decide for the larger network in which they can find more of their friends. Without own content production, a social media provider can do little about this.

The potential for market development in the social media context largely remains with external players who usually do not subscribe to the non-commercial concept of media contributing to political, societal and cultural development or the cohesion of society.

With respect to the revenue model, there are the same options for refinancing available for both legacy and social media. Social media do not feature profoundly different sources of revenue, but network effects have an important influence on the question which revenue models are likely to be profitable. Sources of revenue can be differentiated into direct and indirect sources (Zerdick et al., 2000, p. 25) or by distinguishing the relevant markets in which a media organisation is active and generates revenues (Wirtz, 2011, p. 71). Direct revenues usually are collected from the media users, while indirect revenues can derive from companies (advertising) as well as from the state (subsidies). The consideration of relevant markets differentiates three markets where revenues are generated: the content market, the user market and the advertising market. On the content market (1), content licences and exploitation rights are traded. Media users (2) can be charged a fee based on access or usage. In addition, services or merchandise products can be offered. In the advertising market (3), different advertising formats with their respective potential of relevant information about the consumers can be offered. In addition, under certain circumstances, the state can be an important fourth source of revenue or at least provide opportunities for cost reductions. Legacy media are considered to be important and influential for political and cultural live and the cohesion of society. Thus, in many countries, they benefit from government support. In Germany and the UK, public broadcasting is funded by fees approved by the state; in Spain, it is funded directly from the taxpayers' money. In most countries, legacy media enjoy reduced tariffs of VAT, often the postal distribution of print media is promoted, and film producers can take advantage of tax breaks or direct subsidies. None of these measures exist in the field of social media. Although the relevance of social media in politics is uncontested, for example, in election campaign communication (Cogburn & Espinoza-Vasquez, 2011), the potential importance for the formation of the political will and social development has not yet led to a discussion on the eligibility for public funding of social media. Exceptions can be found in the context of media education, where children shall acquire media literacy in a protected environment. One such example is Watch Your Web, funded by the German Federal Ministry of Food, Agriculture and Consumer Protection. It features a portal with rudimentary social media functionality that shall teach adolescents a responsible use of social media. However, beyond the motive of protecting minors, the provision of social media as a means of (public) communication is usually not regarded as a public responsibility.

Social media offerings are thus in the same situation as those legacy media, who are said to have no relevance for democracy (e.g. commercial fictional TV): In order to diversify risks and to avoid unilateral dependencies, they use a mixed financing based on their three relevant markets. The respective share of the different sources of revenue depends on the good characteristics and the competitive environment (Kind, Nilssen, & Sorgard, 2009).

Direct revenue funding is common for legacy entertainment media such as books, cinema or sound recording media. However, relatively few social media companies can use a revenue model where they rely on direct funding by the users. Since the usefulness of an offer above all depends on the number of participants, a user fee is problematic since it excludes potential users with low willingness to pay and thus limits the value of the network. If users are attractive for advertisers, the loss of value for the network may be greater than the potential income from a fee.

In the media industry, revenues frequently are not directly related to transactions. Readers often pay a subscription fee for their newspaper, and advertisers pay for the advertising space and the assumed associated user attention while they cannot be sure whether their message actually is perceived. The licence fee must be paid regardless of the actual use of public channels. The reason for this can be found in the good characteristics of media products (see Chap. 11). It is hard to set a price for the use of an experience or credence good. Before the use, the willingness to pay is low, as the quality and usefulness of the product cannot be assessed. Conversely, after the use, the quality and usefulness can be assessed, but still the willingness to pay is low, since the experience has already been made. The same principle also applies to social media. The user learns about the value and benefits of a network only after they have signed up and started making contacts. Beforehand, they cannot assess what potentially interesting contacts the network provides unless they are told so by their offline friends. For this reason, no social media platform requires an entry fee. Unlike a TV show where the recreational use ends with the reception, a social media platform can offer on-going benefits. Therefore, social media platform can demand a fee after a trial period. However, since most social media platforms face competitors which offer more or less the same service, and the willingness to pay is said to be lower online, advertising revenue usually constitutes the single most important source of revenue.

The bulk of revenues are generated with small advertisements which are dynamically adapted to the type of content and/or user in order to be more relevant for the recipient.

Since users are forced to create their own profiles, social media providers usually have in-depth knowledge about their users. Thus, they can target advertising messages much more accurately than most legacy media. Facebook as an example offers differentiations by location, language, education, occupation, age, gender, relationship status, birthday, interests and groups of friends. Often, the price is not fixed, but varies according to the demand for a certain advertising space. Advertisers specify how much they are willing to pay and are allocated the demanded advertising space only if no competitor is willing to pay more to reach the same target group. Thus, prices are much more volatile than at legacy media, and available advertising space and willingness of advertisers can be better matched.

Overall, we can summarise that social media depend much more on advertising revenues than legacy media. This has implications for their management as well as for their societal impact.

12.4   The Business Model Approach as Commodification Indicator

Social media are the culmination of a development that has started when legacy media began to pull out of content production and retreated to the packaging and distribution of procured and in some cases commissioned content. These two latter elements of the media business value chain are less distinct from other industries than the business of producing media content. Credit card operators also have to deal with two-sided markets (Rochet & Tirole, 2003), and network effects are a common issue in the telecom and IT sector (Liebowitz & Margolis, 2002). If media companies engage in commissioning content, they may still be involved in the content production, but still they cannot exert the same influence. It is more than just a make-or-buy decision, but organising the flowing networks (Altmeppen, Lantzsch, & Will, 2007) of content production is similar to managing strategic alliances (Emden, Calantone, & Droge, 2006) in other industries. Reduced to packaging and distribution, the media business is not all that special and can be treated as a commodity. The more an analysis of media focuses on technical and tangible aspects of media, the less distinct the media appears to be. From this perspective, the Internet is merely another carrier medium for information, not with the exact same characteristics as a sheet of paper, but receptive to the same means of management. This explains the popularity of the business model concept: As a dominant means of analysing the industry and basis for managerial decision making, the business model approach implicitly reduces the media business to making money with media. External effects for the society (positive or negative) are not really included in the model and thus neglected. On the one hand, this has opened up a much bigger reservoir of potential managers which may be recruited to manage media businesses (Underwood, 1993). On the other hand—for good and bad—this means that certain characteristics of media products are not reflected in the management of media businesses. It can be argued that the proliferation of both social media (understood as retreat from content production) and the concept of business models can be understood as interconnected indicators of a more commoditised media industry.

The business model approach is a useful generic tool to guide media managers to organise their business focusing on economic aspects. If, however, media managers truly want to address the special characteristics of the media products and arrive at objectives beyond the maximisation of profit, they need to add elements from stakeholder management to their management repertoire and try to address the needs and demands of secondary stakeholders (Karmasin, 2002).

References

Achtenhagen, L., Melin, L., & Naldi, L. (2013). Dynamics of business models – Strategizing actions, critical capabilities and activities for sustained value creation. *Long Range Planning, 46*(6), 427–442. doi:10.1016/j.lrp.2013.04.002.

Afuah, A. (2004). *Business models. A strategic management approach.* New York: McGraw-Hill.

Afuah, A., & Tucci, C. L. (2001). *Internet business models and strategies. Text and cases.* Boston: McGraw-Hill.

Altmeppen, K.-D., Lantzsch, K., & Will, A. (2007). Flowing networks in the entertainment business. Organizing international TV format trade. *International Journal on Media Management, 9*(3), 94–104.

Amit, R., & Zott, C. (2001). Value creation in E-business. *Strategic Management Journal, 22* (6–7), 493–520.

Applegate, L. M. (2001). E-business models. Making sense of the internet business landscape. In G. W. Dickson & G. DeSanctis (Eds.), *Information technology and the future enterprise. New models for managers* (pp. 49–101). Upper Saddle River, NJ: Prentice Hall.

Barney, J. B. (2001). Resource-based theories of competitive advantage. A ten-year retrospective on the resource-based view. *Journal of Management, 27*(6), 643–650.

Bechmann, A., & Lomborg, S. (2013). Mapping actor roles in social media: Different perspectives on value creation in theories of user participation. *New Media and Society, 15*(5), 765–781.

Berge, S., & Buesching, A. (2008). Strategien von Communities in Web 2.0. In B. H. Hass, G. J. Walsh, & T. Kilian (Eds.), *Web 2.0. Neue Perspektiven für Marketing und Medien* (pp. 23–37). Berlin, Heidelberg: Springer.

Brousseau, E., & Penard, T. (2007). The economics of digital business models. A framework for analyzing the economics of platforms. *Review of Network Economics, 6*(2).

Casadesus-Masanell, R., & Ricart, J. E. (2010). From strategy to business models and onto tactics. *Long Range Planning, 43*(2–3), 195–215.

Chesbrough, H., & Rosenbloom, R. S. (2002). The role of the business model in capturing value from innovation. Evidence from Xerox Corporation's technology spin-off companies. *Industrial and Corporate Change, 11*(3), 529–555.

Cogburn, D. L., & Espinoza-Vasquez, F. K. (2011). From networked nominee to networked nation. Examining the impact of web 2.0 and social media on political participation and civic engagement in the 2008 Obama campaign. *Journal of Political Marketing, 10*(1–2), 189–213.

Cusumano, M. A. (2011). Platform wars come to social media. *Communications of the ACM, 54* (4), 31.

Demil, B., & Lecocq, X. (2010). Business model evolution. In search of dynamic consistency. *Long Range Planning, 43*(2–3), 227–246.

Dewenter, R. (2004). *Essays on interrelated media markets.* Baden-Baden: Nomos.

Dubosson-Torbay, M., Osterwalder, A., & Pigneur, Y. (2002). E-business model design, classification, and measurements. *Thunderbird International Business Review, 44*(1), 5–23.

Ellison, N. B., & Boyd, D. (2013). Sociality through social network sites. In W. H. Dutton (Ed.), *The Oxford handbook of internet studies* (pp. 151–172). Oxford: Oxford University Press.

Emden, Z., Calantone, R. J., & Droge, C. (2006). Collaborating for new product development. Selecting the partner with maximum potential to create value. *Journal of Product Innovation Management, 23*(4), 330–341.

Gerth, M. A. (2012). *Making Regional News. Ökonomische und publizistische Bedeutung politischer Berichterstattung für regionale Medien.* Baden-Baden: Nomos.

Ghaziani, A., & Ventresca, M. J. (2005). Keywords and cultural change. Frame analysis of business model public talk, 1975–2000. *Sociological Forum, 20*(4), 523–559.

Halliday, J. (2011) Google 'to boost spend on original YouTube content'. Website reported to be planning major overhaul and is in talks with programme-makers in bid to battle internet-connected TV. *The Guardian.*

Johnson, M. W., Christensen, C. M., & Kagermann, H. (2008). Reinventing your business model. *Harvard Business Review, 86*(12), 50–59.

Karmasin, M. (2002). Medienmanagement als stakeholder management. In M. Karmasin & C. Winter (Eds.), *Grundlagen des Medienmanagements* (pp. 279–301). München: Fink.

Kelly, K. (1998). *New rules for the new economy. 10 radical strategies for a connected world.* New York, NY: Viking.

Kind, H. J., Nilssen, T., & Sorgard, L. (2009). Business models for media firms. Does competition matter for how they raise revenue? *Marketing Science, 28*(6), 1112–1128.

Lee, E., Lee, J., & Lee, J. (2006). Reconsideration of the winner-take-all hypothesis. Complex networks and local bias. *Management Science, 52*(12), 1838–1848.

Liebowitz, S. J. (2002). *Re-thinking the network economy. The true forces that drive the digital marketplace.* New York: Amacom.

Liebowitz, S. J., & Margolis, S. E. (2002). Network effects and externalities. In P. Newman (Ed.), *The new Palgrave dictionary of economics and the law* (pp. 671–675). Basingstoke: Palgrave Macmillan.

Lorenz, M.-L., & Hess, T. (2010). Soziale Netzwerke. *MedienWirtschaft, 7*(2), 23–26.

Magretta, J. (2002). Why business models matter. *Harvard Business Review, 80*(5), 86–92.

McGrath, R. G. (2010). Business models. A discovery driven approach. *Long Range Planning, 43* (2–3), 247–261.

Morris, M., Schindehutte, M., & Allen, J. (2005). The entrepreneur's business model: Toward a unified perspective. *Journal of Business Research, 58*(6), 726–735.

Osterwalder, A. (2004) *The business model ontology. A proposition in a design science approach.* Dissertation. Université de Lausanne.

Picard, R. G. (2002). *The economics and financing of media companies.* New York: Fordham University Press.

Porter, M. E. (1985). *Competitive advantage. Creating and sustaining superior performance.* New York: Free Press.

Porter, M. E. (1996). What is strategy? *Harvard Business Review, 74*(6), 61–78.

Rochet, J.-C., & Tirole, J. (2003). Platform competition in two-sided markets. *Journal of the European Economic Association, 1*(4), 990–1029.

Seelos, C., & Mair, J. (2007). Profitable business models and market creation in the context of deep poverty. A strategic view. *Academy of Management Perspectives, 21*(4), 49–63.

Shafer, S. M., Smith, H. J., & Linder, J. C. (2005). The power of business models. *Business Horizons, 48*(3), 199–207.

Shapiro, C., & Varian, H. R. (1999). *Information rules. A strategic guide to the network economy.* Boston: Harvard Business School.

Stähler, P. (2002). *Geschäftsmodelle in der digitalen Ökonomie. Merkmale, Strategien und Auswirkungen.* Lohmar: Eul.

Stewart, D. W., & Zhao, Q. (2000). Internet marketing, business models, and public policy. *Journal of Public Policy and Marketing, 19*(2), 287–296.

Teece, D. J. (2010). Business models, business strategy and innovation. *Long Range Planning, 43* (2–3), 172–194.

Timmers, P. (1998). Business models for electronic markets. *Electronic Markets, 8*(2), 3–8.

Tunstall, J. (1993). *Television producers*. London: Routledge.

Underwood, D. (1993). *When MBAs rule the newsroom. How the marketers and managers are reshaping today's media*. New York: Columbia University Press.

Weill, P., & Vitale, M. R. (2001). *Place to space. Migrating to eBusiness models*. Boston, MA: Harvard Business School Press.

Wirtz, B. W. (2011). *Media and internet management*. Wiesbaden: Gabler.

Zerdick, A., Picot, A., Schrape, K., Artopé, A., Goldhammer, K., Lange, U. T., et al. (2000). *E-conomics. Strategies for the digital marketplace*. Berlin: Springer.

Zott, C., & Amit, R. (2010). Business model design. An activity system perspective. *Long Range Planning, 43*(2–3), 216–226.

Zott, C., Amit, R., & Massa, L. (2011). The business model. Recent developments and future research. *Journal of Management, 37*(4), 1019–1042.

Technology Management and Business Models

13

Gustavo Cardoso and José Moreno

13.1 Introduction

The current revolution in the information and communication technologies is having a huge impact on media companies, both in their processes and workflow and—more importantly—in their business models. Almost all modern companies have seen their businesses transformed by technology, from supply chain to customer interface, but media firms are distinctive because information and digital content *are* the business, and the transformation has been even more radical. In order to adapt to such radical change, managers of media companies must improve their understanding of what is at stake and which alternatives are best suited to face challenges and seize opportunities.

In this chapter, we will argue that the massive changes affecting media work and business models are best understood by examining technological *strata*, rather than at the level of technological products and solutions. Such an approach examines the way that new layers of technology are laid down like layers of sediment. Understanding the potentialities (and constraints) of new technologies is dependent upon accounting for the characteristics of underlying layers and the relationship between them.

Our approach explores, in theoretical terms, how the shift from analogue to digital information and communication technologies forms the basis for both the development of tools and their social appropriation. It is our contention that media companies' work, function and value are determined, in large part, by the social and commercial means by which technologies are adopted and utilised. In doing so, we draw on the theoretical work of sociologists Manuel Castells (2010), Jan van Dijk (2006) and Yochai Benkler (2006) to analyse how the network society and its

G. Cardoso (✉) • J. Moreno
School of Sociology and Public Policy, Lisbon University Institute, Lisbon, Portugal
e-mail: gustavo.cardoso@iscte.pt; jose_carlos_moreno@iscte.pt

© Springer International Publishing Switzerland 2016
G.F. Lowe, C. Brown (eds.), *Managing Media Firms and Industries*, Media
Business and Innovation, DOI 10.1007/978-3-319-08515-9_13

digital information and communication technologies affect the media business and its management strategies.

This chapter attempts a diagnosis of the situation of the media companies in the digital age by examining the aggregated results of 30 reports, published between 2011 and 2012, from 17 consulting firms that studied the issue. We try to identify some of the major trends that are changing the media field and the business of media. We will argue that, in order to manage technology in media companies, media managers need to develop foresight and be able to spot technology trends that influence social uses. Media managers must develop an integrated approach in terms of seizing the opportunities posed by those social uses instead of simply trying to distribute their content using different available technologies.

We will conclude this chapter by proposing an approach to technology management based on what we have termed, Technology Trends Management (T2M), and argue that managing technologies in media companies is not simply an issue of managing technology but rather managing business models within the *framework* of available technology.

13.1.1 From Analogue to Digital: A Theoretical Framework

Much of what is happening in the media right now can be traced back to the conjunction of two combined effects: the massive adoption of digital communication and information technologies and the expansion of broadband telecommunications (van Dijk, 2006). Faced by rapid and profound technological change, media managers often tend to focus upon the functions of specific technological devices instead of the under technologies themselves. Even if they pass the level of the device's capabilities and potentialities, they will still be looking at a partial technology—the smartphone, for instance—instead of the technological basis of the smartphone and other modern information and communication technologies. In order to fully grasp the forces and directions of the technology change that is affecting the media, media managers need to first understand the socio-technical layer that supports the technologies and the devices with which they are confronted.

The single identifiable fact that most extensively explains the way new information and communication technologies are impacting media companies is the shift from physical and analogue technologies to digital (Moreno, 2013). Until the invention and the mass adoption of the computer, the social distribution of information was almost entirely made by physical and analogue technologies like the printing press or the Hertzian television. With the invention of the computer, the manipulation of information quickly became digital at all stages of the process (Manovich, 2001).

The shift from analogue to digital can be viewed as the base stratum upon which all other developments in the digital world (other technological and commercial strata) are layered (Castells, 2010). Such technological sub-layers, to a greater or less degree, determine others. This sub-layer of technology has in itself, prior to any subsequent technological developments, distinctive ways of being appropriated at the social level: a distinctive socio-technical paradigm (Castells, 2010). Those social uses are the result of the intersection between the characteristics of the digital technology and the social structures and connections that incorporate it in daily life.

When considering modern digital communication and information technologies as a whole, we can single out the digital code as the first technological layer upon which all other technological layers are based. The digital binary code is the language all computers and computer-like devices share and on which they operate. Then, each computer or device may have its particular operating system (e.g. iOS), with one or several software platforms (e.g. web apps, web sites or native apps), each with several more specific software packages or programmes and applications (e.g. Skype, Google Maps or Facebook). Each application, software or device it works on can be considered a specific information and communication technology, and many will be viewed by the media manager as potential news outlets or media products and services (see Fig. 1).

We can point five main distinctive characteristics of the digital technologies that influence the way information is socially distributed and the way people use information and information tools in their day-to-day life: metadata, interactivity, flexibility, convergence and global reach (see Fig. 2). These characteristics influence the attributes and design of workflow and business models of media companies.[1]

The first distinctive feature of digital technologies is what has come to be known as 'metadata'. Metadata refers to an additional layer of data, attached to the main data, one that is mostly unknown to the user and serves the purpose of characterising the data itself.

As an example, this 'data about the data' registers your browsing history in a given news website so that it can offer you a personalised news experience the next time you visit. If I, as a user, save a new report in my Delicious bookmark account with my own tags, I am adding different metadata to the original metadata supplied by the author. Likewise, if a number of people bookmarked that particular news report, the Delicious software will register that as metadata and will be able to construct an automatic recommendation service with that metadata.

The concept of 'big data' is, in part, a consequence of this feature of digital technologies. Big data is 'big' not only because of an obvious increase in the information flows in society but most of all because of the astonishing growth of the information collected and managed as information about information.

The digital layer of metadata allows for a wide array of operations to be conducted on the data in question—cataloguing, registration, decomposition, recomposition, correction, multiplication, filtering, ordering, etc.—creating either new types of information or new and innovative ways to present that information.

Furthermore, digital technologies not only act on the metadata layer of information but also provide tools and knowledge to work on the information itself and

---

[1] These characteristics are not listed in any order of priority.

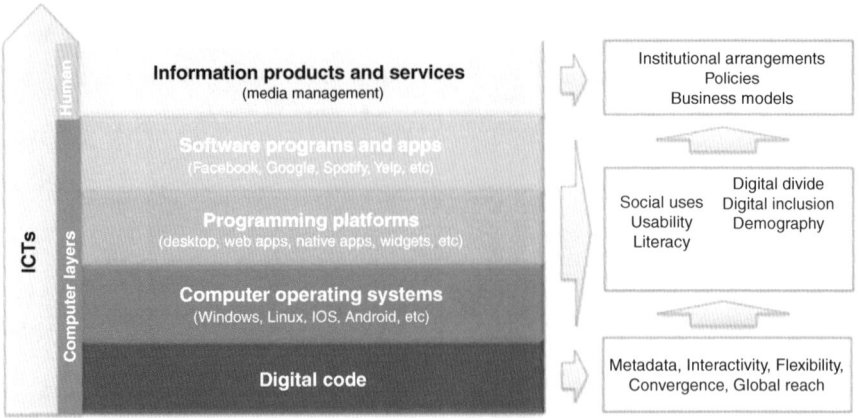

Fig. 1 Layers of digital information and communication technologies

	What it is	**What it means**
METADATA	• Data about the data • Registered by computers • Manual or automatic • Authored or added by the users	• Big data • Data management • Software algorithms • Artifical (information) intelligence
INTERACTIVITY	• Time shifted information comsumption • Place shifted information comsumption • Consumer becomes producer	• Selective (information) comsumption • User empowerment • Prosumer • Challenge on copyright
FLEXIBILITY	• Disassemble/Reassemble • Easy to copy and share • Easy to remix and reuse	
CONVERGENCE	• Text, audio, image, video = bits • All forms of content in one device • One content in multiple devices • "Top-down" and "bottom-up"	• Dominance of screens • New content distribution channels • Diversified authoring tools
GLOBAL REACH	• Digital = computer's common language • "Cloud" is "everywhere" • Cross-effect with bandwith capacity	• Digital reinforces globalization • Abolish frontiers = global reach

Fig. 2 The distinctive features of digital technologies

on its metadata, which means that, with digital technologies, any information user—a website visitor, for instance—can transform that information into something new and out of the control of the original author or proprietary. It's not just the ability to copy and paste but also the more sophisticated ways of managing information. The website IFTTT (if this, then that—https://ifttt.com/), for example, allows the nonprogrammer user of the Internet to instruct many software services to perform automatic actions on information based on its data and metadata. This kind of operations on information and its metadata is something new, with obvious consequences on copyright enforcement but also with potential for new insights to be drawn by media technology managers.

This leads us to a second distinctive feature of all digital technologies: interactivity and flexibility, two ways of looking at the same phenomenon. Interactivity refers to the conditions of action and reaction allowed by digital communications in relation to analogue ones. Flexibility refers to the ability of digital information to be assembled and reassembled in multiple formats. Both ways to look at the phenomenon converge on an empowerment of the individuals in the communication and information process.

Interactivity is greater in digital media than ever was in analogue media, at least at three different levels (van Dijk, 2006). The first level is spatial. Digital media allow a bidirectional or multidirectional communication wherever the individuals may be. In a global network, of course, those who communicate digitally can be anywhere on the planet and maintain a bilateral or multilateral conversation. The second level is temporal. One may choose to consume a particular piece of information whenever he or she chooses and in the context he or she chooses, alone or accompanied, in presence or digitally connected through distance. These two levels of interactivity have huge consequences on the way we consume media and on the way media companies do business. Most traditional media products are conceived on strict time and/or space frame. Newspapers are daily, magazines are weekly or monthly and TV shows go on at a given time, all, mostly, with a national or regional reach. It's not just that the Internet changes the conditions of that media production—you can have a website producing news 24 h that can be 'consumed' anywhere in the world. Most importantly, it puts the control of that consumption in the hands of the consumer.

The third and most important level of interaction is behavioural (van Dijk, 2006). In digital media, sender and receiver can switch roles in the communication process. This constitutes a new feature for traditional media and basically means that all individuals may produce information, which is a 'game-changing' concept (Benkler, 2006; Bruns, 2007). Much of the disruption media face nowadays derives from the fact that individuals are increasingly involved in the production and redistribution of information besides its consumption. Of course, the information and content produced by professionals is very different from that created by amateurs. However, as users become increasingly empowered and involvement in production increases, managers are likely to have to adapt their strategies to incorporate such content and collaborate more effectively with users. Digitally coded information is also easily copied, modified or remixed, a challenge to the media companies' copyright and established business models.

The fourth distinctive feature of digital technologies is what came to be known as 'convergence' (Jenkins, 2006). Content tends to converge in two ways: on the device and by enabling distribution through different digital channels (television, PC, tablet, etc.). This of course opens up obvious opportunities for media companies, because the same content—or different versions of it—can be distributed and marketed through different devices. But what media managers need to understand is that convergence is a 'bottom-up' as much as a 'top-down' process. To the extent that individuals learn to use the authoring tools made available to them by digital technologies, they will increasingly be capable of producing audio, video, image and text, thus seizing for themselves the opportunities created by the convergence process.

The fifth, and final, impact of digital technologies with consequences for the media companies is the global reach and delocalisation. Globalisation is a process that started long before digital technologies emerged, but as the underlying conde is understandable by any computer on the planet (even if interfaces may be language specific), digital technologies tend to massively reinforce the globalisation process. Of course, censorship barriers remain, and governments may seek to control the flow of information by technical means, but the impact remains significant.

These five basic shifts result from the emergence and massive adoption of digital technologies and are the basis of our network society (Castells, 2010). Together, these changes create an entirely new environment for media companies that is fundamental for media managers to understand. In this new media environment, space is increasingly less a space of neighbourhoods, cities or countries and is increasingly a space of flows. What matters are not the confined limits of any geography but the flows of information throughout the networks. Additionally, as Castells suggests, time itself tends to become timeless, in the sense that the processes of digital information cease to be constrained by time—all digital information is available at all times (Castells, 2010). Managers need to develop the capacity to spot technology trends that affect their companies' business models and also to understand the affordances of technologies—their potential uses and modes of interaction—and their impacts.

13.1.2 What Is Changing in Media Technology? A Diagnosis

After analysing the basic theoretical assessments regarding the shift from analogue to digital information and communication technologies, it is now time to look at the changes that shift is producing on the media companies' workflow and business models. An analysis of 30 reports produced between 2011 and 2012 by 17 multinational entities including consultancy firms and think tanks shows the evolution of a new business space in the digital sphere or 'extended media environment' (Cardoso, Mendonça, Paisana, & Lima, 2013).

In this context, it should be stressed that technology migration has initiated new models for creating economic and cultural value. The first feature many reports agree upon is that media businesses now reside within a fully digital age. According to PricewaterhouseCoopers (PwC), we should refer to a 'new normality' of a digital nature. Oliver Wyman (2012) suggests we have already reached the point of no return and we are all connected now. In short, what is argued is that the digital has become the base state to which all media business models must, to a greater or lesser extent, conform.

However, the transition to a digital media environment is complex and requires structural changes that are not easy to implement. If they are to lead the development of new products and overcome procedural problems and limitations, media managers need to better understand technological principles; the full potential of products and digital processes; community and user behaviour; and informational architecture, content management and analytics.

It is necessary to understand the deepest features of digital media in order to avoid adopting a purely cosmetic approach, which is often the case when media managers are pressured to advocate measure to confront the digital revolution. Innovation needs to happen both at the level of products and processes. Ideally, the production of content should itself be influenced by these new dynamics. Managers should consider whether new ventures would be better served by content developed for new platforms and their characteristics rather than simply reversioning archive content or existing products and services.

The same logic should be applied to marketing. In this context, we are already seeing the awakening of the so-called conversational marketing, which places the user at the centre of a strategy oriented towards interactive negotiation with active interlocutors. This new form of marketing is closely linked to social networks; up to 90 % of purchases made by an individual are subject to social influence (Roland Berger, 2012a). At the same time, a connection can be made to the use of marketing dedicated to the analysis of data mining, a trend that guides managers towards a hyper-segmentation of the market. Both changes acknowledge the new active role of consumers and the potential of big data.

As the various media adapt themselves to a ubiquitous electronic context and permanent online connection, a new interactive language gains space in which the consumer is able to choose a specific method of consumption, taking advantage of convergence (increasingly mobile and multimedia) as well as the time when they will consume the information (live/streaming, online/offline, deferred/podcast), using the flexibility allowed by the digital. These are indications of how the profile of the passive media consumer is giving way to one of an active user/producer (Deutsch Bank Research, 2011). An active user/producer values the possibility not only of reacting to a media product, commenting, for example but also maybe of participating (producing) in a platform designed for it. A possible approach for a media company facing such a consumer would be to develop and offer such a platform, very much like what the Guardian and CNN have done with GuardianWitness and iReport, respectively.

Accompanying the paradigm shift here analysed, there has been a widespread uptake of touch-screen technology in which the touch and screen triumph over mouse and keyboard (DB Research, 2012a). In practice, the devices used for online interactions have changed (KPMG, 2012a). Statistics from Deutsche Bank Research (2012a) reveal how the demand for lightweight, portable equipment (connected via cloud computing and network infrastructures) skyrocketed in 2011.

'Cloud'-based products and services are another recurring theme of the reports analysed and a key driver of business model innovation. Cloud-based infrastructure lowers barriers to entry—especially where highly scalable computing and storage resources are required. KPMG places the terms 'cloud' and 'mobile' at the epicentre of change (KPMG, 2012b).

The age of 'Always On' will allow for the renovation of business models and investment in goods and products with a view to minimising client loss and strengthening the user loyalty. Correspondingly, 'push' strategies tend to serve the market better than the traditional 'pull' strategies, both in the distribution of information and in the marketing efforts (Cardoso, Mendonça, Paisana, et al., 2013). For example, applications such as Foursquare allow users to be alerted to offers that are close to where they are currently located.

Faced with the frenetic rhythm of technological advances, the media and tele-communication sectors are the business areas most subject to rapid change. However, they are also the ones in which opportunities could emerge to counter downward trends in profitability. Of course, the current changes in information technologies affect all sectors of business, but disrupt most massively those that use information as its raw material.

The aforementioned importance of multiple screens for the business models of media companies (Deloitte 2012d) highlights the importance of understanding the optimisation of the content, adjusting it to fit the profile and usage characteristic or affordances of each of the available platforms. The Portuguese public television company, for example, recently launched a family of mobile apps, called '5i', designed to work in coordination with some of its most popular TV shows and take advantage of the 'second-screen' use many people are making of their tablets and smartphones when watching television. Those apps have their content optimised to connect with the content of the TV show and integrate with it on the business model with added value phone calls. In this case, both the process of the TV show and its business model integrate with the new social use for a digital technology.

The spread of apps and digital technology is helping to spur the growth of international content markets. It is true that some markets continue to resist services such as Facebook or Twitter, either because they are blocked by national firewalls (e.g. China) or because of the existence of strong national players. However, many of these have seen their share eroded or have been closed down (e.g. in Brazil, the Google-owned Orkut being replaced by Facebook). The same is currently happening with social recommendation engines like Yelp or traffic management services like Waze.

Reference should be made to the role of the aggregators and distributors (Bain & Co., 2012). With privileged access to almost all types of content, they retain the power to orchestrate the selection of content (Bain & Co., 2012), currently a large source of revenue (US$59.8 billion total income in 2013 for Google and US$7.9 billion for Facebook). The network owners and content aggregators—the telcos and the platforms on which users search, filter, produce and distribute information—establish themselves as key players in terms of bargaining power, capable of influencing trends in online consumption and licensing terms prevalent within content markets.

By contrast, content creators and producers are relegated to subordinate levels, something that future business models of content-creating organisations will have to seek to address (as may regulators). They need to analyse the social and user needs that companies like Google and Facebook fulfil and how this allows them to create economic value.

They also need to understand the nature of 'empowered individuals' and the most effective ways of collaborating with them. How can they combine their own proprietary content with that of user-producers, and how can companies make their own content available for users engaged in new forms of content curation and filtering?

Media companies' products and services may, because of their specific characteristics, limit the available options. Some existing models may involve the combination of content and distribution (e.g. pay TV bundles). Media products are also non-excludable and nondepletable goods whose consumption by one individual does not interfere with its availability to others. Most media companies depend on revenue streams from consumers and from advertisers. Some media will be attached to a time window for the release of their products or be geographically based, covering a limited cultural, linguistic and/or geographic audience (Chan-Olsted, & Sylvia, 2006). Some of these practices may have to be abandoned, whilst in other cases, the adoption of technology should acknowledge some of these characteristics.

One final aspect many of the analysed reports mention is the importance of social media in enabling media companies to seize the opportunities created by the digital technologies. In the future, the creation of value within companies will be linked to the way in which social networks are used (McKinsey, 2012). Interaction with content in social media occurs through a multi-experience, multichannel and multi-content environment, within a wider community with cross-border reach and with people who share similar interests (PWC, 2012). Meanwhile, users are curating and discovering content in a new way, not only through search but also increasingly through social media acting as curating and filtering tools.

This new organisation of content consumption and connectivity presupposes a vertical integration according to Oliver Wyman (2012), partnerships between telecommunication companies and leading companies from within specific industries including entertainment but also, potentially, healthcare, financial services and automotive.

The threats and opportunities faced by media companies in the transition to digital information and communication technologies and its related strengths and weaknesses can be summed up in the following SWOT analysis. Although there are certainly specific threats and opportunities in each sector of the media business (television, newspapers, radio, etc.), the central problems and business opportunities are similar.

Strengths	Weaknesses
• High-quality content	• Weak training in the use of new technologies
• Professionalism (management and teams)	• Dependence on advertising revenues
• Strong media brands	• Innovation constrained by dominance of traditional models
• Social institutional relevance	
Opportunities	**Threats**
• Co-opt and acquire user-generated content	• Difficulties in copyright enforcement
• Reuse information products	• Overall revenue decrease
• Put big data/metadata to work for you	• Declining advertising rates
• Curate and filter information abundance	• Competition from content aggregators
• Migrate to 'the cloud' to make information management easier	• Audience decrease in established products and services
• Spread information through multiple channels and devices	• Age gap in the audiences
• Create scale/network effect	• Growth in mobile (difficult to monetise)
• Leverage social media sites	
• Take advantage of global reach	

13.1.3 How Can Media Managers Get Technology to Work for Them? A Prognosis

Armed with an understanding of the social and economic effects of the current digital information and communication technologies and with the knowledge of the disrupting effects they are inducing within the media landscape, media managers are better able to formulate and choose the right strategies to incorporate new media technologies into the workflow and the business models of their companies.

To take advantage of those opportunities, it is important that senior media managers have some understanding of the impact and potentialities of media technologies and that they aren't simply restricted or delegated to technical specialists (Chief Technology Officers, Heads of IT, etc.).

One competence media managers need to develop in this changing media environment is trend spotting. This means going beyond just immediate empirical evidence and examining the underlying nature of trends, such as the growing importance of social media and the increasingly central role of mobile devices. Of course, plenty of empirical evidence points to several key developments in the media landscape, like the growing importance of social media and the emerging central role of mobile devices in the media diet (Stateofthemedia, 2013), to name just two examples. For media companies, it is important to spot such trends.

'Big data' is an increasingly important element of the strategic planning activities of media companies (Cardoso, Mendonça, Paisana, et al., 2013). Privacy concerns on the part of regulators, policymakers and private citizens should not be discounted and may serve as a countervailing factor. Nonetheless, big data offers considerable potential for improved segmentation and product customisation and targeting.

The successful management of technology within media companies is likely to depend on the ability to integrate them into a corresponding business model. Rather than embracing new technologies for their own sake (because they are novel), they should be evaluated in terms of their ability to support and extend existing or new business models.

There is temptation to have a presence in every platform, every channel and every new technology available to distribute information. That may be a waste of scarce resources and assets if that presence is not strategically connected to a viable and sustainable business model. And that may prove more difficult to equate than it seems, because media companies' resources are often still directed at the traditional business models.

The first temptation would be to replicate in the new media environment the business models that were successful in the past. But, given the scope and depth of the transformations analysed above, that may not be the best solution. Most probably the best business models are precisely the ones that respect the basic characteristics of the digital media landscape mentioned above and capitalise them on behalf of media companies (Cardoso, Mendonça, Paisana, et al., 2013).

The most important technology trends emerging are those that correlate several or even all of the basic characteristics of the digital environment:

(a) **Social media**: This is the many-to-many architecture of online networks and the flexibility with which users can share online content. This is an opportunity for media companies to significantly increase the reach of their media brands, although that is not itself easily monetisable. It may, however, increase the potential to generate web traffic (eyeballs) for the content associated with current or new business models. Today, many information brands originating from print already gather a significant part of their online revenues from video (Cardoso, Mendonça, & Neves, 2013).

(b) **User-generated content**: This will continue to grow. Taking advantage of digital authoring tools, people will search for new ways to create and remix content. And they will do so increasingly as they learn to use those tools or as new and improved tools are created, both being permitted and stimulated by the digital technologies (Pascu, Osimo, Ulbrich, Turlea, & Burgelman, 2007). For media companies, this means that, at same time that it disrupts the one-way information flow from media to audience (and its associated business models), digital technologies create a new flow in the opposite direction. The online companies that have been economically successful in the digital age are not creating content but providing the platforms for individuals to create, host and distribute their user-generated content such as YouTube, Blogger, Facebook, Twitter, Instagram, etc. (Accenture.com, 2013a, 2013b; Pascu et al., 2007), which means—again—an obvious opportunity for media companies that are able to act as content platforms rather than content producers or—ideally and transitionally—as both.

(c) **Information overload**: This is increasingly a problem and therefore an opportunity. The combination of the ease with which digital information can be produced and remixed with the network effect of having multiple open channels generates unprecedented amounts of information circulating in a network. In this context, the problem is not the scarcity of information, but its abundance. Users will value ways to manage the abundance, both in the form of tools and of professional curating. Increasingly, user-generated content and social media platforms are doing precisely that, based on the metadata individuals generate when they use those services. Media brands have here a clear opportunity for innovation.

(d) **Big data**: This is still almost entirely ignored by traditional media companies. Rich in metadata, digital information and communication allow the treatment of that information either to better direct marketing efforts of the media brands themselves or to fine-tune the audiences they can present to advertisers. The metadata collected with digital information and communication technologies is something new in the media landscape and therefore suggests opportunities for new business models that can be devised on the basis of the collecting, managing and exploration of those large amounts of metadata.

(e) **Mobile devices**: This expansion in the computing and media landscape is an effect of both the miniaturisation of electronics and the convergence of digital media in a single device. That trend will evolve in the direction of more wearable devices and the so-called Internet of things. Each development will produce trends in the near future. Alongside the current surge in popularity, they also pose real challenges to media companies because adapting their information products and services to such devices is not an easy task. The app environment plays a major role in this trend, not only because it facilitates the mentioned adaptation to the specific characteristics of these devices but also because the current app environment provides an element of scarcity that resembles very much the traditional business models of the media companies. Therefore, that trend will continue to evolve and will present media with additional business opportunities in the future.

(f) **The empowered audience**: This is fostered by digital information and communication technologies and affects the way marketing reaches them. That is relevant to media companies in two ways: first, because it empowers the audience vis-à-vis the media brand itself and secondly, because it empowers the audience that the media brands wish to 'sell' to advertisers. In a digital context in which individuals gain control over the production, distribution and consumption of their information, marketing must become relational (Cardoso, Mendonça, Paisana, et al., 2013). Although advertisers will try that directly with their audiences, media brands still retain the possibility to establish relational marketing channels with their audiences and 'sell' to advertisers the relational access to those audiences. This is yet another trend that can be crossed with new types of business models.

This list does not exhaust all the trends media companies can identify in the foresight of the evolution of digital information and communication technologies. But it covers a lot of potential threats to their current business models, as well as opportunities to expand them or altogether create innovative ones. What is important to retain at this point is that, according to our thesis, the successful avoiding of those threats and seizing of those opportunities will depend on the media manager's ability to understand what the shift to digital technologies means at a deep social and economical level and his or her capacity to identify the trends most relevant to his or her company and cross them with viable business models.

An understanding of socio-technical trends and the intrinsic nature (and benefits) of technologies enables managers to choose technologies that extend their business reach, deepen customer engagement and set a path directly or indirectly towards the generation of revenue streams. Doing that effectively requires an understanding of the strengths and limitations and being able to make a comparative assessment of different technology types. Managers will need to understand how technologies relate to user behaviours and how those, in turn, access the propensity of *someone* (whether user, advertiser or other third party) to spend.

13.1.4 Conclusion

The management of technology in media companies is a greater task than it may seem at first approach. Of course, having a YouTube channel, an iOS news app or a Smart TV app may be immediately attractive for media companies as a way of extending their audience reach. However, several reasons advise a more cautious and *selective* approach. It is probably clear to the reader that the authors regard the embrace of *appropriate* technologies as a matter of importance. However, this needs to take place in a systematic fashion, situated within a broader understanding of socio-technical trends. To not do so entails a number of risks.

First of all, the rate at which technological innovation is happening nowadays is greater than even the broadest company strategy might accommodate. The fundamental disruptive effect those technologies are having on the current work process and business model of media companies makes it urgent to find solutions for the social relevance and eroding revenues of the media (Pascu et al., 2007). Also, the magnitude of the changes imposed by the new digital information and communication technologies imply structural internal transformations that will not come without a cost for the media companies (Cardoso, Mendonça, Paisana, et al., 2013). All of those reasons advise a selective approach regarding the strategies to be pursued in meeting the challenges posed by technology.

In this chapter, we have argued that there are deep changes occurring that call into question the social function of the media and their current business models. Understanding those changes is the first step in meeting the challenges. The second step is to work at spotting emerging trends that are the result of social adoption of new digital technologies. And, finally, the third step is to bring those trends together in practical application by creating new and innovative business models that can compensate for the disruption of current ones.

Both technology and business models (and not just one component) are clearly central in the task of managing media companies. News Corporation's ill-starred acquisition of Myspace is an example of what can go wrong when companies buy into the perceived benefits of new technologies and platforms without understanding their inherent strengths and weaknesses or the degree to which they integrate with companies' strengths, corporative culture and business models (NYT, 2014a).

Rather than adopting an ad hoc approach to technology adoption, its management needs to become more systematic. The management of technology in media companies should be thought as part of Technology Trends Management (T2M), an approach in which the analysis of trends in social appropriation by users of technology is combined with an accurate knowledge of the technological trends available and informs the development and renovation of business models.

References

Accenture.com. (2013a). *The eyes have it: Guess who controls the future of TV. Accenture Outlook [online]*. Accessed December 31, 2013, from http://www.accenture.com/us-en/outlook/Pages/outlook-journal-2013-eyes-have-it-who-controls-future-of-television-media.aspx.

Accenture.com. 2013b. *Taking the pulse: Re-examining digital media and entertainment / Accenture Outlook [online]*. Accessed December 31, 2013, from http://www.accenture.com/SiteCollectionDocuments/microsites/bravemediastudy/Accenture-Taking-The-Pulse-Executive-Summary.pdf

Ashton, W. B., & Klavans, R. A. (1997). *Keeping abreast of science and technology*. Columbus, OH: Battelle Press.

Benkler, Y. (2006). *The wealth of networks: How social production transforms markets and freedom*. New Haven, CT: Yale University Press.

Bruns, A. (2007, June). *Produsage*. In Proceedings of the 6th ACM SIGCHI conference on creativity and cognition (pp. 99–106). ACM.

Burgelman, R. A., & Maidique, M. A. (1988). *Strategic management of technology and innovation*. Homewood, IL: Irwin.

Cardoso, G. (Coord.) (2013). *A Sociedade dos Ecrãs*. Lisboa: Tinta da China

Cardoso, G., Mendonça, S., Paisana, M., & Lima, T. (2013). *Media em Movimento 2013: Perspectivas sobre a evolução do mercado dos Media, a partir de uma (meta-)análise de 30 relatórios de consultoras globais [online]*. Retrieved December 6, 2013, from http://www.obercom.pt/content/834.np3

Cardoso, G., Mendonça, S., & Neves, M. (2013). *Modelos de Negócio Alternativos e Novas Categorias de Jornalismo*. Lisboa: Publicações Obercom. ISSN 2182-6722

Castells, M. (2010). *The rise of the network society. The information age: economy, society and culture* (Vol. I). Malden, MA: Blackwell Publishing.

Chan-Olsted, S. M. (2006). Issues in media management and tecnhology. In A. B. Albarran, S. M. Chen-Olmsted, & M. O. Wirth (Eds.), *Handbook of media management and economics* (p. 251). Manwah, NJ: Lawrence Erlbaum.

Christensen, C. M., Anthony, S. D., & Roth, E. A. (2004). *Seeing what's next*. Boston, MA: Harvard Business School Press.

Digital Tonto. (2013). *5 new principles of strategy for the digital age [online]*. Retrieved December 31, 2013, from http://www.digitaltonto.com/2013/5-new-principles-of-strategy-for-the-digital-age/

Doctor, K. (2014). The newsonomics of NYT Now. *Nieman Journalism Lab*. Retrieved May 10, 2014, from http://www.niemanlab.org/2014/03/the-newsonomics-of-nyt-now/

Filloux, F. (2012). The Atlantic's Quartz: Interesting...but will it make a profit? *The Guardian*. Retrieved May 10, 2014, from http://www.theguardian.com/media/pda/2012/oct/01/the-atlantic-quartz

Insider, B. (2013). How social media is driving massive online video growth. *Business Insider*. Retrieved May 6, 2014, from http://www.businessinsider.com/social-media-driving-online-video-2013-77#!JnJbh

Jenkins, H. (2006). *Convergence culture: Where old and new media collide*. New York, NY: NYU Press.

Manovich, L. (2001). *The language of new media*. Cambridge, MA: The MIT Press.

Moreno, J. (2013). Do Analógico ao Digital: Como a digitalização afecta a produção, distribuição e consumo de informação, conhecimento e cultura na Sociedade em Rede. *Observatório (OBS*)*, *7*(3).

New York Times. (2014a). Retrieved May 10, 2014, from http://mediadecoder.blogs.nytimes.com/2011/06/29/news-corp-sells-myspace-to-specific-media-for-35-million/?_php=true&_type=blogs&_r=0

New York Times. (2014b). Innovation, March 2014. Retrieved May 17, 2014, from http://pt.scribd.com/doc/224608514/The-Full-New-York-Times-Innovation-Report

Pascu, C., Osimo, D., Ulbrich, M., Turlea, G., & Burgelman, J. (2007). The potential disruptive impact of internet 2 based technologies. *First Monday, 12*(3).

Stateofthemedia.org. (2013). *The state of the news media 2013 [online]*. Retrieved November 27, 2013, from http://stateofthemedia.org/

The Economist. (2014). *NewTube*. Retrieved May 6, 2014, from http://www.economist.com/news/business/21601558-media-firms-are-making-big-bets-online-video-still-untested-medium-newtube

van Dijk, J. (2006). *The network society*. Thousand Oaks, CA: SAGE Publications Limited.

White, M. A., & Bruton, G. D. (2007). *The management of technology and innovation*. Mason, OH: Thomson/South-Western.

Consultancy Reports: Accenture

Marshall, C., & Venturini, F. (2011). *The future of broadcasting, a new storm is brewing*. Accenture.

Consultancy Reports: Arthur D. Little

Taga, K., & Schwaiger, C. (2012). *Over-the-top video—"First to scale wins"—Does this mean the return of national heroes?* Arthur D. Little

Consultancy Reports: A.T. Kearney

Gervet, E., & de Matthieu, C. (2012a). *Does advertising still need television?* A.T. Kearney.

Portell, G. (2012b). *Cuts and bruises: What we are learning from the pay TV wars*. A.T. Kearney (www.cmo.com exclusive).

Portell, G., & Gada, K. (2012c, in Foliomag). *The internet economy: Six pence and none the richer*. A.T. Kearney.

Singer, J., Portell, G., Tan, L., & Capp, K. (2012d). *Long live the reader, breaking magazines' dependence on advertising*.

Consultancy Reports: Bain & Company

World Economic Forum Annual Meeting. (2012). (Davos-Klosters, Suíça), Forces transforming the content landscape, Bain & Company.

Consultancy Reports: BCG—The Boston Consulting Group

Rauchfuss, A., Rehse, O., & Stephan, J. (2010). *Lean advantage in media, rethinking operations and building new business models*. BCG.

Dean, D., et al. (2012a). *The connected world—The 4.2 trillion opportunity, the internet economy in the G20*. BCG Report.

Dean, D., et al. (2012b). *Swimming against the tide—How technology, media and telecommunication companies can prosper in the new economic reality*. BCG Report.

Consultancy Reports: Booz & Company

Booz & Company. (2012). *World Telecommunications Outlook 2012+*. Booz & Company.

Consultancy Reports: Deloitte

Asmundson, P., Paul, A., Goswami, D., & Mawhinney, T. (2012a) *Transforming retail: How to improve performance with mobile and digital innovations*. Deloitte.

Davies, M., & Canwell, A. (2012b). *Innovating for a digital future—The leadership challenge*. Deloitte.

Deloitte. (2012c). *Technology and TV, the continuation of a beautiful friendship*. Deloitte.

Lee, P., & Stewart, D. (2012d). *Technology, media and telecommunications predictions 2012*. Deloitte.

Consultancy Reports: Deutsche Bank Research

Dapp, T. F. (2011, Agosto). *The digital society: New ways to more transparency, participation and innovation*. Deutsche Bank Research.

Heng, S. (2012a, Julho). *Media consumption: A mere taste of the actual state of change*. Deutsche Bank Research.

Heng, S. (2012b, Dezembro). *Telecommunications: Volume rising, turnover falling*. Deutsche Bank Research.

Consultancy Reports: Ernst & Young

Ernst & Young. (2010). *Spotlight on profitable growth—Media and entertainment*. Ernst & Young.

Consultancy Reports: IBM—Global Business Services

Berman, S. J. (2012). *Beyond digital: Connecting media and entertainment to future trends*. IBM Global Business Services.

Consultancy Reports: Insead

Dutta, S., & Beñat, B. O. (Eds.), *The global information technology report 2012—Living in a hyperconnected world*. Insead.

Consultancy Reports: KPMG

Matuszak, G., & Lamoureux, T. (2012a). *Mobilizing innovation: The changing landscape of disruptive technologies*. KPMG.
KPMG. (2012b). *Digital dawn—The metamorphosis begins*. FICCI-KPMG Indian Media and Entertainment Industry Report 2012, KPMG.

Consultancy Reports: McKinsey & Company

Chui, M., et al. (2012). *The social economy: Unlocking value and productivity through social technologies*. McKinsey & Company.

Consultancy Reports: Oliver Wyman

Oliver, W. (2012). Painting the bigger picture: An Industry being reshaped—The state of the telecommunications, media & technology industry. Oliver Wyman.

Consultancy Reports: PwC (PricewaterhouseCoopers)

Wilkofsky Gruen Associates Inc., Bothum, D. (Coord.). (2011). *PwC's global entertainment and media outlook 2011-2015*. PwC.
Wilkofsky Gruen Associates Inc., Bothum, D. (Coord.). (2012). *PwC's global entertainment and media outlook 2012-2016*. PwC.

Consultancy Reports: Roland Berger Strategy Consultants

Wittig, M. C., & Bouée, C.-E. (2012a). *Changing the game*. Roland Berger Strategy Consultants.
Wittig, M. C., & Bouée, C.-E. (2012b). *Casual games are for everyone and everywhere*. Roland Berger Strategy Consultants, 2012b.

Consultancy Reports: World Economic Forum (WEF)

WEF. (2007). *Digital ecosystem convergence between IT, telecoms, media and entertainment: Scenarios to 2015. Executive summary*. WEF.

Part IV

Products and Markets

Contents as Products in Media Markets 14

Mercedes Medina, Alfonso Sánchez-Tabernero, and Ángel Arrese

Media products usually comprise two components: a nonmaterial element (journalistic, fiction, persuasive, etc., called content) and a material element (whereby the content is distributed and made accessible to consumers, typically referred to as a platform). While both components function in tandem in the market as regards meeting needs, consumer demand is primarily linked to content; the role of communication or transmission platforms is secondary in this regard, although they may be crucial to such concerns as accessibility (Murphy 2011; Chun 2006).

Hence, the distinguishing feature of media products as such is their capacity to meet the needs and satisfy the desires of potential consumers by providing information, persuasive communication, and entertainment contents. The material elements can influence what kinds of content can be offered and what demand can be fulfilled, but they do not create a demand per se that would be independent from the contents.

Based on this premise, the distinctive nature of media contents may be defined in relation to a set of key concepts that distinguish such contents from other products. On the one hand, these characteristics relate to the status of media products as economic goods, and on the other, such features stem from the special social and cultural significance of media products (Bates 1988).

This chapter addresses media products as economic goods made available in the media market, wherein the management of such products is based on their distinctive nature. Thereafter, the conditions that shape innovation and the production of high-quality contents are explored. Finally, the relationship between contents and target audiences is analyzed because the latter are imbricated (arranged in an

M. Medina (✉) • A. Sánchez-Tabernero • Á. Arrese
School of Communication, University of Navarra, Navarra, Spain
e-mail: mmedina@unav.es; astabernero@unav.es; aarrese@unav.es

© Springer International Publishing Switzerland 2016   243
G.F. Lowe, C. Brown (eds.), *Managing Media Firms and Industries*, Media
Business and Innovation, DOI 10.1007/978-3-319-08515-9_14

overlapping structure) in content management, and this is characteristic of such products from their very beginning.

14.1 Media Contents as Special Products

In light of the two dimensions of media contents cited above, their functioning as information goods, dual (multiple) goods, and talent goods is outlined below.

14.1.1 Information Goods

Media contents are information goods; as such, they share a set of characteristics that are inherent to their nature (Shapiro & Varian, 1999). First, given that their quality and usefulness may only be assessed once they have been consumed, to one degree or another, information goods are experience goods (Nelson, 1970). Hence, the primary objective of media product management in many cases is to gain the client's trust through the experience of an accurate perception of value (for money), which is reinforced or altered over time through a process of continuous learning based on cumulative experiences. Moreover, many media contents also function as credence goods because consumers may find it difficult to assess their degree of quality relative to what they are looking for, and this uncertainty can persist even after consumption of the product (Darby & Karni, 1973).

Second, information goods are subject to economies of scale and economies of scope. These phenomena are related to the normal structure of costs for the production of these contents, characterized by high fixed costs for the initial production of the first copy and low variable costs (in some cases, almost zero) for reproduction. As Doyle observes (2002), this cost structure ensures that marginal costs fall in inverse proportion to the number of units consumed (the basis of economies of scale) and at the same time enables significant savings in multiproduct commercialization strategies and in resale activities for a single product in a variety of formats (the key to economies of scope).

Finally, information goods share to various degrees qualities that are commonly found in public goods, describing goods that depend on the twin characteristics of being both nonrival and nonexclusive in consumption. As far as media is concerned, there are a number of ways to face rivalry and exclusiveness. While free-to-air television and radio have traditionally been regarded as emblematic public goods, the newspaper, music, and cinema industries share many of the defining features of private goods. The traits mean that consumption of the good by one person doesn't prevent consumption also by another (nonrival), and the good is not inherently private (i.e., exclusive).

14.1.2 Multiple Purpose Goods

One of the key characteristics of contents as products is the number and variety of uses to which they may give rise. Hence, it has become common to refer to such contents as multiple purpose goods because they comprise two complementary products targeting two different markets at the same time: contents for audiences and the attention-time of audiences for advertisers (Picard, 1989).

Decision-making in media management must effectively address both the "content product" and the "audience product" (Napoli, 2001), taking into account that each involves specific strategies as regards product design and quality, as well as price, distribution, and promotion. One of the integral criteria of such products in terms of advertising reception and usefulness is their status as attention goods. The media compete in an "attention economy" (Goldhaber, 1997; Lanham, 2006) where variables including consumption time, repetition, and (in)compatibility with other forms of consumption all play a role (Aigrain, 1997).

However, besides the two basic dimensions of most media products (contents for audiences and the attention-time of audiences for advertisers), which imply they be described as dual goods, there is a third dimension that should not be overlooked. This dimension accounts in large part for debates about public intervention in the media sector. To a significant degree, media products have a third target audience: society as a whole. This is especially important for considerations about media effects, or externalities, that can be for good (e.g., promoting greater tolerance) or ill (e.g., promoting violent behaviors).

Thus, media contents are cultural goods—the symbolic products of human creativity. As such, media content pertains to what has come to be known, under varied formulations, as the culture industries. The sociocultural value of media products should not be ignored, which can happen with an exclusive focus on their economic value. Media contents such as films and musical recordings comprise part of the cultural heritage of a society insofar as they have a direct impact on shaping social identities—although how and to which extent certainly vary—and are subject to debate. As regards the information media at the other end of the spectrum (perhaps), the quantity, quality, and variety of information made available may affect the sociopolitical framework of the community in which it is published or broadcast (Picard, 2000). For example, news coverage impacts political election campaigns and results.

The cultural dimension of media products, which is bound up with their potential management as public economic goods, has been used to a significant extent to justify state intervention in the sector, either through ownership or concrete regulations that affect these markets.

In light of the ideas set out above, most media products may be regarded as being multiple by nature—that is, given the number and variety of uses to which they may be put by a multiplicity of clients and target audiences, both individual and collective, they are more than simply *dual* goods.

14.1.3 Talent Goods

The cultural dimension of media content further suggests that they be conceived and assessed as talent goods. Imagination, creativity, and talent are indispensable for the success of media contents, in some cases because of the potential of "star power" to generate extraordinary flows of attention and in other cases because particular teams of professionals succeed in pooling their skills and abilities to produce truly valuable contents in competitive terms. That can happen in sporadically or in a more consistent way over time. In this regard, media contents fulfill the requirements to consider them as creative products. This was defined by Caves (2000: vii) as "the product or service that contains a substantial component of artistic or creative endeavor."

A hallmark of the creative product is a comparatively high degree of unpredictability in market behavior, either in terms of demand (uncertainty as regards the consumption of experience goods as such) or the offer (whereby the reasons for success or failure may not be clear either before or after it takes place)—and, indeed, both. In conjunction with the need to take on high fixed costs, many of which may be unrecoverable, such unpredictability involves a very significant rate of financial risk. At the same time, unlike what may be standard practice in other fields of activity, creative workers are heavily invested in the extent to which they personally care about what they produce. Their "creative inputs" must be internally coordinated within complex work teams, whose members cannot be easily replaced, and must be combined effectively with "humdrum inputs" such as commercialization actions, for instance. Makers of media content typically take the role seriously in terms of its role on professional identity and in terms of its reception and perception among other makers and audiences alike. Factors that may play an important role in the management of media contents when framed as talent goods include market behaviors associated with the so-called economics of superstars (Adler, 1985; McDonald, 1988; Rosen, 1981) and forms of individual brand management linked to "ingredient brands" (Norris, 1992; Venkatesh & Mahajan, 1997).

The specific features of contents as products outlined above mean that media management is a complex process because many of the factors by which the quality and value are assessed will be difficult to measure and because it is also difficult to select the basic and essential resources—above all, talent—in a sector where there is often an (over)abundance of creative pitches and proposals.

To excel in media management, given the relationship with such unique products, companies must practice prudential decision-making at the crossroads between art and commerce, between the creativity of individuals and teams and the firm's corporate financial resources, and between meeting specific audiences' wishes and dealing with both advertiser preferences and society needs in the general interest.

The next two sections discuss how these crossroads are manifested in the management of two key aspects for the success of businesses focused on contents:

one internal, that is, the management of product quality and innovation, and one external, that is, managing relationships with audiences.

14.2   Contents, Quality, and Innovation

Quality is a relative concept because it depends on objective and subjective differences between given contents and the range of other products available. Hence, quality always relates to particular situation at a specific time in a given market context. Indicators (objective standards and the data that measure public perception) reflect the *relative* position of a product or service, which is only known in comparison with equivalent goods produced by rival companies, rather than on some hypothetical, ideal, or theoretically perfect alternative.

In some cases, the link between the objective and subjective aspects of quality emerge in a natural and immediate way: no persuasive process is required to convince consumers that a comfortable, well-furnished mansion is of higher quality than a cold and leaky shack. However, the quality of intangible goods is not nearly as easy to identify: what is the best book, song, or movie of the last decade? The answer will depend on the preferences and backgrounds of each person answering and on the experience they had in consuming the product at a particular time and specific place for each of them.

Framing media products as highly complex goods has a direct bearing on the assessment of the level of quality achieved by the product or range of products that media management decides to offer an audience. As Nieto and Iglesias (2000: 137) pointed out, content quality is a "sum of qualities," many of which are difficult to assess. The fact that media products are basically experience goods and talent goods, whose value is intangible and which encompass a significant creative dimension, renders this issue especially problematic for managers in media industries.

The assessment of content quality ought to at least encompass the following dimensions in a coherent way: objective quality standards (as loosely defined by media professionals: journalists, screenwriters, film directors etc.), subjective quality criteria (the degree to which needs are said to be met and expectations satisfied for particular audiences), and what may be referred to as aspects of social quality (the ways in which such products fulfill symbolic, cultural, political, and social purposes that are regarded as beneficial to and for democratic societies). The inherent difficulty of aligning these three dimensions of quality in a harmonious way, in response to their dependence on experience or trust, results in a spectrum of judgments that range from "Nobody knows" to "I know it when I see it." Thus, it should come as no surprise that products scoring high on objective quality standards sometimes lose out in the market to other, simpler contents that make fewer cultural demands on an audience (Costera, 2005; Ginsburgh & Weyers, 1999).

The quality of media contents is also continually evolving and may be consolidated over time, establishing consumer loyalty behaviors. Habits are formed by repeated acts of consumption that are persistently gratifying—or at least satisfying enough. A particular product may be tried for the first time out of curiosity, on the basis of an effective advertising campaign, or because no more appealing alternative is apparent or available in the market. The endeavor to ensure that the initial reception is eventually consolidated requires media managers to work at molding audience preferences. Only if the audience is "educated," when the public is made to feel comfortable in a particular situation or with a given brand, can a company succeed in establishing an entry barrier to other firms that strengthens its own position in the market. This can mean it not only captures potential clients or customers but also may unseat rival companies in the sector due to the influence it exerts on consumer preferences (Hasebrink, 2011).

Next, then, we will explore quality as the architect of identity, the costs of quality, and the interrelationship between quality and talent in greater detail.

14.2.1 Quality and Identity

In addition to its subjective and objective dimensions, product quality for media content also encompasses a third condition: the construction of an attractive and clearly differentiated identity among competitive alternatives. Growing competition generates noise in the market and creates uncertainty among consumers, who may not know which product to choose or how to distinguish between one offer and another. In this regard, every media outlet needs to have a clearly defined brand identity, which is linked to a well-grounded editorial agenda and communicates a set of instantly recognizable values. As we have explained, media contents are experience goods; as a result, they need credibility to survive.

In a market where there is an overwhelming supply of products, with low entry barriers (especially in relation to creative processes required for their production) and significant volatility in demand, the need for a strong brand identity is becoming more important all the time. That is vital for diverse reasons: to offer a range of different contents as part of a single, coherent brand identity; to create a brand that is continually renewed over time but retains significant values and associations within the market; and to ensure a brand that establishes professional and creative quality norms and sets a standard of public significance, thus facilitating consumer decisions regarding purchase and/or attention.

Brand identity is identified with the company's corporate mission, which grants the organization both a sense of continuity and a capacity for change (Aris & Bughin, 2005; Bogart, 2004). Stability is important because without a fixed point of reference, a company may easily lose its way. Any weakening of identity may give rise to erratic behavior, i.e., one step forward may lead to two steps back and before long the company may be falling far short of the original goal it set when starting out. To all intents and purposes, this risk disappears if company managers base decision-making on clearly established editorial principles (broadly construed, i.e., not restricted only to news content, but certainly especially pertinent there).

The corporate mission also enables a sense of dynamism within the company, since innovation is required if long-term goals are to be met. Internal circumstances (changes in a company's strengths and/or weaknesses) as well as external conditions (emerging opportunities and/or threats in the market) may render what was once regarded as effective and suitable, at a particular point in time to be now outdated and in need of revitalization. Moreover, the corporate mission is comprised of a combination of fixed principles (a particular view of the human being, a set of professional standards, a number of underlying ideas) and other, more variable considerations (market structure, public taste, broader international or domestic developments). Without a well-grounded editorial program that articulates more than merely generic or ornamental statements of good or "politically correct" intention, the company may become paralyzed or unable to change— or even to act. To supply innovative contents, thereby meeting emerging demands from the audience, the company must face challenges head-on and be prepared to leave its comfort zone. It is easier to undertake such a risk for the sake of a particular project that both guides and fosters progress, rather than simply set success itself as the only goal.

To a significant extent, strategies of content imitation stem from the fact that some companies fail to find new ways forward because they do not know where they want to go. This especially happens when their sole concern is not to fall behind or to end up in a cul-de-sac, off the beaten track. However, imitation is often a trap: the strategies that work for some companies may lead to stagnation in other organizations that are limited to merely copying the moves made by the former. It is also possible that the strategy and brand may not be appropriate to either the competencies or the position another firm has enjoyed in the market. On the other hand, in some cases, imitation may make good economic sense because companies are able to save on the costs for R&D, launch products and formats that are already successful in several markets, and realize profits from investment in innovation already accomplished by competitors.

14.2.2 Quality and Talent

There are two "brakes" on quality, the first of which is intangible. A lack of talent, of motivated professionals, and of a spirit of teamwork and a culture that promotes both excellence and innovation comprise one significant brake. The second limiting factor relates to the financial resources available to a firm because many forms of progress are "capital intensive"—that is, significant investment is required to bring about the expected results (Berry & Waldfogel, 2010).

The intangible "brake" on further development lies in the difficulty in building teams of outstanding professionals. The margin of error in this regard is almost unlimited, covering the selection and training of employees, a poor use of tools which, in turn, compromises professional teamwork, as well as policies relating to hiring and firing. Deficiencies in any of these fields tend to produce disenchantment among professionals as regards the companies for which they work, prompting them to write and speak to the interests of management personnel (what the managers want to hear) rather than consider how their work may have a positive or negative impact on the public. Given a workplace dynamic of this kind, innovative change and progress become impossible.

In part at least, the second "brake" is linked to the first: companies may mistakenly hire mediocre employees who have neither appropriate principles nor a particularly refined capacity for storytelling. This situation tends to occur in situations where the preeminent concern is to keep salaries low, rather than as a result of poor employee selection procedures (Martin, 2006).

In sum, then, it should be clear that quality does not come cheaply in media products. It requires the use of a lot of resources (more resources than those used by competitors offering a lower-quality product) and of many types in the hope that such investment may be recovered in the long term, at least. A generous budget enables companies to recruit good employees, to reach beneficial agreements with the best suppliers and distributors, to access the best production tools, and to devise a wide range of different products and/or services to meet the needs and preferences of every consumer group. But it is also safe to say that big budget productions have routinely failed, as well (Picard, 2011). Again, then, the unpredictable nature of media markets, competition, and product performance are particular to media industries—and their management.

The latter aspect is crucial for three reasons: first, the production systems are more flexible, and therefore the cost of implementing variations in each model or prototype is lowered. Second, rival companies endeavor to expand their presence in the market by seeking out less adequately covered market niches, and thus offering a very generic range may involve a major risk in terms of lost sales. Finally, the audience is now accustomed to making its own decisions in consumer choices and, as a consequence, a limited range of options may lead to rejection.

Every rule has relevant exceptions: sometimes, extraordinary talents are able to produce a blockbuster with a small budget. This is the case of "The Blair Witch Project," "Paranormal Activity," or "Super Size Me": all of them spent less than 100,000 dollars and got earnings of more than 30 million dollars. Similar cases can be found in music, television production, or publishing industries.

14.2.3 Quality and Competition

In practice, a balance tends to be struck within the market between the number of competitors and the range of products and/or services on offer. The destruction of competition in media industries is contrary to the public interest because an unregulated monopoly generally leads to an abusive pricing system while also severely limiting incentives that may favor innovation. But it is equally contrary to the public interest to see the emergence of too many competing companies in these industries: if the market becomes too fragmented, the gaps for companies to potentially exploit may be reduced, leading to an increase in prices because of the higher unit cost of production and stifling the drive to innovate. Here again the concept of media contents as special products is implied: for the most part, media products are public goods characterized by a nonexclusive consumption.

Balance in the range on offer is related to how well audience preferences are met. But this must be measured against the fact that too many offers will exceed the potential for a sufficiency of consumers, which results in a loss of productivity. The counterweight of greatest production efficiency is keyed to cost savings realized by producing a generic product for many consumers. This may fail to satisfy the needs of a large part of the public, however, thus both lowering the rate of consumption and undermining entry barriers that prevent or inhibit new competitors.

In this regard, an historical analysis of what a specific company has done in the past, and what other similar organizations have done previously, may disclose very useful insights into what future commitments should be made (Gershon, 1997). Managers and administrators must strike a successful balance between the variety of products and/or services they make available and the need for production efficiency. Internal corporate debates often center on disputes between those who favor supporting consumer preferences and those pressing for greater cost savings.

The factors cited above (technological development, an increase in competition, and a more ingrained habit of choice among consumers) have an extraordinary impact in all media today—print, audiovisual, and interactive. In particular, technology has fostered high levels of specialization and segmentation in communications media, giving rise to what might be referred to (in terms of theoretical possibility at least) as the "Daily Me" or "Personal TV." In fact, limitations on the range of products or services on offer in many fields are now solely economic in nature. As noted above, excessive personalization might place too high a cost burden on many users.

Here it is useful to consider three stages in the process of innovation: (1) identify potential improvements or advances in products and services, often based on the development of new technologies and knowledge; (2) discover whether such changes are of interest to the public, how and to what extent; and (3) devise a business model that would (as much as possible) guarantee that making such change is sustainable (Rao, 2009). Given that quality is a relative concept, the lack of innovation marks a step backward because it weakens a company's position in relation to its competitors and gives rise to dissatisfaction among consumers whose demands and preferences are subject to ongoing change (the two are correlated, obviously). Thus, to maintain and reinforce its competitive edge, the media company must avail its self of the services of many alert professionals who are capable of discerning opportunities for continuous improvement that may be enacted via actions designed to meet the needs of the audience. These professionals may be in-house employees or specialists contracted on some basis from the wider market of service providers.

The decisions taken may also be inspired by some notable activity among outstanding professionals in a field. Professionals in every field explore the newest possibilities afforded by technological and scientific developments, by what other firms and sectors in the industry (and adjacent industries) are doing, and by listening to the advice and suggestions of consultants and experts. However, the most effective way of bringing about significant innovation is to listen carefully to, and strive to understand, the public as people express their thoughts, desires, and preferences by many and varied means. It is vital for media managers these days to be cognizant of social and cultural change, able to trace implicit demands, competent to interpret consumer decisions, and capable to address the causes of success and failure in their firms and industries.

In summary, it is extremely difficult to ensure efficient quality control systems in and for media industries. The best way to foster quality is to build up excellent teams, to ensure a culture of innovation, and to allow some "waste" and failure because that is necessary to explore and discover new territories. For this reason, the management of media companies is particularly challenging; such work requires more creativity than technical knowledge, although the later is also important.

14.3 Audience Products

The most important aspect of media management is to manage audience reach (quantitative) and public satisfaction (qualitative). This means that decision-making in media companies is determined by considerations of and about audiences. However, media are interested in audience as a measurable entity, not for altruistic reasons. They are dependent on the "audience product." The values supplied by the media are not primarily designed to meet audience needs or satisfy public demands, but rather to hone their competitive edge in relation to competitor. Media companies must produce high-quality content not only to achieve audience ratings but also to engage audience attention. In the emerging digital media markets, how media products can become more interactive, how the attention of publics may be engaged, and how audience satisfactions may be measured have become key issues for media managers and all of that needs to be understood in this light.

14.3.1 Audience Participation

The availability of digital broadband presents telecommunications operators with new business opportunities, as well as other suppliers outside the industry who have expanded their business into the booming media sector. Media companies are no longer the only providers of content. Users have begun to play an increasingly significant role in content development—as evident in the Web 2.0 model (Davidson & Rees-Mogg, 1997; Shapiro, 1999). User-generated contents receive high viewer ratings on global online platforms such as YouTube. New technologies have given individual citizens the status of coeditors involved with shaping public opinion via blogs, chats, online communities, and instant messaging. Neither the traditional media nor politicians can afford to turn a blind eye to this shifting influence.

The potential for personalization enabled by new technologies may lead to the paradox described by Carlson (2006). While the new media grants users the power to enjoy media contents when and as they choose (see also Albarran, 2010) and to avoid advertising, such technologies also enable the collection of valuable audience-related data of great interest to content providers and advertisers, such as demographic information and viewer preferences, that facilitates a more targeted form of advertising.

Online media products are characterized by peer collaboration, transparency, audience participation, segmentation, and globalization (Kozinets, 2006; Tapscott & Williams, 2006). Some of these features are complementary to traditional media, and therefore they may enrich their potential. Siapera (2004: 164) believes the Internet brings to the media the possibility to control fans' activity, ascertain their preferences and promote the creation of communities, thereby strengthening audience loyalty to the media. Of course this causal link is not certain and there is a lot that can go wrong. Again, as already discussed, media goods and their performance in markets are characterized by high uncertainty.

Digital media audiences tend to be more passionate and engaged: they do not simply enjoy what they like by themselves; they typically share it with others (Newman, 2012). Hence, communities that are based on shared interests, tastes, and knowledge have emerged and proliferated. At the same time, the evaluation of contents continues to rest mainly on popularity—in general, a spontaneous form of popularity—which media managers may find difficult to either plan for or predict. In the new media scenario, it seems necessary to develop efficient tools to know and understand audience behaviors and interests.

14.3.2 Engaging the Audience

Media audiences are defined on a scale of quantitative parameters that advertisers use to budget their investments. These are based on viewer ratings, shares, and circulation measures. Media managers are keenly aware that users have a variety of tastes, feelings and critical perspectives as regards different media products. The critical attitude among many in the audience today is especially acute in relation to contents for which they have to pay. Audiences that pay, known in commercial circles as subscribers, tend to pay only for contents they regard as indispensable (Herrero, 2003; Picard, 2011).

Pay-per-view media make available a wide range of consumer options and foster user evaluation and personalization of the contents on offer. Users can pay to view the basic package, select specific contents, or pay to access exclusive contents. Pay-per-view options grant the subscriber a decisive role in establishing which contents ought to be offered and which withdrawn. The later especially happens when few users express a willingness to pay for the offer. The pay-per-view model facilitates an almost perfect match between supply and demand, at least in theory, taking into account the tastes and needs of subscribers.

For media companies in many cases and types, the meeting point with consumers, a key location for all companies in the service sector, is not a physical space where direct interaction takes place. This can happen, for example, when a radio or TV channel is broadcasting from a remote location or at the head sales office of a book publisher. But for many media, and media products, ratings figures amount to an implicit, indirect form of contact, wherein the role of users tends to be minimized. This tends to be problematic, however, as insightful discussed by Ien Ang (1991) in a seminal volume titled *Desperately Seeking the Audience*.

Westerlund, Rajala, and Leminen (2011) highlighted two aspects of the new digital business model: the revenue paradigm and customer-driven strategy, both of which foreground the role of the audience. The transformation of business practice brought about by new technologies has prompted a shift from something-for-everyone to everything-for-selected media consumers—that is, spectacular growth in specialized and personalized contents that respond to particular consumer profiles. The internal structure of media companies has likewise been transformed (or is being, depending on context) by this radical change, leading to a focus on market research and on building new organizational capabilities and operational skills. The company-driven or competitor-driven strategies approach that shaped media operations for many years is being replaced by customer-driven strategies. This shift also requires business organizations to be more versatile and adaptive than historically characteristic (Sánchez, 1995).

In addition to allowing users to choose their favorite programs or channels, the type of interactivity enabled by new media technologies fosters what Bordewijk and van Kaam (1986) referred to as interactivity of register, which denotes the media's capacity to register user information and to adapt or respond to user needs. Prahalad and Ramaswamy (2000) draw a distinction between "customization," a production strategy whose purpose is to meet the needs of a particular client, and "personalization," in which the client is a cocreator or the content (s)he uses. Digital media are significant here because of their capacity to foster a more active attitude to and engagement with contents among users. By means of technologies integrated into a platform, rather than external devices such as mobile telephones or the Internet, the audience can take part not only in content creation but also in its evaluation.

Online digital media also enable new and richer data to be collected (Napoli, 2011). Although the Internet is still a comparatively new media and its audience-measurement tools are not yet fully developed, it is clear that far more than only the number of users or the amount of time spent on a given website can be quantified. Analysis can reveal where users come from, what they like, how they behave, and when they make choices. Thus, the Internet provides more detailed knowledge of the audience.

In the new digital media context, profitability is more closely related to nearness, identification, satisfaction, entertainment experience, and branding than to mass audiences and large revenues. A number of scholars have used the term "social capital" (Burt, 2005) in this regard, described as "the benefits individuals derive from their social relationships and interactions: resources such as emotional support, exposure to diverse ideas, and access to non-redundant information" (Ellison, Steinfield, & Lampe, 2010: 873). However, social capital is very difficult to monetize, even among users. Rather than revenues, social media provide media companies with traffic to their sites and information about how people are thinking and responding to products. This depends on the degrees to which media firms are able to capture the data, analyze it, and do something useful in response. This indicates a range of new challenges and also opportunities for media managers. Engagement and branding, closely related to identity ant talent, would appear to be the most valuable benefits to be monetized; some say these are the real social capital (Doyle, 2010).

14.3.3 Audience Satisfaction

The audience does not simply consume media contents: implicitly or explicitly, the public acknowledges the value of such contents as information goods insofar as they add to their knowledge and/or meet their expectations. If contents succeed in holding the public's attention, audience satisfaction can increase. However, establishing a yardstick against which such satisfaction may be measured is not a straightforward task in media management.

In 1995, the annual report issued by AEDEMO (the Spanish Association of Market, Marketing and Opinion Research) included an assessment scale devised to optimize program scheduling in audience satisfaction terms. This was based on viewer predictions in relation to programming (see Pascual & Navia, 1995). To ensure that these predictions are accurate, the assumption was that every individual is watching what (s)he likes in any given moment—the so-called coefficient of coherence. Further research disclosed that this was not in fact the case, and so researchers began to ask why viewers don't always consume the content they might like most. The reasons for this apparent contradiction are many and various and often lie beyond the control of media managers. For instance, the consumer's choice may depend on someone other than the individual viewer; viewers may be unaware of other, more appealing program options; broadcast schedules may prevent viewers from watching the programs they most like; and loyalty to a particular program may lead viewers to ignore more highly rate programs scheduled for broadcast at the same time. This suggests a level of complexity that is quite high for managers of media firms.

Frank and Greenberg (1980) carried out a series of inquiries exploring the interrelationship between audience attention, program types, and the reasons why viewers watch different programs. Among the significant potential factors they identified are social stimulus—that is, sharing ideas with others, the desire to retain a certain social status and/or to impress others, effort to assert leadership, seeking to escape one's problems, trying to build closer family bonds, wanting to better understand others, to be entertained, to improve one's knowledge in educational terms, and an intellectual desire simply to learn. As Frank and Greenberg pointed out, this research facilitates program scheduling based on audience interests, program promotion, and the evaluation of existing shows. But of course, it also suggests the complications in establishing which interests to prioritize in making those decisions and the need to juggle varied and potentially contradictory interests.

Hooking and holding the audience's attention marks success in understanding what audiences need, likes, and tastes. Meeting audience needs and interests involves fulfilling their wishes, thus raising their spirits and prompting them to share what they like with others. In the new digital media economy, sharing is both a sign and measure of satisfaction. Satisfaction cannot be assessed only in terms of audience ratings; it can also be evaluated by reference to the number of individuals who talk about the content; how many view the contents repeatedly; how many download or record contents for later viewing; how many register as fans or access other media to find out more about given contents; and how many are prepared to pay for related products (Medina, 2009).

14.4   Conclusions

The distinctive nature of media contents as products is complex. Their threefold definition as information goods, multiple goods, and talent goods creates particular demands on the decision-making process as regards the range of contents on offer and gives rise to a significant number of distinctive consumer behaviors, which render the management activity in media companies more complex and more complicated than in many other industries.

On the one hand, media contents as products cannot be managed merely by reference to conventional quality standards. Rather, the multiplicity and variety of factors that comprise content or service quality must be taken into account. In this regard, aspects relating to brand and corporate identity and mission and the talent of professional and management teams, as well as their ability to innovate contents in response to audience indications and needs, are especially noteworthy.

At the same time, media contents as products require increasingly refined management competency insofar as these are framed by and depend on audience as product. This form of management goes beyond the established approach to traditional management, or even of legacy media products, because it involves offering high-profile products whose competitive edge draws on such factors as audience participation, engagement, and satisfaction.

In short, then, the management of media contents framed as high-quality products and as audience products requires investing significant resources in the knowledge that such investment will only be recovered in the long term, if at all. In fact, it requires taking calculated risk to a very high degree because success is so unpredictable. This locates the audience (i.e., meeting the public's needs and demands) at the heart of the business decision-making process and calls for the design of an editorial project that renders the diverse skills, talents, and labor of many kinds of professionals internally coherent and consistent and sets out a path toward progress that is clear and compelling for most. This both arises from and is reinforced in companies with highly trained and motivated staff who are committed to bringing about a "peaceful transition" more or less as a continual project today— a process that neither unnerves the audience by making abrupt changes nor rests on the laurels of past success when the fundamentals no longer facilitate sustaining the causes of that success.

References

Adler, M. (1985). Stardom and talent. *American Economic Review, 75*(1), 208–212.

Aigrain, P. (1997). Attention, media, value and economics. *First Monday, 2*(9). Retrieved from http://www.firstmonday.dk/issues/issue2_9/index.html.

Albarran, A. (2010). *The transformation of the media and communication industries.* Pamplona: Media Market Monographs.

Ang, I. E. N. (1991). *Desperately seeking the audience.* London: Routledge.

Aris, A., & Bughin, J. (2005). *Managing media companies.Harnessing creative value.* Chichester: Wiley.

Bates, B. J. (1988). Information as an economic good: Sources of individual and social value. In V. Mosco & J. Wasko (Eds.), *The political economy of information* (pp. 76–94). Madison, WI: University of Wisconsin Press.

Berry, S., & Waldfogel, J. (2010). Product quality and market size. *The Journal of Industrial Economics, 58*, 1–31.

Bogart, L. (2004). Reflections on content quality in newspapers. *Newspaper Research Journal, 25* (1), 40–54.

Bordewijk, J., & van Kaam, B. (1986). Towards a new classification of tele-information services. *Intermedia, 14*(1), 16–21.

Burt, R. S. (2005). *Brokerage and closure: An introduction to social capital.* Oxford, New York: Oxford University Press.

Carlson, M. (2006). Tapping into TiVo: Digital video recorders and the transition from schedules to surveillance in television. *New Media & Society, 2*(8), 97–115.

Caves, R. E. (2000). *Creative industries. Contracts between art and commerce* (p. vii). Cambridge, MA: Harvard University Press.

Chun, W. H. K. (2006). *Control and freedom: Power and paranoia in the age of fiber optic.* Hong Kong: MIT.

Costera, M. I. (2005). Impact or content? Ratings vs. quality in Public Television. *European Journal of Communication, 20*(1), 27–53.

Darby, M., & Karni, E. (1973). Free competition and the optimal amount of fraud. *Journal of Law and Economics, 16*, 67–88.

Davidson, J., & Rees-Mogg, W. (1997). *The sovereign individual: How to survive and thrive during the collapse of the welfare state.* New York: Simon and Schuster.

Doyle, G. (2002). *Understanding media economics.* London: Sage.

Doyle, G. (2010). From Television to multi-platform: Less form more or more from less? *Convergence, 16*(4), 431–449.

Ellison, N., Steinfield, C., & Lampe, C. (2010). Connection strategies: Social capital implications of Facebook-enabled communication practices. *New Media & Society, 13*(6), 873–892.

Frank, R. E., & Greenberg, M. (1980). *The public's use of television: who watches and why.* Beverly Hills: Sage.

Gershon, R. (1997). *The Transnational Media Corporation: Global messages and the free market competition.* Mahwah, NJ: Erlbaum.

Ginsburgh, V., & Weyers, S. (1999). On the perceived quality of movies. *Journal of Cultural Economics, 23*, 269–283.

Goldhaber, M. H. (1997). The attention economy and the net. *First Monday, 2*(4). Retrieved from http://www.firstmonday.dk/issues/issue2_4/goldhaber/.

Hasebrink, U. (2011). Giving the audience a voice: The role of research in making media regulation more responsive to the needs of the audience. *Journal of Information Policy, 1,* 321–336.

Herrero, M. (2003). *Programming and direct viewer payment for Television.* Pamplona: Media Markets Monogaphs.

Kozinets, R. V. (2006). Click to connect: Netnography and tribal advertising. *Journal of Advertising Research, 46*(3), 279–288.

Lanham, R. A. (2006). *The economics of attention.* Chicago: The University of Chicago Press.

Martin, G. (2006). *Managing people and organizations in changing contexts.* Amsterdam: Elsevier.

McDonald, G. M. (1988). The economics of rising stars. *American Economic Review, 78,* 155–166.

Medina, M. (2009). *Creating, producing and selling TV shows. The case of the most popular dramedies in Spain.* Lisbon: Media xxi.

Murphy, S. (2011). *How television invented new media.* New Brunswick, NJ: Rutgers University Press.

Napoli, P. (2011). *Audience evolution: New technologies and the transformation of media audiences.* NY: Columbia University Press.

Napoli, P. (2001). The audience product and the new media environment: Implications for the economics of media industries. *Journal on Media Management, 3*(11), 66–73.

Nelson, P. (1970). Information and consumer behavior. *Journal of Political Economy, 78,* 311–329.

Newman, M. (2012). Free TV: File-sharing and the value of television. *Television and New Media, 13*(6), 463–479.

Nieto, A., & Iglesias, F. (2000). *Empresa Informativa* (2nd ed.). Barcelona: Ariel.

Norris, D. G. (1992). Ingredient branding: A strategy option with multiples beneficiaries. *Journal of Consumer Research, 9*, 19–31.

Pascual, J., Navia, C. (1995). Una aproximación a la predicción de audiencias: panel de valoración de programas. *11° Seminario de Audiencia de Televisión*, 69° Seminario de AEDEMO, pp. 201–218.

Picard, R. G. (2011). Mapping digital media: Digitization and media business models. *Open Society Media Program, 5*, p 23.

Picard, R. G. (2000). *Measuring media content, quality, and diversity: Approaches and issues in content research.* Turku, Finland: Turku School of Economics and Finance.

Picard, R. G. (1989). *Media economics. Concepts and issues.* Newbury Park, CA: Sage.

Prahalad, C. K., & Ramaswamy, V. (2000). Co-opting customer competence. *Harvard Business Review, 78*, 79–87.

Rao, H. (2009). *Market rebels. How activists make or break the rules of the game.* Princeton, NJ: Princeton University Press.

Rosen, S. (1981). The economics of superstars. *American Economic Review, 73*, 757–775.

Sánchez, R. (1995). Strategic flexibility in product competition. *Strategic Management Journal,* *16*(Summer), 135–159.

Shapiro, A. (1999). *The control revolution.* New York: Public Affairs.

Shapiro, C., & Varian, H. R. (1999). *Information rules: A strategic guide to the network economy.* Boston: Harvard Business Press.

Siapera, E. (2004). From couch potatoes to cybernauts? The expanding notion of the audience on TV channels' websites. *New Media & Society, 6,* 155–172.

Tapscott, D., & Williams, A. (2006). *Wikinomics: How mass collaboration changes everything.* New York: Portfolio Trade.

Venkatesh, R., & Mahajan, V. (1997). Products with branded components: An approach for premium and partner selection. *Marketing Science, 16*(2), 146–165.

Westerlund, M., Rajala, R., & Leminen, S. (2011). Insights into the dynamics of business models in the media industry. In *Next Media*. Finland: TIVIT. March 8.

The Audience as Product, Consumer, and Producer in the Contemporary Media Marketplace

15

Philip M. Napoli

15.1 Introduction

One of the most distinctive characteristics of the media marketplace—and thus one of the most important points of focus for media managers—is the role and function of the audience. In the dual-product marketplace that characterizes media, in which content is sold (or given) to audiences and audiences are, in turn, sold to advertisers, audiences occupy the unique position of being the customer in one market and the product in the other market. A substantial literature—some of it critical, some of it strategic/managerial—has developed around the dynamics of this dual-product marketplace, in which the audience occupies this prominent dual role (see, e.g., Ang, 1991; Meehan, 1984; Napoli, 2001, 2003; Owen & Wildman, 1992; Smythe, 1977; Webster, 1998).

New media technologies related to the Internet have contributed to an unprecedented transformation of the media marketplace on a variety of levels (see, e.g., Garfield, 2009; Wirtz, 2011). One of the most significant aspects of this transformation is that it has further expanded the role of the audience (Napoli, 2011). Today, the audience as consumer/product dynamic is being further complicated by the ways that digital, interactive media are increasingly providing audiences with the opportunity to also serve as content *producers,* capable of making and distributing content that can be of significant value to other media consumers—and to advertisers (Benkler, 2006; Livingstone, 2003; Napoli, 2010; Shirky, 2010). That is, media users now regularly produce and distribute content that reaches, and is consumed by, audiences. In addition, media users often produce content, such as social media comments and endorsements, that assist advertisers in delivering brand messages and that can also be used as data in assessing the effectiveness of advertising campaigns.

P.M. Napoli (✉)
School of Communication and Information, Rutgers University, New Brunswick, NJ, USA
e-mail: phil.napoli@rutgers.edu

© Springer International Publishing Switzerland 2016
G.F. Lowe, C. Brown (eds.), *Managing Media Firms and Industries*, Media Business and Innovation, DOI 10.1007/978-3-319-08515-9_15

The traditional dual-functionality of the "audience" in the media marketplace has taken on an increasingly prominent third dimension, thereby further entrenching the audience as perhaps the most significant of the various key stakeholders (including content producers and distributors, advertisers, media buyers, and research companies). Clearly, understanding the nature of the media audience is fundamental for media managers looking to effectively navigate the unique complexities of the media marketplace.

When addressing the question of what is so special about media management, an important part of the answer is in our understanding of the audience, as the audience is much more than the traditional consumer of goods that characterizes most other product markets. The audience serves a number of additional roles, all of which are interconnected and all of which can have profound implications for the management of media organizations. This chapter outlines key distinctive characteristics of the audience as product in the media marketplace and the implications of these distinctive characteristics for media management. The chapter also examines audiences as both consumers and producers of media products. In exploring these various dimensions, the chapter will pay particular attention to what these various dimensions of the audience mean for the management of media organizations, as well as how they have been addressed in media management scholarship.

15.2   The Audience as Product

Many (though not all) media organizations derive at least part of their revenue from the sale of audiences to advertisers. The transaction essentially involves selling the attention (hopefully, but not certainly) of potential consumers to advertisers seeking to sell products to them. When talking about this "audience marketplace" (see Napoli, 2003), we are basically discussing something that is grounded in the rather murky economics of human attention (see, e.g., Davenport & Beck, 2001; Goldhaber, 1997).

The extent to which media organizations participate in this audience marketplace varies by industry sector and even by individual media organizations within sectors. Today some of the key strategic decisions that media managers must make involve questions of if and how they are going to attempt to monetize audiences through collecting advertising revenue. We have seen some social media organizations, such as Twitter, migrate to a business model that is increasingly dependent upon advertising revenues (Lee, 2010), and others, such as Facebook, engage in significant reconfigurations in terms of how they sell their audiences' attention to advertisers (Heine, 2012; Williams, 2012).

One of the most important aspects of the audience as product is the fact that not all audiences have the same value for the consumers of audiences (i.e., advertisers). The value of an audience varies across a wide range of criteria (see Napoli, 2003). The most significant and well-known criteria are, of course, the essential demographic characteristics of age and gender. For many years, the audience marketplace has been driven by a powerful demand among advertisers to reach men and women in the 18–49 age bracket (Napoli, 2003). In many cases, an even narrower audience segment is highly desired (men and women age 18–34). And for many advertisers, the relative scarcity of young men in the media audience (they tend to consume less media) has made them particularly valuable. Other related factors that have been shown to bear directly on advertisers' valuations of media audiences include income, education, and race/ethnicity (Napoli, 2003).

Why are certain demographic groups worth more than others? The answer lies in the fact that these demographic characteristics have historically served as the best available (or at least the most economically viable) proxy for what advertisers presumably care about the most, which is audiences' product purchasing preferences and behaviors. And so, at the most general level, audiences in certain age/income/education categories have been valued more than others largely on the basis of an assumption that these audiences are more likely to spend money on the products being advertised, for reasons ranging from having a greater amount of disposable income to spend, to being more susceptible to advertisements, to a lack of established brand loyalties that might be built up over time to the advantage of the advertiser (Napoli, 2003).

However, it is important to emphasize that audience demographics are an imperfect proxy for the genuine source of the value of audiences and that this approach is an effort by the key stakeholders (commercial media and advertisers) in the marketplace to bring a manageable level of simplicity and efficiency to a very complex process. Advertisers have tended to value certain demographic groups well beyond the extent to which these groups can be empirically demonstrated to warrant such interest (for reviews of this literature, see Napoli, 2003, 2012a). There has always been a fair bit of what we might call "slippage" between those characteristics of the audience that genuinely matter most to advertisers (what products they buy or are likely to buy) and characteristics that actually serve as the key valuation criteria (demographics) in the audience marketplace (see, e.g., Seles, 2010). Yet, advertisers and content providers have for years persisted in relying on this established template for making decisions in the audience marketplace.

As stakeholders have recently begun to meaningfully confront dramatic changes taking place in the population as a whole, we are beginning to see buyers and sellers of audiences move away from heuristics that have long guided their decisions and behaviors. Thus, for instance, the aging of the sizable Baby Boom generation has compelled some advertisers and content providers to rethink their strategies of largely ignoring older audiences (in the 60-plus age range). That is partly because Baby Boomers continue to demonstrate behavioral characteristics that are appealing to advertisers, being more active consumers than previous generations of older audiences (because of better health and more wealth), and partly because they represent a very large (and too large to ignore) percentage of the overall population (BoomAgers, 2012; Elliott, 2009; Moses, 2011).

It is important to emphasize that the reason for the historical disconnect between *how* audiences are valued and purchased and *why* audiences are actually valuable is to some extent a function of the ways in which media audiences have traditionally been measured in the audience marketplace. The process of quantifying human attention for sale in the audience marketplace brings us into the realm of audience measurement as an institutionalized practice (see, e.g., Bermejo, 2007, 2009; Napoli, 2011). One cannot discuss the audience as product without discussing audience measurement. Audience measurement systems are the means by which a product as intangible as human attention is made tangible. Traditionally, audience measurement systems have focused on recruiting a relatively small—though, ideally, representative—sample of a total population and asking that sample to participate in whatever measurement system the firm relies on for information about them (Bermejo, 2007; Webster, Phalen, & Lichty, 2013). Sample-based audience measurement continues to dominate most media platforms, including radio, television, and magazines.

More interactive technologies such as the Internet and digital cable television have contributed to an ongoing migration away from this traditional sample-based process (at least within these platforms), as consumption data can be gathered from virtually every user (see Napoli, 2011). However, even in these contexts, sampling still maintains a prominent role as a control mechanism intended to enhance the generalizability of the findings and to provide the necessary demographic data that advertisers continue to demand (Napoli, Lavrakas, Callegaro, & Mane, 2014).

Considering, then, the role of demographics in this process, it is important to emphasize that, given the many complexities involved in such processes (sample recruitment, retention, proper participation, etc.), emphasizing demographic distinctions has been the most cost-effective means that measurement firms could implement for categorizing the audience as product. More complex categorizations that are based, for instance, on product affinity and purchasing behaviors of individual audience members would introduce a much higher (and perhaps unworkable) degree of complexity into the decision-making processes for buying and selling audiences. Equally important is that attempts to systematically link audiences' media consumption activities with their product purchasing behaviors have failed on a number of occasions, due largely to the measurement challenges and costs. These challenges and costs are associated with the difficulty of maintaining a sufficiently large and representative sample of participants who are willing to engage in all of the activities that are necessary to have their media consumption and product purchasing behaviors accurately measured (Napoli, 2011). Thus, the default system for measuring and valuing media audiences has long been focused on demographics.

This traditional approach to producing the audience product is further challenged by dramatic transformations affecting the media environment. Of particular importance is the increased fragmentation both within and across media platforms, which is a result of the increasing bandwidth and channel capacities with the various media, and the proliferation of new devices and platforms that are changing the media landscape (see Napoli, 2011). Fragmentation makes it increasingly difficult for sample-based measurement systems to fully capture the complete range of audience's media usage. As the number of channels available to a typical television household or the number of Web sites available online increases, the extent to which audiences are spread across these available content options increases as well (though certainly not proportionally). The result is that a growing proportion of the available content options have audiences that are quite small (the well-known "long-tail" phenomenon; see Anderson, 2006).

This situation poses real problems for audience measurement. A sample of say 25,000 television households, or even a million Internet households, becomes increasingly inadequate to provide accurate and reliable audience projections for all of the content options that are available. Consequently, advertisers' trust in the audience estimates is reduced, and thus the value of those small audiences declines. But increasing the sample size increases the costs, and there are limits to what can be charged to clients. Essentially, then, an increasing proportion of total audience attention falls through the measurement cracks. This "dark matter" of audience attention (see Napoli, 2011) cannot be effectively monetized. This ongoing process has been perhaps one of the key issues confronting media managers—and audience measurement firms—over the past decade, as it involves a disruption in the very economic foundation of the audience marketplace (see, e.g., Garfield, 2009).

It is important to emphasize that the realm of audience measurement is a dynamic landscape, particularly in light of the abovementioned changes in the media environment that require effective responses for the audience marketplace to operate as efficiently as possible. Alterations to existing audience measurement systems can recast the nature of the audience—and its value—in significant ways (see, e.g., Barnes & Thomson, 1994; Buzzard, 2002). New systems of audience measurement can emerge that illuminate new potential sources of audience value.

Thus, for instance, in recent years, we have seen the emergence of "social TV analytics," in which data from social media conversations about television programs is collected, aggregated, categorized, and reported in ways that allow the volume and valence of social media discussion about programs to serve as an alternative, or supplement at least, to traditional ways of measuring and valuing television audiences (Napoli, 2012b). Obviously, how many people are discussing a television program online (and how positive or negative their sentiments) represents a very different representation of the audience than the traditional approach of measuring (via a representative sample) the size and demographic characteristics of the audience exposed to the program. Not surprisingly, participants in the contemporary television audience marketplace have been engaged in a fairly detailed examination—and sometimes contentious discussion—of whether social TV analytics represent a meaningful approach for measuring and valuing the television audience (Napoli, 2012b).

This social TV example is just one of the many ways in which the new, interactive media environment has disrupted established approaches to understanding audiences. To address this increased complexity, media organizations and advertisers are now drawing upon a wider array of information sources, ranging from the use of various forms of "big data" (consumer purchasing and lifestyle data, server logs, etc.) to more granular forms of qualitative and ethnographic data that seek to understand the ever-changing dynamics of audiences' media usage across a growing array of platforms. These approaches create new information flows that are contributing to a dramatic reconfiguration of how media organizations and advertisers go about understanding and valuing their audiences.

These patterns and dynamics are part of a much broader transition away from measuring and valuing audiences merely on the basis of their *exposure* to media content and/or advertisements to instead measuring and valuing audiences on the basis of their demonstrated level of *engagement* with the content and/or advertisement (Napoli, 2011, 2012a). Inherent in such a transition is the institutionalization of the value of a dimension of audience behavior that had been largely neglected under the established parameters of the audience marketplace. How this situation is resolved remains to be seen.

The first point here, however, is that various technological and institutional changes can contribute to reformulations of the key criteria of audience value, but any such reformulation must ultimately emerge from—and be supported by—systems of audience measurement that all of the relevant stakeholders in the audience marketplace perceive as sufficiently accurate and reliable to be useful (Balnaves & O'Regan, 2010; Buzzard, 2002). The second important point here is that the value of the audience product is inextricably intertwined with the ways in which the audience is measured. The mechanisms of audience measurement have the power to uncover or unlock previously untapped sources of audience value. These systems also have the potential, via the particular methodological approaches they employ, to neglect potentially important sources of audience value.

From a management standpoint, there are a number of important implications that emerge from the nature of the audience as product and these rapidly evolving dynamics of the audience marketplace. The first is that audiences are a uniquely intangible product. Because the audience product is often the projection of a particular (potentially fallible) measurement system, buyers and sellers of audiences face a high degree of uncertainty about the product that is central to their transaction. Media managers must therefore maintain a comprehensive understanding of the strengths and weaknesses of the specific measurement systems that are being used to translate audience attention into something tangible that can be bought and sold in the marketplace.

Second, as the recent evolutionary patterns discussed above illustrate, the process of understanding and capturing the true sources of audience value is ongoing, which creates an important opportunity for media managers. What is particularly interesting about the contemporary media environment is the extent to which stakeholders are embracing alternative sources of audience value and thus institutionalizing a greater diversity of success criteria in the audience marketplace. This creates greater opportunities for new and innovative types of content to potentially take hold and can actually serve as an incentive for experimentation and innovation.

15.3 Audience as Consumer

The second dimension of the dual-product marketplace that characterizes the media sector involves the audience as consumer of media products. It is important to emphasize the overlap between this dimension and the audience as product dimension, given that audiences' behavioral patterns as consumers factor directly into how they can be packaged and sold to advertisers. But here the focus is on audiences in terms of the dynamics of how they consume media products (rather than how these dynamics are measured and valued). Of particular emphasis will be the role that audiences can play as a direct source of revenue for media organizations (i.e., as paying customers) and the associated range of complications for managers of media companies.

The media sector is characterized by a wide range of strategic approaches within and across platforms in the extent to which media organizations seek to capture revenue directly from audience members. Different strategic approaches have been employed over time even by the same organization. Thus, for instance, the story of the *New York Times* (along with many other online newspapers) in the digital age has been an ongoing saga of the company imposing and then removing paywalls and experimenting with other payment and access variations (see, e.g., Salmon, 2011).

These activities reflect the changing dynamics of the contemporary media marketplace, an environment in which, due largely to the increased availability of "free" content via both legal and illegal channels, audiences' willingness to pay for content has diminished (see Anderson, 2009). Capturing revenue from audiences today therefore involves a complex and dynamic strategic challenge as media managers must determine whether audiences' demand for content is sufficiently high to sustain consumer payment and develop pricing and access strategies that can effectively parse low value and high value content in ways that maximize revenues.

To illustrate, we see sites such as ESPN.com and Hulu making the bulk of their content available for free but withholding some higher value (premium) content for those willing to pay a monthly subscription fee. This "freemium" strategy (see Anderson, 2009) for pricing access to content is increasingly common and depends on an accurate assessment of how audiences value different types of content. This strategic approach can be difficult to implement, however, particularly on a global scale. Particular strategies and access models adopted in one domestic market may not work across geographic boundaries or (as in the case of "windowing") may require that content access models and platforms shift over time. This suggests the need to maintain a dynamic and fluid perspective, but of course that is no recipe for stability and predictability—which are important for business. Moreover, such strategic differentiations can be undermined all too easily by the ways in which pirated content often circulates freely online.

Questions about if, when, where, and how much to charge for content need to be assessed in conjunction with an understanding of how the different pricing strategies interact with potential advertising revenues. Thus, the interaction between the audience as product and the audience as consumer has obvious importance. Content made available for free will usually attract a larger audience than paid-for content, and a larger audience stands a better chance of being successfully monetized in the audience marketplace. However, it is possible that more revenue could be derived from imposing a requirement to pay directly for access than would be obtained purely from advertising if the content is made freely available. So the choice is not always straightforward or self-evident. The revenue captured on a per capita basis from paying customers can be significantly higher than what individual audience members are worth to advertisers. Media managers today frequently find themselves trying to ascertain how best to navigate this dual-product marketplace at a time when both the content and audience marketplaces are in a period of profound change.

It is important to understand, as well, that the audience as a consumer of media products goes beyond the fairly narrow issues regarding the dynamics of consumer payment. Whether content is free or not, audiences are still engaged in processes of searching for, learning about, selecting, and consuming media products. Increasingly today, this also involves sharing their media consumption experiences with others. Media managers must have a thorough understanding of the dynamics of all of these components of the diverse and complex processes by which audiences consume media.

There's a long tradition of research that has sought to enhance media managers' (and scholars') understandings of how and why audiences consume media. Early research in this vein examined issues such as consumer satisfaction with various media products (see, e.g., Lazarsfeld & Field, 1946; Steiner, 1963). Over time, the study of media consumers has come to increasingly focus on understanding how consumers choose various media products (see Owen & Wildman, 1992). This body of primarily theoretical work has sought to develop predictive models for consumer content selection and the associated content provision decisions of media organizations under varying consumer preferences, channel capacities, and competitive conditions.

Empirical work inspired to some extent by the program choice literature has delved into a wide range of factors that impact consumer choices. The findings include both audience factors (i.e., the characteristics of the media consumers, such as tastes, preferences, and awareness of various content options) and media factors (i.e., the quantity of content options, the range of media consumption technologies available). This research seeks to account for both the structural-level and individual-level factors that impact consumers' choices in the media marketplace (Webster & Phalen, 1997).

This research has addressed questions such as the extent to which media consumers' individual genre or format preferences drive media consumption, how content selection is impacted by changes in the technological environment (such as increased channel options, or increased technological choices), and, more broadly, the extent to which media consumers exhibit passive versus active tendencies in their media consumption behaviors (and how such tendencies may vary across different media types and across different demographic categories). The primary objective is to identify consistent and predictable patterns in consumer choice that can have both applied utility for media managers and yield theoretical insights into the dynamics of media consumption.

Another important behavioral pattern among media consumers, from a media management standpoint, involves the "one-way flows" of media products (see, e.g., Kim, 2006; Wildman, 1994). Research on one-way flows has illustrated enduring patterns in media consumer behavior involving (as the name suggests) the tendency for the consumption of media products to flow from large markets to small markets (both nationally and internationally), but seldom vice versa. Such patterns illuminate an important tendency among media consumers to gravitate toward content produced for larger markets, due in large part to the higher production budgets that result in more appealing products (Owen & Wildman, 1992). Many of the recurring patterns we see in the distribution of audience attention in the contemporary media environment, such as the well-known "long-tail" phenomenon (see Anderson, 2006; Brynjolfsson, Hu, & Smith, 2006; Elberse, 2008), can be explained in large part by audiences' tendencies to gravitate to content options with very large production budgets—i.e., the "big head."

Despite some general predictable patterns and tendencies in the consumption patterns among media audiences, it is important to emphasize an inherent unpredictability. Although audiences exhibit fairly predictable patterns across the *aggregate* of content options, and of course those patterns vary across cultures and media environments in different countries, everywhere there remains a tremendous amount of uncertainty about audience selection of *individual* content options. From the "nobody knows anything" mantra that has long permeated the film industry, and research into motion picture audiences (e.g., De Vany, 2004), to the "all hits are flukes" perspective that has emerged from research on the production and consumption of television (see Bielby & Bielby, 1994), media consumers have been, and continue to be, very difficult to predict with regard to specific content options.

For these reasons, media managers often conceptualize consumption as a two-stage process (see, e.g., Webster & Phalen, 1997). The first stage is about making the decision to consume content via a particular medium. This stage is reasonably predictable and exhibits fairly stable behavioral patterns. The audience is going to watch TV, go to the movies, read a newspaper, or go online. The second stage is about the selection between individual content options, and this is highly unpredictable. Which TV channel to watch, which movie to see, which paper or even which article to read, and which site to visit?

This explains todays' keen interest in, and increasingly sophisticated uses of, the ever-growing amounts of data that can be gathered about audiences' media consumption processes, in efforts to develop more predictive models of audience behavior. As was noted above, in today's increasingly interactive media environment, audiences frequently leave measurable traces of their media consumption choices—digital footprints, of sorts. These traces can be aggregated and analyzed in a variety of ways that can, presumably, reduce uncertainty about audiences' media consumption patterns. And so, for instance, motion picture studios increasingly rely on sophisticated algorithms to predict the likely performance of films well before they are even produced (Davenport & Harris, 2009). Predictive tools are derived not only from historical patterns in moviegoing but also from analyses of the sentiments expressed online about individual films. Similarly, online "buzz" is used to predict the likely audience sizes for new television programs (Napoli, 2011). In these and many other ways, mining the vast and growing troves of data about audiences' media consumption has become a vital tool for media managers seeking to effectively anticipate and serve audiences' content preferences.

The key point here is that audiences' media consumption decisions are uniquely difficult to predict, which makes most sectors of the media industry very high-risk endeavors. From a management standpoint, this situation emphasizes the importance of developing the necessary analytical tools for effectively predicting audience behavior. While, as was noted above, the industry is developing a wide range of data-based tools for making such predictions, there are others who would argue that understanding and anticipating audiences' tastes and preferences is more art than science and that the most successful media managers have been those with an innate sense of what types of content will succeed and what types will fail.

And here, of course, is where the unique dual-product marketplace of the media sector comes into play once again. Whereas the manager of an automobile factory can make a very accurate prediction about how many cars the factory will produce in a given day, the producer of audiences for sale in the audience marketplace often lacks any such certainty, given the unpredictable nature of audiences' media consumption. This situation imposes levels of risk and uncertainty that are, in many ways, defining characteristics of the media sector that media managers must learn to effectively navigate.

15.4   Audience as Producer

In recent years, the role of the audience in the media marketplace has expanded significantly, in ways that further distinguish media management from other managerial fields. No longer does the audience serve only as consumer and product in the media marketplace. Today, in a media environment of increased interactivity, in which audiences' opportunities to engage in the production and distribution of user generated content are increasing well beyond those that were available in the "traditional" media era, audiences are increasingly able to operate alongside traditional media companies as content producers, competing with them for audience attention and, to some extent, advertising revenues (see, e.g., Napoli, 2010; Shirky, 2010). To return to the automobile industry comparison, automobile manufacturers generally don't have to worry about their customers deciding to produce and distribute their own cars. In the media sector, in contrast, the contemporary environment is one in which every media consumer can also become a competitor for audience attention and advertising dollars.

Prominent new media platforms such as YouTube place traditional, institutionally produced media content alongside user-generated content emerging from what some characterize as "the people formerly known as the audience" (see Rosen, 2006). While it seems a bit extreme to claim that the concept of the "audience" is fundamentally outmoded, it is important to understand and appreciate the ongoing expansion of the audience's role in the media marketplace and how it is factoring into media managers' decision-making.

At the most basic level, the rise of user-generated content can be seen as both threat and opportunity for media organizations (see, e.g., Bughin, 2007; Mabillot, 2007). The threat arises largely from the extent to which this content can serve as competition for audience attention (and advertising dollars) in an already highly fragmented and competitive media marketplace. Aggregators and facilitators of user-generated content, such as Facebook and YouTube, have proven tremendously powerful in attracting and retaining audience attention—and increasingly in capturing advertising dollars. But such platforms also represent inherent opportunities in user-generated content, as clearly evident in the fact that there is substantial revenue potential for media companies that manage to effectively aggregate and package user-generated content for audience consumption. And, of course, a particularly appealing aspect of user-generated content is that media organizations that find effective ways of aggregating it and monetizing do not have to incur the substantial production costs associated with traditional types of content.

There are a variety of additional roles that user-generated content can play in the strategies of media organizations. Many news organizations are utilizing such content to supplement content produced by their often-dwindling news-gathering resources (i.e., fewer journalists) and as a means of providing a more interactive, and thus more appealing, experience for their audiences (see, e.g., Gal-Or, Geylani, & Yildirum, 2010). Advertisers have, in some instances, relied upon consumers to generate advertisements for them (Burstein, 2012). And a variety of television programs are drawing upon the ever-growing amount of user-generated video posted online (Reinhard & Amsterdam, 2012). In these and many other ways, the effective integration and interplay of user-generated content with traditional, institutionally produced content has become a strategic imperative (Mabillot, 2007).

To date, however, advertisers tend to value media content produced by the audience much less than professionally produced content (Rosenbaum, 2011). It is important to emphasize this is not to say that the audiences are intrinsically less appealing than those for more professionally produced content, but rather that advertisers are wary—or at the very least uncertain—of the "context" (i.e., the nature of the content) in which their advertisements are likely to appear. Here is another instance of the problem of unpredictability in media industries, and thus as a key dimension in their management.

Here we also have an example of the type of emergent (and still evolving) market dynamics characteristic of user-generated content. Other emergent issues include revenue sharing, liability, and the as-yet unclear dynamics surrounding audiences' long-term demand for opportunities to both produce and consume user-generated content in conjunction with traditional media content. All of this highlights a new set of strategic imperatives that media managers are faced with when thinking about "the audience."

Finally, media managers need to be cognizant of the ways in which the audience's role as content producer can interact with its role as product and consumer. Thus, for instance, as the social TV example discussed above illustrated, some forms of user-generated content can be aggregated to serve as data that inform and affect decisions about the buying and selling of audiences. Similarly, various forms of online conversation, such as user-generated reviews and recommendations, are playing an increasingly influential role in audiences' media consumption decisions, creating an important and influential form of "word of mouth" that becomes a vital point of focus for media managers.

15.5 Conclusion

This chapter has addressed a variety of interacting functions that the audience serves in the media marketplace as a key driver explaining why and how media management is fundamentally different from management in other industries. Certainly conceptualizing and understanding consumers for the products of most industries is inherently challenging; it seems rather clear that the degree of complexity and uncertainty involved with this requirement for managing in the media industries is greater than most others. On the face of it, the idea of the "audience" seems rather simple, but in fact media managers must contend with a complex, abstract, and unpredictable entity that is fundamental to their successes and capable of simultaneously being a product, consumer, and producer in the media marketplace.

Fortunately, media managers have a growing array of analytical tools at their disposable for trying to understand, predict, and value audiences in their multiple roles. This also makes it clear that the work of the media manager is increasingly specialized, given the range of dedicated tools for measuring, engaging, valuing, and monetizing media audiences and the fact that these tools continue to grow and become more sophisticated. In this regard, a persistent theme in the media trade press is the increasing analytical sophistication and analytical skill sets that need to be brought to bear on all aspects of the process of buying, selling, attracting, and monetizing audiences (see, e.g., Allen, 2012; Kaye, 2012; Soloff, 2011). Thus, as the nature of the media audience continues to evolve, so too do the necessary conceptual, analytical, and practical skills required of media managers in their persistent need to understand audiences in their diverse roles.

As noted at the outset, media management can be distinguished from other fields of management in large part by the centrality of the dual-product marketplace. As this discussion makes clear, it is further distinguished by the comparatively unique degrees of ambiguity, malleability, and persistent unpredictability of the audience product. Moreover, as this chapter has illustrated, the media audience is a rapidly evolving construct and its evolution is driven by technological changes that impact not only how audience use media but how those usage patterns are perceived and valued by industry stakeholders. Keeping apace of this evolution is a central challenge for media management practitioners and researchers.

References

Allen, L. (2012, January 17). The traditional media buying agency is dead. *Business Insider.* Retrieved January 10, 2013, from http://articles.businessinsider.com/2012-01-17/news/30634372_1_agency-media-clients.

Anderson, C. (2006). *The long tail: How the future of business is selling less of more.* New York: Hyperion.

Anderson, C. (2009). *Free: The future of a radical price.* New York: Hyperion.

Ang, I. (1991). *Desperately seeking the audience.* London: Routledge.

Balnaves, M., & O'Regan, T. (2010). The politics and practice of television ratings conventions: Australian and American approaches to broadcast ratings. *Continuum: Journal of Media & Cultural Studies, 24*(3), 461–474.

Barnes, B. E., & Thomson, L. M. (1994). Power to the people (meter): Audience measurement technology and media specialization. In J. S. Ettema & D. C. Whitney (Eds.), *Audiencemaking: How the media create the audience* (pp. 75–94). Thousand Oaks, CA: Sage.

Benkler, Y. (2006). *The wealth of networks: How social production transforms markets and freedom.* New Haven, CT: Yale University Press.

Bermejo, F. (2007). *The Internet audience: Constitution and measurement.* New York: Peter Lang.

Bermejo, F. (2009). Audience manufacture in historical perspective: From broadcasting to Google. *New Media & Society, 11*(1/2), 133–154.

Bielby, W. T., & Bielby, D. D. (1994). "All hits are flukes": Institutionalized decision making and the rhetoric of network prime-time program development. *American Journal of Sociology, 99*(5), 1287–1313.

Nielsen & BoomAgers (2012). *Introducing Boomers: Marketing's most valuable generation.* Retrieved January 13, 2013, from http://www.nielsen.com/us/en/insights/reports-downloads/2012/introducing-boomers--marketing-s-most-valuable-generation.html.

Brynjolfsson, E., Hu, Y. J., & Smith, M. D. (2006). From niches to riches: Anatomy of the long tail. *MIT Sloan Management Review, 47*(4), 67–71.

Bughin, J. R. (2007, August). How companies can make the most of user-generated content. *The McKinsey Quarterly.*

Burstein, D. D. (2012, February 3). Five lessons in participator marketing from Doritos' "Crash the Superbowl" and CMO Ann Mukherjee. *Fast Company.* Retrieved January 10, 2013, from http://www.fastcocreate.com/1679605/5-lessons-in-participatory-marketing-from-doritos-crash-the-super-bowl-and-cmo-ann-mukherjee.

Buzzard, K. S. (2002). The Peoplemeter wars: A case study of technological innovation and diffusion in the ratings industry. *Journal of Media Economics, 15*, 273–291.

Davenport, T. H., & Beck, J. C. (2001). *The attention economy: Understanding the new currency of business.* Boston, MA: Harvard Business School Press.

Davenport, T. H., & Harris, J. G. (2009). What people want (and how to predict it). *MIT Sloan Management Review, 50*(2), 22–31.

De Vany, A. (2004). *Hollywood economics: How extreme uncertainty shapes the film industry.* New York: Routledge.

Elberse, A. (2008). Should you invest in the long tail? *Harvard Business Review,* July/August, 88–96.

Elliott, S. (2009, April 19). The older audience is looking better than ever. *New York Times.* Retrieved January 11, 2013, from http://www.nytimes.com/2009/04/20/business/20adcol.html?_r=1&.

Gal-Or, E., Geylani, T., & Yildirum, T. P. (2010). *User-generated content in news media.* Retrieved January 12, 2013, from http://www.pitt.edu/~esther/papers/Gal-Or_Geylani_ Yildirim_User-Generated%20Content%20in%20News%20Media_July%2021%202010.pdf.

Garfield, B. (2009). *The chaos scenario.* New York: Stielstra.

Goldhaber, M. H. (1997). The attention economy and the net. *First Monday, 2*(4).

Heine, C. (2012, October 1). Facebook: Our ads are just like TV. *AdWeek.* Retrieved January 10, 2012, from http://www.adweek.com/news/technology/facebook-our-ads-are-just-tv-144118.

Kaye, K. (2012, December 3). Not just for Google: CPGs, Sony seek out data scientists. *Advertising Age.* Retrieved January 10, 2013, from http://adage.com/article/digital/google-cpgs-sony-seek-data-scientists/238578/.

Kim, E. M. (2006). Market competition and cultural tensions between Hollywood and the Korean film industry. *International Journal on Media Management, 6*(3–4), 207–216.

Lazarsfeld, P. F., & Field, H. (1946). *The people look at radio.* Chapel Hill, NC: University of North Carolina Press.

Lee, E. (2010, April 19). Chat, stats, secrets about Twitter. *Advertising Age.* Retrieved January 12, 2013, from http://adage.com/article/special-report-digital-conference-2010/chat-stats-secrets-twitter/143352/.

Livingstone, S. (2003). The changing nature of audiences: From the mass audience to the interactive media user. In A. Valdivia (Ed.), *Companion to media studies* (pp. 337–359). Oxford, UK: Blackwell.

Mabillot, D. (2007). User generated content: Web 2.0 taking the video sector by storm. *Communications and Strategies, 65,* 39–49.

Meehan, E. R. (1984). Ratings and the institutional approach. *Critical Studies in Mass Communication, 1*(2), 216–225.

Moses, L. (2011, October 24). For advertisers, older people are the new youth. *AdWeek.* Retrieved January 10, 2013, from http://www.adweek.com/news/advertising-branding/advertisers-older-people-are-new-youth-136023.

Napoli, P. M. (2001). The audience product and the new media environment: Implications for the economics of media industries. *International Journal on Media Management, 3*(2), 66–73.

Napoli, P. M. (2003). *Audience economics: Media institutions and the audience marketplace.* New York: Columbia University Press.

Napoli, P. M. (2010). Revisiting "mass communication" and the "work" of the audience in the new media environment. *Media, Culture & Society, 32*(3), 505–516.

Napoli, P. M. (2011). *Audience evolution: New technologies and the transformation of media audience.* New York: Columbia University Press.

Napoli, P. M. (2012a). Audience evolution and the future of audience research. *International Journal on Media Management, 14*(2), 79–97.

Napoli, P. M. (2012b). Program value in the evolving television audience marketplace. *Time Warner Cable Research Program on Digital Communications.* Retrieved January 3, 2012, from http://www.twcresearchprogram.com/pdf/TWC_Napoli.pdf.

Napoli, P. M., Lavrakas, P. J., Callegaro, M., & Mane, S. (2014). Internet and mobile audience ratings panels. In Callegaro, et al. (Eds.). *Online panel research: A data quality perspective.* West Sussex, UK: Wiley.

Owen, B. M., & Wildman, S. (1992). *Video economics.* Cambridge, MA: Harvard University Press.

Reinhard, C., & Amsterdam, P. (2012, June). *Virtual world television: Case studies in the emergence of user-generated participatory television.* In Paper presented at the Web Science 2012 Conference, Evanston, IL.

Rosen, J. (2006, June 30). The people formerly known as the audience. *Huffington Post.* Retrieved January 2, 2012, from http://www.huffingtonpost.com/jay-rosen/the-people-formerly-known_1_b_24113.html.

Rosenbaum, S. (2011, November 23). YouTube and the death of user-generated content. *Fast Company.* Retrieved January 12, 2013, from http://www.fastcompany.com/1796573/youtube-and-death-user-generated-content.

Salmon, F. (2011, August 14). How the New York Times paywall is working. *Wired*. Retrieved January 2, 2012, from http://www.wired.com/business/2011/08/new-york-times-paywall/.

Seles, S. (2010). *Turn on, tune in, cash out: Maximizing the value of television audiences*. Retrieved December 12, 2012, from http://convergenceculture.org/research/c3-turnon-full.pdf.

Shirky, C. (2010). *Cognitive surplus: Creativity and generosity in a connected age*. New York: Penguin.

Smythe, D. (1977). Communications: Blindspot of Western Marxism. *Canadian Journal of Political and Social Theory, 1*(3), 1–27.

Soloff, (2011, December 5). How big data analytics can save publishing. *Advertising Age*. Retrieved January 5, 2013, from: http://adage.com/article/digitalnext/big-data-analytics-save-publishing/231363/.

Steiner, G. A. (1963). *The people look at television: A study of audience attitudes*. New York: Knopf.

Webster, J. G. (1998). The audience. *Journal of Broadcasting & Electronic Media, 42*(2), 190–208.

Webster, J. G., & Phalen, P. (1997). *The mass audience: Rediscovering the dominant model*. Mahwah, NJ: Erlbaum.

Webster, J. G., Phalen, P. F., & Lichty, L. W. (2013). *Ratings analysis: The theory and practice of audience research* (4th ed.). New York: Routledge.

Wildman, S. S. (1994). One-way flows and the economics of audience making. In J. S. Ettema & D. C. Whitney (Eds.), *Audiencemaking: How the media create the audience* (pp. 115–141). Thousand Oaks, CA: Sage.

Williams, D. (2012, July 5). Untangling the implications of Facebook's new ad exchange. *Advertising Age*. Retrieved January 3, 2013, from: http://adage.com/article/digitalnext/untangling-implications-facebook-s-ad-exchange/235780/.

Wirtz, B. W. (2011). *Media and Internet management*. Wiesbaden, Germany: Gabler Verlag.

Audience Experiences and Emotional Economy

16

Annette Hill

Audiences are at the heart of an emotional economy. From the perspective of media industries, an emotional economy is about ensuring that a live event, programme or format not only has economic value but emotional value as an interactive experience that becomes embedded in people's lives (Pine & Gilmore, 2011). Audiences are able to experience media in such a way that they play diverse roles: as consumers, performers, participants and producers. In many ways, audience experiences of media parallel those cultural experiences offered to fans for live sporting events. Audiences are positioned as supporters rather than consumers, as part of and not extra to an event (Boyle & Haynes, 2009). Emotions are a striking feature of media products, compared to other types of goods and services, and this has implications for the management of an emotional economy within media firms.

Philip Napoli claims in *Audience Evolution* (2010, and also in his chapter in this book), that media managers must understand audience practices if they are to survive changes occurring in the marketplace. Media professionals are entering into a complex relationship with their consumers–audiences–producers. Content producers and media managers face a series of challenges in creating cross-media content with economic value, aesthetic value and sociocultural value. This is a challenging balance between executive producers, advertisers, sponsors and broadcasters looking to ensure an economic return on a product, creative producers working to ensure the quality of content that connects with consumers, and audiences and users, who engage with content they find meaningful. From a managerial perspective, balancing different types of value is no mean feat. Tensions arise over different practices surrounding value within media management and creative production and the value media has for audiences.

This chapter explores the case of reality entertainment as an example of an evolving audience for complex mediascapes. Reca (2005) cautions against an

A. Hill (✉)
Department of Communication and Media, Lund University, Lund, Sweden
e-mail: annette.hill@kom.lu.se

© Springer International Publishing Switzerland 2016
G.F. Lowe, C. Brown (eds.), *Managing Media Firms and Industries*, Media
Business and Innovation, DOI 10.1007/978-3-319-08515-9_16

overly generalised perspective on media product management, and to that end, the chapter looks specifically at challenges facing media professionals involved in the making, management and distribution of the reality genre. The focus here is on the development of global reality entertainment formats and the role of audiences as consumers, producers and users in their success or failure. The research draws on quantitative and qualitative empirical data that tells us a great deal about audience engagement with this kind of popular entertainment. We shall see that an overly general approach to media management in a multisite project of brand, format and cross-media content can work against the situated practices of audiences as consumers–producers (see Reca 2005). This suggests that in the case of reality entertainment, there is need for flexible management practices that can respond to the fast and furious changes among audiences for this kind of popular culture. The capacity to adapt quickly and effectively to volatile markets is significant to media management.

Göran Bolin notes that the value of media is not so much in content but in how value is produced from that content (2011). The value of reality television often lies beyond the content on offer. For example, the value of mega format *Idols* is about its economic value as an international entertainment format with multiple revenue streams, its aesthetic value as live entertainment for cross-media content and its cultural, social or emotional value. The connections across these different types of value are constantly shifting positions. *American Idol* (Fox, 19 and FremantleMedia) capitalises on an experience economy so that audiences can be both consumers and participants in an immersive media environment, able to support and vote for contestants during live broadcasts, perform during auditions and live events, produce and create mobile and online media content and consume merchandising, music and other media, such as spin-off shows, magazines and newspapers. The brand of *Idol*, then, is connected to consumer interaction and emotional attachment to this form of talent show across a diverse range of media content and experiences. For the past decade, *American Idol* outperformed other television series, including drama, sports and rival talent shows, to be a ratings juggernaut of American network television. Its success in this region helped in the global reach of the format around the world. And yet for all its rating success, *American Idol* also regularly tops 'love to hate' charts and is the butt of jokes on Internet sites like Television Without Pity. One of the reasons for the low cultural and social value attributed to *American Idol* is the perceived overproduction and manipulation of contestants 'formerly known as the audience' (Rosen, 2006). Thus, reality TV's innovation as a genre—real people as entertainment—is also its downfall at this historical juncture as the media become saturated with people performing themselves.

Audiences' evolving experience of reality entertainment is richly suggestive for thinking about the tensions surrounding different notions of value within media management and different modes of emotional engagement with specific forms of entertainment. In terms of media innovation, there are tipping points for media content that can be successful and then fall out of favour with audiences. It is of critical importance that media managers adapt and cope with change in uncertain media markets.

16.1 Emotional Economics

The idea that emotional impact matters for media product success is not new in itself. It is a common assumption in cultural industries (such as sports, leisure and media) that there is money to be made from emotional experiences. A global industry has developed over the past few decades in sports that capitalises on fans of football, for example, and their emotional identification with players and teams. The sporting industry works in close relationship with media industries in representing these fans and their passionate commitment to sport, on TV, in newspapers and in social media. A book on media and sports titled *We Love to Hate Each Other* (2012) neatly encapsulates the use of fans and anti-fans in the business of sports as a consumer experience. In tourism and leisure industries, there is the development of emotional tourism aimed at consumers looking for memorable experiences. A variant on experience-driven holidays is dark tourism, where people specifically travel to nuclear hot spots or visit the site of the 9/11 terrorist attacks in New York City, to experience a holiday with a difference they find remarkable (Sheller & Urry, 2004). Successful tourist operators and leisure managers do not just sell holidays these days, they sell memorable and unusual experiences (Hill, 2011).

In media industries, there has long been an understanding that generating emotional reactions to a film, radio and TV shows is one crucial element in achieving successful ratings. Genres such as soap opera or melodrama rely on a range of emotions (love, hate, pity, jealousy, etc.) to create a backdrop for the multiple narratives and characterisations that are a feature of these genres. If the maker can get audiences to react strongly, then they most certainly have their attention. Recently, popular television has expanded the range of audience reactions from identification with characters, or a storyline, in soap opera say, to shiny floor shows such as *Strictly Come Dancing* (BBC Worldwide) where emotional identification works alongside audience interaction and participation.

Variously, business trends called attention economy, time economy or talent economy are about harnessing time and audience feelings in correlation with consuming products and services. Philip Napoli (in this book) refers to an attention economy to indicate the way media managers have to think about their consumers as dividing their attentions between different genres and across platforms. Albarran and Arrese (2003) in *Time and Media Markets* signal the significance of an attention or time economy. Reca (2005) noted how celebrities and stars become a talent economy in a busy media market. Such talent can draw audiences and consumers to a celebrity performer, programme or product again and again, potentially generating a personal investment and emotional connection with a brand over time. This ability to catch viewers and users and to persuade them to devote precious time to a media product is a significant feature of an attention economy and quite evident today as a key feature of media markets. Thus, it is not surprising that managing product commissioning and acquisition, scheduling, branding and marketing and cross-platform production are core competencies for media managers—especially in broadcasting companies.

Arlie Hochschild (2003) noted how time is a scarce commodity in commercial society. She calls the commercialisation of intimate life 'the time bind'. The phrase perfectly encapsulates the pressure people feel in having enough time given the routines of work, family and households in contemporary society. Hochschild sees a time bind as a negative aspect of the development of American society that is in large part the result of its being so overwhelmingly commercialised. Companies that offer services to help in managing time, such as childcare and relationship advice, capitalise on the time bind to produce revenue. But such a perspective on time, essentially reduced to a commodity, arguably leaves the community and civic values of American society in short supply. Hochschild shows the problems and tensions that arise in families and relationships when people feel the time bind and, perhaps grudgingly, turn to companies that capitalise on the commercialisation of intimate life. She also shows how such negative political, economic and social trends can be worked around or resisted through people's practices on a daily basis. This combination of macro trends and micro practices creates contradictory meanings and values surrounding our relationship with time and has significant implications for media.

These broader trends in an attention economy, an emotional economy or a time bind in commercial society relate to industry audience research. Napoli (2010) analyses the transformation of audience information systems, such as ratings, audience appreciation and measures of engagement. Analyses of industry audience research highlight engagement as attention, memory, emotions and social relations (2010: 100). In particular, 'audiences' emotional responses to content have also been posited as a central element of the broader concept of engagement' (ibid: 104). Performance metrics are applied to television content, for example, emotional engagement in drama, recall of adverts or mood detection for Twitter feeds. Napoli describes the current state of institutional audience research as chaotic attempts to respond to changing dynamics of media consumption, especially increased fragmentation, interactivity and autonomy. He predicts a future of 'greater narrative complexity and ambiguity in our cultural products' where 'the narrative experience associated with any media product extends beyond the primary medium for which it was produced' (ibid: 155).

This state of play regarding media products as narrative or emotional experiences within an attention economy means that media managers need to develop relationships with their audiences that go beyond brand attachment or customer satisfaction. Managers at varied levels—especially in the making of content—must be concerned about creating memorable experiences, moments that stand out in a noisy media market. Good content is partly that because it stimulates emotional responses that audiences find satisfying. It is not nearly enough to fill schedules with content that is cost-efficient—it must also be emotionally effective. The balance between the economic value of a product and the aesthetic, emotional and cultural values of a product becomes crucial when attracting consumers in a time bind. This means that media managers should understand that their competition is not only with other media firms and products but with the wider range of demands on everyone's shrinking amount of 'free time'. People want to spend precious time on products that have a cultural and emotional resonance, whether in drama, factual programming or entertainment. And people's practices shift depending on their engagement with a dramatic narrative like *The Walking Dead* (AMC, USA) or participation in a cultural phenomenon like live sporting events. What follows is a case study of the rise and current decline in reality entertainment formats and audience reactions keyed to the shifting values of these live events as both cultural formations and media experiences.

16.2 Reality Entertainment

The Experience Economy (Pine & Gilmore, 2011) charts business trends that go beyond goods and services. The subtitle of the first edition spells out the message: 'work is theatre and every business a stage' (1999). In the 2011 update, they write, 'The greatest opportunity for value creation resides in staging experiences' (ix–xviii). Examples include tourism and boutique hotel experiences, the Apple Store modelled on hospitality experience design and food and drink industries—e.g. the Heineken Experience. Pine and Gilmore argue that the experience economy comes at a key moment when knowledge, attention and creativity are of high social and economic value. They give the example of birthday parties; whereas only a few decades ago, parents would bake a cake, decorate a home and organise games for their children's birthday parties, now time-poor parents are willing to pay for a birthday party experience organised and managed by event companies, fast food outlets or petting zoos. 'Staging compelling experiences begins with embracing an experience-directed mindset' (2011: 27). This mindset includes 'sensorialising the goods' on offer by heightening the sensory experience for customer interaction and increasing opportunities for membership and participation (ibid). Companies can also 'stage goods events', often through live and interactive experiences (ibid). Although Pine and Gilmore emphasise the staging of experiences for companies, they acknowledge the role of 'cocreation in the formation of experiences' using terms such as participation and prosumer to highlight the multiplicity of dimensions to engaging, multisensory and memorable experiences (2011: xx).

The Experience Economy was first published at a time when reality TV took off as formatted entertainment. It is no coincidence that the reality genre shifted from infotainment in the early 1990s to an emphasis on drama and performance, with multiple points of narrative, characterisation, engagement and interaction (see Glynn, 2000; Hill, 2005, 2007). Around the turn of the millennium, Napoli (2010) described a media industry in crisis, with audience fragmentation across different kinds of content, media ownership and regulation in flux and the rise of the

Internet as a major rival to audience attention. Reality TV producers finely tuned an already existing interplay between fact and drama and formatted this mix into live mediated experiences.

Format is a decisive feature of media products. A format is a way of taking a creative idea, like the reality game show *Big Brother* (created by Endemol), and crafting that idea as a series with characteristic features that is produced in different countries and regions. In an article on reality entertainment formats, the fashion term 'made to measure' has been used to convey the way formats have a certain pattern that can be adjusted for different regions (Hill & Steemers, 2011). Reality formats from the 2000s are household names worldwide today (see Kraidy & Sender, 2011). There are live formats that recruit public votes for each media event (*The X Factor*, produced by Syco and FremantleMedia) and pre-recorded formats that mobilise audience attention and public debate through the scheduling of the series (*MasterChef*, produced by Endemol Shine).

Reality formats utilise many kinds of cross-media content. The formats rely on the mothership, which is the television programme, and that is linked to votes via telephones, mobiles and second screens, to audience interaction via live events and social media and public debate (and discussion) on radio and in newspapers and magazines (Oren & Shahaf, 2012). The biggest formats have spin-off events, like a sister programme that focuses on gossip and interviews with contestants and judges (e.g. *Big Brother*), a national tour or a reunion show (e.g. *Idols*), and extra products, like mobile applications, games and songs. These global formats span a variety of themes including survival competitions like *I'm a Celebrity. . .* (ITV, UK), talent competitions like *The X Factor*, cooking competitions like *Hell's Kitchen* (ITV Studios) and business competitions like *The Apprentice* (Mark Burnett Productions). The roll-out of a format like *Idols* across the media landscape, in each country or region, is a professionally managed juggernaut.

There were reality formats before the global successes of *Big Brother* or *Idols*. The following viewers (aged 18–44) commented on lifestyle TV like *Changing Rooms* (produced in the UK by the BBC) in the late 1990s:

Mark: I find that too orchestrated now, it's the same format every time. . . you know what's coming and you know how it's going to end and I don't enjoy it for those reasons, really.

Andrew: It's had its day really, hasn't it? It was all right at first, weren't it?

Mark: Yeah, you watch the first two minutes and you watch the last two minutes and you've seen the programme.

But, in the words of producer Peter Bazalgette (the manager behind *Changing Rooms*), reality formats 'changed the face of television' when they first appeared (2005).

There are several reasons why formats such as *Big Brother* became 'a billion dollar game' at the turn of the millennium. Briefly, independent producers were able to sell shows to broadcasters whilst retaining rights to the idea itself—the format. From this new kind of intellectual property rights, format-driven companies were able to grow into powerful international businesses that acquire, create, produce, market and distribute formats around the world. Rather than create an idea for a new show from scratch, networks, broadcasters and cable channels can reduce their economic risks through buying a show with a proven track record elsewhere. These programmes have a certain look and feel that is elaborated in a 'production bible' that comes from the format originator but can (with negotiation) be made to measure for other regions, countries and cultures (Hill & Steemers, 2011). In terms of the experience economy, reality formats transformed 'people TV' into live events where audience interaction was embedded in the format and increasingly offered additional revenue streams.

Some companies have to think creatively about how to sensorialise their goods and services. Pine and Gilmore talk in awe about transforming a household product into duct tape experiences. Reality formats put emotion and performance centre stage. Here the drama of a live entertainment show for a large crowd is utilised for maximum affect. There are emotional, physical and vocal performances, judging performance skills and the performance of people participating in the show as themselves, as contestants and as live crowds and audiences. Interactive elements include phone and Internet voting, chatting, creating and sharing content through social media or gaming. The sensorialising of the format and the interactive elements like public voting are steps towards the central staging of live media experiences, key to the success of many reality shows. One viewer defined these kinds of reality formats as follows:

> I've got this tight interactive section—*The X Factor*, *Big Brother*... they rely basically, totally, on viewer participation as much as watching. You've got to call. These shows couldn't work if they didn't have people calling and stuff like that. That's how they make their money. (21-year-old male writer)

Tight interactivity is a good way of describing reality formats such as competitive reality or talent shows. For example, from the moment auditions begin, *The X Factor* relies on a high degree of audience and performer interaction. In the first iterations of the format, these auditions were filmed behind closed doors. In later seasons, the producers recognised a new opportunity in opening up the auditions process to a live audience in theatrical venues to heighten interaction. The feeling of liveness is produced even in these pre-recorded segments through the participation of the contestants and their family and friends as supporters, coupled with the judging panel positioned in front of the stage and backstage presenters and producers. Once the live shows begin, the interactive elements are part of an event that carries audiences through to the season finale. Tight interactivity is a key driver for audience engagement through a long season that can include as many as 20–30 shows. As one viewer explained:

> *The X Factor*, *The Apprentice*, which you have to kind of watch it every week to appreciate it... You have to know the characters to appreciate it more. It's more of an investment. And you kind of decide 'yeah, I'm going sign up for that.' (38-year-old female office assistant)

Reality talent formats are examples of the way media managers and producers can extend narrative experiences beyond the show itself into a global brand and immersive environment. When Reca (2005) talks of a talent economy, these formats take that idea of talent to the very core of the format. Following Aaker's (1997) work on brand personality, the symbolic value of ordinary people performing social roles such as pop star, or dance star, adds to the personification of the brand for these talent formats. These stars in the making are produced by media professionals and audiences who vote in their millions to support or reject the next winner of a talent format. However, the media management strategies for harnessing a talent economy in these formats can backfire as consumers can also feel manipulated into voting for certain personalities. Too much producer intervention into the casting and management of ordinary people in these entertainment programmes can lead to audience disengagement not only with a particular series but a brand as well.

Take *American Idol*, for example. According to the official FremantleMedia (2014) website, *Idols* has been 'watched by over 460 million viewers worldwide since it first launched in 2001' and 'the *Idols* format has aired 207 series across 47 territories to date'. Producers of *American Idol* construct a narrative of consumer power where the public vote is seen to make a difference to the larger dramatic narrative of the competition. As viewers vote for their top ten singers in *American Idol*, their votes are reflected back to the audience in the changing faces of the remaining singers. The live elimination shows have dramatic presence, an unfolding narrative where votes make a difference to people's lives—'America has voted'. Try to watch these elimination shows a few weeks or months later and the drama has faded—the emotional connection is largely gone. This is where the national tour acts to extend the narrative experience beyond the live event. Viewers are invited to vote for their favourite performers who they can see for themselves if they buy tickets to the live tour after the season finale.

Such an embedding of a commercial agenda into a reality entertainment experience can backfire with audiences who tire of a branded talent format. According to the *New York Times* (Stelter, 2012), the 2012 season of *American Idol* saw the format 'grappling with its own competition'. Rival talent shows challenged the juggernaut (e.g. *The Voice*), although *American Idol* still remained number one after eleven seasons on Fox. TV critics and social media chatter suggested the series had lost its cultural value, however, suffering from 'format fatigue'. A commentator for the now defunct website, Television Without Pity, noted how contestants 'probably can't remember a world without *American Idol*' and noted that training for the competition from a young age is 'like watching somebody who was grown in a vat for this purpose' (Stelter, 2012). For 2013, the season dropped its pole position by 40 % compared to 2012, with 14.3 million viewers, in particular losing younger viewers. The average audience age is around 50 now: 'it's become your grandparents *American Idol*' (Halperin, 2013). For 2014, the ratings dropped further still, with 8.4 million for a mid-March show. The show has now been cancelled. The ratings decline marks 'the fall of the house of *Idol*' (Carter, 2014). Such an example illustrates the tricky balance between different kinds of value that a media manager must be aware of and handle within the industry and its connections to wider trends in society and culture.

16.3   Emotional Engagement

To understand future audience trends, a good place to start is with emotion because that is fundamental to human experience. Emotion is traditionally associated with narrative, performance and audience reactions to popular cultural artefacts. For media managers, a crucial aspect of emotional engagement is to consider emotions within marketing strategies as something different from the construction of emotion as representing universal human truths within a drama or entertainment programme. In turn, the ways audiences engage with emotion will sometimes connect and more often disconnect with a marketing approach or a creative producers' construction of emotion. A key point is that emotions are messy and trying to harness emotions in a united project can miss the inherent contradictions surrounding emotional engagement.

In some media companies, the marketing and executive end of a media product is kept separate from the creative content producers. This sensitivity to different production practices allows for creative drive within media content that is relatively unfettered from the marketing or executive teams selling, distributing and promoting content. Similarly, a strategy to allow social media trends to develop as a cross-fertilisation of creative producer and audience conversations allows for audiences and users to feel a sense of ownership for their own emotional engagement with media content. To interfere with Twitter chatter, for example, can send the wrong signals to audiences and fans, indicating they are not in control of their own feelings. Certainly, Twitter analytics for second-screen activities suggest that positive reactions to media content arise from an open conversation between creative producers and audiences. The more media managers intervene in this process, the more likely audiences will disengage as they feel manipulated into an emotional experience that is not their own.

The issue of professional ethics for media managers becomes a clear and compelling issue in relation to strategies and practices surrounding emotional engagement. Emotions work across a spectrum from positive and negative feelings, to the expression of those feelings in social situations. As Arlie Hochschild (2003) points out in her seminal research on emotion work, there is a world of difference between registering an emotional feeling and expressing that feeling. In everyday society, the market of emotions primarily deals in positive expressions of internal feelings, putting negative emotions in short supply. But in the media, there is a market for both positive and negative emotions. Some genres like reality entertainment trade in more negative emotions, including the performance of negative emotions like jealousy, deception and betrayal or even hate. These genres can offer an entertainment space for a market in negative emotions that is not socially acceptable in everyday life.

The construction of emotions in reality TV involves the cultural practices of producers, participants and audiences working together. We can say this is a co-production of emotional performances. There is the production of performances through characterisation, narrative and editing. For example, one producer of a docusoap described the casting of 'big characters with small stories to tell' (Kilborn, 2003: 97). Another series producer of a formatted reality show in the late 1990s noted how participants adapted to the contrived situation of the programme. *Living With the Enemy* (BBC2, UK) challenged people with wildly different values to spend a week together—animal rights activist versus hunter. The producer observed people improvising their roles as antagonists. Participants rehearsed during the week, sounding each other out, identifying the emotional triggers that would create disagreement: 'they don't just turn up and start arguing' (Kilborn, 2003: 165).

Research on performances in theatre or documentary that are based on real people emphasise the centrality of emotions to ways audiences engage in the authenticity of a drama (see Lipkin, 2002, Cantrell & Luckhurst, 2010). Whereas actors performing real people invite audiences to think about how fact might become fiction, reality TV also asks audiences to reflect on how fiction might become fact. In a representative survey of nearly 10,000 people in Britain in 2000, around seventy per cent of respondents thought people acted up for the cameras in reality TV (Hill, 2005). In another survey of 4,500 people in 2003, the results were the same, with around 70 % of respondents expecting people to perform in reality shows (Hill, 2007). When asked if it was important people did not act up for the cameras, only a third of respondents in the 2003 survey agreed with this statement. Key is the genre expectation that reality TV is dramatised. As little as 11 % of respondents in this sample claimed reality formats were true to life. As this woman explained, 'programmes such as *Big Brother* are not factual because the contestants are in a false environment and are acting up for the camera' (aged 25–34).

Reality performances are distinct from actors performing in docudrama. But they are not entirely fictional. One viewer said: 'I think the way in which people speak is more realistic than scripted. The kind of active style dialogue. I think that's one thing that makes it feel much more realistic' (22-year-old female bar staff). Active-style dialogue is a good description of emotional performances in reality TV. Another viewer noted:

> I mean, when the camera's on you all the time it's boring because it hasn't got a plot. We haven't rehearsed something. But when you've been, when you rehearse and you say 'well, we have to do this and we have to do that, the cameras are going to point at us', then... you know, you give something to the people. (29-year-old male electrician)

Kilborn (2003: 102) calls this the 'actuality plus' frame of reference for audiences: 'an acknowledgement of the fact that producers will have dramatically and creatively enhanced the reality being projected'.

Alongside 'active-style dialogue', voice and dance are significant performative modes in reality entertainment formats. Paget and Roscoe (2006) in their research on another hybrid form, the documusical, argue for greater attention to sound in documentary studies. 'Music, as in drama, has a linking/commentating function, driving narrative and providing emotional texture. As John Corner has observed, music in documentary "greatly *intensifies* our engagement with...images"' (2006).

For Paget and Roscoe, music extends the range of emotional colour within documentary; in particular, voice performance can feel more authentic to audiences, a short cut to an 'emotional hub' (ibid). Shows like *The X Factor* draw on vocal performance to intensify that sense of 'emotional truth' producers are looking for in reality TV performances. These viewers (aged 20–30) commented:

Emma: Some of them are real feelings as well. I mean, these, what's it called... for example, *The X Factor*, all of those, that's real feelings. People are in there for a reason. It's that they want to become famous.
Chris: That's the driving thing, everybody wants to be famous.
Emma: So, they are really emotional, passionate.

Physical performances are another shortcut to an emotional hub. In sports, attention has been paid to 'point of contact' or a kinetic energy to physical performances. For example, one sports critic commented, 'boxing has a smell coming off it, and a feel... the taste and sometimes the stink of sweat, snot and blood as bodies clash and clinch' (Boyle & Haynes, 2009: 142). To really experience boxing, one has to be at ringside. For televised boxing, drama is enhanced in the preshow build-up and postshow commentary, where a serial narrative is created through, for example, 'the ritual of the pre-fight weigh in, the menacing eye-to-eye stares' or theatrical entrances to the boxing ring (ibid: 142).

Similarly, physical performance is enhanced in televised live reality shows. In *Got to Dance* (Shine, Sky One, UK, 2012), a teenage boy talked about his love of contemporary dance and how this private passion was a cause of bullying in school. When he performed his dance routine, everyone was moved to tears; the studio audience, the presenter and judges and the viewers were invited to extend their own range of emotional engagement through responding to his dance. As with so many physical or vocal performances in reality entertainment formats, it is not so much this performer's technical skill or level of professionalism that is at stake but their ability to express something that feels authentic, to move us in some way.

In the 2012 season of *American Idol*, the judges repeatedly emphasised that vocal skill was not enough to win; contestants needed to make an emotional connection with audiences through their vocal performances. In one live show (episode 19), several contestants broke down whilst performing. As Jennifer Lopez said 'I feel you baby'. So powerful were their vocal performances that the panel of judges stood up countless times in appreciation. For a professional singer, there is a balance between expressing emotion and losing control of their voice. One contestant Joshua was unable to hit the final high note to his song because he became upset and his throat tightened up. Judge Steven Tyler said Joshua had an emotional breakdown. For producers and audiences, this emotional moment was a breakthrough in the live show and the contestant was voted to the next round. Time and again, viewers will vote for contestants who have struggled with a vocal performance or tripped up in a ballroom dance routine, as long as they can express through physical and vocal performances their 'real feelings', what's driving them to win and how 'really emotional, passionate' they are.

In the same season of *American Idol* (season 11, 2012), we can also see the manipulation of emotional performances by producers and judges in the series. Judge Randy Jackson commented on Phillip Phillips' performance: 'Finally, in the end, in this moment, when you need moments ...you had a giant moment' (Herman, 2012). For Jackson, a contestant's emotional investment in a live performance (the moment) is combined with the framing of this performance as a memorable moment within the television show and across media. The 'moment's moment' is a strategic move by producers to deliver a big emotional performance. This 'moment's moment' then becomes an aggregation of moments that feature in a live show, 'best of' segments from the series, YouTube videos and social media chatter. It takes something that has an emotional truth in a person's vocal or physical performance and transforms it into a faux emotional hub that viewers can perceive as illegitimate.

This focus on feelings is a product of both media professionals and audiences working together. 'Emotional labour' (Hochschild, 1983) is not limited to the media and cultural industries. Professionals working in care homes, for example, are working with emotions on a daily basis: listening, sympathising and empathising with others. Sociologist Viviana Zelizer (2005) in her book *The Purchase of Intimacy* highlights the close relationship between emotions and economics in health and well-being and care industries. We can say that media managers and creative producers are co-workers in an emotional economy, so that when producers script or stage emotional performances, they are working with performers to create a connection with audiences. Similarly, audiences are also co-workers in an emotional economy, where the tight interactivity of reality entertainment formats, for example, only work when producers, performers and audiences are in concert with each other. In this way, emotional engagement does not happen in isolation, but can be co-created by producers and audiences with often different results. Producers can manage emotions within a television show or social media community, through the work of hosts, performers, moderators and users, but audiences also manage their emotions, through the work of attention, user interaction or fan activities. For contemporary audiences, they are aware of the commercialisation of feelings within media industries, but they are still looking for an emotional truth, passions they can tap into and make their own, as shared moments or collective experiences.

It is worth briefly unpacking what is meant by the cocreation of media content. The idea of a cocreation of producer, participant and audience practices is a term that is situated within political economics and production studies, where structural factors are a basis for producer–market–consumer relations. And it is a term that is situated within audience studies, where media content can be used as cultural resources for understanding agency, identity and power. We should be wary of using a term like cocreation without qualifying both the structural factors that can lead to political interpretations of the media production–consumer relations and the resource factors that can lead to cultural interpretations of production–audience relations. Rather than see cocreation as a co-operative endeavour, it is often a tense relationship between different groups of people who are engaged in multiple practices.

Zelizer (2005: 306) calls the mingling of economic activity and social relations 'connected lives' and observes that 'people are continually involved in maintaining, reinforcing, testing, and sometimes challenging their relations to each other'. For Zelizer, 'there is not one strategic actor moving against another. Instead, we find people locating themselves within webs of social relations' (ibid). This idea of connected lives is suggestive of the ways producer–consumer–audience relations can be located within economic and social or cultural contexts. This is not one power player moving against another, but people maintaining, reinforcing, testing and challenging the relations between each other in a push–pull dynamic.

The relations between producers, consumers and audiences are complex practices. For every successful format that becomes a talking point, there are many failures. For all the preparation by producers in the staging of a reality event, there are still a dozen ways audiences can react in unforeseen circumstances. According to one viewer, 'these programmes are created by us. We create demand for them, we create the justification for them, we create their success and we create therefore their continuity' (34-year-old male mobile phone seller). The success and continuity of reality entertainment in an emotional economy is situated in these shifting relations between producers, participants and audiences.

16.4 Conclusion

Media audiences are at the forefront of an emotional economy where consumer engagement, performance and experience are centre stage. This mix helps to create individual and collective cultural experiences that people will pay for again and again. If we look at the example of reality entertainment formats such as *American Idol*, they contain tight interactivity in the form of public auditions, voting or social media that function as a driver to increase audience investment in the live event as it builds momentum through the season and is rolled out around the world. A reality entertainment experience is a co-production between producers, performers and audiences. Format producers and participants work on enhancing drama, tragedy and comedy, rehearsing and scripting certain types of characters and their emotional journey. The 'active-style dialogue' of reality performances works alongside vocal and physical performances, creating emotional hubs for audience engagement. Reality entertainment makes consumers, audiences and publics visible and audible, through participating in shows as live crowds and in auditions as contestants and as themselves, through voting or making and sharing content for social media and through gossiping, people watching and public debate. The immersive, interactive elements of media such as reality entertainment suggest a widening point of consumption for all things emotional.

A note of caution among media managers can be seen in the ways talent formats are now in a decline with their target audience of 18–49-year-olds. This decline is partly because of format fatigue and partly because there has been an overproduction of participants in these talent shows. Producer intervention and participant's overtly emotional performances can make audiences disengage with the brand. The emotional hub so significant to narrative experiences for a talent show can be overproduced to the point of saturation with a target audience. This highlights the crucial importance of managing a balance between the varying economic and emotional and social values of a media product across difference spaces within the industry and for media audiences, consumers and participants. Emotion can be a revenue source, and it can be a creative or narrative construct, but it also signals more universal human truths such as authenticity or truth that matter to audiences.

The trends in experience and emotional economics are an example of a development in business management, highlighting the commercialisation of feeling as part of a canny repositioning of an industry and economy in crisis. Interactive and participatory media is also an example of the development in the future of media audiences, highlighting evolving practices for immersive mediascapes. The tight interactivity, emotional hubs and participatory elements of much media content suggest that audiences have evolved from recipients or spectators to a hybrid form where they can be consumer, participant and producer at the same time. And yet this development narrative can overshadow the bigger picture of media and audiences. The focus on emotion is a testament to audiences' traditional engagement with human nature, mediated across different historical junctures, genres, platforms and spaces. There is something familiar and traditional about emotional hubs in TV shows or social media forums, where vocal and physical performances are short cuts to 'real feelings'. As one person explained, 'it's like an ancient formula in a different format. It's just human nature. That's what it is' (25-year-old male student).

Research Note

The audience research in this chapter draws on a range of methods: quantitative surveys with representative samples, semi-structured focus groups and in-depth interviews in households in Britain and Sweden. Research from 2000 to 2001 included a survey, distributed by the Broadcasters' Audience Research Board (BARB) to a representative sample of 8216 adults (aged 16–65+) and 937 children (aged 4–15) during August 2000; twelve semi-structured focus groups (7–8 participants), with children (aged 11–14), young adults (aged 15–18) and adults (aged 18–44), who defined themselves as regular viewers of popular factual television and were in the C1C2DE social category (lower middle class and working class), during 2000–2001; and in-depth interviews with ten families, with children of varying ages, over a six-month period in 2001, living in the Greater London area and in the C1C2DE social categories. For 2003–2004, the data included a quantitative survey with a representative sample of 4516 British people aged 16–65+, carried out by Ipsos RSL. In Sweden, a quantitative survey was conducted with a random sample of 2000 people, in co-operation with the SOM Institute, Göteborg University, and carried out by Kinnmark Information AB. The net sample was 1,854 people, with 944 respondents and a net response rate of 51%. The distribution among responses was compared with the Swedish population as a whole and also compared with another representative survey (National SOM study 2004). During 2003–2004, a series of semi-structured focus groups were conducted in Sweden and Britain. There were 24 groups, 12 in each country, with a total of 129 respondents aged 18–60. The sample was based on the criteria of age (roughly split into two groups of 20–30-year-olds and 40–60-year-olds), gender (even mix of male and female) and socioeconomic status (working and middle class and educational levels from school to university). There was also an ethnographic, longitudinal study of media and interactivity in thirty households in the Greater London area (2005–2007).

The research for this chapter was funded by the public organisation the Economic and Social Research Council, the regulatory bodies the Independent Television Commission and Broadcasting Standards Commission (now Ofcom) and the television companies BBC, Channel 4 and Channel 5; Jonköping International Business School; the Society, Opinion and Media Institute, Göteborg University, Sweden; and the University of Westminster, UK.

References

Aaker, J. (1997). Dimensions of brand personality. *Journal of Marketing Research, XXXIV*, 347–356.

Albarran, A. B., & Arrese, A. (2003). *Time and media markets.* Mahwah, NJ: Lawrence Erlbaum Associates.

Bazalgette, P. (2005). *Billion Dollar Game: How three men risked it all and changed the face of Television.* Britain: Time Warner Books.

Bolin, G. (2011). *Value and the media: Cultural production and consumption in digital markets.* London: Ashgate.

Boyle, R., & Haynes, R. (2009). *Power play: Sport, the media and popular culture* (2nd ed.). Edinburgh: Edinburgh University Press.

Cantrell, T., & Luckhurst, M. (2010). *Playing for real: Actors on playing real people.* London: Palgrave Macmillan.

Carter, B. (2014, March 21) Once a hit, it's ratings make idol an also-ran. *The New York Times, 22.*

Glynn, K. (2000). *Tabloid culture: Trash taste, popular power and the transformation of television.* Durham and London: Duke University Press.

Halperin, S. (2013, May 17) American idol finale's ratings free fall: what went wrong. *The Hollywood Reporter, 4.*

Herman, J. (2012, 18th May). American idol castoff Joshua Ledet talks favourite moments. *Hollywood Reporter.* Accessed online, http://www.hollywoodreporter.com/idol-worship/american-idol-joshua-ledet-phillip-phillips-326691.

Hill, A. (2005). *Reality TV: Audiences and popular factual television.* London: Routledge.

Hill, A. (2007). *Restyling factual TV, audiences of news, documentary and reality genres*. London: Routledge.

Hill, A. (2011). *Paranormal media: Audiences, spirits and magic in popular culture*. London: Routledge.

Hill, A., Steemers, J. (2011). Big formats. Small nations: Does size matter? In G. Lowe, N. Christian, and P. Robert (Eds.), *Why size matters*. Gothenberg: Nordicom.

Hochschild, A. (1983). *The managed heart: The commercialisation of human feeling*. Berkely: University of California Press.

Hochschild, A. (2003). *The commercialisation of intimate life: Notes from home and work*. Berkley: University of California Press.

Kilborn, R. (2003). *Staging the real*. Manchester: Manchester University Press.

Kraidy, M., & Sender, K. (Eds.). (2011). *The politics of reality television: Global perspectives*. London and New York: Routledge.

Krøvel, R. (2012). *We love to hate each other. Mediated football fan culture*. Gothenberg: Nordicom.

Lipkin, S. N. (2002). *Real emotional logic: Film and television docudrama as persuasive practice*. Carbondale and Edwardsville: Southern Illinois University Press.

Napoli, P. (2010). *Audience evolution*. NY: Columbia University Press.

Oren, T., & Shahaf, S. (2012). *Global television formats*. New York: Routledge.

Paget, D., & Roscoe, J. (2006). Giving voice performance and authenticity in the documentary musical. *Jump Cut: A Review of Contemporary Media, 48*(Winter). Online, Accessed 19 June 2012. http://www.ejumpcut.org/archive/jc48.2006/MusicalDocy/text.html.

Pine, J., & Gilmore, J. (2011). *The experience economy (1999 updated edition)*. Boston: Harvard Business Review.

Rosen, J (2006, 30 June). The people formerly known as the audience. *Huffington Post*. Accessed 21 June 2014 http://www.huffingtonpost.com/jay-rosen/the-people-formerly-known_1_b_24113.html.

Sheller, M., & Urry, J. (2004). *Tourism mobilities: Places to play, places in play*. London: Routledge.

Stelter, B. (2012). Idol Grapples with its own competition. *New York Times*. Accessed May 22, from www.nytimes.com/2012/05/23/arts/television/American-idol-ponders-a-ratings-dip-on-fox.html?_r=o

Zelizer, V. (2005). *The purchase of intimacy*. New York: Princeton University Press.

Dynamic Media Management Capabilities: A Case Study

17

John Oliver

17.1 Why 'Dynamic Capabilities' Matter for Media Firms Today

The new media environment that has emerged in the past decade or so has paved the way for new technologies keyed to digitalisation that has fuelled the proliferation of television channels and changes in audience consumption patterns, as is evident in time-shifted viewing and multiple platform uses of television content. Albertazzi and Cobley (2010, p. 179) noted that the 'transformational changes' in this new competitive environment may have felt like an unwelcomed revolution to some television broadcasters, whilst to others, it is likely to have provided them with a unique sequence of evolutionary opportunities. In fact, we don't know enough about this because, as Albarran (2006, p. 17) noted, the 'literature devoted to television management is extremely limited', and researchers need to engage in this area in order to understand the 'rapid change as a result of regulatory and technological changes'.

This transformational context raises a number of questions for media management researchers that also have implications for practitioners. Firstly, how do media companies manage their businesses in this context, and how are they responding to the challenges of a media environment characterised by sweeping change and high uncertainty? Secondly, how do they manage and adapt their resources and capabilities to remain competitive? This chapter will argue that the concept of 'dynamic capabilities' is useful and important for answering these questions. This discussion will be illustrated by a study about BskyB in the UK because the case demonstrates how one influential firm has adapted to a competitive landscape that is characterised by rapid market changes. Colapinto (2010, p. 60) sets the tone for our

J. Oliver (✉)
The Media School, Bournemouth University, Dorset, UK
e-mail: joliver@bournemouth.ac.uk

discussion in arguing that traditional media companies have been required to 'adopt dynamic responses to the challenges of a multiplatform television market', and as such, the concept of dynamic capabilities is ideally placed to investigate the management practices of media firms.

The 'dynamic capabilities theory' (DCT) is based on empirical research about the renewal of company resources and capabilities (Ambrosini, Bowman, & Collier, 2009). Four premises underpin the concept:

1. It is concerned primarily with change at the organisational level.
2. It suggests that change involves a process of adaptation that is centred on an organisation's ability to renew capabilities and competencies.
3. It positions adaptation as a project that requires deliberate resource investment in organisational learning with processes that aim to produce positive results in corporate performance and strengthen competitive advantage.
4. It envisions the adaptation process as occurring in a compressed timescale because the focus is on success in the operational context of the fast changing market conditions.

DCT is distinguished from more general notions of change and firm adaptation by its emphasis on the renewal of resources and capabilities with the aim of delivering superior firm performance in the near term, not only much later (Garud & Van de Ven, 2007).

17.2   Overview of Dynamic Capability Theory

DCT has a relatively long history of inquiry in strategic management literature, but has only recently been investigated by media management researchers. What makes this concept especially relevant to this field is the application to 'high-velocity' markets (Oliver, 2012). Media industries are challenged with change at a pace and scope that is relatively unique. The literature on dynamic capabilities describes a concept linked to the resource-based and knowledge-based paradigms of strategic management. In essence, these paradigms argue that the effective management of tangible and intangible resources can provide a firm with sustainable competitive advantage in the form of unique capabilities and competencies.

Whilst this theoretical base presents an array of definitions, interpretations and even claims and counterclaims about the existence of dynamic capabilities, the inspiration for this concept arose from theorists questioning how firms were able to sustain competitive advantage and superior performance in the context of changing market conditions where 'the increasing dynamism of the environment' (Pettigrew, Thomas, & Whittington, 2007, p. 143) makes it increasingly difficult to remain competitive. Many scholars (Leavy, 1998; Mintzberg, 1987; Senge, 1990; Zollo & Winter, 2002) concluded that superior performance was driven by a firm's ability to learn, adapt and change their resource configurations in order to produce a series of typically temporary competitive advantages. Lawton and Rajwani (2011, p. 167) concluded that 'dynamic capabilities are the bridge between firm resources and business context' and, as such, believe this concept provides a useful lens for examining superior organisational performance. Thus, DCT has a strong practical footing that media managers ought to find especially useful and important.

The central tenet of 'dynamic capabilities' is that tangible resources are (re) configured and consistently utilised to generate value and secure rents and that intangible, knowledge-based resources (in the form of skills, experience, learning, organisational and managerial processes) provide the 'know what and know how' (Pettigrew et al., 2007, p. 143) to organise these tangible resources in a way that create competitive advantages that cannot easily (or at all) be imitated by competitors.

Ambrosini, Bowman, & Collier (2009, pp. 30–35) argued that dynamic capabilities 'specifically focus on how firms can change their valuable resources over time'. They further argued that dynamic capabilities refer to the drive and enthusiasm of a firm in their 'renewal of resources'. This perspective echoes the earlier work of Teece and Pisano (1994), and also Zollo and Winter (2002), who emphasised that in a changing external environment, firms needed to adapt and reconfigure internal resources, assets, operating routines and competencies in order to improve their effectiveness and grow competitiveness that depend on, and account for, superior corporate performance. In a sense, the idea that firm capabilities need to be dynamic prioritises alignment with the competitive environment, taking into account its future direction and establishing how a firm can take advantage of the opportunities provided by environmental change today and for tomorrow.

The theoretical frame for this discussion identifies and differentiates the concept of dynamic capabilities by considering the discrete but interrelated definitions of 'capability', 'core competence' and 'dynamic capabilities'. Whilst Ljungquist (2007, p. 394) noted that these terms are often amalgamated in literature, there is greater value in understanding each concept and 'distinguish(ing)...their characteristics'. 'Capability' assumes that many organisations have access to similar resources, but that one, or some, has a superior ability to manage, as Grant (1991, p. 119) suggests, 'a team of resources to perform some task or activity' better than competitive rivals and to extend the resource potential that differentiates the organisation's capability and performance from competitors.

In their review of strategic management literature, Pettigrew et al. (2007, p. 39) noted that understanding a firm's 'capability' should be extended to a consideration of competition in the marketplace and how this influences long-term corporate performance. It is one thing to succeed for a while, and there are lessons worth learning from that, but even more when studying about firms that have enjoyed long periods of success in contexts that required frequent adaptation and continuous development. Such firms are evidently 'dynamic' in the management of their capabilities. A firm's dynamic capabilities can be considered as a minimum threshold of resources that are required to satisfy market requirements that are in flux. Bitar and Hafsi (2007) support this view and suggested that capabilities arise from a range of organisational elements that prioritise the interaction of people, structure, systems and values. This conceptualisation of organisational capability provides a route to competitive advantage that gives rise to the notion of unique and distinctive business processes that provide value for the customer, thus extending the debate into the realm of core competence.

A generation of researchers has been developing the conceptual framework proposed by Prahalad and Hamel (1990, p. 82) that is focused on core competencies as 'the collective learning in the organization, especially how to coordinate diverse production skills and integrate multiple streams of technologies'. Core competencies ground sustainable competitive advantage because they facilitate unique abilities to provide customer value. However, one must acknowledge that all competitive environments change over time, and this raises the question of whether organisational capabilities and competencies can continue to leverage competitive advantage in high-velocity media markets (Oliver, 2012) when 'market boundaries are blurred, successful business models are unclear, and market players (i.e., buyers, suppliers, competitors, complementers) are ambiguous and shifting' (Eisenhardt & Martin, 2000, p. 21).

Whilst investment in, and development of, resources and core competencies are embedded in operational routines and facilitate learning that create opportunities for a firm (Leonard-Barton, 1992), in fast changing markets, those routine behaviours can also present a dilemma, and this certainly applies to media firms today. On the one hand, they need to invest in the exploitation of existing capabilities and competencies, whilst at the same time, they need to be mindful of the necessity to refresh and adapt their resource base to align with environmental changes that have strategic importance. Otherwise, existing competencies become core rigidities and function as barriers to change. In contrast, to give a sense of balance to this area of discussion, Danneels (2002, p. 1097) provided a more encouraging perspective on embedded operational routines, arguing that rather than restricting the firm, existing core competencies could be successfully used to 'leverage' new competencies. But it's arguably the case that the degree to which those possibilities will be realised in practice depends largely on the firm's development of dynamic capabilities.

The work of Teece, Pisano, and Shuen (1997, p. 516) is seminal in the elaboration of the concept of dynamic capabilities. They were the first to explain superior organisational performance through the lens of dynamic capability, arguing that firms needed to renew competencies in line with changing competitive conditions and that it was 'the firms ability to integrate, build and reconfigure internal and external competencies to address changing environments' that explained variations in interfirm performance. Although differences in the definitions of capability, core competency and dynamic capabilities may at first glance seem a small matter of semantics, closer scrutiny draws attention to two words that suggest dynamic capabilities can be differentiated from core competence and capability. The words 'reconfigure' and 'changing environments' suggest that core competencies, whilst providing unique customer benefits, may in fact decay or even become irrelevant due to structural changes in the competitive environment. As a consequence, they would not provide a means of sustaining competitive advantage. This line of reasoning has subsequently been supported by a number of scholars including Eisenhardt and Martin (2000) and Ambrosini, Bowman, & Collier, (2009).

Another focal point in literature is concerned with whether it is possible for organisations to reconfigure the resource base without having a dynamic capability. Winter (2003, pp. 992–993) argued that organisational change can occur outside the realm of dynamic capabilities where unusual environmental challenges in the form of 'force majeure' act as a driver for change. What differentiates these acts from dynamic capability is that the latter requires 'long-term commitments to specialised resources' which incur higher investment costs for the organisation that adapts to, and benefits from, opportunities presented by new competitive conditions. This point is illustrated in the account of how the Wall Street Journal built dynamic capabilities for the online provision of journalism content. Steinbock (2000, p. 184) noted that building these new capabilities required 'bold resource commitments' and 'innovative responses in times of market turmoil and technological change'. Thus, whilst it is possible to reconfigure without master of dynamic capabilities, it isn't likely that reconfiguration can happen as a continual and consistent practice that is successful more often than not in its absence.

17.3   A Conceptual Framework for Dynamic Capabilities in Media Firms

There is no doubt that traditional media firms and markets have been characterised by turbulence, complexity, unpredictability and often what amounts to seismic change since the emergence of the new media environment that is the consequence of digitalisation combined with networked communications. DCT provides a clear and relevant lens through which to examine the causes of superior firm performance over time.

The previous discussion acknowledges that media firm resources should be managed in a way that delivers capabilities to compete by meeting minimum market requirements and that these resources can be managed with a focus on developing unique core competencies that create sustained competitive advantage and superior firm performance. At the same time, however, high-velocity environmental change dictates that these resources, capabilities and core competencies can decay and lose relevance, and, as such, they need to be reconfigured and adapted for the firm to remain competitive. This is the heart of the matter that DCT addresses.

Interestingly, Miller and Shamsie's (1996, p. 519) study found that the management of tangible resources and intangible knowledge-based resources provided different outcomes of firm performance in relation to different market dynamics. They concluded that the management of physical resources 'contributed most to performance in stable and predictable settings', whereas the management of knowledge-based resources was more effective in uncertain and unpredictable markets since they are more adaptable and more flexible. This suggests that the managers of media firms would be wise to invest more resources and efforts in developing knowledge-based competencies and capacities.

The answer to why some media firms are more successful in the adaptive process than others would, in this view, suggest that some are more dynamically capable than others. Jarzabkowski (2004, p. 533) argued that whilst the environment sets a context for change and adaptation, there is tension with the recursive nature of some firms that exhibited 'path dependence, persistent organizational routines and organizational memory' that resulted in unique competencies. However, in fast changing conditions, this type of behaviour could result in what Pettigrew et al. (2007, p. 217) described as a 'competency trap' which promotes organisational stability to a degree that causes inertia. In contrast, some firms may exhibit adaptive behaviour and 'capability dynamism' (Chmielewski & Paladino, 2007, p. 466), and that has been found especially valuable in high-velocity markets. This type of behaviour is manifest in flexible organisational structures, routines and processes, organisational learning, willingness to experiment, market sensing and opportunistic behaviour, and informal management and strategy processes. Such behaviour seeks the serial realisation of temporary competitive advantages over time, with the timeframe of advantage varying of course.

The conceptual framework in Diagram 17.1 illustrates a linear process explaining how resources develop over time and in response to changing environmental conditions. In the first stage, all firms have access to resources. The management and utilisation of these resources create capabilities to deliver at minimum market requirements. Over time and with experience, and further resource investment, firms can develop core competencies that are unique and deliver higher value to customers. However, when the competitive environment undergoes structural change, turbulence and uncertainty, firms are driven to adapt and reconfigure their resource base, assets, operating routines and competencies to improve effectiveness in the pursuit of competitive advantage and to realise superior performance. Thus, in a low-velocity and predictable environment, firms are not motivated to change, adapt and reconfigure their resource base, whilst in a high-velocity and unpredictable environment, they are.

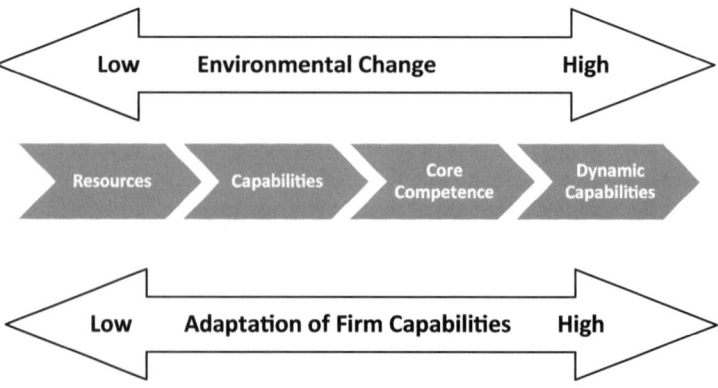

Diagram 17.1 A conceptual framework for understanding dynamic capabilities

The bibliographic and co-citation analysis of dynamic capabilities research by Di Stefano, Peteraf, and Verona (2010) presented several significant areas of inquiry from researchers over the past decade. Firstly, researchers have tended to focus their activities on strategic organisational change, adaptation and the transformational processes that deliver these changes. Secondly, the creation of dynamic firm capabilities requires a long-term commitment to resource renewal that bears higher costs over a sustained period of time. Thirdly, there are certain factors that enable or inhibit the development of dynamic capabilities, organisational renewal and adaptation.

Factors that enable the development of a dynamic capabilities have been presented by numerous authors (Colapinto, 2010; Danneels, 2002; Eisenhardt & Martin, 2000; Helfat, 2000; Karim & Mitchell, 2000; Macher & Mowery, 2009; Steinbock, 2000; Tripsas & Gavetti, 2000; Winter, 2003). Taken together, they have argued that reconfiguration to refresh a firm's resource base can be achieved by:

- Setting corporate objectives and strategy at an aspirational level
- Managerial cognition of the environmental and competitive context
- Investment in product innovation and development
- Investment in more general R&D
- Significant investment in people and (or) processes
- Corporate acquisitions, joint ventures and mergers

To illustrate, we'll look at a UK firm, BskyB, using two methods of research: firstly, comparative financial analysis that relies on both horizontal and vertical analysis to understand how an organisation is performing when compared with its past achievements (Ellis & Williams, 1993) and, secondly, a content analysis of BskyB annual reports, including the statements made by the respective chairmen and chief executive officers (Miller & Shamsie, 1996).

In the year 2000, BskyB was a market-leading pay-tv broadcaster. More than a decade later, they have not only held their market-leading position; they have enhanced their competitive position in the UK market and adapted their business into a multiplatform, multiproduct media firm. The discussion that follows will provide a 'vignette' on how they developed dynamic capabilities, adapted their business and delivered superior financial performance.

17.4 Analysing BskyB as a Case of Dynamic Capabilities

17.4.1 Setting Corporate Objectives and Strategy at an Aspirational Level

At the start of the new millennium, BskyB chairman Rupert Murdoch set an aspirational tone for the company as it entered the dawn of the new media environment. He said they were 'changing the way people watch TV and the way we communicate, empowering consumers with tomorrow's technology today' and that they will 'anticipate what consumers want and how they want to access it' (Rupert Murdoch, CEO, 2000).

With a record breaking 21 % increase in subscribers to reach 3.6 million in 2000, BskyB was not content to rest on its success and continued to set ambitious subscriber figures, looking to reach 7 million by 2003–2004 and setting a target of 10 million subscribers by 2010. Their ambition of 'sky in every home' would seem to be an aspiration too far; however, they continued to achieve their subscriber targets ahead of schedule and argued in 2005 that pay-tv sector penetration in the UK and Ireland was only 44 % and that in the 'long-term penetration levels can increase to around 80 %' (James Murdoch, CEO, 2005).

The statements made by three successive BskyB chief executive officers over more than a decade are testament to a corporate culture capable of taking risks that finds opportunity in the seismic challenges presented by the new media environment. The words *risk taking*, *opportunity*, *adaptable* and *invest* act like beacons of confidence in successive annual reports. These aspirations are illustrated in the following statements:

> Sky therefore seeks to invest and adapt in order to remain competitive.
> Rupert Murdoch, CEO (2003)

> This has been a year of significant changes- not just for Sky, but for the entire industry. Throughout the year, our focus has been on setting the pace of change, and re-affirming our appetite for doing so.
> James Murdoch, CEO, (2006)

> We challenge ourselves constantly to be a business that is adaptable and embraces change.
> Jeremy Darroch, CEO (2008)

17.4.2 Managerial Cognition of the Environmental and Competitive Context

Tripsas and Gavetti (2000) and Winter (2003) argued that the cognitive ability of managers to seek out, take advantage of and capitalise on market opportunities can be regarded as an intangible resource that could deliver superior firm performance. Over the decade, the management of BskyB made various strategic decisions that in the main appear to have been successful. These included formulating strategy for navigating an uncertain media environment, making successful resource investment decisions, developing new products and making corporate acquisitions and divestments. These variables will be explored in more detail later, but how the management of BskyB have viewed the competitive environment is interesting. On the one hand, they have invested heavily in new capabilities, made corporate acquisitions and been robust in their view of accrued losses, such as the £55 million in British Interactive Broadcasting Limited and £11 million in KirchPay TV in

2000. The reasoning was voiced by CEO Rupert Murdoch in 2005: 'In a dynamic market place it is the work of the business to continue to adapt and refresh itself...over the years Sky has reintroduced itself, reinvented itself and revitalised its appeal'. The corporate optimism is reflected in a statement from CEO James Murdoch in 2008 on the global economic crisis: 'These changes are creating significant opportunities for companies that have the capability and appetite to adapt their businesses'.

Thus, the senior management of BskyB manifests the first two criteria for success in developing dynamic capabilities: aspirational goals and management cognition.

17.4.3 Investment in Product Innovation and Development

Many researchers including Helfat and Raubitschek (2000), Winter (2003), Danneels (2002) and Eisenhardt and Martin (2000) have argued that product development is an important characteristic of dynamic capabilities and, to be successful, requires 'bold resource commitments' (Steinbock, 2000, p. 184) made over the long term. It is evident that BskyB has been transformed from one of the UK's leading television (only) broadcasters into a multiplatform, multiproduct entertainment and communications enterprise. Achieving this was described by CEO Jeremy Darroch in 2007 as '...a step change in our capabilities...'.

Over a period of more than a decade, BskyB innovated an impressive range of new products, including Sky Active services that incorporated shopping and betting on certain broadcast channels; interactive features on Sky Sports and Sky News; distribution of news and sports content on the Orange mobile phone network (2000); the UK's first personal television recorder in Sky+; the Sky Guide advanced electronic programme guide (2001); Sky Multiroom subscription; an enhanced version of Sky+ (2004); Sky Gnome, the portable device to listen to audio content (2005); Sky HDTV; Sky Broadband; Sky Talk; Sky+ access from customer mobile phones (2006); Sky Anytime, an on-demand service (2007); Sky 3D television (2010); Sky Go, the live and on-demand service that allows subscribers to watch programmes on iPhone, iPad, smartphones and PCs (2011); and their internet TV service Sky Now TV (2012). Thus, the third criterion is certainly fulfilled: investment in product innovation and development.

17.4.4 Investment in General R&D

Studies by Helfat and Raubitschek (2000), Steinbock (2000) and Macher and Mowery (2009) argued that the creation of dynamic firm capabilities required a long-term commitment to resource renewal that results in higher costs over a sustained period of time in order to fully realise the best potential for superior performance and competitive advantage. Accessing information on BskyB's research and development costs is difficult because this information is largely obscured in their annual reports. However, a good indication of strategic intent in this area can be identified in statements such as Rupert Murdoch's (Chairman) 2000 statement, 'Opportunities for companies to acquire true market leadership are rare, and BSkyB are uniquely placed to achieve this on the back of our investment in hardware, programmes and technologies'. Although one can presume such investment over time and in general, this hasn't yet been confirmed. What we can say, and all we can say for certain, is that statements by Mr. Murdoch indicate awareness and intention to do so.

17.4.5 Significant Investment in People and (or) Processes

Zollo and Winter (2002) and Winter (2003) reported that this type of investment was a good platform on which to build a dynamic capabilities through the reconfiguration of firm resources. Accessing this type of information in a consistent manner over time is difficult, but we can obtain a good indication from statements like the following:

> We continue to invest consistently in capital expenditure as required to support our growth strategies. . .this included £341 m invested in core services; information system infrastructure; broadcast infrastructure, broadband and telephony infrastructure, new product development. . .and customer service improvements. In addition, £114 m was invested in new property and property improvements.
> BskyB Directors Report (2010)

It is evident from BskyB's performance and general financial records that there has been significant investment in processes, at least. Although getting the details is difficult for an outsider, it's clear that this criterion is satisfied.

17.4.6 Corporate Acquisitions, Joint Ventures and Mergers

The renewal and reconfiguration of firm capabilities and competencies may be achieved through two means: (1) organic resource investment and/or (2) the acquisition of another organisation's capabilities (Colapinto, 2010; Danneels, 2002; Eisenhardt & Martin, 2000; Helfat, 2000; Karim & Mitchell, 2000; Macher & Mowery, 2009; Steinbock, 2000; Winter, 2003). BskyB has invested in numerous joint ventures as part of their corporate strategy since the early 2000s. They made significant investments (£1,512 million in 2000 and £1,163 million in 2001) in interactive services, customer relationship management and interactive broadcasting services. They recognised an opportunity for leadership in the pay-tv market noting what Rupert Murdoch (chairman) spoke about in 2000: 'We are now moving decisively into new media through organic development and acquisitions, partnerships and joint ventures'. Between 2002 and 2007, BskyB consolidated earlier investment spending with relatively small investments in the range of £22–£34 million per annum. Thus, the final criterion is also satisfied.

17.5 Dynamic Capabilities and Superior Firm Performance in Action

The vignette we have described distils the key aspects of DCT in action. But it remains to be addressed as to how does dynamic capabilities relate to superior firm performance. The question hinges on the issue of how best to measure dynamic capabilities and superior firm performance? That is an under researched area. This discussion acknowledges the practice-led approach to media management and suggests that measuring superior firm performance can be demonstrated using corporate financial analysis. For our discussion here, three such ratios have been used to illustrate superior firm performance.

Firstly, return on capital employed (ROCE) was used as an overall measure of corporate performance because it reflects the assets used by BskyB to generate profit. For example, a business that has a lot of assets but little in the way of profit will have a smaller ROCE. By comparison, a company with the same level of assets but producing profits will have a higher ROCE. Secondly, we look at net profit margin (NPM) to measure the percentage of profit compared to turnover (after direct and indirect expenses have been deducted). Interfirm comparisons of this ratio are likely to reveal a number of media management issues, including the way a firm competes in the marketplace, their pricing strategy and their ability to manage costs. Thirdly, we look at asset turnover (AT) as a measure of how efficiently a business uses their assets to generate sales revenue. A high AT figure indicates that the firm is generating a high level of sales from its resource base, although a note of caution should be addressed. High AT figures can also be an indicator of 'overtrading' where sales volumes are too high to be sustained on the basis of existing resources. Equally, a low AT figure is a good indication that the company may not be reaching the level of sales that it should given its resource base.

The analysis of ROCE for BskyB (see Diagram 17.2) indicates an impressive and superior performance in leveraging their assets over a sustained period of time. In the early 2000s, the company made significant investments of nearly £3 billion in joint ventures, interactive services, customer relationship management and interactive broadcasting services. These bold resource commitments, combined with the efficient management of costs and a decrease in operating expenses (programming costs down to £75 million following the renegotiating sports contracts and a reduction in movie costs down to £37 million), saw a rapid improvement in ROCE between 2001 and 2005, followed by sustained returns over the course of the decade.

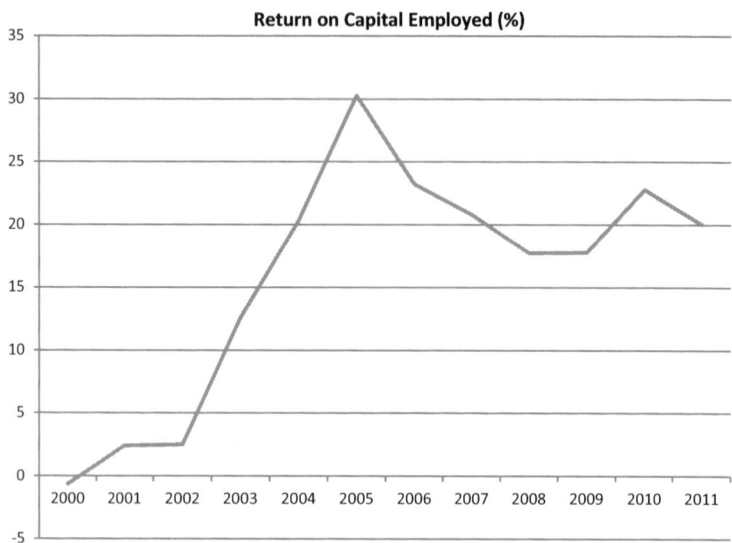

Diagram 17.2 BskyB return on capital employed (ROCE) 2000–2011

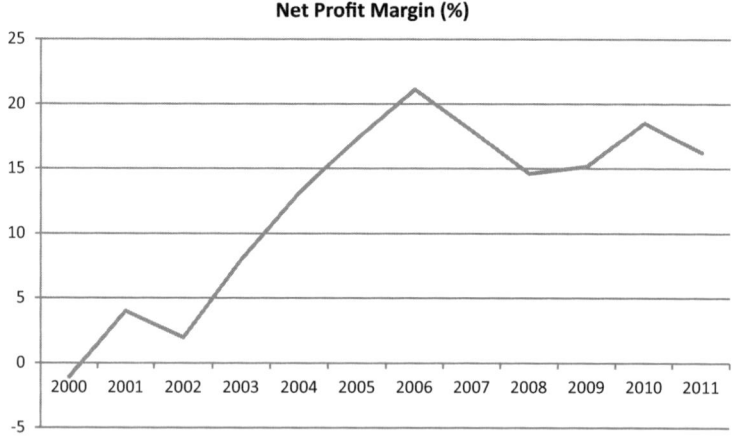

Diagram 17.3 BskyB net profit margin (NPM) 2000–2011

As stipulated, net profit margin (NPM) measures the percentage profit of each unit of turnover after direct and indirect expenses have been deducted. Once again, we see a similar pattern in BskyB's ability to deliver impressive returns in the form of net profit margin (see Diagram 17.3).

Finally, as also stipulated, asset turnover (AT) measures how efficiently a business uses their assets to generate sales revenue. Once again, we see a familiar pattern in the analysis (see Diagram 17.4).

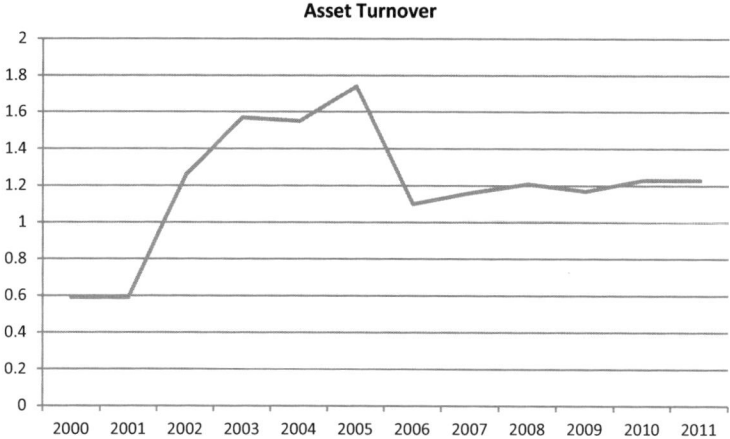

Diagram 17.4 BskyB asset turnover (AT) 2000–2011
BskyB has been able to generate a high level of sales from its resource base during the period
between 2000 and 2005 as a result of the investments made at the turn of the century. They have
also managed to sustain a good level of sales from their resource base from 2006 onwards, despite
evident complications caused by the general economic downturn that began in 2008

17.6   Conclusions

At the start of this chapter, two questions were posed. Firstly, and more generally,
how do media organisations manage their businesses under uncertain and high-
velocity market conditions? Secondly, how do media organisations manage and
adapt their resources and capabilities to remain competitive? An insight into the
answers to both of these questions has been illustrated by dynamic capabilities
theory (DCT) and the example of BskyB.

The aim of dynamic capabilities is to produce positive effects on corporate
performance and competitive advantage over time. Four premises underpin the
theory. The first three relate to the following: (1) the need for organisational
change; (2) this change process is centred on an organisation's ability to adapt
and refresh their resource base and renew capabilities and competencies; and
(3) this process of adaption requires deliberate resource investment in new
organisational learning and processes.

These principles have been illustrated using the BskyB case, a UK firm that has
successfully adapted their business from being a television broadcaster to a
multiplatform, multiproduct media firm. Their successful adaption has been driven
by a number of activities that are characteristic of dynamic capabilities theory, such
as seeking opportunities in a changing media landscape, setting aspirational corporate objectives, taking risks and investing in R&D and corporate acquisitions that
renew, refresh and leverage new capabilities and competencies. These activities

have delivered new products and services to consumers who perceive higher or better value than the competitive alternatives.

BskyB's corporate mantra of 'invest and adapt' has resulted in a step change in their business that has delivered superior financial corporate performance. As a comparison, one of their major competitors, ITV, produced an ROCE that ranged from −81.42 % in 2008 and peaked at 13.83 % in 2011 and an NPM of −130.46 % in 2008 and 18.87 % in 2011. So in terms of comparative advantage, BskyB has produced a superior financial corporate performance over a sustained period.

However, it is the fourth premise of dynamic capabilities theory that needs further interrogation: (4) dynamic capabilities require the process of adaptation to occur in a compressed timescale due to the fast changing nature of market conditions. The literature on this aspect of dynamic capabilities is ambiguous. On the one hand, the reconfiguring of a firm's resource base requires significant and bold resource commitments over a long period of time. Continually investing and reconfiguring a firm's resource base, therefore, leads to a process of incremental organisational adaptation. Yet, one of the central tenets of DCT is that a firm's ability to reconfigure their resource base, capabilities and competencies needs to be done in a short timescale due to the fast changing nature of market conditions. One of the most striking aspects of the financial analysis presented above is that of the transformative, not incremental, results achieved in ROCE, NPM and AT between 2002 and 2006 by BskyB. These impressive results were largely the result of the significant investments between 2000 and 2001 in joint ventures, interactive services, customer relationship management and interactive broadcasting services. The renewal and reconfiguration of BskyB's capabilities and competencies largely occurred in a short timeframe.

This leads us to consider an interesting question and one that may prove to be a fertile ground for media management researchers in the future. The question is 'How do we differentiate between dynamic capabilities and more general notions of organisational adaptation, strategic flexibility and continuous morphing?' In the view of Garud and Van de Ven (2007), DCT is distinguished by its emphasis on the renewal of resources, and capabilities with the aim of delivering superior firm performance in the short term appear to be a useful starting point. But this view does not necessarily open as fertile a field for focused development of understandings that would deliver higher theoretical and practical value. Further research needs to be undertaken to establish dynamic capabilities theory as a transformative instrument and especially as useful in high-velocity markets to deliver competitive advantage and superior firm performance in a short timescale. Even in the absence of greater maturity at present, however, it should be clear that media management is in key respects unique because of the scope and speed of changes that characterise the environment.

That is precisely the reason that dynamic capabilities theory has such evident importance for this field and media industries.

References

Albarran, A. B. (2006). Historical trends and patterns in media management. In A. B. Albarran, S. M. Olmsted, & M. O. Wirth (Eds.), *Handbook of media management*. New Jersey: Lawrence Erlbaum Associates Inc.

Albertazzi, D., & Cobley, P. (2010). *The media: An introduction*. England: Pearson Education Limited.

Ambrosini, V., Bowman, C., & Collier, N. (2009). Dynamic capabilities: An exploration of how firms renew their resource base. *British Journal of Management, 20*(S1), S9–S24.

Bitar, J., & Hafsi, T. (2007). Strategizing through the capability lens: Sources and outcomes of integration. *Management Decision, 45*(3), 403–419.

Chmielewski, D. A., & Paladino, A. (2007). Driving a resource orientation: Reviewing the role of resource and capability characteristics. *Management Decision, 45*(3), 462–483.

Colapinto, C. (2010). Moving to a multichannel and multiplatform company in the emerging and digital media ecosystem: The case of Mediaset. *The International Journal on Media Management, 12*, 59–75.

Danneels, E. (2002). The dynamics of product innovation and firm competences. *Strategic Management Journal, 23*(12), 1095–1121.

Di Stefano, G., Peteraf, M., & Verona, G. (2010). Dynamic capabilities deconstructed: A bibliographic investigation in the origins, development, and future directions of the research domain. *Industrial and Corporate Change, 19*(4), 1187–1204.

Eisenhardt, K., & Martin, J. (2000). Dynamic capabilities; what are they? *Strategic Management Journal, 21*(Special Issue), 1105–1121.

Ellis, J. R., & Williams, D. (1993). *Corporate strategy and financial analysis: Managerial, accounting and stock-market perspectives*. NY: FT Prentice Hall.

Garud, R., & Van de Ven, A. H. (2007). Strategic change processes. In A. Pettigrew, A. Thomas, & R. Whittington (Eds.), *Handbook of strategic management*. London: Sage.

Grant, R. M. (1991). The resource-based theory of competitive advantage: Implications for strategy formulation. *California Management Review, 33*(3), 114–136.

Helfat, C. E. (2000). Guest editor's introduction to the special issue: The evolution of firm capabilities. *Strategic Management Journal, 21*, 955–959.

Helfat, C. E., & Raubitschek, R. S. (2000). Product sequencing: Co-evolution of knowledge, capabilities and products. *Strategic Management Journal Special Issue, 21*(10/11), 955–959.

Jarzabkowski, P. (2004). Strategy as practice: Recursiveness, adaptation, and practices-in-use. *Organization Studies, 25*(4), 529–560.

Karim, S., & Mitchell, W. (2000). Path-dependent and path-breaking change: reconfiguring business resources following acquisitions in the U.S. medical sector, 1978–1995. *Strategic Management Journal, 21*(10–11), 1061–1081. Special Issue: The Evolution of Firm Capabilities.

Lawton, T., & Rajwani, T. (2011). Designing lobbying capabilities: Managerial choices in unpredictable environments. *European Business Review, 23*(2), 167–189.

Leavy, B. (1998). The concept of learning in the strategy field. *Management Learning, 29*(4), 447–466.

Leonard-Barton, D. (1992). Core capabilities and core rigidities: A paradox in managing new product development. *Strategic Management Journal, 13*, 111–125. Summer, Special Issue.

Ljungquist, U. (2007). Core competency beyond identification: Presentation of a model. *Management Decision, 45*(3), 393–402.

Macher, J. T., & Mowery, D. C. (2009). Measuring dynamic capabilities: Practices and performance in semiconductor manufacturing. *British Journal of Management, 20*, S41–S62.

Miller, D., & Shamsie, J. (1996). The resource-based view of the firm in two environments: The Hollywood film studios from 1936 to 1965. *Academy of Management Journal, 39*(3), 519–543.

Mintzberg, H. (1987). Crafting strategy. *Harvard Business Review, 65*(4), 66–75.

Oliver, J. J. (2012). Winning in high velocity markets: the case of BSkyB. *Strategic Direction, 28* (10), 3–5.

Pettigrew, A., Thomas, A., & Whittington, R. (2007). *Handbook of strategic management.* London: Sage.

Prahalad, C. K., & Hamel, G. (1990). The core competence of the corporation. *Harvard Business Review, 63*(8), 79–91.

Senge, P. M. (1990). The leader's new work; building learning organisations. *Sloan Management Review, 32*(1), 7–22.

Steinbock, D. (2000). Building dynamic capabilities. The Wall Street Journal Interactive Edition: A successful Online Subscription Model (1993–2000). *Journal of Media Management, 2* (III/IV), 178–194.

Teece, D. J., & Pisano, G. (1994). The dynamic capabilities of firms: An introduction. *Industrial and Corporate Change, 3*(3), 537–556.

Teece, D. J., Pisano, G., & Shuen, A. (1997). Dynamic capabilities and strategic management. *Strategic Management Journal, 18*(7), 509–533.

Tripsas, M., & Gavetti, G. (2000). Capabilities, cognition, and inertia; evidence from digital imaging. *Strategic Management Journal, 21*(10/11), 1147–1161. Special Issue.

Winter, S. G. (2003). Understanding dynamic capabilities. *Strategic Management Journal, 24*, 991–995.

Zollo, M., & Winter, S. G. (2002). Deliberate learning and the evolution of dynamic capabilities. *Organization Science, 13*, 339–351.

Part V

Leadership and Labour

Leadership in Media Organisations: Past Trends and Challenges Ahead   18

Ghislain Deslandes

> *Who would still want to rule? Who would still want to obey?*
> *These two tasks are too painful.*
>   Nietzsche, *Thus Spake Zarathustra.*

18.1   Introduction

The question posed by Nietzsche could well concern the media more particularly than other industries. Who would still want to rule? Media companies, especially those that deal with information, have in the past few years been shaken by radical changes in business and technology and by the roles they are expected to play in facilitating the civic functioning of a democratic society. The scope of this quite recent revolution is unmatched since the advent of mass media (Picard, 2006a). Its impact has been so strong that their very existence and sociocultural mission are called into question. Ultimately, two contestants face each other: On the one hand, traditional players may feel overwhelmed by the changes brought about by the digital revolution and whose vocation is severely challenged. On the other hand, new entrants, particularly companies spawned by the telecom industry, are struggling to apply their 'recipes' in a sector that is averse to implementing automated processes.

Accordingly, who would still want to obey? The players in the media environment are practitioners, journalists, producers and entrepreneurs who view their professions as an avocation and are therefore reluctant to accept the imposition of external authority or controls (Auletta, 1991; Perez-Lattre & Sanchez-Taberno,

English translation by: Lionel Dahan (em), Language and Culture Department, ESCP Europe Business School, Paris, France; e-mail: dahan@escpeurope.eu

G. Deslandes (✉)
ESCP Europe Business School, Paris, France
e-mail: deslandes@escpeurope.eu

© Springer International Publishing Switzerland 2016   311
G.F. Lowe, C. Brown (eds.), *Managing Media Firms and Industries*, Media
Business and Innovation, DOI 10.1007/978-3-319-08515-9_18

2003; Underwood, 1993). Newsrooms, much like the sets and locations where films are made or TV shows are shot, are filled with people who consider themselves 'opinion leaders' (Lazarsfeld et al., 1944). Such individuals feel disinclined to listen to voices coming from the top of the hierarchical ladder. This is all the more true since management, whose rationale focuses on effectiveness and performance, is not overly popular among 'entertainers' and individuals operating in this industry. Consequently, the customary disobedience of practitioners is compounded by the emergence of a newfound rebelliousness among audiences themselves. Indeed, the latter no longer complacently accept a top-down imposition of linear programming to determine their consumption practices.

Yet, to the artists and entertainers that resist a stronger management presence, one should reply that the communication industry's uninterrupted growth for over a century is at an end. This is reflected especially in the latest developments in the field of audiovisual technology that has thoroughly undermined the historic stability of these media industries, leading to increasing audience fragmentation and economic contraction. This suggests that an approach compelling managers to monitor every stage of production in order to both facilitate and direct operations may not be the worst method for balancing the need to nurture creativity and to generate and allocate resources that are required for its expression. Management theory needs to be clearly and specifically formulated for application to the distinct characteristics of media industries, moving away from the functionalist perspectives that characterise traditional approaches to management. Today one should rely on a strategic management perspective by 'focusing on the long-term growth of firms, not only on immediate financial goals [that] ignore the future' (Picard, 2006b, p. 171).

Consequently, in such a context why would anyone question the major role played by the industry's 'leaders', referring to the women and men who steer media organisations? From Rupert Murdoch to Silvio Berlusconi, from Michael Bloomberg to Harvey Weinstein, figures traditionally described as 'tycoons' or 'moguls' consistently stand at the helm of media groups. Few doubt that such leaders have played prominent roles throughout the history of media—especially as industries (Knee, Greenwald, & Seave, 2011). The list could include such renowned figures as NBC's Brandon Tartikoff, Fox's Barry Diller and Pearson's Marjorie Scardino who—although not necessarily moguls in the common sense of the word—have been prime movers in the development of their media corporations. They are, so to speak, the descendants of the founder of *The Times* that was portrayed by Jeanneney (1998, p. 80) in his *Histoire des Médias*:

> In January 1785, a Scotsman named John Walter, a former coal merchant who had turned a profit by speculating on the insurance business when British colonies experienced a boom, intended to diversify his operations. He decided to venture into the press. He was the first person in this special category which might be dubbed "*entrepreneurs spellbound by the media*": business people who having demonstrated their knowhow in trade or industry and, when reaching middle age, feel the desire to prove that they could be effective in the world of information, while enjoying the social prestige they derive from playing with this instrument.

These preliminary elements lead us to approach leadership in the media industry from two opposing angles. On the one hand, the sector needs, more than ever, leadership and strategic vision to survive the profound economic, societal and editorial changes brought about by the digital revolution. On the other hand, it's clearly true that the concept of leadership in the media, with its vertical representation based on the unique personality and character traits of a 'great man/woman' (Hang, 2006), deserves a second look or, at the very least, is worth reviewing. As summed up by Küng (2007b, p. 11):

> The task of leadership in the media sector contains many inherent paradoxes. The span of competencies and talents required is best served by multileader structures, yet these complicate and dull decisiveness, the power, influence and responsibility place huge requirements in terms of self-knowledge and emotional maturity, yet individuals possessing such characteristics are unlikely to be able to stomach the temperamental, ego-driven, hard-nosed, power-hungry individuals who populate the sector.

In the present chapter, we shall first emphasise reasons that explain why the number of scholarly studies on these issues is quite limited. We shall then summarise the most significant analyses, which essentially deal on the one hand with the leader's personality and on the other with understanding the specific context of the media. At the end, we rely on a critical approach to stress the ethical nature of leadership and endeavour to open new avenues for research and practice that are likely to lead to a better understanding of leadership in the context of media organisations. In all of this discussion implies quite a lot that is special about media management in comparison to other industries.

18.2   A Weak Link in Research on Media Management

Although leadership is now recognised as a full-fledged discipline in research on business administration (Northouse, 2004), the same is not true in *media studies*. In our field the global corpus has not devoted much room for this topic (Küng, 2008, p. 200). Although the role played by leaders operating in the industry is undisputed, as testified by articles devoted to the subject in all types of media, specialised or not, in the estimation of Mierzejewska and Hollifield (2006), study about leadership is the most neglected field of research and theoretical analysis in media management scholarship.

There could be at least two reasons. The first is related to the specificities of the characteristic power structure (Bjurstedt, 2006) within the media industry, broadly construed. This structure accords a large degree of autonomy to individual workers (especially for journalists and artists). This differs from industries such as manufacturing or construction where hierarchy is clearly and strongly top-down. Even though a hierarchical structure is represented in the media organisation charts for most firms, these don't always reflect where real power is located. Power is typically quite diffused and multilayered in media firms, especially big outfits. Leadership issues therefore seem more difficult to grasp. The second reason has to do with the specificities of research about leadership in general, which poses methodological problems.

Concerning the first difficulty, power relations between top managers, employees and partners aren't very comparable with common practices that prevail in other sectors. For instance, the fame enjoyed by some employees (i.e. 'stars') is sometimes much greater than that of prominent organisation leaders, a difference that is likely to exert a strong influence on internal power relations. Likewise, the actual decision-making power of a young manager, when newly appointed (especially in a governmentally administered system such as public television), might not be at all strong in comparison to the power enjoyed by a popular news anchor who has been on the air for decades. At this point one should distinguish between administrative power (i.e. the power of shareholders) and managerial power—which acts on behalf of the former—and not forgetting editorial power, which is just as legitimate and important (Lavine & Wackman, 1988).[1] Clearly there are many and varied levels and kinds of power in the typical media organisation, and this is arguably more complex than in most other industries. The power to make decisions and to influence decision-makers is complicated in media firms.

For example, in a newspaper, the decision-making power of the publisher is distinct from that of the editor. Typically the former is accountable for the newspaper's economic performance, while the latter is viewed as the guardian of its editorial policies. This separation of powers is intended to guarantee sound ethical practice for a free and independent press that is also accountable to shareholders and readers. But the separation in practice is difficult to monitor and can be disregarded when the publisher decides to interfere in editorial choices for various political and economic reasons. Thus, the common relational dynamic between leaders and followers that prevails in other industries doesn't hold as well or as clearly in this area of the media industry.

In addition, complications in the publisher-editor relationship—which is by its essence peculiar, as the types of personalities are likely to be quite different and backgrounds may prove very heterogeneous[2]—can be compounded when stakeholders desire to play a leadership role. Politicians are frequently eager to interfere, or at least attempt to influence, the programming of public TV stations; advertisers want to influence the processing of information and its presentation for their own interests; a newspaper's society of readers or editors (the French daily Le Monde is a case in point) can table a no-confidence motion against the top manager or threaten to appeal to an 'assignment clause' in the event of a change in ownership. Such a clause authorises journalists to resign yet still keep their social/unemployment benefits should there be a presumption of substantial change

---

[1] As defined by Aris and Bughin, editorial power consists in discovering and evaluating talent, without applying standardised processes, as it can hardly be measured objectively; it distinguishes itself from the powers of shareholders and managers whose performance can be quantified more easily (2005).

[2] In a study bearing on the track records of top managers operating in the media in France, Dagnaud and Mehl (1990) distinguished between three categories: a "professional elite" comprising chiefly former hosts/producers or journalists having moved to managerial positions; a "managerial elite" pursuing an entrepreneurial vision; and a "political-administrative" elite made of senior officials with experience as top government aides who opted for administrative jobs within business organizations.

in the editorial line. The dual nature of mass media is exemplified in such cases: editorial and creative staff serve audiences and readerships with content, while publishers, senior managers and the heads of advertising sell inventory and audiences (as commodities) to advertisers. In such contexts, power should be viewed as a constantly negotiated balance between conflicting demands. This balance results from agreements between stakeholders, not from orders 'coming from the top' (Perez-Lattre & Sanchez-Taberno, 2003).

The second reason why the scope of studies on leadership is so limited is to a large extent due to the scarcity of available information. Academic research in leadership is confronted with methodological problems, especially in the stage of data collection (Bryman, 2004; Cohen, 1999; Painter-Morland & Deslandes, 2012). Although access to information is a recurring question in all studies on leadership, this difficulty is a crippling problem in the media where information is by definition a key resource and vital characteristic. It is particularly difficult to approach industry leaders who are reluctant to divulge their plans, have extremely busy schedules and are not necessarily conversant with the stakes and challenges of particular interest for academic research. Second-hand literature is available for data on figures and personalities (producers, CEOs of TV stations, editors in chief, entrepreneurs, etc.) because they are more on display through varying degrees of media exposure. But first-hand information, which is so crucial to ensure the quality of field studies, is hard to come by.

At this point it will be useful to clarify what is meant by 'leadership', and how that applies specifically to the management of media companies. This is important for understanding what's special about media management.

18.3   Orientations of the Major Research Work to Date

Leadership is generally defined as a process *by which a person influences several individuals, so that they voluntarily strive to achieve the goals set for the group that they form* (Koontz & Weihrich, 1993). The leader guides individuals within some framework that defines the nodes and boundaries of formal authority and is in the best position to perceive (and conceive) the purpose of an organisation (Bennis & Nanus, 2003). His or her approach is typically entrepreneurial and power is relational. Such characteristics set the leader apart from the manager, who essentially endeavours to achieve goals assigned by his or her superiors. A leader focuses on the accomplishment of collective tasks: 'As chief strategist and 'official interpreter' of the environment, the leader must perceive changes, puzzle out their importance, and then decide how the organization should adapt' (Küng, 2007b, p. 6).

Accordingly, it follows that all managers are not leaders. Leaders have a developed capacity for steering and are adept in handling the cross-currents of divergent stakes and related conflicts. They are vital for organisations' capacity to anticipate changes in the environment and for ensuring employee morale and motivation in periods of change. No wonder the profiles of significant leaders are especially sought after, as testified, for instance, by the leadership programme developed by Landale (2005) for the executives of the NDS group, a subsidiary of the News Corp. group.

This traditional understanding raises as many questions as it answers. Can a manager become a leader, and how? Are leaders born or made? Aren't leadership qualities generally essential for managers? Can a 'natural leader' be an effective manager if he or she is unaware of the real-life constraints inevitably handled as a routine requirement for management? It is difficult to arrive at conclusive, convincing answers. We can make a reasonable attempt by recognising that leadership generally includes two aspects that are often treated as a contradiction: the leader's personal dimension and a contingent and relational dimension.

18.3.1 The Personal Dimension

We can begin with an overview of distinctions between three types of leadership as traditionally defined in the literature on the subject (Deslandes, 2008):

- **Visionary leadership** focuses on the leader's vision and his or her ability to mobilise his or her employees. The visionary leader develops a particular charisma, and his or her behaviour reflects the values he or she claims to embody. The self-confidence and positive view of leaders in this category is based upon their own communication skills, their non-conformist behaviours and their power of conviction (Kets De Vries, 2006).
- **Transactional leadership** resorts to the motivation and management of their subordinates through variable practices based on reward (Bass, 1973). Priority is given to employees' performance to determine compensation.
- **Transformational leadership** encourages employees to transform their own vision of the world and of the organisation in which they operate. The purpose in this case is to enable each worker to go beyond his or her own personal interest and to overcome his or her fear of change (Avolio & Bass, 1985; Conger, 1998).

In the field of media management research, these three models have been alternately applied. For example, a study conducted with top managers active in Greek media companies demonstrated that most leaders nowadays resort to a subtle combination of transactional and transformational styles as a means of better anticipating changes (Dekoulou, Tsourvakas, & Zotos, 2007). Girdauskienė and Savanevičienė noticed that these types of leadership are frequently found in collaborative work within creative teams: 'Transformational leadership encourages people to perform and increase their demands to respect hierarchy of values, to raise the cultural level of development. Transactional leaders try to carry out effectively its activities as well as evaluate their employees, but their criteria for evaluation is the existing competence of the workers rather than future potential' (2012, pp. 17–18). According to these researchers, knowledge transfer abilities are a key factor for the success of projects; in its transactional form, leadership plays a central role in fostering the technical and structural conditions for transfer, whereas in its transformational form, the dissemination of information and knowledge may be effected in a more informal mode.

The type that has drawn most of the attention in our scholarly community is clearly based on 'the leader as individual' (Hang, 2006; Norback, 2006; Shaver & Shaver, 2006; Wickstrom, 2006). In elaborating this model, scholars essentially emphasise the leader's personality traits. Lucy Küng illustrated the tendency: 'Murdoch, it is claimed, has built his entire empire by defying convention and taking risks, and Turner's appetite for risk is said to be insatiable. He further claims: 'if you are going to try to change things in a big way you have to be willing to go against the odds and sacrifice everything'. This suggests the leader has a sophisticated facility in handling risk, and that is proposed as a shared trait by high profile leaders in the field' (2007b, p. 7). The general purpose is to study the leadership phenomenon through the physical, cognitive and emotional characteristics of an individual who stands at the top of an important company's organisation (Garcia, 2011).

In fact, respondents to most empirical studies about leadership in media companies focus on the (presumed) central role of charisma and the 'personal factor' (see Frame 1). This is particularly prominent in visionary and transformational types. As stated by a respondent interviewed by Küng in the course of her study on CNN's organisational culture: 'Ted Turner *is* the strategic planning department' (2000, p. 119). A leader's personal dimension and assets, be they technical, human or conceptual (Küng, 2008), seem to be the central element that fosters emotional endorsement among his/her followers' (Howell, 2005).

Frame 1. Portrait of Marin Karmitz
The founder and CEO of the MK2 Group offers another example of an entrepreneur who, through his life and work, so to speak embodies his group's strategy. In the early 1970s, he indeed directed two committed films, *Camarades* and *Coup pour coup*. Four years later, he opened the first MK2 multiplex movie theatre in the Bastille district in Paris. Marin Karmitz defines himself first as a producer: 'Someone who is accountable for financial problems. . . and does not pretend to be an 'artist' when it comes to money matters' (ibid, p. 151). He has been the producer of the most prestigious directors of French cinema (Chabrol, Malle, Godard) and European filmmakers (Angelopoulos, the Taviani brothers, Kieslowski for whom he produced the *Three Colors* trilogy masterpiece). Want to know his secret trick? Art-house cinema, his so-called *Passion Pieces* to be played at seasonal festivals (Sundance, Cannes, Venice, Berlin) and his productions dubbed *Commercials* (to be released in the form of films and DVDs) with shoestring budgets. He makes sophisticated, often arty films, released in the cinema

(continued)

houses which he runs preferably in Paris neighbourhoods where essentially urban culture prevails. A strong social commitment is part and parcel of its vision of the film industry: 'Those who are lucky as I am to be working in this industry are vested with obligations. In the field of culture, private financing has a responsibility to society' (*Le Monde*, March 13, 2007). As a champion of independence, he turned down offers from Warner Bros. and Paramount in 1986, preferring a network model, especially in international operations, which are performed in collaboration with Channel 4 in the UK, for example. He is always likely to cause surprise, most often as a master of cultural communication: he did so when he banned the screening in his movie theatres of Mel Gibson's *The Passion of the Christ*, which he deemed too violent. Karmitz has made his life dream come true by succeeding in making a 'tool that created a fresh and bold vision of the cinema industry' (*Libération*, May 22, 2004): the world's largest network of art-house cinema theatres whose turnover is yet much lower than the production budget of *Pirates of the Caribbean*—a tell-tale clue on the status of culture in a world of globalised entertainment.

Findikli and Yozgat (2012, p. 235), who studied leadership in teams that were responsible for the creation of fiction for Turkish television stations, emphasised the crucial role played by charisma among directors:

> The directors as charismatic leaders follow their own dreams and have passion to realize them. They also follow trends but they try to create their own differentiated works. They think that they still do not perform their bests and that there is time for their masterpiece work. (. . .) Their leadership philosophy includes belief, positive perspective, professional competency, honesty, courage, and creativity. The directors possess certain degree of sensitivity to their external environment and scan for trends that will cause them to adapt their vision as charismatic leaders.

Another method, relying on the psychoanalytical approach of Stora (1987), defines four psychological types of leaders in the media (Deslandes, 2008):

- **The narcissistic leader** who 'is focused on the perpetuation of himself or herself', desires to make a mark in history and is characterised by a feeling of invulnerability (e.g. Jean-Marie Messier, former CEO of Vivendi Universal).
- **The seductive leader** who fascinates people around him or her and seduces them by his or her speech. He or she is surrounded by a legion of followers who are dedicated to his or her cause (e.g. Jean-Jacques Servan-Schreiber, founder of the French newsmagazine *L'Express*).
- **The possessive leader** is a person who does not tolerate people who resist him or her, whatever the cost may be (e.g. Rupert Murdoch, CEO of News Corp.).
- **The benevolent leader** likes to convince people and does not hesitate to trust them (e.g. Richard Parsons, former CEO of Time Warner).

So there are diverse approaches that are all based on the leader's personality, and this arouses strong interest. In comparison, scholarship in organisation studies often pay less attention to individual agency and more to problems related to structures. So whereas researchers in media management mainly focus on managerial problems characteristic of a specific professional environment, contextual factors are more strongly emphasised in the wider field of leadership studies. In fact, context is a significant factor in determining leader influence and success in media firms, as well. One of the reasons why Jean-Marie Messier became undoubtedly narcissistic is that the French media consistently built a flattering image of his personality while Vivendi Universal was being created. The context of coverage partly accounts for the kind of leader he became, even if the seeds might already have been present. One reason that Jean-Jacques Servan-Schreiber proved attractive is that he developed an innovative and attractive product—the American-style news magazine—in a context that had not earlier embraced that type. One reason that Richard Parsons is portrayed as benevolent is that he assumed responsibilities at a time when the industry was consolidating, when conflicts seemed less acute than in the previous period. In short, when taken out of the context in which their actions unfold, the study of media company leaders quickly reaches its limits. This insight encourages opening the debate to dimensions that less often taken into account in scholarship on media leadership because they do not privilege the individual but rather the context.

18.3.2 The Contingent and Structural Dimension

Leadership in the media cannot be limited to individual factors (Hersey, 1995). As Richard Parsons said in *Business Week* (issue # 3833, 2003): 'I am not Moses coming down from the mountain with the Tablets in his hand. It's all about collaboration. When all is said and done, gathering a team around oneself is what is most important'. Arguably concentrating too much authority in the hands of a single individual, based on a paternalistic model of management and leadership, may prove to be a negative factor in fast changing and creative environments, which are characteristic of media industries today (Küng, 2008). In view of the model suggested by Küng (2007a), we need to consider a 'contextualist' approach, one that is designed to study the management of media in an ever-changing and 'pluralistic' environment with complex historical, sociological and economic dimensions.

The corollary requires acknowledging the specific complexity of media organisations, notably from an editorial,[3] political and cultural standpoint. Leadership in media industries cannot shun the analysis of contingency factors that are so specific to it, especially the evident in the importance of editorial creation and the

---

[3] Especially the essential distinction existing between information media and entertainment media, as well as between 'hard news' and 'soft news'.

need for constant innovation. Based on Schein's theoretical work (1985), Küng shows how, at the BBC, the orientation of strategic planning has been influenced not only by the top executive's personality but also by beliefs shared by other key managers (2000). This strongly suggests the importance of a thorough analysis of corporate culture as a prerequisite for comprehending power relations in media organisations.

In the same light, I conducted a study on a children's television network that broadcast programmes in classical Arabic language (Deslandes, 2011). The findings underscored the fact that this station's *organisational identity* was less dependent on its CEO's character traits than on the explicit, reflexive and self-avowed interpretation of cultural values. This grounded an insistence on recognising the central role played by external parties. Dal Zotto (2005) analysed human resource management in three companies publishing newspapers in Germany. The results of her work also present leadership less as a personal attribute and much more as a contextualised process (p. 57). This general approach goes further than only focusing on the leader-follower relationship to view leadership primarily as the coordination of efforts made within a community (see also Van Weezel, 2006).

Here we can also highlight the fact that leadership contributes to strengthening the cooperative spirit of work communities and securing a degree of needed autonomy within teams. What is accomplished is less the managers' would-be 'leadership' than the intrinsic motivation of team members being eager to share a common cause. This is particularly obvious among journalists. In the words of one of the scholars who founded the discipline of leadership research, Mary Parker Follett, the media industries seem especially prone to a form of 'reciprocal leadership'. Indeed, the priority is to understand and integrate the 'invisible leader', which in her work means the 'common purpose' rather than a specific individual (Follett, 1928/1970, p. 137). Such analyses represent a stream of research that essentially considers leadership as a shared, distributed and 'systemic' ability belonging to all the members of an organisation (Collier & Esteban, 2000; Uhl-Bien, Marion, & McKelvey, 2007).

There has been frequent mention of power in our discussion. That construct and practice will benefit from a critical approach[4] that is based on analysing the nature of power in media organisations. It is not, however, much evident in media management research so far. It is mainly only obvious that the notion depends on the way that each individual comprehends it, according to his or her sensitivity and inventiveness (Alvesson, 1996; Alvesson & Spicer, 2011). Such consideration is certainly needed to open promising avenues for potential research on leadership in media organisations where so much of what happens as a consequence of operations has much to do with power, as especially evident in the tradition of political economy. Insofar as this industry shuns authoritative modes of management, such a critical approach allows redefining important constructs that continue

---

[4] See also Chap. 5 by Charles Brown.

to animate debates about traditional media leadership semantics, stances and gestures. These considerations are pointedly important to the field of media management as a social science. Indeed, chances are slim of being able to teach a 'great man' how to be great since he already seems to know that by himself (or she herself as a 'great woman'). Nonetheless, lessons may be drawn from the manner in which teams of employees can learn how to better manage power issues for the benefit of innovation and creativity (Bilton, 2006).

Before drawing conclusions, it is useful to consider how the two approaches we've considered can be included in a global analysis of leadership phenomena in the media sphere.

18.4 Bridging the Approaches: 'Shared Charismatic Leadership'

At the present stage of research development, one notes the emergence of work that combines the leader's charisma with the teams' participation and mobilisation and from which it cannot be separated. This is especially important because the focus is on subtle but significant forms of interdependency. The study conducted by Murphy and Ensher (2008) is a case in point because it aims at bringing closer the two seemingly contradictory notions of *charismatic leadership* and *shared leadership* (Pearce & Conger, 2003).

Firstly, this approach reasserts the importance of charismatic leadership among professionals in charge of television shows. The authors interviewed 21 top-level directors, with 10–40 years of professional experience in the industry, and who had received numerous prizes (Emmy Awards, Director Guild Awards, etc.). The referential shows are widely screened TV series like *Scrubs*, *Ally McBeal*, *Crossing Jordan*, *Third Watch*, *West Wing*, *Law & Order* and *NYPD Blue*. These scholars first rely on the model developed by Conger and Kanungo (1994), which identifies six behavioural factors characterising charismatic leaders. They then focus on processes of mutual influence between leaders and followers, which are often observed in creative environments where urgency and complexity of tasks is commonplace.

The notion of 'shared charismatic leadership' (which is less paradoxical than it would seem) allows Murphy and Ensher to claim: 'the leader of a very talented creative team is in a position to take turns with his or her followers in assuming the leadership role. This approach may be particularly appropriate in television production where there are a variety of specialised functions that must be integrated to create the programme. A leader demonstrating shared charismatic leadership may set the stage by beginning with a compelling vision and then standing aside as the team members take the lead throughout the production as necessary' (2008, p. 338). However, the authors specify that, in the cases they studied, *shared leadership* first relies on *self-schema leadership*. The idea (schema) is the basis on which the leader expresses himself or herself (personality) and takes a social role that demonstrates an ability to mobilise other individuals and conduct a discussion with them in a non-verbal form of ongoing collaboration, which is characteristic of media environments.

In a study focusing on television show directors (Painter-Morland & Deslandes, 2013), vision and sensitivity to the needs of the group were identified as prominent behavioural factors. This was testified by a film director: 'I feel like people on film crews are more sensitive than your regular employees. Everybody has their own gripes about their job...on a show, everybody's bringing their own stuff about [previous work], 'oh, I got screwed on the last job by that producer.' Or 'Oh, I got screwed by that director who is so lazy and took credit.' A lot of these people bring baggage and they're more sensitive. So you have to be constantly on your toes and trying to make it better' (ibid., p. 343).

18.5   Conclusion: 'Blended Leadership' and Ethical Leadership in the Media

Emphasising especially the findings and prospects offered in connection with the notion of 'blended leadership' provides a useful way to conclude. The intention is to raise a few highly pertinent questions in relation to ethics because this aspect of the specificity of leadership in the media is especially central—and sometimes underestimated. Thus, conclusions focus on the ethical dimension.

Deciding whether primacy in the field of leadership in the media is predicated on the personality of the leader or on collaborative phenomena isn't really new. It is evident, for instance, at the core of heated debates raging in France when the *Nouvelle Vague* bloomed (with Godard, Varda, Rohmer, Truffaut etc.) and had a direct bearing on what should be the definition of art-house cinema (*cinéma d'auteur*), which relies mainly on the vision of a particular director as opposed to industrialised forms of cinema. Perhaps new is that the historic dualism is being overcome today. That is hopeful because, as noted by Collinson and Collison (2009), these are actually fictitious dichotomies that do not correspond to what is practiced in reality.

In fact, industrial forms show ceaseless variations in the leader's distance and proximity vis-à-vis employees and in delegation to others and the fullness of exercising personal power. The 'blended leadership' approach (Murphy & Ensher, 2008) contends that leadership effectiveness cannot be adequately measured by using only the yardstick of a leader's 'heroic performances'. Neither can it be adequately measured only by focusing on its collective origin (the 'post-heroic' perspective). Undoubtedly media companies are especially interesting examples of the need for and utility of overcoming such dualisms (or dichotomies) because these are too simple to be explained enough about what needs understanding. This holds true, in my opinion, despite the fact that the dualism or dichotomy is found in most leadership studies, including as we have seen in the transactional/transformational difference suggested earlier.

Adopting the blended leadership perspective and taking into account the provisional nature of some of the insights encourage the community of researchers interested in the management of media firms to prioritise an inclusive perspective rather than favouring one option or the other as if dealing with an opposition. On the contrary, media management scholars are well advised reconcile diverse perspectives in order to better understand the twin necessities facing a leader: in line with Nietzsche's opening quotation, the need to be obeyed and for obeying—what Mary Parker Follett refers to as the common purpose and law of the situation.

It seems useful to insist that what distinguishes the mission of top managers in media companies is a *triple bottom line* represented by the economic, editorial and societal stakes involved in this enterprise and which both burden and truly define their jobs. The recent crisis in the global economy has put financial responsibility in the limelight, seeing the end of many of the most prestigious print publications (the case of *Newsweek* is the most striking example) and the inability of News Corporation's tablet-based *The Daily*, which closed after less than 2 years in business. Even worse, the recession had a tremendous impact on society at large and has taken a heavy toll on citizens. A professional crisis affecting journalists is fuelled by the development of new forms of creation such as blogs, amateur documentaries or community information websites (Deslandes, Fonnet, & Godbert, 2009) that increasingly compete against traditional means of distributing content and jeopardise their societal function. The media must redefine their roles and models if they are to survive (Picard, 2006a). In the face of this de facto situation, we think that media professionals need to question the 'depreciative vision' (Picard, 2006b, p. 171) held by the people destroying them within their ranks and reassert their role by upholding high ethical standards. Consequently, in the years to come, leadership should play a key role in building audience loyalty.

This dilemma and the need for a satisfactory resolution are supported by recent research. In a series of *focus groups* with media managers in France, Africa and the USA (Deslandes & Painter-Morland, 2012), researchers found that in the USA, managers described themselves as 'architects' or 'curators', which wasn't surprising, but more surprisingly also as 'providers of fast food' or even 'sluts' (sic). They thereby express the idea that their decisions depend less on the personal beliefs they may cherish or on the professional responsibilities they need to discharge than on the ever-changing expectations of the general public in the context of unstable markets. Such metaphors suggest that media managers face conflicting demands between offering the public *what they need* and being content with providing them with *what they want* (Picard, 2006b). This also emphasises the dual nature of such organisations, indicated in being simultaneously expected to improve profitability while also satisfying audiences.

From an ethical standpoint, the *News of the World* phone hacking scandal, which was a sensation worldwide, revealed what the public should expect from media industry leaders: professional ethics worthy of that name. In a preliminary report released on 1 May 2012, Brian Leveson, commissioned to investigate such practices, claimed that: 'Rupert Murdoch. . . turned a blind eye and exhibited wilful blindness to what was going on in his companies. . . We conclude that (he) is not a fit person to exercise the stewardship of a major international company' (*Financial Time*, May 2, 2012). A strong verdict suggesting the vital role of leadership for a media manager, which is first and foremost defined by adhering to an ethical approach to solving problems as an inherent responsibility for firms in media industries (Brown & Treviño, 2006; Knights & O'Leary, 2005, 2006; Trevino, Brown, & Hartman, 2003; Trevino, Hartman, & Brown, 2000).

Moreover, Rupert Murdoch himself, sincerely or not, seems to agree that ethics should prevail over charisma. In an article in the *Herald Tribune* of 26 April 2012 reporting on the inquiry, the reporter observed: 'On occasion, he seemed laconic and cautious in his responses, mildly disputing suggestions that he ran his company as a charismatic figure. "Aura? Charisma? I don't think so," he said'. In the long term an ethical approach to leadership has a central role in the management of media firms and will hopefully be reasserted at the top of companies operating in these industries. That, in turn, would prompt further research. In my view, this emphasis is crucial for fighting disinformation and the prevailing climate of cynicism and would be facilitative for restoring confidence that has been lost among many publics. Failing that, as predicted by Robert G. Picard already some years ago, 'the media will eventually lose their specific status and the benevolent attitude towards them among politicians' (2006b, p. 172). The countdown has already started.

Acknowledgements The author is grateful to his colleague, Pr. Lionel Dahan, for the English translation of this chapter.

References

Alvesson, M. (1996). Leadership studies: From procedure and abstraction to reflexivity and situation. *Leadership Quarterly, 6*(4), 455–485.

Alvesson, M., & Spicer, A. (2011). *Metaphors we lead by: Understanding leadership in the real world*. London: Routledge.

Aris, A., & Bughin, J. (2005). *Managing media companies: Harnessing creative value*. West Sussex: Wiley.

Auletta, K. (1991). *Three blind mice: How the TV networks lost their way*. New York: Random House.

Avolio, B. J., & Bass, B. M. (1985). *Transformational leadership, charisma and beyond, Work paper*. Binghamton: State University of New-York.

Bass, B. (1973). *Leadership: Psychology and organisational behaviour*. Westport, CT: Greenwood Press.

Bennis, W., & Nanus, B. (2003). *Leaders: Strategies for taking charge* (2nd ed.). New York: Harper Business Essentials.

Bilton, C. (2006). *Management and creativity: From creative industries to creative management*. Oxford: Blackwells.

Bjurstedt, A. (2006). A study of power in media leadership. In *Leadership in the media industries: Changing context, emerging challenges*. JIBS Research Report Series, 2006–1. pp. 179–186.

Brown, M., & Treviño, L. (2006). Ethical Leadership: A review and future directions. *Leadership Quarterly, 17*, 595–616.

Bryman, A. (2004). Qualitative research on leadership: A critical but appreciative review. *Leadership Quarterly, 15*, 729–769.

Cohen, S. (1999). *L'art d'interviewer les dirigeants*. Paris: Presses Universitaires de France.

Collier, J., & Esteban, R. (2000). Systemic leadership: Ethical and effective. *The Leadership and Organizational Development Journal, 21*(4), 207–215.

Collinson, D., & Collinson, M. (2009). 'Blended leadership': Employee perspectives on effective leadership in the UK further education sector". *Leadership, 5*(3), 365–380.

Conger, J. A. (1998). Qualitative research as the cornerstone methodology for understanding leadership. *Leadership Quarterly, 9*(1), 107–121.

Conger, J. A., & Kanungo, R. N. (1994). Charismatic leadership in organizations: Perceived behavioural attributes and their measurement. *Journal of Organizational Behaviour, 15*, 439–452.

Dagnaud, M., & Mehl, D. (1990). *Patrons de chaînes*. Cent: Réseaux.

Dal, Z. C. (2005). Human resources leadership in highly dynamic environments: Theoretically-based analyses of 3 publishing companies. *Journal of Media Business Studies, 2*(1), 51–70.

Dekoulou, P., Tsourvakas, G., & Zotos, Y. (2007). Leadership styles in the top Greek media companies: Leading people with mixed style. *The International Journal on Media Management, 9*, 77–86.

Deslandes, G. (2008). *Le Management des médias*. Paris: La Découverte, Collection Repères.

Deslandes, G. (2011). Corporate culture versus organizational identity: Implications for media management. *Journal of Media Business Studies, 8*(1), 23–38.

Deslandes, G., Fonnet, L., & Godbert, A. (2009). Ethique des médias sociaux et économie de la participation: Vers une nouvelle approche éditoriale? Une étude comparative. *Global Media Journal—Canadian Edition, 2*(1), 41–61.

Deslandes, G., & Painter-Morland, M. (2012). Rethinking accountability in contemporary media organizations. *Studies in Communication Sciences, 12*, 1–6.

Findikli, M. A., & Yozgat, U. (2012). A qualitative analysis of charismatic leadership in creative teams: The case of Turkish TV series directors. *Procedia—Social and Behaviour Sciences, 41*, 227–236.

Follett, M. P. (1928/1970). The teacher–student relation. *Administrative Science Quarterly 15*(1), 137–148.

Garcia, E.-J. (2011). *Leadership. L'exercice du pouvoir dans les entreprises* (p. 378). Oxford: De Boeck.

Girdauskiene, L., & Savanevičiene, A. (2012). Leadership role implementing knowledge transfer in creative organization: How does it work? *Procedia—Social and Behavioural Sciences, 41*, 15–22.

Hang, M. (2006). Do traits matter? Applying the leadership trait approach to Rupert Murdoch. In *Leadership in the media industries: Changing context, emerging challenges*. JIBS Research Report Series, 2006–1, pp. 159–169.

Hersey, P. (1995). *Le leader situationnel*. Paris: Actualisation.

Howell, J. M. (2005). The role of followers in the charismatic leadership process: Relationships and their consequences. *Academy of Management Review, 30*(1), 96–112.

Jeanneney, J. N. (1998). *Une histoire des médias, des origines à nos jours,* Ed. « Points » Seuil, Paris.

Kets De Vries, M. (2006). *La face cachée du leadership*, Village Mondial, 2ème édition.

Knee, J, Greenwald, B., & Seave, A. (2011). *The curse of the Mougul*, Portfolio trade.

Knights, D., & O'Leary, M. (2005). Reflecting on corporate scandals: The failure of ethical leadership. *Business Ethics: A European Review, 14*(4), 359–366.

Knights, D., & O'Leary, M. (2006). Leadership, ethics and responsibility. *Journal of Business Ethics, 67*, 127–137.

Koontz, H., & Weihrich, H. (1993). *Management: Global perspectives* (10th ed.). Singapore: MacGraw-Hill.

Küng, L. (2000). *Inside the BBC and CNN*. London and New York: Managing media organisations, Routledge.

Küng, L. (2007a). Does media management matter? Establishing the scope, rationale and future research agenda for the discipline. *Journal of Media Business Studies, 4*(1), 21–39.

Küng, L. (2007b). Strategic leadership in the media industry. *The Ashbridge Journal, Autumn*, 6–11.

Küng, L. (2008). *Strategic management in the media*. London: Sage.

Landale, A. (2005). Managers become leaders at NDS: Program integrates formal learning, coaching, mentoring and project work. *Human Resource Management International Digest, 13*(7), 15–18.

Lavine, J., & Wackman, D. (1988). *Managing media organizations: Effective leadership of the media*. New York: Longman.

Lazarsfeld, P. F., Berelson, B., & Gaudet, H. (1944). *The people's choice: How the voter makes up his mind in a presidential campaign*. New York: Columbia University Press.

Mierzejewska, B., & Hollifield, C. A. (2006). Theoretical approaches in media management research. In A. Albarran, S. Chan-Olmsted, & M. O. Wirth (Eds.), *Handbook of media management and economics* (pp. 37–65). Mahwah, NJ: Erlbaum.

Murphy, S. E., & Ensher, E. (2008). A qualitative analysis of charismatic leadership in creative teams: The case of television directors. *The Leadership Quarterly, 19*, 335–352.

Norback M. (2006) The staging of "Captain Outrageous versus the Australian Scumbag' – An Analysis of Media Mogul Ted Turner and his Feud with Rupert Murdoch". In *Leadership in the Media Industries: Changing Context, Emerging Challenges*. Research Report Series, 2006–1, pp. 1195–1202.

Northouse, P. (2004). *Leadership theory and practice* (3rd ed.). London: Sage.

Painter-Morland, M., & Deslandes, G. (2012, July 5–7). Redesigning leadership "design": A redefinition of "leadership" in the media environment. In *Proceedings of the 28th European Group for Organizational Studies Colloquium*, Aalto University, Helsinki, Finland.

Painter-Morland, M., & Deslandes, G. (2013). Gender and visionary leading: Rethinking "vision" with Bergson, Deleuze and Guattari. *Organization*. doi:10.1177/1350508413488636, pp. 1–23.

Pearce, C. L., & Conger, J. A. (2003). *Shared leadership: Reframing the hows and whys of leadership*. Thousand Oaks, CA: Sage.

Perez-Lattre, F., & Sanchez-Taberno, A. (2003). Leadership, an essential requirement for effecting change in media companies: An analysis of the Spanish Market. *The International Journal on Media Management, 5*(3), 199–208.

Picard, R. (2006a). Les médias au risque du Management et du Marketing. *Le Temps des médias, 6*, 164–174.

Picard, R. (2006a). Journalism, value creation and the future of news organizations. Working Paper Series, Joan Shorenstein Center of the Press, Harvard University.

Schein, E. (1985). *Organizational culture and leadership* (3rd ed.). San Francisco, CA: Jossey-Bass.

Shaver, D., & Shaver, M. A. (2006). Credentials, strategy and style: The relationship between leadership characteristics and strategic direction in media companies. In *Leadership in the media industries: Changing context, emerging challenges*. JIBS Research Report Series, 2006–1, pp. 123–136.

Stora, J. (1987). *Identité psychique et styles de leadership: approche psychanalytique*. Cahier de recherches du Centre HEC-ISA, n 297.

Trevino, L. K., Brown, M., & Hartman, L. P. (2003). A qualitative investigation of perceived executive ethical leadership: Perceptions from inside and outside the executive suite. *Human Relations, 55*(1), 5–37.

Trevino, L. K., Hartman, L. P., & Brown, M. (2000). Moral person and moral manager: How executives develop a reputation for ethical leadership. *California Management Review, 42*(1), 128–142.

Uhl-Bien, M., Marion, R., & McKelvey, B. (2007). Complexity leadership theory: Shifting leadership from the industrial age to the knowledge era. *Leadership Quarterly, 18*, 298–318.

Underwood, D. (1993). *When MBAs rule the newsroom*. New-York: Columbia University Press.

Van Weezel, A. (2006). A behavioural approach to leadership: The case of Michael Eisner and Disney. In *Leadership in the media industries: Changing context, emerging challenges*. JIBS Research Report Series, 2006–1, pp. 169–178.

Wickstrom, P. (2006). Transformational leadership in practice? The case of Steve Jobs and Pixar animation studios. In *Leadership in the media industries: Changing context, emerging challenges*. JIBS Research Report Series, 2006–1, pp. 187–194.

Managing Media Workers

19

Mark Deuze

19.1 Introduction

People spend more time with media today than at any previous point in history. The number of media channels, forms, genres, devices, applications, and formats is proliferating—more media get produced every year. Yet at the same time, the news about the media as an industry is less than optimistic. Reports about massive layoffs in all the creative industries—most notably film and television entertainment, journalism, digital game development, and advertising—are paramount.[1] This suggests a fascinating paradox: As people engage with media in an increasingly immersive, always-on, almost instantaneous, and interconnected way, the very people whose livelihood and sense of professional identity depend on delivering content and experiences across such media seem to be at a loss on how to come up with survival strategies—in terms of business models, effective regulatory practices (e.g., regarding copyrights and universal access provisions), and perhaps most specifically the organization of entrepreneurial working conditions that would support and sustain the creative process needed to meet the demands of a global market saturated with media. This puts the emphasis on management—of media as a business as well as the management of one's individual career. One needs a roadmap to navigate the unruly seas of the creative industries.

---

[1] For ongoing news about layoffs across the creative industries, I rely on reports such as regularly provided by IWantMedia (http://www.iwantmedia.com/); Journalism (in the UK; see http://www.journalism.co.uk/); the International Labour Organization (see, e.g., http://www.ilo.org/sector/Resources/publications/WCMS_161547/lang--en/index.htm); the Twitter feed of themediaisdying (https://twitter.com/themediaisdying).

M. Deuze (✉)
Department of Media studies, University of Amsterdam, Amsterdam, The Netherlands
e-mail: mdeuze@uva.nl

© Springer International Publishing Switzerland 2016
G.F. Lowe, C. Brown (eds.), *Managing Media Firms and Industries*, Media Business and Innovation, DOI 10.1007/978-3-319-08515-9_19

This contribution is based on previous research integrating different fields of study regarding media management and media work (see Deuze, 2007, 2011; Deuze & Lewis, 2013; Elefante & Deuze, 2012; some of the current work is adapted). The chapter can be understood as an attempt to integrate theories of how media industries function in society with theories of how media professionals manage their individual careers and professional identity in this context and case-based work on how media industries and professionals alike manage creativity and innovation. The assumption is that the combination of these perspectives assists in articulating a bridge between theory and practice in media management. This approach to managing media work stems from a few key considerations about the field of media management:

- Media management tends to be underexplored and undertheorized (Mierzejewska, 2011);
- Most media management research does not look across boundaries between media professions or academic disciplines (Aris & Bughin, 2012).
- The traditional tendency in much of the field has been to artificially maintain distinctions between management and creativity, which seems unhelpful (Bilton, 2007).
- Media management (studies and practice) should take an integrative, holistic approach—something advocated by many yet practiced by few.

Of crucial importance here is a conceptualization of media management as the management of companies as well as careers in the media. Particularly the latter part of this equation has been somewhat absent from the literature in the field, as it tends to focus on either specific industries (e.g., journalism or Hollywood), specific aspects of businesses within these industries (copyright enforcement, revenue models, product differentiation, concentration of ownership), or specific cases of company and firm projects (change management, work floor culture). The focus on (individual or group) careers is of added value for two key reasons: first, the ongoing casualization and individualization of labor and working conditions of professionals throughout the creative industries and, second, a motivation based on pedagogy. Schools, departments, programs, and courses in information science, (tele) communication, journalism, and media studies attract more students every year who are seeking careers in "the" media. Generally, such departments don't actually teach or train students for this purpose, instead focusing on the theories and methods of media and communication research. A broad perspective on media as careers may address this particular oversight.

Beyond the popularity of the media industries as degree programs and career perspectives, it must be said that the trends affecting media management are not particular to the creative industries. A new world of work is taking shape across the manufacturing, service, and creative industries that seems to be premised on individual- rather than industry-level responsibility, requiring a high degree of skillset flexibility, and with an implicit expectation of portfolio careerism. Media industries are special in this context for a longer history manifesting these broader trends (such were not characteristic of manufacturing, especially). Moreover, the media industries are unique with regard to the powerful link between work and self-realization that is generally evident in the motivation to pursue creative careers. This individualization of work (in motivations and careers) makes people in creative labor settings both easier and harder to manage: easier, because they are less likely to engage in collective action and bargaining, but harder because managing a more or less temporary network of fragmented individuals can be quite complicated and time-consuming.

It is difficult to adequately convey the complexity and dynamics of the typical work experience (anywhere) in the creative industries if relying on a traditional pedagogical focus that privileges the industry as the domain of corporations and companies. Such an institutional approach is reinforced by relying on the literature, which has generally omitted the individual from its consideration of media management, and by delegating "real-world" experience to the encouragement of internships and apprenticeships within media institutions. This is not to say that the characteristic approach is wrong or that it should be reversed. But it is to acknowledge that the work companies and firms do has increasingly less to do with the lived experience of an individual working in the media, and that the models for studying media management and managing careers in the media merit reconsideration. This chapter is an attempt to articulate a general context for managing media workers across creative industries and makes such a context specific to what generally defines and also drives cultural workers: their sense of self in terms of a professional identity (for more detail, see Deuze, 2007; Deuze & Lewis, 2013).

19.2   The Context of Managing Media Work

Driving contemporary media management and media work in all the creative industries is a shift in power away from professional content creators to users on the one hand and to owners on the other. Control over storytelling (including authority over what kind of stories is told and how) as well as the resources needed to creatively and effectively convey these stories are flowing away from professionals toward audiences. That is exemplified by decision-making processes that are increasingly governed by ratings and market research and a push toward including more user-generated content by and for corporations (see Napoli, 2010). Companies are exerting, or attempting to exert, increasingly control over financing arrangements, copyrights, and access to distribution platforms. For media workers, this means a loss of (negotiating) power in two directions at the same time, further contributing to what I characterize as an alienation process. In this context, the current shift toward individualized entrepreneurialism in creative labor can be considered the result of an increasingly precarious character of media work as well as a tactic to counteract its consequences.

As the industry, and especially its business models, focuses on user-generated content and consumer engagement, and as corporate media owners gain stronger control over their workforce via outsourcing production to loosely affiliated networks of professionals and firms or by abandoning production altogether in a bid to control the marketing and distribution of content produced elsewhere, those who professionally create content are often left (or made to feel) more or less powerless. In this way, work is being outsourced to both ends of the labor spectrum, leaving many media professionals far more isolated that has historically been the case. This is exemplified by a constant and ongoing struggle for work and the loss of any direct sense of creative autonomy.

Further, managing media work must be seen within the larger social architecture of which it is part, and this means taking into consideration every factor that contributes to the organization of media companies and careers. Such would certainly include content, processes, people, technology, and a range of implicit and unconscious aspects of organizational life such as beliefs, values, affects, and emotions, all of which can have a tremendous influence on planning as well as behaviors. Thus, managing media work is necessarily made up of both material and immaterial factors, and these must be considered in conjunction. Simply put, a key approach to media management requires focusing on the many resources (both human and nonhuman) that combine to form the source of all media action. By thinking in terms of such factors that comprise the broad context within which media work takes place, one cannot emphasize enough both the distributed and the hybrid nature of media work in comparison to other industries.

Media work does not simply involve the transfer of information (of books into treatments into screenplays into movies into franchises into…) but is situated in and involved with complex networks of information and understanding, including those related to competition, markets, organization and structure, industry standards, technologies, and the evolving media environment. All of that is not unique to media industries. Most of these variables are evident in the literature on general management work in determining the best strategy for a firm. But a singularly important aspect about media work remains the keen relevance of personal motivation, dedication, and identity investment that practitioners invest in their contributions—i.e., in the fruits of their labors. Media professionals tend to identify first and foremost with how they see themselves as a practitioner—as a filmmaker, a beat reporter, or television producer, for example—and only in the second or third instance would their professional identities be related to a particular company or brand.

Arguably the most powerful factor to be considered in managerial strategy for media firms is the role of technology. The plethora of technological innovations being developed and incorporated into and by society on a routine basis serves to supplement and undermine previous technologies. This shift presents media companies and individual professionals alike with the constant challenge of adaptation to a continually emerging range of new technologies and the progressive realignment or abandonment of older ones. In turn, the media as an industry (including its professionals) are at the forefront of supercharging the development of, and demand for, technological innovation. Again, I would like to underline the intertwined nature of human and nonhuman factors in the management of media industries—technologies are not neutral, "cold" machines nor is human talent something that exists in a vacuum (Winston, 1998).

Similar to the process of adaptation to technological development is the equally daunting challenge of adapting to the evolution of media content models. Business models are, like media technologies in general, always already remediated. That is to say, when new models emerge, the old models are supplemented and only rarely displaced. In media, traditional business models are perhaps not obsolete, but their effectiveness, which is based on markets and determined by channel scarcity and corresponding control over access, is diminished. This happens due to technologies that flatten the playing field and an overall tendency by management to cling to the familiar ("tried and true") when interpreting change that is disruptive. Media industries are experiencing a broad shift in the formulation of business models from an emphasis on mass media to personalized content and to participatory and user-generated content. Media products are becoming increasingly hybridized and are thus difficult to place into neat categories that can be isolated and therefore more effectively managed. Overall, however, communication between phases of the creative process, between elements of the global production network, and between technologies and practices, as well as between producers and consumers, is just as important a function as content itself.

Adaptation to technological development and the evolution of media content models are driving an increasing strategic emphasis on niche-oriented and also participatory media. A third influence on media strategy design is keyed to consumers' relationships with content. With technological advances facilitating the provision of custom products and an increased level of user participation in the production of content and experiences, the industry-driven construction of audiences is progressing from a mass of static objects conceived in passive terms to an unruly mob of active cocreators and people variously labeled by industry observers and scholars as "pro-ams," "amafessionals," "produsers," and "prosumers." Although this trend seems to be supported by data showing a growing group of people (especially teenagers) who are actively sharing, making, and up- and downloading content online, the audience construct is as much a product of industry rhetoric as behaviors (Napoli, 2010). But the changing nature of perceptions of and audience uses and relationships with media is forcing managers and workers alike to rethink their processes and practices when making content and designing experiences.

The contextual challenges that contribute to managing media work as discussed above are contributing to a different and far less stable environment than in the past. Additionally, rising costs, declining revenues (especially from advertising), and increasing competition (on a global scale) require companies and individuals to adapt to working with scarce resources for all elements of the production process: financing, conceptualizing, creation, marketing, and distribution. This leads to an increased focus on "creativity" as a real or perceived necessity to rise above the many challenges and win the ongoing competition for market demand—a trend that contributes to a global policy shift toward creative economies and creative industries (Flew, 2011). In short, more creativity and innovation on both the firm and the individual level means more success and a greater competitive advantage, even though such "advantages" fit in a broader context of precarious labor, technological complexity, and shifting power dynamics between employers, employees, and audiences.

19.3   A Model for Media Work

The ways in which media professionals give meaning to what they do—as documented in the literature, articulated in interviews, and visible in how they express themselves in trade magazines and online—are a primary source for understanding what it is like to work across the creative industries. This does not necessarily mean that people's lived experience of cultural work describes what actually happens, nor does it translate easily across the different types of media industries and areas of production involved with each type. But it is noteworthy to observe striking similarities in these self-expressions. Here it is useful to collapse the discourse of media workers into several categories of values, goals, and priorities that feature prominently in their everyday strategies and tactics. Regardless of whether a media worker is (or considers herself or himself to be) successful, or whether the measure of that "success" conforms to traditional notions of good (or bad) work, the set of values she or he deploys to articulate that struggle (or joyride) remains largely constructed out of the same principal components. For a broad discussion on notions of good and bad media work, see Hesmondhalgh and Baker (2011).

Doing cultural work shows that the market does not rule with an iron fist and that informal networks exist alongside sedimented structures and routines. It's also clear that the production process includes and also excludes both commercial aspiration and creative impulse and that the democratic nature of what Henry Jenkins (2006) effectively describes as *convergence culture* is both bottom-up (user-generated content) and top-down (cross-media marketing and franchising). Within this complicated frame of reference, the individual worker tends to stand alone—both in terms of labor protections (or rather the lack thereof) and regarding sense-making processes. Media work today is not only about what gets produced in terms of spoken and written words, audio, still, or moving images but (and increasingly) also is about providing platforms for people to make, edit, and exchange their own content. Four constituent elements comprise one's professional identity within today's creative industries: **content, connectivity, creativity**, and **commerce**. Professionals in media industries in particular, and creative industries more generally, produce content. That is obvious. But they also invest in platforms for connectivity where fans and audiences provide free labor. Media work is culture creation that tends to take place within a distinctly (and increasingly) commercial environment.

Within a context of destabilized legacy industries and dissolving boundaries between media consumption and production, the media worker may understandably feel individually isolated. However, this isolation can give some creative control to the media professional as well. Managing a boundary-less career can be considered to be the best, if not only, way to survive in the current work environment. To some extent, individuals can thus be seen as taking control of their career paths, resulting in a new type of self-directed job security. It is also possible that those who are willing to train themselves to become more attractive to management and employers. By being proficient in various methods of media production, workers can use multiple creative talents to their advantage—and are increasingly expected to be doing that. At the same time, however, it must be noted that existing ways of organizing labor and the current system of worker protections (both in the work-place and in terms of public policy and legislation) tend to overlook or even harm the ability of the individual to chart her or his own career path. Labor laws, unions, and other working arrangements tend to protect those who are already "inside," i.e., employees already contracted with a specific employer, often as part of a long-term package. The legal (including tax) context of individual or independent entre-preneurship in the creative industries often adds complexity to an already precari-ous work-life.

The contingency and casualized nature of media work is not necessarily new, nor does it occur similarly across all creative industries. On the other hand, ongoing digitalization and globalization of production and distribution have impacted careers in media significantly, amplifying an already fragmented labor experience (from the perspective of the individual worker). For management, this process has accelerated the level of complexity that must be handled when addressing workflows and assessing strategies needed to adapt to fast-changing and often uncertain circumstances. Nowhere is this felt more acutely than in the software sector (including digital games), where a small number of publishers and a sprawling field of small-sized businesses (including many individual entrepreneurs) try to keep up with a global market where producers and consumers are literally everywhere.

Whereas for most workers in temporary and contingent settings the employment situation is far from ideal, many in the higher skilled knowledge-based areas of the labor market, which certainly includes media, seem to prefer such precarious working conditions, associating this with greater individual autonomy, the acquisi-tion of a wide variety of skills and experiences, and a reduced dependence on a single employer. This, too, may be comparatively unique to media industries. The portfolio workstyle of the self-employed information or cultural worker/entrepre-neur can be characterized by living in a state of constant change, and flux, while at the same time seemingly enjoying a sense of control over one's own career. But Zygmunt Bauman warns against overtly optimistic readings of the relative freedom the beneficiaries enjoy in a context of inequitable globalization: "We are called to believe today that security is disempowering, disabling, breeding the resented 'dependency' and altogether constraining the human agents' freedom. What is passed over in silence is that acrobatics and rope-walking without a safety net are an art that few people can master and a recipe for disaster for all the rest" (quoted in Bauman & Tester, 2001, p. 52).

Freedom and security, often seen as mutually exclusive, become ambiguous in the context of how different people from different walks of life deal with, and give meaning to, the consequences of not having either. It is perhaps the perfect paradox: all the trends in today's work-life quite clearly suggest a rapid destabilization of social bonds corresponding with increasingly disempowering effects of a fickle and uncertain global hi-tech information economy, yet those workers caught in the epicenter of this bewildering shift also express a sense of mastery over their lives, interpreting their professional identity in this context in terms of individual-level control and empowering agency. Melissa Gregg (2011) shows how this interpretative process is part and parcel of being part of a community of peers in cultural work that sometimes quite willingly includes self-delusions of "making it work" while, from an outsider's point of view, the professional involved clearly does not.

We are describing a more or less deliberate negotiation of otherwise debilitating forms of labor exploitation that is characterized by rampant unpaid ("spec") work, expectations of 24/7 engagement, a mutually enforced always-on mentality, and experiencing no control over one's future under the guise of a "nobody knows" mantra and the disempowering effects of generally operating in a labor context without traditional lines of feedback and support. What explains this? In my view, it is the fact that media work tends to be affective. The professional identity of a job in the creative industries tends to have meaning beyond the instrumental functionality of doing something that earns a living. The fact that people who do media work often care so deeply about what they do (as, increasingly, also evident in many other sectors and industries) not only opens more opportunities for exploitation; it can also be seen as raising the stakes for a personalized sense of professional identity as a coping mechanism that can be self-delusional as well as self-empowering (see Neff, Wissinger, & Zukin, 2005).

In the everyday construction of a media professionals' sense of self—that which leads to a more or less coherent (at least imagined) professional identity—it is the interplay between the values of providing content, organizing connectivity, handling creative freedom, and being commercially successful (which is not necessarily an expression in monetary terms) that influences one's negotiations. The external factors intervening and complicating these everyday negotiations are many and certainly beyond the contemporary context sketched earlier. Key elements that are historically continuous include the uneven structure of ownership over cultural products and the control of its modes of distribution (where in all industries, a handful of major corporations and holding firms operate vis-à-vis many smaller or independently operating enterprises), the mentioned lack of adequate legal protections for atypically employed workers, as well as a profound age, gender, and life phase imbalance throughout the creative industries—featuring a workflow that tends to privilege young men living in unmarried and childless circumstances (Creedon & Cramer, 2007). These structural elements of the identity equation are not particular to the early twenty-first century and are not experienced in the same way by everyone involved. However, their omnipresence codetermines deliberations about one's choices and priorities when considering a career in media.

Although the role of technology impact is continual, there can be said to be something quite particular about the current media ecosystem within which media work takes place. This primarily has to do with the disruptive potential of increasingly ubiquitous and pervasive information and communication technologies, wresting control over all aspects of the media value chain—especially production, marketing, and distribution—away from gatekeepers such as record labels in the music industry, distributors in the film industry, and publishers in the game industry. In a real sense, these trends further contribute to the individualization process in cultural work because the artist—whether a fashion designer, intrepid reporter, or aspiring moviemaker—is considered to be individually empowered by relatively cheap and easy-to-use technologies to do "their own thing" and be successful at that. Celebratory accounts of formerly unknown individuals striking it "big" through suddenly popular songs or viral videos on YouTube obscure the significant investments made by individuals to *make it work* both within and outside of creative industries and thus tend to highlight product over process. Notions of long-term affective investment in one's craft or art get sidelined in favor of often one-time oversized success (in turn generally only assessed through rather traditional industrial metrics, such as number of hits/visitors/likes/re-tweets/copies sold).

It is within this system of variables that media professionals can be expected to be outlining their sense of professional identity in terms of the stories they want to tell (content), their relationship with audiences and publics (connectivity), their particular perception of what kind of work they aspire to (creativity), and the role success in whatever shape or form plays in all of this (commerce).

19.4 Professional Identity in Practice

The work of authors in various fields signals an increased prevalence of consumer-generated, customer-controlled, or user-directed media content and experiences across the creative industries (see Jenkins, Ford, & Green, 2013). Researchers in different disciplines signal a corresponding industry-wide turn toward seeing the consumer as cocreator in cultural work, particularly where the cultural industries' core commodity is (mediated) information. Online, media participation can be seen as the defining characteristic of the Internet in terms of its hyperlinked, interactive, and networked infrastructure and digital culture. None of this is essentially new, nor is it necessarily tied to the Internet. Yet it must be argued that continuous blurring of the real or perceived boundaries between making and using media by professionals as well as amateurs has been supercharged in recent years—particularly in terms of its omnipresence and visibility online.

I say supercharged because historically we find that people who make media have often collaborated with those who use media. Much of the great works of art came about because rich patrons commissioned painters and sculptors to make specific portraits, decorations, and other representations signifying status and prestige in society. Often such works were not created by single art "producers" but came to be through intense collaboration and exchange among dedicated teams of artists, their apprentices, sponsors, and visitors.

Participation as a value and expectation in journalism was first established through letters to the editor sections in newspapers and later expanded to include functions like newspaper ombudsmen and reader representatives that became an accepted part of news organizations worldwide. All areas of the creative industries from advertising, marketing communications, and public relations through journalism, architecture (visual and performing), arts and crafts, design, fashion, film, video and photography, software, computer games, music, publishing, television, and radio—all have historical trajectories that show how the oft-maintained distinction between production and consumption is quite artificial, largely serving to sustain discursive structures of power and control within hierarchies. This is manifest in the proclivity to see the "artist" as intrinsically more enlightened than the "audience" or, in the case of a radical democratization theory of digital culture, the other way around (see Benkler, 2006).

As discussed before, a significant consequence of the new media environment is the shifting of power to the audience, both in power of resources and power of selection. This presents a double-edged sword to professional media workers. For established professionals, it generally becomes more difficult to utilize their power in the industry, of course depending on their relative position in the (often informal) hierarchy of their field and the platform within which they work. For newcomers, there are more tools and opportunities to break into the field. The lines between production and consumption continue to be drawn, erased, and redrawn, all of which takes place within an industrial context offering a fascinating blend of large multinational corporations and grassroots initiatives. This predicates an hourglass structure of cultural employment where a few networked companies employ thousands of people worldwide, while most of the production of content and experiences in media takes place in thousands of tiny companies often employing a handful of people, or less.

This trend highlights the pressure on media workers to strike a balance for every project and therefore as a benchmarking element of their professional identity. That balance is between the "auteur" ideal of creating content and compelling user experiences versus the (often considered as oppositional) value of providing people with platforms for connectivity and sharing their own free labor. Participatory media production and individualized media consumption are two different yet co-constituent trends that typify an emerging media ecology that is determining the direction of media workers' professional identities in practice.

In today's media environment, consuming some kind of media also involves producing media because people's media behavior so often involves some level of participation, cocreation, and collaboration, depending of course on the degree of openness or closedness of the media involved. In this context, the concepts of "open" and "closed" media refer to the extent which a given media company or site of media work shares some or all of its modes of operation with its target publics. A media organization can, for example, increase the level of transparency about how it works, or can opt to give its customers more control over their user experience. Yet the same communication technologies that enable interactivity and participation are wielded to foster the entrenchment and growth of a global corporate media system that can be said to be anything but transparent, interactive, or participatory. The creativity of workers—paid and unpaid alike—throughout the creative industries must therefore be always considered within the competing as well as enabling framework of commerce.

It is crucial to note, however, that the delicate dance of media work in convergence culture is not a phenomenon particular to the contemporary context. The stranglehold of major business entities in most creative industries over financing, organization of labor, mode of distribution, as well as promotion and marketing is a structural phenomenon. However optimistic some of the readings of media workers' individual agency and cultural productions' convergence are, uneven and exploitative relationships remain a significant structural factor in determining how one's professional identity gets shaped and correspondingly shapes the political economy of both media management and media work. This last point is significant in suggesting that much of the precariousness of media work is in fact maintained by individuals trying to "make it work" within the system by not collectively organizing or by acquiescing to free labor and speculative work, as examples. In this view, one cannot simplistically conclude that "the corporation" is the source of all constraints on the development of a professional identity in cultural work.

19.5 Discussion

In this contribution, I've attempted to connect the worlds of theory and practice in media management and media work. At the same time, I have tried to steer clear of explanations that either suggest work across the creative industries is necessarily benchmarked by exploitation (Ross, 2009) or celebrate the supposedly new and improved chances for creativity and success in the current cultural economy (Jenkins, 2006). In my view, it is crucial to follow the lead of scholars such as David Hesmondhalgh and Sarah Baker, who benchmark their analyses of interviews with media workers across three cultural industries with the deliberate intent "to take creative workers' accounts seriously" (2011, p. 50).

An important question when considering the current practice and future of managing media work is why we still talk so much, even entirely, about firms, companies, and organizations in an era that seems to celebrate looseness and non-commitment? The framing of this question suggests that the answer lies in looking at media management somewhat differently than is typical, as described early in this contribution. Here the perspective on media management is marked by an appreciation of the lived experience of media work. In order to generate a systematic way of understanding the individualized "workstyle" (meaning the way of working and being at work) in media work—I have framed the everyday negotiations a media worker makes within the axes of content, connectivity, creativity, and commerce. The daily deliberations that oscillate between these variables and values have been framed by both continuous and contemporary trends across creative industries. This taxonomy of individual lived experience, professional identity formation, and structuring factors should help to unpack the particularities of media management within and beyond organizations and firms as well as between and across different areas in the creative industries.

When thinking about the practice of media management, a couple of closing considerations remain to be briefly addressed. First of all, let me reiterate something stressed at the outset: media management is about individual talent. This talent is either present in the company or network, or it is available otherwise to manage deliberately. What this also means is that the company in and of its self is not special—rather, the talent it manages is special. Although this may seem obvious, it is striking that the literature on media management calls for more attention to be paid to media workers and the creative process alongside business models and flowcharts (Aris & Bughin, 2012). So even if obviously important, it has been too often neglected.

Second, it seems clear that the trends affecting media are similar across the creative industries and that different disciplines—journalism, advertising, digital games, film, and so on—address such issues in a variety of ways. This should make it similarly obvious for people inside these industries that it is wise to consider each other's best (and worst) practices. However, such cross-pollination is so far rare.

Finally, media management today seems to be, perhaps now more so than ever, a reminder to all of us that the boundaries between commercial acumen and creative enterprise need to be erased. Furthermore, to deny or even downplay the role of the user in the life cycle of the media product or service seems equally misguided. Arguably missing from all of this is an appeal to ethics to serve as a warning against exploitation as well as an appeal to aesthetics to protect the art of producing culture.

References

Aris, A., & Bughin, J. (2012). *Managing media companies: Harnessing creative value* (2nd ed.). Hoboken, NJ: Wiley.

Bauman, Z., & Tester, K. (2001). *Conversations with Zygmunt Bauman*. Cambridge: Polity Press.

Benkler, Y. (2006). *The wealth of networks*. New Haven: Yale University Press.

Bilton, C. (2007). *Management and creativity: From creative industries to creative management*. Malden: Blackwell.

Creedon, P., & Cramer, J. (2007). *Women in mass communication* (3rd ed.). Thousand Oaks, CA: Sage.

Deuze, M. (2007). *Media work*. Cambridge, UK: Polity Press.

Deuze, M. (Ed.). (2011). *Managing media work*. London, UK: Sage.

Deuze, M., & Lewis, N. (2013). Professional identity and media work. In M. Banks, S. Taylor, & R. Gill (Eds.), *Theorizing cultural work: Transforming labour in the cultural and creative industries* (pp. 161–174). London: Routledge.

Elefante, P., & Deuze, M. (2012). Media work, career management, and professional identity: Living labour precarity. *Northern Lights: Film & Media Studies Yearbook, 10*(1), 9–24.

Flew, T. (2011). *The creative industries: Culture and policy*. London: Sage.

Gregg, M. (2011). *Work's intimacy*. Cambridge: Polity Press.

Hesmondhalgh, D., & Baker, S. (2011). *Creative labour: Media work in three cultural industries*. London: Routledge.

Jenkins, H. (2006). *Convergence culture: Where old and new media collide*. New York: New York University Press.

Jenkins, H., Ford, S., & Green, J. (2013). *Spreadable media: Creating value and meaning in a networked culture*. New York: NYU Press.

Mierzejewska, B. (2011). Media management in theory and practice. In M. Deuze (Ed.), *Managing media work* (pp. 13–30). London: Sage.

Napoli, P. M. (2010). *Audience evolution: New technologies and the transformation of media audiences*. New York, NY: Fordham University Press.

Neff, G., Wissinger, E., & Zukin, S. (2005). Entrepreneurial labour among cultural producers: "Cool" jobs in "Hot" industries. *Social Semiotics, 15*(3), 307–334.

Ross, A. (2009). *Nice work if you can get it: Life and labor in precarious times*. New York: NYU Press.

Winston, B. (1998). *Media, technology and society: From the telegraph to the Internet*. London: Routledge.

Managing Creativity in Media Organisations

20

Paul Dwyer

20.1 Can Creativity Be Managed?

Much conventional management thinking has been concerned with standardising work practices and reducing worker autonomy (see Taylor, 1911; Weber, 1915; Mintzberg, 1979). From this conventional perspective, bureaucratic management and creativity are antithetical: 'bureaucracies are supposed to operate "by the rules". They are places where individual initiative, enterprise, and *creativity* are supposed to take second place—if they are permitted at all!—to the policies and procedures that have been defined or authorized by those in charge of the organization as a whole' (Morgan, 1989: 49). One of the leading authors in this field, Teresa Amabile (1996b), argues many managers design organisations that—unwittingly but systematically—'kill' creativity. Regarding the media industries, some influential studies have suggested that creative personnel are 'unmanageable' because creative work, by definition, cannot be 'taylorised' (Florida, 2002).

This idea of a tension, or even a zero-sum game, between management and media creativity poses a challenge to the very idea of a field of media management research. To address this challenge, it is necessary first to try to define what is meant by 'creativity'.

20.2 What Is Creativity?

It is somewhat ironic that despite a general consensus on the importance of creativity—in media industries as elsewhere—as a precious resource in media industries, there is no consensus on what creativity actually is. Simply put, there

P. Dwyer (✉)
CAMRI, University of Westminster, Harrow, United Kingdom
e-mail: p.dwyer@westminster.ac.uk

© Springer International Publishing Switzerland 2016
G.F. Lowe, C. Brown (eds.), *Managing Media Firms and Industries*, Media
Business and Innovation, DOI 10.1007/978-3-319-08515-9_20

is no 'theory of creativity'. As Hennessey and Amabile (2010: 569) recently observed, there is instead a 'staggering array of disciplinary *approaches* to understanding creativity'. They conclude that 'What we need now, are all encompassing *systems theories* of creativity, designed to tie together and make sense of the diversity of perspectives found in the literature—from the innermost neurological level to the outermost cultural level'.

In the absence of a theory of creativity, there is surely no agreed theory of managing creativity. Instead the literature, and management practice, evidences a range of often conflicting approaches. As I will try to show, the debates about managing creativity, and the differences in approach, are (sometime unwittingly) a reflection of the 'staggering array' of fundamentally different conceptions of creativity adopted in their development.

The first part of this literature review focuses on approaches to managing creativity drawn from the creative and media worlds. The second section reviews literature on the topic drawn from conventional management and organisation theory.

20.2.1 Managing Talent

At the most basic level, media organisations try to manage creativity by identifying and recruiting creative individuals (Zafirau, 2008). This approach reflects the earliest conception of creativity—the idea of exceptionally creative individuals (or 'talent') who contribute, to a disproportionately large degree, to the success of media organisations. Although this approach is now a common practice across media and cultural industries, its roots are found in our fundamental understanding of the characteristics of the artistic temperament. Much psychological research in the field of creativity has involved attempts to identify the personality traits of creative individuals via analysis of the lives and careers of significant contributors to a range of disciplines in the arts and sciences (the modern classic is Gardner, 1993).

This conception of creativity as an individual process of self-expression where irrational, unconscious or childlike cognitive processes are more likely to produce creativity than rational ones is often attributed to Freud. It is significant for media management researchers that his most frequently cited example is drawn from drama: 'Language has preserved this relationship between children's play and poetic creation. It designates certain kinds of imaginative creation concerned with tangible objects and capable of representation. As "plays"; the people who present them are called players' (Freud, 1908/1958: 45). Freud's ideas have been hugely influential in the development of a discourse around a proposed opposition between creativity as an expression of the irrational unconscious and Weber's view of management and organisation as the ultimate expressions of means-end rationality. As we shall see, however, this view of creativity as embodied in especially talented individuals (the 'genius myth') has been subjected to considerable criticism. This is not to neglect the ample evidence that identifying and managing talented individuals is indeed central to the practice of media management (Caves, 2002; Perry, 2009).

20.2.2 Facilitating Creative Thinking

The Freudian description of non-rational cognitive processes ('play') involved in creativity raised questions about whether anyone and everyone could learn to be creative by developing capability to think in this way. This approach originated in the media industry and is usually credited to Alex Osborn, whose hugely influential *Applied imagination* (1953) codified his insights into the way the advertising industry managed creativity by 'facilitating' nonroutinised, unconventional, divergent thinking. The appeal of Osborn's book was its apparent ability to resolve the Weberian tension between management and creativity. Conventional management thinking tends to encourage means-end 'convergent' rationality that discourages the consideration of alternative 'out-of-the box' possibilities. Resolution of this problem requires the introduction of techniques to promote 'divergent' thinking.

Proponents of this approach have tried to manage creativity by increasing the *quantity* of ideas ('ideation') by using techniques (most famously the brainstorm) to generate multiple options to solve a problem. Osborn established the Creative Problem Solving Institute to promote his approach by publishing practice-based literature advising businesses on facilitating creativity. A range of techniques in this general vein have emerged in the decades since Osborn—including Edward de Bono's (1971, 1987) concepts of lateral thinking and his six 'thinking hats' (see Runco, 2010 for a recent review). Whilst these techniques for creative thinking and creative problem solving have been very popular in business applications, the empirical evidence for their efficacy in stimulating creativity is much disputed (Puccio, Murdock, & Mance, 2006).

20.2.3 Manageable Creativity

Chris Bilton (2007, 2010) is an increasingly influential contemporary voice in scholarship about creativity, especially in media and creative organisations. Whereas the writers discussed thus far have accepted the neo-Weberian tension between conventional management and creativity, Bilton argues that management and creativity are not in conflict. 'Creativity and management, having been positioned historically as opposing concepts, are increasingly converging in new models of cultural policy and business management' (Bilton, 2010: 255). Noting the existence of a large number of people prepared to do creative work for free, Bilton reformulates the central problematic: management does not 'kill' creativity.

In fact there is *too much* creativity: 'the problem is, if anything, the over-supply of creative ideas and talent, not scarcity' (Bilton, 2010: 260).

Bilton's approach originates from a critique of the 'talent management' approach discussed above. He argues that this approach rests on a heroic conception of creativity, focused on the personality traits of creative individuals (he references Robbie Williams) and contends that this idea has been 'effectively debunked'. In support, Bilton cites Weisberg's work (1986, 1993, 2010) which emphasised the *rational* cognitive processes involved in the development of creative talent through practice. Weisberg (2010: 246) argues that 'recent research on expertise has raised the possibility that deliberate practice is the critical factor in reaching world-class levels of performance in many domains'. He prioritises interaction and social differentiation within a community of professionals as the essential stimuli and context for creativity.

Bilton's 'manageable creativity' approach appears to have a number of inherent problems. First, there is his proposal that the tension between management and creativity has been resolved. The logic of Bilton's (2007, 2010) argument for the convergence of creativity and management into a 'manageable creativity' appears to derive not from his use of Weisberg's definition of creativity but from the emergence of 'new models of cultural policy and business management' at the end of the twentieth century. Cultural policymakers in the UK (influenced by the 'cultural industries' theories of the Frankfurt School, see Adorno & Horkheimer, 1979) identified 'the creative industries' as a new area for economic growth. This influenced the adoption of a similar policy framework in many countries, particularly in Europe. But as Garnham noted, the assumptions about the economic growth of the creative industries were ideologically rather than empirically motivated: 'the term "creative" was chosen so that the whole of the computer software sector could be included. Only on this basis was it possible to make the claims about size and growth stand-up' (Garnham, 2005: 26). The apparent emergence and growth of the 'creative industries' thus represents a questionable basis for the argument that creativity and management have converged.

Bilton argues that media organisations continue to use the talent management approach—despite its flawed conception of creativity—because this 'myth' provides 'a glimmer of hope for the vast army of underpaid and exploited hopefuls who feed the industry machine' (Bilton, 2007: 16). Thus media managers are either mistaken or cynically exploitative in continuing to support the myth of 'heroic' creativity. However, there is a central problem in the alternative conception of creativity he proposes.

Bilton's development of Weisberg's critique of ('heroic') talent management leads him to a conception of creativity that ultimately appears to dispense with the analysis of creativity altogether—and to redefine creativity as innovation. He does not so much present an argument that management and creativity have converged, as define this conflict away. The problem with 'heroic' creativity, he says, is that it rests on 'a definition of creative processes and people, weighted towards the process of *ideation* rather than the longer process of idea development and *application* and favouring the individualistic, irrational process of "divergent thinking" over the collective, deliberate processes of "convergent thinking" which convert new ideas into valuable *innovations*' (Bilton, 2010: 259, my emphasis). In the end, then, Bilton's argument appears to accept the notion that creativity (or in his definition 'ideation') is 'irrational' and (presumably) unmanageable and instead focuses on the process of managing innovation. In focusing on innovation management (which is an important discipline), Bilton offers little help in understanding how to manage the creative process itself.

20.3 Creativity and Conventional Management Thinking

This section reviews the literature on managing creativity within the field of conventional management studies. Here the approach to managing creativity has often developed from a neo-Weberian critique of the dysfunctions of bureaucratic management rather than an explicit concept of creativity. This argument follows Weber in suggesting conventional management techniques (rationalising work, restricting worker autonomy) create 'human factor' dysfunctions (alienation and boredom among workers) reducing the motivation to work (Mayo, 1933; Herzberg, 1959). This resulted in a subdiscipline of management thinking aimed at restoring human factors and thus motivation, principally through teamworking.

20.3.1 Creative Management

Xu and Rickards (2007) argue that the natural evolution of this school of thought is a new paradigm they term 'creative management'. The cases they analyse suggest that 'the creative manager re-invents his or her corporate self and the organization', and they offer examples of senior managers leading change in organisational cultures (op. cit: 223).

The 'creative management' approach has two principle weaknesses. First, the 'paradigm' unfortunately is not defined in detail. Secondly, whereas the writers discussed above appear to derive their approach to managing creativity from a particular concept of creativity, the 'creative management' approach lacks a clear conception of creativity. The original 'human factor' approach was much criticised from both pluralist and Marxist perspectives as an essentially ideological device, appearing to 'humanise' work whilst actually legitimating conventional management exploitation (Braverman, 1974). Xu and Rickards' (2007) focus on changes to organisational culture, and the work environment, rather than the actual nature of work processes, leaves their approach open to similar criticism.

20.3.2 Teresa Amabile's Model of Creativity

However, the focus on motivation identified by Xu and Rickards has also been central to the work of Teresa Amabile (see especially, 1996a), the most widely cited theorist within discussions of managing creativity in the field of conventional management. The strength of Amabile's approach is that it is derived from a clear and explicit theoretical model of creativity (see Fig. 20.1). The model comprises three key elements: domain skills, creative thinking processes, and intrinsic motivation. Amabile addresses the conflict between creativity and management by connecting the problems of facilitating creativity with the critique of the impact of bureaucratic management on motivation. Conventional management practices 'kill' creativity, she argues, because they inhibit employees' intrinsic motivation to work creatively: 'people will be most creative when they feel motivated primarily by the interest, satisfaction, and challenge of the work itself—and not by external pressures' (Amabile, 1996b: 79).

Amabile's model has significant advantages over all the approaches reviewed above because her conception of creativity incorporates many of the valuable elements of the other approaches. Specifically, the requirement for 'domain skills' addresses the media manager's search for individual talent; Osborn's creative thinking skills are explicitly included; and the tension between conventional management and creativity is addressed by her proposals to provide for 'human factors' that can enable intrinsic motivation.

Amabile also hypothesises a logic organising the way the three elements may interact and proposes that this should enable managers and researchers to use the

Fig. 20.1 Amabile's model of creativity. Source: Adapted from Amabile (1996b)

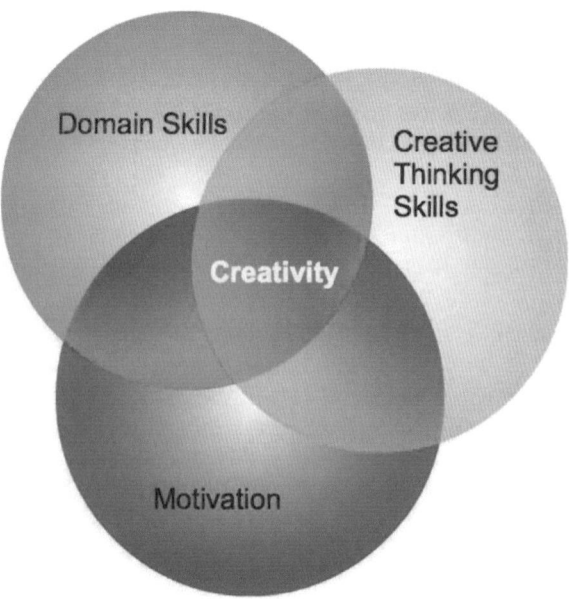

model to predict the level of creativity that may be expected to result in a particular work context. Thus, an individual or group possessing in high degree all three elements of the model (domain skills, creative thinking skills and intrinsic task motivation) is the most likely to be high in creativity (op. cit: 104–105). Similarly those who have the expertise and thinking skills, but aren't motivated, would not create as well or as much. Hence, it is the combination and interaction of these elements that co-determine the degree of creativity likely to result in the workplace.

For these reasons, I believe Amabile's model offers the best available approach to analysing the management of creativity in media organisations. In the final section of this chapter, I attempt to show how Amabile's model can be applied to analyse and evaluate the BBC's attempt to improve creativity. But before embarking on this analysis, it is important to identify and address certain weaknesses within Amabile's approach and to show how the model may be modified to improve its utility in describing, analysing and evaluating the management of creativity in media organisations.

The chief weakness of Amabile's model is in the method proposed for measuring the creativity of an organisation or individual. Amabile outlines a method she calls the Consensual Assessment Technique that is according to Baer and McKool (2009: 3) 'based on the rather simple idea that the best measure of the creativity of a work of art, a theory, or any other artefact is the combined assessment of experts in that field'. Such a subjective measure may have some utility but, ironically, returns to Amabile's under-theorised concept of domain expertise as the best means of assessment.

This lack of an objective method of measuring creativity is clearly a very significant weakness. Without some objective means of measuring the results of the process, there is no way to assess the success of a particular approach to, or empirical instance of, managing creativity. Resolving this problem is a broader challenge for the field of creativity research and may require the development of a generally agreed definition of creativity. For the purposes of media management research, I suggest that Amabile's model may be operationalised using contextual proxy measures of creativity. The analysis of the BBC case, below, attempts to show how this may be done.

The second weakness of the model is that although Amabile emphasises the importance of the combination and interaction of the elements of creativity, in practice the most influential aspect of her work has been the techniques she has developed for managing creativity. These have focused on one element of this model—intrinsic motivation (1996a: 230–36). It isn't immediately clear why having developed a clear tripartite model, in practice she focuses so much on one element. One reason may be her assessment of the differing stages of the conceptual and empirical development of the three elements. She seems to suggest that applying the concept of domain skills is problematic because 'there has been virtually no research directly examining the role of domain-relevant skills in the production of creative work' (1996a: 87). But lack of research would not explain her relative neglect of the third element in her model, creative thinking skills.

As noted above, a large field of practice-based research has developed since Osborn founded the Creative Problem Solving Institute.

There may also be a more pragmatic explanation for Amabile's decision to focus on intrinsic motivation. After noting that she believes managers *could* improve the domain skills and creative thinking of employees, she confides, 'the fact is that the first two are more difficult and time consuming to influence than motivation' (1996b: 79–80). The implication, at least, is that intrinsic motivation offers managers 'a quick fix' that can 'yield more immediate results' (ibid.).

This neglect of two core elements of creativity must surely weaken the potential of the model in analysing the management of creativity in practice. To try to demonstrate this, this section refers to Küng's (2004, 2008) analysis of HBO, 'an industry leader in creative original programming' (2004: 71) which follows Amabile in concentrating on the role of intrinsic motivation. Küng shows how HBO's secure business model and related employment and compensation policies fostered intrinsic motivation. HBO is 'unique in the industry in offering writers a 5 year contract, with the explicit goal of providing creative stability and the psychological freedom to take risks' (Küng 2008: 156). But Küng also notes that the heads of HBO's original programming division had 'deep expertise in both entertainment (both had considerable prior experience as talent scouts) and a deep knowledge of the cable sector' (2004: 72). This suggests that a fuller description and analysis of HBO's management of creativity would be obtained through greater attention to other elements of the model—particularly domain skills. One might hypothesise, for example, that this talent-scouting expertise enabled HBO to recruit writers (and other creatives) with particular 'domain skills'. Looking further ahead in our argument, we might suggest that the less stringent regulation and niche audience offered by a cable channel helped 'loosen' the domain of network TV drama production. Given the importance of creativity in media organisations, further research on the role of domain skills should give us an even better understanding of how HBO achieves creative results on such a persistent and remarkable basis.

This section has suggested that Amabile's model offers the best available method of improving our description and analysis of the process of managing creativity. However, three important weaknesses of Amabile's model have been identified; no objective measures of creativity are proposed; the role of critical thinking and in particular domain skills has been neglected; and the effect on creativity of the *interaction* of the elements is not precisely specified.

Before the model can be applied to analyse practice, therefore, it is necessary to sketch out how these weaknesses may be addressed by modifying the model. The case study section, below, illustrates how contextual elements (proxy measures and empirical data on specific interactions) may be added to the model to try to address the specifics of measuring creative results and illustrating the interaction of elements in a specific context.

The discussion of the weakness of the model suggested that an area of future media management research may be key to making further progress in developing the model to analyse and guide practice. The neglect of domain skills was identified as a weakness both of the conceptual development and, especially, the application of Amabile's model. The following section attempts to show how further research might develop our understanding of the concept and role of domain skills in creativity to modify Amabile's model to enable it be applied successfully. The final section uses this modified model to test for the presence of the three elements of creativity and to analyse their interaction, in order to evaluate and account for the success or failure of the BBC's attempt to improve creative performance.

20.4   Developing Amabile's Model

20.4.1 Domain Skills

This first part of this section attempts to show how Amabile's concept of domain skills might be developed by reference to the work of Mihaly Csikszentmihalyi (1996, 1998), the other most widely cited theorist in the field of creativity. One of the weaknesses of Amabile's model is that 'domain skills' are, by definition, domain specific, whereas the other two elements of the model are generalisable to any field. Amabile's discussion of domain skills is brief but helpfully clear in positioning talent as something both special and specific, but not 'heroic' in the sense Bilton is concerned to 'debunk'. Amabile combines Weisberg's idea of creativity through practice with the media manager's commonsense understanding of talent. For Amabile, domain skills require 'special training or experience; certainly a talent can be developed' (1996a: 86). A creative worker has 'a special skill for which an individual appears to have a natural aptitude... (which) clearly distinguishes him or her from the general population' (ibid).

Csikszentmihalyi's (1996, 1998) idea of a domain may be a fruitful avenue for further media management research in this area. For Csikszentmihalyi, workers' ability to be creative *varies* depending on the stage of development of the domain. In very 'loosely organised' domains, it may be difficult to determine whether a new development is an improvement on existing practice, while other domains may be 'so tightly organized that no new development seems possible' (1998: 319). By examining the 'stage of development' of a domain, we may develop an understanding of the role of domain skills in creativity which is more sophisticated than that provided by Amabile's model. Based on Csikszentmihalyi, we can hypothesise that domain skills will exercise a *variable* role in creativity—contributing most to creativity when they reach a stage of maturity but before they become institutionalised.

Csikszentmihalyi enables a further contextualisation of the concept of domain skills by suggesting that the stage of development is not a linear, historical process. Instead changes in the broader culture or society will affect the stage of development of a particular set of domain skills, loosening tight skills and vice versa. This enables a more sophisticated understanding of the logic organising the interaction of domain skills with the other elements of Amabile's model. At very early ('loose') or very late ('tight') stages of development of the domain, creativity may be difficult to achieve *regardless* of the level of intrinsic motivation—or indeed the talent or domain expertise of an individual worker. In such circumstances, however, we could hypothesise that the interaction between domain skills creative thinking skills may be important for opening up space for creativity within tightly organised domains or in figuring out ways to develop a perception of improvement in loosely organised domains.

20.4.2 Domain Skills and Media Creativity

A second weakness of Amabile's model is that whilst motivation and thinking skills are generalisable to almost any business, domain skills are specific to a creative context—in our case media industries. To apply Amabile's model to the management of creativity in *media* domains, we need to identify and understand the role of those domain skills that are specific to the creation of media content. This is another important area for future media management research. The rest of this section attempts to illustrate how this could be done in relation to the skills of creating content for film and TV.

Thus far, media management research has not made great progress in the study of media skills. One reason for this may be that, as Küng (2008: 150) notes, media expertise 'tends to rest on tacit rather than codified knowledge' stemming not from qualifications but from 'a combination of experience derived from exposure to the field and individual judgment and intuition'. The difficulty for researchers and managers is that such tacit skills are rarely articulated or even acknowledged by media workers. Many researchers who have interviewed media workers will recognise Becker's (1982) account of the typical kind of rationale media workers give for their creative decisions: 'an undefinable but perfectly reliable standard like "it swings" or "it works"' (Becker, 1982: 200). One difficulty in identifying media domain skills, therefore, is that media workers are rarely able to articulate what knowledge or skills they are applying in making creative judgments; they simply 'know' after the fact when they have made the right or wrong creative decision.

Much of what we know about media skills in general, and film and TV in particular, is derived from the study of drama—ideas first expressed in detail in Greek poetics (Aristotle, 1996). Subsequent theories of narrative and genre have helped distinguish types of storytelling and to discern the loose design blueprint that forms the 'domain' of drama. Neale (1990: 46) draws on Todorov (1973) to argue that genres 'involve a knowledge of... verisimilitude, various systems of plausibility, motivation, justification and belief'. Genres therefore work as 'systems of conventions' that enable both creative workers and audiences to understand a story. They describe (to audiences and creatives alike) the different emotional experiences they can expect and help them decide which to prioritise, manifest and stimulate. In this way, genres are similar to brands in that they enable managers to make rough predictions of the demand for products and to control investment and production risks (Terry et al., 2005). Thus genre knowledge is a key element of the so-called Hit or blockbuster strategy of media management (see Picard 2005 on portfolio management and efforts to control risk). Küng (2008: 85) argues that 'a blockbuster strategy imposes a template on content creation... to appeal to the largest number of audience groups and eliminate the risk that particular market groups might reject the project'. Rose (1985: 5) say genres are 'commodities manufactured for and utterly dependent upon public consumption and support... the formulas which have endured are those which have managed to yield a profit'.

As noted above, by directing our attention to the interaction between the development of the domain and the broader culture, Csikszentmihalyi (1988, 1996) helps contextualise the concept of domain skills. This enables us to examine changes in the 'stage of development' of particular domain skills in the media. Broader changes in the environment or ecology of the media industries do indeed appear to correlate with periods of intense creativity in media genres (Rose & Alley, 1985). The impact of TV on movie audiences and the emergence of digital technologies are generally considered crucial to the creative development of science fiction/fantasy genres using spectacular visual effects and the emergence of the 'blockbuster strategy'. Following Csikszentmihalyi, we might hypothesise that these broader changes 'loosened' the previously 'tight' domain of Hollywood filmmaking, enabling creative workers with specific expertise—particularly Stephen Spielberg and George Lucas—to make a hugely significant creative contribution (Biskind, 1999).

A similar argument could be made, two decades later, for television. The advent of digital multichannel media drove media organisations to seek new audiences, markets, and sources of revenue. Again, we might argue that these changes in the culture loosened the domain of factual TV production and enabled individuals with particular expertise—like John de Mol, Mark Burnett or Simon Cowell—to pioneer the development of the reality TV genre (Biressi & Nunn, 2005).

This section has modified Amabile's model to emphasise the importance of all three elements of the model and, in particular, to enable a more detailed and sophisticated understanding of the role of domain skills. The contextually specific nature of this concept has been addressed by sketching out how domain skills might be conceptualised in the specific media sectors of film and TV. It has been possible to suggest how elements of the model may interact; for example, broader social and cultural changes may 'open up space' for creativity within a 'tight' set of domain skills; or creative thinking may help focus a previously loose set of domain skills.

This version of the model can be applied to analyse practice because it enables us to test for the presence of all three creativity variables in the work of individuals and groups. It also suggests how the elements of the model may interact to produce creative results. This modified version of the model would hypothesise that (ceteris paribus) a strategy for managing creativity will be more successful if it includes all three elements rather than focusing on any single one. An approach based on this version of the model should, in theory, be expected to yield greater creativity than one based on a single element—whether 'talent management' or Osborn's creative thinking skills or even Amabile's own focus on intrinsic motivation.

The test of the model is its ability to describe, analyse, evaluate and explain the success of attempts to manage creativity in practice. The next section attempts to do this for the case of the BBC.

20.5 Managing Creativity at the BBC

The previous section illustrated how Amabile's model might be modified to develop the concept of domain skills and apply it to the skills of media production. This section attempts to show how this modified version of the model may be used to describe, evaluate and explain the results of an attempt to manage an increase in creativity in a media organisation. The case chosen is former Director General Greg Dyke's attempt to make the BBC 'the most creative organization in the world'. This case represents a good test of the model first because it was such an explicit attempt to manage an increase in creativity (rather than media managers and creators instinctively achieving exceptional creativity). Secondly, as we shall see, in the BBC case, all of the elements of the model are apparent. Thirdly, as a participant-observer in the process (see end note), I have access to relevant original data that supplements what is currently available from published sources. For the sake of brevity, background information about the BBC and its management has been excluded (for this, the reader is referred to two excellent contemporary accounts of this period in its history—Dyke in 2004 and Born in 2005, both included in the references).

Describing Greg Dyke's intended strategy is complicated by the difficulty of accurately identifying his own working definition of creativity—in public, at least, he made few explicit statements about creativity (see especially Dyke, 2004). It is clear, however, that he explicitly departed from what I have described as the commonsense 'talent management' approach to managing creativity: 'There was a recognition [at the BBC] that single acts of creative genius were the exception... and that BBC people needed to learn how to work together in creative teams to come up with and improve on good ideas' (Dyke, 2004: 218). Dyke's team appears to have developed his critique into a conception of creativity that is close to Amabile's idea of expertise and also shares Bilton's critique of the myth of heroic creativity.

As Caroline van den Brul (one of the leaders of Dyke's creativity working group) explained, 'for years there had been a reliance on named individuals — creative geniuses with reputations for delivering outstanding quality. But there were simply not enough of these rare and talented people to supply the increasing demands for high quality output from all the new channels' (Spindler & van den Brul, 2006). Multichannel TV created an increased demand for content which left Dyke's team with a problem: 'how we could get more and better everyday creativity and how we could get "blockbuster" innovation?' (op. cit: 43).

A third objective of the strategy seems to have been related to creating more diverse content which would appeal to particular target audiences which the BBC had failed to attract. At the launch of his strategy for managing creativity, he 'threw down challenges from recent audience research: with a few exceptions the BBC seriously underserved the young—defined as people under-55—and the younger they were, the more marginal the BBC was in their lives; ethnic minorities in the U.K. were disproportionate under-users of services and did not think the BBC was for them; many BBC services were still seen as aimed at audiences living in the South of England' (Spindler & van den Brul, 2006: 34).

In trying to achieve these objectives, Dyke and his team followed the Amabile's model of managing creativity quite closely—although Dyke (2004) does not appear to have been personally aware of her work. Van den Brul, however, attended both Osborn's Creative Problem Solving Institute and the Stanford Research Institute (SRI). SRI had developed the 'Watering Hole'—a tool to enable and improve creative thinking processes by overcoming the acknowledged problems in the brainstorming technique. The Watering Hole incorporated ideas from both Osborn (1953) and De Bono (1971) and was designed to 'leverage reactions from a disparate audience in a structured format to create customer value' (Carlson and Wilmot, 2006: 107), achieving results 'through the *compounding* of ideas... a process to improve your initial idea—over and over' (ibid.).

The introduction of Watering Holes at the BBC involved linking TV producers with practitioners from other 'domains' across the organisation—including non-production departments like accounting and legal. Applying Amabile's model, as modified above, we might expect this would help 'loosen' the domain of PSB TV production and (assuming this domain was at a tighter stage of development) we could predict this would broaden the space for creativity within the domain and result in increased creativity.

The second element of Dyke's strategy for managing creativity was a drive to create an 'open and inclusive' culture. This seems clearly to have been aimed at improving intrinsic motivation. Dyke believed the very conventional management practices of his predecessor, John Birt, had been 'killing' creativity at the BBC. He mocked Birt's declared aim of making the BBC 'the best managed organisation in the public sector', joking about the effect of such a statement on motivation: 'I have to admit that wouldn't have got me out of bed in the morning' (BBC, 2002). His account of cultural change at the BBC (Dyke, 2004) is peppered with stories about making many and various inexpensive changes to the working environment of the kind Amabile contends will improve intrinsic motivation. Dyke also invested considerable sums (Daily Telegraph, 2003) in developing a leadership programme, run in partnership with Ashridge Business School, to train hundreds of BBC producers in strategic thinking, effective communication, giving feedback, coaching others and working collaboratively. Again we might expect the effect of such training to lessen the extent to which conventional management kills creativity and to improve intrinsic motivation.

Dyke also invested in developing media domain skills, as evident in appointing and supporting genre commissioners who were given the power to commission content in partnership with channel controllers. The genre commissioners were supported by an expanded and proactive Marketing, Communications and Audience Directorate in interpreting audience research and cultural trends and in translating these insights into 'creative briefs' articulating a single creative vision for each to both independent and in-house producers. The modified version of Amabile's model would predict that this investment in deepening the BBC management's understanding of contemporary TV genres and broadening their understanding of social and cultural changes would improve the creative potential of the domain skills within each genre. The next section uses proxy measures of creativity to assess whether the implementation of the elements of the model did, in the BBC case, actually produce the intended creative results.

20.6 Measures of Creativity at the BBC

The discussion of Amabile's model above identified as its principal weakness the lack of an objective method of measuring creativity—the purpose and results of managing creativity. It was suggested that, until such time as objective measures are identified, the model should be modified by the addition of contextual proxy measures of creativity. The next section attempts to illustrate how such proxy measures might be identified in the BBC case.

We have seen that the objectives of Dyke's strategy for managing creativity were to generate more 'everyday creativity' and more 'blockbusters' and to attract underserved audiences.

Van den Brul (Spindler & van den Brul, 2006) does not cite any rating figures that could help evaluate success but does give a (single) example of success. She points out that *World Class*, a web platform enabling children in schools around the world to communicate with one another, was an idea conceived by a junior radio producer rather than an already acknowledged 'creative genius'. This does appear to be evidence (albeit a single instance) of the success of the strategy in enabling 'everyday creativity'.

To get a better test of the success of the strategy, we may examine quantitative data to try to identify a proxy measure, but of course these data must be interpreted carefully. For example, we might hypothesise that an increase in the number of ideas being commissioned from the in-house production teams of the BBC compared to independent producers would be a good proxy measure of an increase in 'everyday creativity'. However, this would be invalidated by the existence, during this period, of a guaranteed quota of commissions from independent producers. A better proxy measure of everyday creativity would be to measure the 'conversion rate'—the percentage of ideas developed that are also commissioned—before and after the introduction of the strategy.

Data from the BBC Factual and Learning directorate allows us to perform this test for increased 'everyday creativity' in this division of the corporation. Koenig (2005) analysed commissions in the Documentaries and Contemporary Factual department of the BBC before and after the introduction of the SRI methods and compared the rate of conversion of programme proposals into commissions (i.e. programme ideas that went into production). He found that 'proposals developed according to the SRI formula fared no better or worse than those that were not' (op. cit: 33). He noted that van den Brul was 'disappointed by this outcome, and had hoped the conversion rate [of proposal to commission] might have been improved by the use of the approach... (she) remarked that conversion rates were higher in more recent commissioning rounds, probably due to better understanding and implementation of the SRI process' (ibid). It is not possible to assess this claim, however, as van den Brul does not include any details of these later conversion rates in her account (Spindler & van den Brul, 2006). On the basis of the available data, therefore, we have van den Brul's single example of 'everyday creativity', whilst our proxy measure (conversion rates) shows no increase in 'everyday creativity' as a result of the strategy.

Staiger (2000: 3) defines 'blockbusters' as 'ratings busting programmes (which) are garnering audience attention beyond normal viewing behaviors, evidenced by the disparity between their ratings numbers and those of the average success'. Van den Brul appears to suggest that *World Class* meets her definition of a blockbuster as 'an ambitious core public service idea that did not fit neatly into any single department of the BBC. It was an idea that would need to involve many people across dozens of departments in the BBC (and outside) if it were to be developed' (op. cit: 54). In this, she seems to suggest that *World Class* also demonstrates the success of the strategy in producing a 'blockbuster'. However, as a web platform rather than a TV programme, it is not possible to assess it against Staiger's definition.

BBC Factual and Learning data allow us to identify other candidates for the 'blockbuster category' and test against ratings and commissioning data. The two most regularly cited candidates for this were not *World Class* (presumably because it was not a TV programme) but *Coast* and, in particular, *Fat Nation*: '*Fat Nation* is a fantastic example of how the development process can work. We knew we wanted to develop something big around the obesity epidemic, but our ideas were entirely predictable until we met one of the key members of the development team... [a young person from an obese family] was the trigger for *Fat Nation*. Not only did he help us identify a fresh way into obesity, he reminded us that often ideas are not the brainchild of one person' (BBC, 2004a).

As well as being TV programmes, both projects had the qualities van den Brul identifies in *World Class*—they enabled the BBC to use its multiplatform presence to extend an idea beyond broadcast. However, F&L data demonstrates that *Fat Nation* failed to meet Staiger's definition of a blockbuster, achieving relatively modest ratings compared to the channel average for successful BBC1 shows in that genre (3.3 m viewers and 14 % share compared to *Ground Force's* 4.5 m and 19.1 % share), and the series was not commissioned for a second run (BBC, 2004a). However, *Coast*, on the minor channel BBC2 did achieve above average ratings (3.5 m and 15 % share) compared with the channel's undisputed blockbuster *Top Gear* (4.5 m and 19 % share). Indeed *Coast's* performance was more exceptional given that *Top Gear* is in the factual *entertainment* rather than the purely factual genre (BBC, 2006). For this reason, the series was recommissioned and became the kind of returning blockbuster Dyke's team wanted.

Turning to the type of audience attracted, however, demonstrates the limitations of the success of *Coast*. Two thirds of the audience of *Coast* were over 55 years old and 43 % were over retirement age. *Fat Nation* performed better in this respect with only a third of its audience over 55 years old and a third under 34 years old. By contrast, three quarters of *Top Gear's* audience were under 55 and 44 % were under 34 years old (BBC, 2006). No data was available to assess the ethnicity or locality of the audiences.

This section has analysed BBC Factual and Learning data to evaluate the three proxy measures of creativity (everyday creativity, blockbusters, youth audience). Our measure of everyday creativity, the conversion rate of ideas into commissioned, showed no improvement following the introduction of Dyke's creative strategy. Two programmes identified as blockbusters emerging from the strategy were tested against Staiger's definition of a blockbuster. Whilst *Fat Nation* was judged a failure in this respect, *Coast* was judged a success. Finally, the measure of attracting underserved audiences was applied. Here *Fat Nation* was more successful than *Coast*, which failed spectacularly in this respect, but this appeared to have been achieved at the expense of the blockbuster ratings required.

Of course it could be that the Factual and Learning directorate is a poor test of the strategy and that other in other directorates the strategy enabled greater improvements in creativity. Although no comprehensive quantitative data are available, a look at the BBC's Drama, Entertainment and Children's directorate would reveal two series produced in-house at the BBC during this period which pass Staiger's test of a 'blockbustes'—*The Weakest Link (TWL)* and *Strictly Come Dancing (SCD)*. Indeed the latter was, at least for a period, the world's most successful TV format (Daily Telegraph, 23 November, 2010). However, a brief study of the history of the development of these ideas suggests it would be unfair to claim them as successes of Dyke's strategy. *TWL* does seem to have benefited from being 'batted around' by a development team, providing some support for the SRI-influence approach (Brown, 23 October, 2000). However, *SCD* was famously 'turned down' at a brainstorm and only commissioned as a result of the very traditional process of two 'heroic' talents meeting the BBC's Head of Entertainment (Daily Telegraph, 12 January, 2012) and pitching a compelling creative idea.

Overall then, the results from Dyke's creative strategy were very modest. Analysis of Factual and Learning data suggests no increase in everyday creativity and only mixed success even for the two programmes most regularly cited as the 'blockbuster' achievements of the strategy.

The next section attempts to show how the modified Amabile's model may be used to try to explain why a strategy for managing creativity results in a particular level of creative performance. In this case, the analysis will try to explain why the Dyke strategy appears to have achieved very minimal success, at least in the Factual and Learning Division, despite Dyke's team broadly implementing the key elements of the model.

20.7 Explaining Creativity at the BBC

As noted earlier, Amabile's model predicts creativity will be highest when the three model elements are all present. Yet the description of the BBC's creative strategy presented above suggested that although Dyke's team implemented all three elements of the model, they did not achieve their objectives. One might be tempted to conclude from the BBC case that implementing Amabile's model does not, in practice, *always* result in increased creativity. There is an alternative interpretation, however. The modified version of Amabile's model hypothesised that to ensure creative results, media managers may not merely have to ensure that the three elements of creativity are present but may also be required to manage the *interaction* of these elements in the workplace. This section tests this alternative hypothesis against the BBC case.

Dyke's team faced a problem common to many PSB organisations in the early twenty-first century—attracting underserved audiences (young, ethnic minority, outside the capital city) to PSB channels. Dyke's team saw creative thinking skills, and the SRI approach in particular, as a way for BBC producers to think 'outside the box' to create content to meet this market need. They supported this by giving producers greater access to market data through an internal reorganisation that placed audience planners (members of the Marketing, Communication and Audience department) inside production teams with a brief to analyse and interpret audience data to help identify audience needs around which ideas could be developed. The audience data confirmed the views of Dyke's team that the target audiences were attracted by 'blockbuster' reality shows and factual formats like *Big Brother* and *Wife Swap* (BBC, 2004b).

A close analysis of Dyke's strategy demonstrates that the management of the creative thinking skills element of the model (SRI approach) *disrupted* the positive interaction between this variable and the actions intended to encourage intrinsic motivation (the creation of an inclusive culture). Although the SRI approach did encourage the use of creative thinking skills, it also fundamentally and *actively discouraged* intrinsic motivation. This is most noticeable in the second key technique the BBC adopted from SRI—the 'elevator pitch'. This approach manages creativity by focusing on an identifiable market 'need'. Only when an audience need has been identified should a TV programme be developed. Van den Brul makes clear that the Dyke's team saw this approach as a technique for reorienting BBC producers *away from* an intrinsic motivation and towards an *extrinsic* motivation. 'The BBC had always valued individual creative geniuses and given them space to pursue their own projects. But this had been widely interpreted as a right of all producers to pursue subjects and make programs ***they*** found interesting and to resist input from anyone outside their own small circle who might challenge their views. Too often their programs were not compelling *to audiences*' (Spindler & van den Brul, 2006: 45, my emphasis).

Van den Brul's statement makes clear that Dyke's team believed encouraging intrinsic motivation would only exacerbate the problem the BBC faced—by creating *more* programmes which did not attract the young, ethnic minority, outside-London audience they needed. Dyke's team therefore implemented creative thinking skills (SRI approach) as a means of motivating BBC producers to meet *external* demands. In this way, the implementation of creative thinking skills clearly conflicted with the efforts to encourage intrinsic motivation. Amabile's model would predict, therefore, that Dyke's team's own decisions undermined the potentially positive interaction between the elements of the model. Amabile (1996b) is emphatic about the negative effect such external demands have in killing creativity.

This analysis suggests that managing the *interaction* of the key creativity variables is crucial to the success of managing creativity. But it also returns us to a central question. Were Dyke's team correct in their assumption that intrinsic motivation would encourage *the wrong kind* of creativity? Were they, in effect, forced to choose either improving the creativity of their staff or meeting the needs of their audience (who pay for the BBC)?

20.8   Media Domain Skills at the BBC

The analysis above posed what may seem to be an intractable problem for managing creativity in media organisations. Where an organisation, like HBO, for example, can target and meet the needs of a niche audience, then a virtuous circle of intrinsic motivation, creativity and a satisfied audience seems achievable. But in other contexts, where the audience is more diverse, the need to satisfy audiences may appear as an external demand, reaffirming the Weberian means-end rationality of conventional management and thus 'killing' the intrinsic motivation required for creativity. However, this final section hypothesises that by paying particular attention to the specific nature of media, domain skills media managers may be able to resolve the apparently intractable audience/motivation, means-end/creativity dilemmas facing many media managers. This section concludes by testing this hypothesis in the BBC case.

The discussion of domain skills above identified a particular problem with this element of Amabile's model. Where creative thinking skills and motivation techniques are generalisable to many organisational contexts, domain skills are by definition *specific* to a particular domain. The discussion illustrated how Amabile's model could be modified to allow for the specific role of domain skills in particular contexts. The discussion illustrated how research on specifically *media* domain skills (in this case film and TV) could be used to modify of model to provide better description, analysis, explanation and guidance of the management of creativity in media organisations. Attention was drawn to the role of broader cultural trends in altering what Csikszentmihalyi called 'the stage of development' of a particular set of domain skills. The model was modified to define more precisely how domain skills may act as a *variable,* in interaction with the other elements—for example, when previously 'tight' domains became loosened or vice versa. It was suggested that the move to multichannel TV had 'loosened' the previously 'tight' domain of factual TV production enabling talented individuals to achieve greater creativity in the area of reality shows and factual formats.

How then might management of media domain skills have enabled Dyke's team to resolve the dilemmas which appear to have undermined, or at the very least weakened, the effectiveness of their implementation of the model in improving creativity? The problem the faced was that they believed intrinsic motivation would improve creativity—but the *wrong kind* of creativity. Intrinsic motivation would lead to BBC producers creating more of the programmes *they* liked rather than the 'blockbuster' reality shows and factual formats which could attract the target audience. Dyke's team sought to resolve this dilemma by the SRI approach, encouraging producers to create ideas for programmes which would meet identified audience needs. However, the Factual and Learning data showed (as Amabile's model would predict) that their proposed solution—*external* motivation—did not produce increased creativity. The conversion rate of ideas into commissions did not improve. And the two formats most often cited as successes of the strategy either failed to achieve blockbuster ratings or failed to attract the target audience. Analysis of the interaction of the model elements suggested that the reason the strategy had such limited success was that the implementation of SRI creative thinking skills deliberately oriented producers away from intrinsic towards extrinsic motivation, thus undermining the other work (inclusive culture) to promote intrinsic motivation.

Rather than simply accept that conventional, means-end management objectives will *always* kill creativity, our modified version of the model allows us to propose an alternative hypothesis. The modified version of the model enables us to hypothesise that it was the *specific* nature of media skills in this domain which formed the core of the problem Dyke's team faced. As briefly discussed above, the domain skills required to produce reality shows and factual formats were developed largely in medium-large independent production companies in Europe. Since the late 1990s, companies like Endemol, Fremantle and RDF had begun developing and producing hugely profitable reality shows like *Big Brother, The Apprentice* and *Wife Swap*. This period of creativity loosened the 'tight' domain of documentary and factual TV production introducing elements from entertainment—particularly game show elements and the casting of celebrity talent.

Suppose, for example, Dyke's team had decided to address the domain skills of the producers rather than their motivations. One objection to even considering such an approach might be to argue that no rational, means-ends oriented managers would make the investment required to achieve such a transformation. This certainly seems to be the reason Amabile focuses on motivation rather than domain skills—(see Sect. 20.3.2 above). However, Dyke was clearly prepared to invest significantly in creative thinking skills and in leadership training (intrinsic motivation) (Daily Telegraph, 2 October, 2004).

Such domain skills were in short supply in the BBC's in-house factual production departments where production was more focused on traditional public service (read "tight") forms—observational documentary, natural history and educational features. The modified version of the model would thus predict a further conflict—between the SRI/audience research attempt to identify audience needs (reality and factual formats) and the domain skills of in-house producers (observational documentaries, science and natural history features).

My own experience, as a development producer and later leader of a development team in Factual and Learning, suggests that this conflict was as important in explaining the limited success of the strategy. Even when in-house producers and development teams created factual formats which channel controllers believed would meet the 'blockbuster criteria'—series like *My Week of Dressing Dangerously* or *Full on Food*—in-house producers lacked the domain skills to turn these concepts into the kind of ratings required for a blockbuster. This created a 'vicious' circle where channel controllers would not commission promising ideas for reality shows or factual formats because they believed in-house producers would not have the required domain skills to realise the idea to the required level of quality.

Dykes team were almost certainly correct in their assumption that intrinsic motivation would not create blockbuster formats to reach the target audience. However, if they had identified the *specific* domain skills of reality TV and factual format production as the core of the problem they faced, they might have altered their strategy of managing creativity and potentially achieved greater success. They might have decided, for example, to redirect their investment in training and development away from general management and leadership skills, aimed at encouraging intrinsic motivation, towards training developing and recruiting producers with mastery of the domain skills required to produce the desired blockbusters—reality shows and factual formats.

The effect of this might have been to improve the interaction of the other elements of the model. The Dyke's strategy created two sets of conflicts: between creative thinking skills and intrinsic motivation and between creative thinking skills and domain skills. Addressing the problem of specific domain skills might have produced a 'virtuous' circle by encouraging in producers an intrinsic motivation to use creative thinking skills and new domain skills to create new programmes in the genres that could attract the target audience. Producers would be creating content '*they* found interesting', which would also attract the target audience.

Ultimately, then, the BBC case may provide support for the modified version of Amabile's model. Applying this model allows us to hypothesise that if Dyke's team had reoriented their investment from leadership skills to specific domain skills (in the area of reality and factual formats), this might have enabled positive interaction between the model elements, resolving our central tension between the external demands of management and the intrinsic motivation required for creativity.

20.9 Managing Creativity in the Media: Future Research

This chapter has suggested that the central tension in managing creativity in media organisations is between conventional (means-end) management (the neo-Weberian view) and intrinsically motivated creativity. The argument has illustrated how this tension may be managed using a model first proposed by Amabile, with suggested modifications, because it is helpful for describing, analysing and evaluating three key variables involved in managing creativity: domain skills, creative thinking skills and intrinsic motivation.

The chapter has illustrated how this modified version of the model can be used to analyse and explain the success of a particular approach to managing creativity—in this case at the BBC. The case study illustrated how the modified model can be used to measure creativity using contextual proxies and to analyse the interaction of model elements to *explain* a particular level of creative performance. Even in the case of a strategy which did not succeed, it has been possible to use the model to suggest how media managers facing similar problems might manage the interaction of the creativity variables to improve performance in a media organisation.

The chapter has indicated where future research in the media management field could develop understanding of the management of creativity by producing clearer more detailed descriptions of a range of specific media domain skills and by studying how these interact with creative thinking skills and intrinsic motivation to foster creativity in media organisations. Further empirical studies will help understand the nuances of managing the creativity variables in specific media contexts. The chapter also identified serious weaknesses in the Amabile model. In the longer term, media management research may be able to develop more sophisticated, theoretically mature and operationally useful conceptual models of creativity that can replace Amabile's model (already 30 years old).

The chapter began by proposing a central problem of managing creativity—the tension between conventional management and creativity—and ended by suggesting a key role for domain skills in resolving this century old tension. Media management research that develops a better understanding of how to enable creativity at work should lead to better management practice, not just in media organisations but in modern society as a whole.

Research Note: Participant Observation
I was able to observe management of creativity at the BBC under John Birt (from 1995 to 2000), Greg Dyke (2000–2004) and Mark Thompson (2004–2008). I was based first in the news (initially in radio and then in TV) and then in Factual and Learning. Between 2006 and 2008, most of my work was as a member and then leader of a development team creating and 'pitching' new content ideas directly to BBC channel controllers and genre commissioners.

References

Adorno, T., & Horkheimer, M. (1979). *Dialect of enlightenment*. New York: Continuum.
Amabile, T. (1996a). *Creativity in context*. Boulder: Westview Press.
Amabile, T. (1996b). How to kill creativity. *Harvard Business Review* September–October 1998.
Aristotle. (1996). *Poetics* (Malcolm Heath, Trans.). London: Penguin.
Baer, J., & McKool, S. (2009). Assessing creativity using the consensual assessment technique. In C. Schreiner (Ed.), *Handbook of assessment technologies, methods, and applications in higher education*. Hershey, PA: IGI Global.
BBC. (2002). *Greg Dyke's speech*. BBC, http://www.bbc.co.uk/pressoffice/speeches/stories/dyke_makingithappen.shtmlyke
BBC. (2004a). *Creativity crash course*. Internal BBC Training Document.
BBC. (2004b). *Audience composition: Factual youth strategy: Digging deeper for more tangible strategies BBC One and BBC Two*. Marketing, Communications and Audiences, BBC
BBC. (2006). *Factual series averages features*. BBC Factual and Learning MC&A.
Becker, H. (1982). *Art worlds*. Los Angeles, CA: UCLA Press.
Bilton, C. (2007). *Management and creativity*. Oxford: Blackwell.
Bilton, C. (2010). Manageable creativity. *International Journal of Cultural Policy, 16*(3), 255–269.
Biressi, A., & Nunn, H. (2005). *Reality TV*. London: Wallflower.
Biskind, P. (1999). *Easy riders raging bulls: How the sex-drugs-and rock 'n roll generation saved Hollywood*. New York, NY: Simon & Schuster.
Born, G. (2005). *Uncertain vision*. London: Vintage.
Braverman, H. (1974). *Labor and monopoly capital*. New York: Monthly Review Press.
Brown, M. (23 October, 2000). He ain't heavy. *The Guardian*.
Carlson, C., & Wilmot, W. (2006). *Innovation*. New York: Crown.
Caves, R. (2002). *Creative industries*. Cambridge, MA: Harvard University Press.
Csikszentmihalyi, M. (1988). Society, culture and person. In R. J. Sternberg (Ed.), *The nature of creativity* (pp. 325–339). Cambridge: CUP.
Csikszentmihalyi, M. (1996). *Creativity*. New York, NY: Harper Collins.
Csikszentmihalyi, M. (1998). *Finding flow*. New York, NY: Basic Books.
Daily Telegraph. (2003, May 15). BBC to spend millions on leadership training courses. *Daily Telegraph*.
Daily Telegraph. (2 October, 2004). BBC's £35m training course is a fiasco, says expert. *Daily Telegraph*.
Daily Telegraph. (23 November, 2010). Strictly Come Dancing is 'world's most successful reality television format.' *Daily Telegraph*.
Daily Telegraph. (12 January, 2012). Richard Hopkins: Obituary. *Daily Telegraph*.
De Bono, E. (1971). *The use of lateral thinking*. Harmondsworth: Penguin.
De Bono, E. (1987). *The use of lateral thinking*. Harmondsworth: Penguin.
Dyke, G. (2004). *Inside story*. London: Harper Perennial.
Florida, R. (2002). *The rise of the creative class*. New York, NY: Basic Books.
Freud, S. (1908). The relationship of the poet to daydreaming. In S. Freud (Ed.), *On creativity and the unconscious* (pp. 44–55). New York, NY: Harper.
Garnham, N. (2005). From cultural to creative industries. *International Journal of Cultural Policy, 11*(1), 15–29.
Hennessey, B. A., & Amabile, T. (2010). Creativity. *Annual Review of Psychology, 61*, 569–598.
Herzberg, F. (1959). *The motivation to work*. New York: John Wiley.
Koenig, N. (2005) *Promiscuous hybridity: The commissioning process*. In British Broadcasting Reuters Foundation Paper No: 258. Oxford: Green College.
Küng, L. (2004). What makes media firms tick? Exploring the hidden drivers of firm performance. In R. Picard (Ed.), *Strategic responses to media market changes*. Jonkoping International Business School: Jonkoping.

Küng, L. (2008). *Strategic management in the media*. London: Sage.

Mayo, E. (1933). *The human problems of an industrial civilization*. Cambridge: Harvard University Press.

Mintzberg, H. (1979). *The structuring of organization*. Englewood Cliffs, NJ: Prentice-Hall.

Morgan, G. (1989). *Creative organization theory: A resource book*. Newbury Park: Sage.

Neale, S. (1990). *Genre and Hollywood*. London: Routledge.

Osborn, A. (1953). *Applied imagination*. New York, NY: Scribners.

Perry, B. (August, 2009). How Hollywood manages talent. In *Talent Management*.

Picard, R. G. (Ed.) (2005/2014). *Media product portfolios: Issues in management of multiple products and services*. London: Routledge.

Puccio, G., Murdock, M., & Mance, M. (2006). *Creative leadership*. London: Sage.

Rose, B. (1985). Introduction. In B. Rose & R. Alley (Eds.), *TV genres: A handbook and reference guide*. Westport, CT: Greenwood Publishing Group.

Runco, M. (2010). Divergent thinking, creativity and ideation. In J. Kaufman & R. Sternberg (Eds.), *The Cambridge handbook of creativity* (pp. 413–446). New York, NY: Cambridge University Press.

Spindler, S., & van den Brul, C. (2006–2007). Making it happen. *NHK Broadcasting Studies 5*, 29–55.

Staiger, J. (2000). *Blockbuster TV: Must-see sitcoms in the network era*. New York: NYU Press.

Taylor, F. W. (1911). *The principles of scientific management*. New York: Harper Brothers.

Terry, N., Butler, M., & De'Armond, D. (2005). The determinants of domestic box office performance in the motion picture industry. *Southwestern Economic Review, 32*(1), 137–148.

Todorov, T. (1973). *The fantastic*. Cleveland, OH: Case Western Reserve University Press.

Weber, M. (1915/1947) *The theory of social and economic organization* (trans. Talcott Parsons). New York: Free Press

Weber, M. (1912/1968). *Economy and society*. New York: Bedminster Press.

Weisberg, R. (1986). *Creativity: Genius and other myths*. New York: WH Freeman/Times Books/Henry Holt & Co.

Weisberg, R. (1993). *Creativity: Beyond the myth of genius*. New York: WH Freeman.

Weisberg, R. (2010). The study of creativity: From genius to cognitive science. *International Journal of Cultural Policy, 16*(3), 235–253.

Xu, F., & Rickards, T. (2007). Creative management. *Creativity and Innovation Management, 16*(3), 216–228.

Zafirau, S. (2008). Reputation work in selling film and television. *Qualitative Sociology, 31*(2), 99–127.

Projectification in the Media Industries

21

Rolf A. Lundin and Maria Norbäck

21.1 What Is a Project Really?

To analyse and describe the effects that projects have on media industries and vice versa, the concept needs to be defined and scrutinised. What does a 'project' look like? The easy way to answer that question is to reference well-known texts in the field. The Project Management Institute has supplied a well-cited definition: 'A project is a temporary endeavor undertaken to create a unique product, service or result' (Project Management Institute, 2013: 3). This is from the so-called PMBOK Guide which is now into its fifth edition! Each word has intended emphasis. *Time* is important (since the effort is temporary) as well as the *task* (the focus of the endeavour). The element of uniqueness can and has been debated because each project is unique to varying degrees, although similarities exist so that some projects are fairly similar. The origin of project management can be traced to the engineering sciences (see e.g. Pinney, 2001), leading some to suggest that a *plan* for how to achieve the desired results (i.e. it is *undertaken*) in an efficient way with a minimum use of scarce *resources* is also characteristic (cf. Packendorff, 1995).

The notion of efficiency in project work has been the main focus for most classical project management textbooks (like Meredith & Mantel Jr., 2000), with the support of professional organisations (for practising project managers, like the Project Management Institute, PMI). Various ways of developing and ensuring project efficiency have been developed and spread, mainly for engineers by PMI. Attempts to construct good project management and work procedures account for a

R.A. Lundin (✉)
Media Management and Transformation Centre, Jönköping International Business School, Jönköping University, Jönköping, Sweden
e-mail: rolf.a.lundin@jibs.hj.se

M. Norbäck
Gothenburg Research Institute, Gothenburg University, Gothenburg, Sweden
e-mail: maria.norback@handels.gu.se

© Springer International Publishing Switzerland 2016
G.F. Lowe, C. Brown (eds.), *Managing Media Firms and Industries*, Media Business and Innovation, DOI 10.1007/978-3-319-08515-9_21

focus on planning techniques, and addressing various and typical concerns that project managers have over the life cycle of projects has been at the heart of what the professional project management organisations (like PMI) have been doing.

The scope of projects is undergoing a change in relation to the traditional way of regarding projects, and this is where projectification comes in. To our knowledge the term projectification was used for the first time by Midler (1995) who was covering the case when the development of a new car model changed from being handled in the line of Renault to be separated and handled as a project.

21.1.1 The Project as a 'Plan' or an 'Organisation'

Understanding about what a project really is has developed over time and is no longer confined to the traditional engineering context. Research on projects has covered a wider area of concerns. In a seminal article, Packendorff (1995) scrutinised articles on projects in research-oriented journals published before 1995 and found that the use of the word 'project' in research settings could be roughly divided into two fairly separated groups distinguished between 'project as plan' and 'project as organisation'.

Project as plan refers to projects of an engineering type, which are characterised by the task, the time allotted to complete the task, the people and other resources needed to do the project, and (most importantly) the plan to go from where it starts to where we are to be when it is done. The managerial task is to do this as efficiently as possible in the sense that the task is completed on or even before the expected delivery time and/or with less used resources than included in the plan. This is the normative, how-to-do-it version, although not to say cookbook version. The alternative conceptualises project as a temporary organisation. Whereas research work on project as plan is mainly concerned with giving advice about achieving higher efficiency to practitioners, the alternative focuses on what people actually do when they work in projects or manage them. That approach has subsequently been reformulated as a focus on project-as-practice. What happens in a temporary organisation as a result of its character as an organisation, albeit a temporary one? The approach is mainly descriptive and the ambition seeks explanation for improved understanding of development over time.

The two approaches to project conceptualisation are the manifestation of different research activities in engineering and the social sciences. But this also implies that a project manager needs to take a stand on how to regard the task. The approach can be either to regard it as a 'plan' or as an 'organisation'. Andersen (2014) has made the point that the person responsible has to make a deliberate choice. In general, one might prescribe that the use of the project as plan approach is appropriate when the project is well defined, where uncertainties are not particularly strong and where the understanding of what the project is all about is undisputed for those who will work with it. On the other hand, if the task is not well defined and there is lack of consensus about the task and/or on the process and objectives, then an organisational perspective is more appropriate. But it is important to remember that what a project is about evolves and is developed as the project process moves forward—a phenomenon called 'progressive elaboration'. In practice, then, the two approaches should not be thought of as clear-cut and exclusive. A key implication is that the best a project manager can do is to remain flexible and to balance the two approaches and do so based on the situation at hand project by project or indeed phase by phase within a project.

As noted, project as organisation is characterised by an implicit assumption that the organisation of a project will be inherently temporary, a stance that is more descriptive than normative as also mentioned. Researchers preoccupied with this approach tend to be based in business studies or the more general social sciences rather than those based in engineering. In the past the focus of this kind of research tended to be on how these temporary organisations could be understood for organisational theory. Since there are so many different types of social scientists, the variation in studies related to this approach is a lot wider than in the first approach (as a plan). Although the project as organisation approach was born in what is nowadays considered project-as-practice (Blomquist et al., 2010; Söderholm, 2008), there are practical implications for how to manage projects.

The essential differences are illustrated in Table 21.1. Task is the *raison d'être* for the project. Time speaks for itself, we think. Transition is about what happens in the project over time. A fourth dimension concerns management or leadership, with the planned approach characterised by formal and more traditional management practice and the latter a team-based practice. The table demonstrates how the two alternatives differ (for detailed discussion, see the 1995 article by Packendorff).

A few typical examples of the two types in connection with media will be helpful. An example of the project as plan approach is shooting a TV show. In general, the efficiency requirement dominates and in that respect TV production companies are very good indeed. There is persistent pressure to get the task done at standards and on time. A typical example of the temporary organisation approach is in strategy development work in media companies, which nowadays is often related to technological or market changes. Most of the time strategy work isn't amenable to being handled as a programmable effort, and the task might even be abandoned before any reasonable conclusion has been reached. But whether we look at the typical practices as plan oriented or organisation oriented, media companies tend to be 'project based'.

Most people have adopted the word 'project' to meet their needs for communication in daily life and aren't really concerned about the detailed variations in

Table 21.1 Comparing characteristics of project

As	Plan	Temporary organisation
Task	Given	Given but often adapted over time
Time	Predetermined	Aspired but depending on evolution
Transition	Accordance with plan	Adjusted to circumstances
Team leader	Project manager (PM)	PM open to informal leadership

meaning. For most, perhaps, the general meaning is about doing something as a 'focused endeavour'. There is often a plan but perhaps not very elaborate. An undertaking is described as a project if it is a named endeavour. Although in project management literature the definition of the task needs to be very precise, in practice it is often enough to have a reasonably clear direction. If the focus of a project is to save an endangered species, for example, then the task is inherently imprecise because it is very difficult to know when the species will no longer be endangered or precisely when the threshold to non-endangered is crossed. One can only know if the project has come to a complete failure and the species is now extinct.

This idea that a project is a focused direction rather than a fixed goal to be achieved has been treated using a concept taken from the military in connection with peace-supporting or peace-keeping operations (Lundin & Söderholm, 2013). When scrutinising peace-supporting operations run by the United Nations, we find they are initiated using a very vague description of the end goal for operations. The task is referenced as the 'end state', and the particulars are worked out and adapted over time as changes occur. So, for example, the project to guarantee peace and stability in the Congo develops over time as a result of the various (and often unpredictable) activities of the government, of the rebels and of the UN itself. So one characteristic is that knowledge and capability grow as a result of learning from ongoing practice. Examples of such open-ended approaches to project work are evident in the media field as well. The efforts are involved in the BBC's Creative Futures project, which is an internal BBC venture concerning how the future should be tackled. It includes reinventing the BBC's outputs for a digital era and was important in the context of charter renewal in 2004 and is a relevant example of a case when the direction is clear but no definite end point is set initially.

Thus as we have seen in the varied examples, media industries practice all the various approaches to project work, from those where demand for efficiency is very high to the other extreme where creativity and freethinking is a must. In some cases there is a precise plan, but in many cases only a clear direction. The end results or goals are often figured out in a process of progressive elaboration, meaning these are keyed to learning and knowledge development as the project evolves. But projects of all the varied types we find in media industries are typically based on temporary organisations, however long or short the 'temporary' aspects—there is a start date and mostly also an end date. Each project is managed as an entity. This is what is labelled as project management or management of a project. But when there are many projects of various kinds as in the example above, management by projects might be an appropriate concept to describe what the leadership of the organisation needs to do (cf. Gareis, 1991).

In what sense, then, are projects in the media industries more precise in comparison with the general guidelines and characteristics alluded to above? The answer depends very much on what characterises particular industries. In general, most organisations and companies in media need to be both efficient and effective—that is, in a sense, the crunch point that makes project work in media industries potentially unique compared with more general societal development projects. At this point it is useful to address the phenomenon of 'projectification'. We need to have a fair understanding of the origins of the idea and levels of projectification in society at large.

21.2 Projectification: A Trend

As mentioned already, Midler (1995) most likely was the first one who used the concept 'projectification' in a scholarly context in describing how the development of a new car model was transformed at Renault. For this car manufacturer, the idea implied a fundamental shift from handling car development efforts in the traditional line organisation to handling it as a project with a definite start point and an end point and with the focus on the end result of product development. Nowadays, almost all product development or innovation efforts are organised as projects, not only at Renault but at most car producers in the world.

The terminology indicates an aspiration to make the development process more rational in the sense of being more streamlined and systematic and requires a change in focus for the time aspect as well as use of other resources. The same ambitions have been spreading to a lot of industries, not only in manufacturing but also in construction where work seems to have been done in a project-based manner all along (even though the specialist terminology was not used).

Thus, projectification has ramifications going well beyond product development in individual companies and in companies in other fields related to the historical development of project management. There is a projectification trend not only for operations in individual companies or organisations but also related to society at large.

The projectification trend is parallel to the development of professional organisations specialised in project management. By far the most influential is the Project Management Institute (PMI), a US-based organisation whose membership has almost exploded during the last decade. PMI started from 0 in 1969 and now counts around half a million individual members worldwide. There are also others like IPMA (International Project Management Association), which is primarily European. IPMA is an association of national associations with no individuals as members and with a size in headcount that varies widely year by year, but it has also been increasing. These professional organisations promote the development of the project management field by certifying project managers and by accrediting project management programmes at educational institutions.

The statement that projects are more prevalent nowadays compared to earlier periods in the past is certainly regarded as true. The rapid growth of membership in the project management profession is one kind of 'proof' of that. Although there are inherent difficulties in measuring the prevalence, one possible explanation is that the word 'project' is more used in daily life. It has become an 'in word' or 'buzz term' not only among engineers and business people but also among people in general. We sometimes hear people talking about 'working on their marriage' or an important relationship as a project or an endeavour related to self-improvement as a project. One effect of this general popularity and related dispersion into different applications is that the definition has become blurred, especially in the light of the prescriptions put forward by professional organisations and scholars in the area. Thus, the projectification of various industries is affected by general trends in society, by professional organisations (trying to convert proselytes in new industries) and by industry-related characteristics.

A major factor explaining the growing popularity of projectification among the general public hinges also on the remarkable successes that engineering projects have enjoyed in producing results on time and according to predetermined specifications. It is evident to most that many major accomplishments around the world affect the thinking of those involved. The trend is aligned with the development of managerialism as well. A strong belief in the efficacy of projects has developed as a consequence of the push for productivity and the expanding role of information technology adoption. At this point we can relate the general concept to media and describe developments in these industries.

21.3   Projectification in the Media Industries

Traditionally many media industries have been project based, especially in the production mode. This would include television and film (DeFillippi, 2009; Lundin & Norbäck, 2009; Sydow, 2009), video game development (Davis, 2011), the recording industry (Wikström, 2009) and book publishing (Greco, 2005). Previously in these industries, production projects took place within a company, as in the Hollywood studio system that organised production as a series of projects as a kind of 'portfolio' undertaken under the same company roof where media workers were hired on permanent contract by the studio. Public broadcasting corporations liked the BBC in Britain and SVT in Sweden were organised to facilitate production by permanent employees working in-house (Küng-Shankleman, 2000; Norbäck, 2012). For some time, however, project production of content has been standard for film and TV (Perren, 2011: 156), not only in the USA but also in Europe and elsewhere. Studies from Germany (Windeler & Sydow, 2001) and the UK (Starkey, Barnatt, & Tempest, 2000) show how production of film and TV content is being organised in networks where many different organisations are cooperating, instead of under the roof of one, big organisation. Bilton (2011: 37) describes this change in production logic:

> Here creative and media enterprises have moved from value chains to value networks, based on clusters of firms and individuals working together. /.../ Many of these changes in the value chain reflect industrial restructuring, usually summarized under the heading of *post-Fordism*. The term describes a shift from vertically integrated firms to networks of smaller, specialized firms collaborating together, a shift from mass production to customization, and a shift in the balance of power from producers to consumers, driven by

changing technologies, changing markets, legal and political challenges to monopolies, and the emergence of a more sophisticated and discriminating consumer.

The discussion points to another mechanism for projectification as this relates to efforts to bring more efficiency into big organisations by adapting or changing the production logic. Rather than working with large integrated firms where production staff is permanently on payroll, many small individual companies provide flexibility to the production process as the commissioning organisation (such as a TV broadcaster or a film studio) can hire the specialists needed for the short duration of a particular project without having to employ them full time.

It is not only in the screen-based media industries that projects have become the dominant organising mode. Increasingly also other media industries that have not typically been regarded as 'project based' are becoming 'projectified' as so much of the work in these industries is done in project forms. As noted earlier, this applies to both production and strategic work. Even in newspapers, work (both kinds) that traditionally has not been organised in projects is now handled in project-like forms, such as strategic development projects that are set up for a limited period of time or production work of a specific digital application or print supplement that is organised in projects with a limited time span and specifically assigned production resources (Raviola, 2010). The saying in the media industries in general is now that 'know-who' becomes as important as 'know-how' in these increasingly project-network structured industries (Bilton, 2011), since the competence to put together a good project group becomes an important skill for media professionals.

The drivers of projectification in the media industries are manifold, but the most important include decreasing financial resources (caused by diminishing ad revenues, decrease in product sales as subscription and purchasing declines and decrease in public financing as budgets tighten), customisation of media content and technological development. The combination has encouraged (some might say forced) media organisations to look for new business models, including new partnership arrangements with other media actors and organisations in other industries where activities are often organised in project forms. Changes in media industries have also meant increased competition (lower barriers of entry and traditionally 'non-media' actors entering the industry) that has increased cost for quality content and talent (Küng, 2007). Projectification of activities in media organisations (as well as in networks outside the organisation) allows for decreased fixed costs for labour as well as increased flexibility. Another contributing factor is the deregulation trend in many European labour markets that has facilitated a boom in commercial staffing agencies that make it easier for media organisations to use itinerant personnel (Bergström, 2003).

21.4   Project Networks

The project literature has described how 'project networks' (Sydow & Staber, 2002; Windeler & Sydow, 2001) or 'latent organisations', as Starkey et al. (2000) call them, evolve in industries where projects are the prevailing approach to organising production. Manning (2005: 410) described project networks as 'dynamic sets of project-based inter-organizational and inter-personal relationships which sustain beyond particular projects.' The commissioning organisation in charge of the endeavour is part of a broader project network consisting of long-term and reciprocity-based relationships between firms that are legally autonomous but functionally interdependent. As the case in single projects, activities in a project network are limited in duration. But since networks form on the basis of previous projects as well as on the anticipation of future ones, project networks come to have a more continuous and enduring character—hence the rationale for referring to them as 'latent organisations'. In this sense, project networks provide both flexibility and stability for conducting activities such as the production of media content, and they allow for customisation and specialisation of content as well as the skills of producers.

In the television content production industry, project networks are a common way of structuring production within the industry (see Davis, Vladica, & Berkowitz, 2008; Starkey et al., 2000; Windeler & Sydow, 2001 for examples from Canada, the UK and Germany, respectively). Past experience and future anticipation in collaboration help to coordinate the projects and create norms and routines. Davis et al. (2008) report findings from a study of Canadian independent TV producers that show these producers find the organising and management of projects as relatively unproblematic (at least compared to other issues such as business and product development or marketing). Other studies (e.g. Lundin & Norbäck, 2009) support these findings and show that small independent TV producers (with dozen or fewer employees) can organise large production projects with relative ease once they secure contracts from buyers. This relies on their extensive knowledge and relationships with other small firms and freelancers in the industry.

Project networks are also a common feature in advertising, film and game production industries. Kerr (2011: 225) found that 'game production networks flow beyond firm boundaries, and certain functions are outsourced (e.g., human resources, middleware, testing, marketing, community support, content creation)', but noted the paucity of studies of these kinds of networks and how they are managed.

As for other media industries, such as news and magazines, where production projects have not traditionally been the modus operandi for the production of goods and services, there are signs indicating a projectification of these industries (Bilton, 2007; Gill, 2011; Singer, 2011). Bilton highlights the complexity, specialisation and individualisation of skills and labour in media production industries and how this has created a production industry with very high levels of self-employment and many small businesses. He writes that:

...microenterprises and individuals converge around temporary projects—the project-based, flexible, and unpredictable nature of creative projects makes this more efficient than working in large, permanent organizations. Advertising, film, and television have long been characterized by this mode of working, with networks of specialists collaborating for one project, breaking up, and regrouping around the next one. (Bilton, 2011: 38)

The organising of production in project networks has a bearing on the mode of employment and the character of work in the media industries. Where production is increasingly organised in such networks instead of as internal labour markets with comparatively stable hierarchies, the labour markets have been made external and groups of professional media workers have become flexible suppliers to media industries described as an 'hourglass' shape where there is a handful of big companies, a few middle-sized organisations and many small producers (Born, 2004; Deuze, 2007; Randle, 2011).

As the organising logic in the media industries changes from a hierarchical, bureaucratic mode to a dispersed or 'distributed' project mode, the logic of employment and work changes. The mode of working in project networks poses special demands on the individual media worker. We next elaborate what the 'network competencies' mean for the individual worker and for the media organisation.

21.5 Project Network Competencies

The organising logic of project networks, as stated earlier, means that 'know-who' becomes as important as 'know-how' (Bilton, 2011). This is as true for producers looking to put a crew together to make the best possible product—be it a programme, film, campaign, book, or game—as it is for workers in the industry aiming to secure the next contract. Gill writes about how the organising principles in the 'new media' sector seem to be based on informality:

> ...informality is the structuring principle on which many small and medium-sized new media companies seem to operate: Finding work, recruiting staff, and getting clients are all seemingly removed from the formal sphere governed by established procedures, equal opportunities legislation, or union agreements and located in an arena based on informality, sociality and "who you know". (Gill, 2011: 256)

This approach is increasingly prevalent not only in sectors renowned for precarious labour markets, especially new media, film and television, but increasingly also for the news industry (newspaper, magazines, broadcast). In the West journalists are faced with a very different employment and production logic than was characteristic even a decade ago. Deuze and Fortunati (2011: 111) demonstrate that although there are still many news reporters employed full time by one company, there is an evident trend in journalists nowadays having to 'parachute in for a period of time to work on a certain aspect of a project (a special issue or supplement, a specific program or reportage, a part of a news Web site)'. Thus, news media organisations are also headed in the direction of a project-based orientation. Like in the TV and film industries, the production of news is being transformed by organisations that are downsizing and outsource their production facilities and instead commission and package news that is produced by other companies and freelance external workers. To offer an example, the chief editor at the Swedish daily newspaper *SvD* has argued that newspapers need to start imitating broadcasters in terms of outsourcing the production of their content. She highlighted sports news and said that newspapers ought to focus on the analysis and compilation of sports news, not the actual production of articles covering sports events (Samuelsson & Karén, 2013). If this trend takes off, the historical vertically integrated news media organisations will disintegrate and become aggregators and distributors of news content produced by others and mainly capitalise instead on their respected brand names for implied trustworthiness and prestige while cutting fixed costs and increasing flexibility.

Such a development puts pressure on both workers and managers in media industries and will require specific competencies to be successful in this new projectified world. For the individual media worker, this means that she/he needs to either be in possession of a very specific, sought-after skill or talent that differentiates her/him from other workers in the labour market or that she/he should make sure to be part of what Blair (2003) calls 'semi-permanent work groups' that migrate from project to project. In such a group, the responsibility of generating continued jobs for the entire group usually falls heavily on the most senior and experienced members of the team (in film this is typically the director or first photographer) who, having secured a job in a new project, takes the whole group along (Randle, 2011).

21.6   Project Careers and Management in the Media: 'Life Is a Pitch' and 'Know-Who'

The nature of the increasingly projectified media industries means that media workers will be increasingly occupied with managing their careers in detail and as ongoing practice. That will involve continually finding new projects to work in, as well as individually having to update their skills and competencies (which, in bureaucratic organisations, used to be the responsibility of the employer). In her study about workers in new media, Gill (2011) characterises their lives as 'a pitch' because they must constantly be on the lookout for a new gig and pitching themselves to get it, either as an applicant for something announced or acting in an entrepreneurial manner when spotting a potential opportunity. The boundary between work and private life (if ever actually valid) is dissolved. Georgina Born (2004) offers an example in her study of the BBC and the UK TV market. An independent producer apparently moved his child to the same kindergarten attended by a commissioner at the BBC in hopes of forming a connection that might secure a commission. Deuze (2007) calls this work-life structure 'the portfolio career', where one is only as good as the last job and a livelihood is the responsibility of the individual worker, rather than the employer as historically understood in organisational and contractual terms.

For the management of media organisations, the key to success in a projectified industry is the ability to bring together workers of all types and manage business opportunities, which often depend on new technology, in order to create a viable enterprise. As Deuze and Steward put it: '. . .in an age of remix and convergence culture and cross-media and multiplatform integration, bringing together the work of others in a meaningful and creative way seems not just a valuable but increasingly crucial skill' (Deuze & Steward, 2011: 8). Küng (2008) expects the media industries to become less a cultural field and more 'business oriented' as a rule because of such great need for new and innovative business models. Media managers will have to be more business savvy and entrepreneurial than in the past; it is no longer sufficient to be 'just' an expert in their baseline profession (e.g. journalism). With this development, it follows that a keener understanding of technology and constant sensitivity to spotting the opportunities new developments create are crucial for the success of media managers already today and even more in the future. As Küng (2008: 221) observed: 'A news organization, for example, needs to understand developments in citizen journalism and social networking sites, mobile content, interactive television, free newspapers and podcasting. To name but a few'.

Other media management skills that will be increasingly valuable are in the area of 'contract and negotiation' (Norbäck, 2012). Those are needed for securing the growing range and amount of contracted labour and dealing with rights management issues. In the era when media companies employed their own makers and made most of the products in-house, the employer owned the rights to those contents by default. In the era and context of projectification, intellectual property rights are of utmost importance because ownership and the proceeds must be divided among the involved parties, and this is handled according to increasingly intricate revenue sharing models. In a media industry with many platforms and windows of distribution, some media content has a long shelf life (see Anderson, 2006 for discussion about the 'long tail') and can be repackaged and resold repeatedly. This means that talent agents and actors with royalty-collecting functions become even more important in a projectified media industry and are therefore factors that media managers must deal with on a regular basis.

As stated earlier, drivers of projectification in media industries are mainly the perceived need for these organisations to reduce fixed costs that are largely linked with personnel, facilities and equipment in order to increase the latitude for flexibility. The responsibility for career progression, pensions, job security and professional development are transferred to the individual worker and small independent producers. When companies are commissioning content from independent producers, they can and often do make higher demands and exert more pressure because the supplier is conceived as a subcontractor, implying a very different relationship than companies have with employees (Christopherson, 2011; Norbäck, 2012; Randle, 2011).

While this construct certainly brings evident advantages for incumbent media organisations, there are also risks keyed to the increase use of projects involving competencies from outside the organisation and reliance on 'casual labour' (Deuze, 2007). The characteristic loyalty and related worker motivation that companies have enjoyed, and to an extent counted on, will be harder to find. Valuable talents previously secured by long-term contract commitments are free to go where they choose and when they like and may be also harder to contract even on a temporary basis—and when available, potentially at higher cost. Temporary labour can be expected to pursue the most stimulating professional opportunities and to chase the biggest fees. Media organisations in a projectified industry will be hard pressed to sustain competitive advantage based on employed competencies—an issue of essential concern in a resource-based view of the firm (see Conner & Prahalad, 1996). However, it is conceivable that future competitive advantage may arise from the type and robustness of a firm's project network and the management competencies that are essential to that, as discussed earlier. The ability to sustain a project network that can recognise, create and exploit new business opportunities is already of evident general importance.

But another danger in the projectification of personnel may be more difficult to offset. The unsecure working conditions can undo the capabilities for higher and more sophisticated degrees of creativity. As Küng (2007, 2008, 2011) reports, precarious working conditions appear to be rather detrimental to creativity because much of that capability is environmental and relational. Yet another thorny problem relates to the trustworthiness of media companies, something especially important to news organisations. When such organisations no longer have the type of internal control that they once had over producers of content and the production process, they run a more pronounced risk of running afoul in scandals when people connected to them are found out as unethical practitioners, for example, as in the *New York Times* case where a reporter was found out fabricating stories over a long period of time (Sullivan, 2013). Such scandals will most likely hurt the value of media companies by eroding prestige and damaging credibility associated with their brands, which are proving to be an important competitive advantage in the media landscape (Chan-Olmsted, 2006; Ots, 2008; Tungate, 2004).

21.7   If Projectification Is Where the Media Industries Are Going, What Does This Mean for Media Management?

In this chapter we have argued that a developing trend in the media industries is evident in the increasing projectification of content production, and this has many and diverse implications for media management today and even more for professional practice in the future. Although the roots of this trend are in the traditional project-based industries of TV, film and advertising, it has been deepening there and spreading to industries not characterised by this mode of production until now. What does the trend mean for the researching and teaching of media management? What do media managers need to know to be successful at their jobs in this context? And what does it mean for professional media workers?

Media managers in charge of content production will need to become more 'project fluent', both in the sense of having expertise in knowing how to assemble projects and in how to manage them as a process and professional practice. Media managers in many cases will work less with in-house employees and more with diverse and scattered networks populated by small firms and individuals. Media managers must therefore develop some mastery of skills and competencies not only in production but also in many areas that aren't traditional for media companies. We have highlighted a few, including skills in negotiation and communication, scanning for opportunities, managing networks and so forth. We could add multiplatform knowledge and understandings and respect for audience participation (e.g. utilising the audience as cocreators (Norbäck & Raviola, 2013). Certainly there is need for greater skill and fluency in acting in an entrepreneurial fashion, such as finding new and innovative ways of collaborating with advertisers (Aris & Bughin, 2009; Küng, 2011).

Professional media workers need to become accustomed to, even comfortable with, the fact that a projectified logic in production means that one cannot only be excellent at what he/she does in the 'know-how' of making content, but needs to develop other skills and competencies that are necessary for cumulative success in a project context. Again, this obviously involves requirements to think and act more entrepreneurially and to learn how to handle the dynamics of collaboration. It will also inherently mean developing competence in networking (the 'know-who').

Media firms need to adapt to rapid and ongoing changes in technology, customer preferences and consumer behaviour, advertising business models, globalisation of content and consumption and so on (Aris, 2011; Küng, 2011). That has been obvious for some time now. Firms need to adjust to a changing environment and need to develop new business opportunities and wean themselves from faltering business models. They need to keep track of varied important actors that include not only competitors but also policy makers, regulators, workers, advertisers and suppliers. The urge to renew and to do so swiftly is therefore strong—arguably stronger as a package than in many other industries.

We have argued that the projectification of production processes is an increasing feature of media industries. This may also become a useful idea and characteristic for other, more strategic activities in media industries. Given the present popularity of the project approach to work, projectification may well come to represent most of what is done at the management level in media companies. What does 'management by projects' provide in terms of new levels of efficiency and effectiveness in media industries? In the light of our discussion about networking, there is evidently room for more experimentation in the field. However, previous research results (e.g. Lundin & Norbäck, 2009) suggest that project competence does not easily spill over from one area (for instance, content production) to other management areas (like strategy formulation). This suggests a need to renew managerial processes in these industries in order to renew many and significant activities routinely conducted by the media firm. Arguably, applying management by projects on a grand scale may be a useful, even necessary, mechanism to achieve that change. How to preserve what is good today and combine it with what is possibly needed for tomorrow (Aris, 2011) is the key challenge that media management faces. And we conclude by observing that there will certainly be other routes that can be taken and that everything won't realise its best results in a project-based approach. Projectification has limits.

References

Anderson, C. (2006). *The long tail: Why the future of business is selling less of more*. New York: Hyperion.

Andersen, E. (2014). Two perspectives on project management. In R. Lundin & M. Hällgren (Eds.), *Advancing research on projects and temporary organizations*. Copenhagen, Denmark: CBS Press.

Aris, A. (2011). Managing media companies through the digital transition. In M. Deuze (Ed.), *Managing media work*. London: Sage.

Aris, A., & Bughin, J. (2009). *Managing media companies harnessing creative value* (2nd ed.). West Sussex: Wiley.

Bergström, O. (2003). Introduction. In O. Bergström & D. Storrie (Eds.), *Contingent employment in Europe and the United States*. Northampton, MA: Edward Elgar.

Bilton, C. (2007). *Management and creativity: From creative industries to creative management*. Malden, MA: Blackwell.

Bilton, C. (2011). The management of the creative industries. In M. Deuze (Ed.), *Managing media work*. London: Sage.

Blair, H. (2003). Winning and losing in flexible labour markets: The formation and operation of networks of interdependence in the UK film industry. *Sociology, 37*(4), 677–694.

Blomquist, T., Hällgren, M., Nilsson, A., & Söderholm, A. (2010). Project-as-practice: In search of project management research that matters. *Project Management Journal, 41*(1), 5–16.

Born, G. (2004). *Uncertain vision: Birt, Dyke and the reinvention of the BBC*. London: Vintage.

Chan-Olmsted, S. M. (2006). *Competitive strategy for media firms. Strategic and brand management in changing media markets*. Mahwah, NJ: Lawrence Erlbaum.

Christopherson, S. (2011). Connecting the dots. Structure, strategy, and subjectivity in entertainment media. In M. Deuze (Ed.), *Managing media work*. London: Sage.

Conner, K. R., & Prahalad, C. K. (1996). A resource-based theory of the firm: Knowledge versus opportunism. *Organization Science, 7*(5), 477–501.

Davis, C. H. (2011). New firms in the screen-based media industry. Startups, self-employment and standing reserve. In M. Deuze (Ed.), *Managing media work*. London: Sage.

Davis, C. H., Vladica, F., & Berkowitz, I. (2008). Business capabilities of small entrepreneurial media firms: Independent production of children's television in Canada. *Journal of Media Business Studies, 5*(1), 9–39.

DeFillippi, R. (2009). Dilemmas of project-based media work: Contexts and choices. *Journal of Media Business Studies, 6*(4), 5–30.

Deuze, M. (2007). *Media work: Digital media and society series*. Cambridge: Polity Press.

Deuze, M., & Fortunati, L. (2011). Atypical newswork, atypical media management. In M. Deuze (Ed.), *Managing media work*. London: Sage.

Deuze, M., & Steward, B. (2011). Managing media work. In M. Deuze (Ed.), *Managing media work*. London: Sage.

Gareis, R. (1991). Management by projects: The management strategy of the 'new' project-oriented company. *International Journal of Project Management, 9*(2), 71–76.

Gill, R. (2011). "LIfe is a pitch": Managing the self in new media work. In M. Deuze (Ed.), *Managing media work*. London: Sage.

Greco, A. N. (2005). *The book publishing industry* (2nd ed.). Mahwah, NJ: Lawrence Erlbaum.

Kerr, A. (2011). The culture of gamework. In M. Deuze (Ed.), *Managing media work*. London: Sage.

Küng, L. (2007). Does media management matter? Establishing the scope, rationale, and future research agenda for the discipline. *Journal of Media Business Studies, 4*(1), 21–39.

Küng, L. (2008). *Strategic management in the media: Theory to practice*. Los Angeles, CA: Sage.

Küng, L. (2011). Managing strategy and maximizing innovation in media organizations. In M. Deuze (Ed.), *Managing media work*. London: Sage.

Küng-Shankleman, L. (2000). *Inside the BBC and CNN managing media organisations*. London: Routledge.

Lundin, R. A., & Norbäck, M. (2009). Managing projects in the TV production industry: The case of Sweden. *Journal of Media Business Studies, 6*(4).

Lundin, R. A., & Söderholm, A. (2013). Temporary organizations and end states: A theory is a child of its time and in need of reconsideration and reconstruction. *International Journal of Managing Projects in Business, 6*(3), 587–594.

Manning, S. (2005). Managing project networks as dynamic organizational forms: Learning from the TV movie industry. *International Journal of Project Management, 23*, 410–414.

Meredith, J. R., & Mantel, S. J., Jr. (2000). *Project management – A managerial approach* (4th ed.). New York: Wiley.

Midler, C. (1995). "Projectification" of the firm: The Renault case. *Scandinavian Journal of Management, 11*(4).

Norbäck, M. (2012). *Making public service television—A study of institutional work in collaborative TV production*. Jönköping, Sweden: Jönköping University.

Norbäck, M., & Raviola, E. (2013). Digitization of newspaper and magazine publishing: The contribution of technology to the construction of the world. In R. DeFillippi & P. Wikström (Eds.), *Business innovation and disruption in publishing* (Vol. 1). Media XXI Formalpress.

Ots, M. (Ed.). (2008). *Media brands and branding*. Jönköping: Jönköping International Business School.

Packendorff, J. (1995). Inquiring into the temporary organization: New directions for project management research. *Scandinavian Journal of Management, 11*(4), 319–333.

Perren, A. (2011). Producing filmed entertainment. In M. Deuze (Ed.), *Managing media work*. London: Sage.

Pinney, B. W. (2001). *Projects, management, and protean times: Engineering enterprise in the United States, 1870–1960*, MIT. PhD thesis.

Project Management Institute. (2013). A guide to the project management body of knowledge (PMBOK Guide) (Fifth Edition).

Randle, K. (2011). The organization of film and television production. In M. Deuze (Ed.), *Managing media work*. London: Sage.

Raviola, E. (2010). *Paper meets web: How the institution of news production works on paper and online Jönköping*. JIBS dissertation series, Jönköping International Business School, ISSN 1403-0470; 065.

Samuelsson, L. K., & Karén, F. (2013, 6 March 2013). Kvalitetsjournalistik, *Svenska Dagbladet*.

Singer, J. B. (2011). Journalism in a network. In M. Deuze (Ed.), *Managing media work*. London: Sage.

Söderholm, A. (2008). Project management of unexpected events. *International Journal of Project Management, 26*(1), 80–86.

Starkey, K., Barnatt, C., & Tempest, S. (2000). Beyond networks and hierarchies: Latent organizations in the U.K. television industry. *Organization Science, 11*(3), 299–305.

Sullivan, M. (2013, 2013-05-04). Repairing the Credibility Cracks, *The New York Times*.

Sydow, J. (2009). Path dependencies in project-based organizing: Evidence from television production in Germany. *Journal of Media Business Studies, 6*(4), 123–140.

Sydow, J., & Staber, U. (2002). The institutional embeddedness of project networks: The case of content production in German television. *Regional Studies, 36*(3), 215–227.

Tungate, M. (2004). *Media monoliths: How great media brands thrive and survive*. London: UK Kogan Page Limited.

Wikström, P. (2009). *The music industry*. Cambridge: Polity Press.

Windeler, A., & Sydow, J. (2001). Project networks and changing industry practices collaborative content production in the German television industry. *Organization Studies, 22*(6), 1035–1060. doi:10.1177/0170840601226006.

Printed by Printforce, the Netherlands